9th Brief Edition

PRINCIPLES OF SPEECH COMMUNICATION

9th Brief Edition

PRINCIPLES OF SPEECH COMMUNICATION

DOUGLAS EHNINGER

BRUCE E. GRONBECK
The University of Iowa

ALAN H. MONROE

Scott, Foresman and Company   Glenview, Illinois
Dallas, Texas   Oakland, New Jersey   Palo Alto, California
Tucker, Georgia   London, England

An Instructor's Manual to accompany *Principles of Speech Communication*, Ninth Edition, is available. It may be obtained through a Scott, Foresman representative or by writing to Speech Communication Editor, College Division, Scott, Foresman and Company, 1900 East Lake Avenue, Glenview, Illinois 60025.

Photo Credits: page 4, George Bellerose/Picture Group; page 31, Susan Lapides/Design Conceptions; page 52, Glen Donahue/Atoz Images; page 79, Ulrike Welsch; page 109, George Zimbel/Monkmeyer; page 128, Victoria Arlak; page 154, Richard Henley; page 177, Courtesy Dallas Police Department; page 188, Perry Ruben/Monkmeyer; page 189, Martha Stewart/The Picture Cube; page 214, Courtesy of the Bell System; page 226, Susan Lapides/Design Conceptions; page 268, Courtesy WTTW/Chicago; page 295, Sybil Shelton/Monkmeyer; page 313, Courtesy First National Bank of Chicago.

Library of Congress Cataloging in Publication Data

Ehninger, Douglas.
    Principles of speech communication.

    Includes bibliographies and index.
    1. Public speaking.   I. Gronbeck, Bruce E.   II. Monroe, Alan Houston,
1903-   III. Title. PN4121.E36 1984   808.5′1   83–11578
ISBN 0-673-15877-2
ISBN 0-673-17959-2 (embossed ed.)

PREFACE

For fifty years, *Principles of Speech Communication* has been an eminently practical guide to public speaking. This Ninth Brief Edition, like the ones before it, emphasizes both principles and skills. It is based on the belief that the principles of speech communication can be applied to a great variety of speaking situations. And it stresses the preparation and presentation skills which everyone needs at work, in social situations, and in the public marketplace of ideas.

USING THE PRINCIPLES OF SPEECH COMMUNICATION

Principles of Speech Communication, Ninth Brief Edition, allows a variety of instructional approaches. It is intended as a guide to speech construction and presentation, and so each chapter—through the vocabulary, the advice, and the exercises—is designed to help people construct and deliver clear and convincing messages. But we have also been sensitive to the needs of listeners; the advice and exercises on analyzing and criticizing speeches emphasize listening skills. Therefore, after reading this book, students should be able to use the principles of speech communication in three ways: to prepare and deliver effective speeches, to listen to them in a discriminating manner, and to analyze more critically the speeches of others.

The book's flexibility is enhanced by its organization. Although the chapters are ordered to match the sequence of most public speaking courses, each chapter is relatively self-contained, so that instructors can reorder the chapters to suit their own preferences.

TEACHING SPEECH PRINCIPLES AND THEIR APPLICATIONS

It was Alan Monroe (1903–1975), really, who "invented" the principles approach to the teaching of public speaking in this book's first edition, *Principles and Types of Speech* (1935). The book became an immediate classroom success because its format allowed students (1) to gain an overview of the process of public speaking, then (2) to learn the basic principles of speech preparation, and then (3) to apply those principles to producing speeches tailored to different occasions and audiences. The "Monroe formula" for teaching public speaking is both time-honored and time-tested; it still governs this edition. Thus, Chapter 1 offers an overview of the process of speech communication; Chapter 2, an overview of listening; Chapter 3, an introduction to all of the steps in speech preparation; Chapters 4–7, more detailed treatment of the key steps; Chapters 8–10, an examination of each of the primary channels (linguistic, vocal, bodily, and visual aids) of public oral communication; and Chapters 11–15, advice on how to apply all of those principles in preparing and delivering speeches with different purposes, settings, and occasions.

This approach to public speaking allows students to understand communication principles individually before combining them in "complete" speeches. It also allows instructors to stress particular aspects of speech preparation and delivery without sacrificing coherence.

ADAPTING THE NINTH EDITION
TO THE CONTEMPORARY CLASSROOM

While *Principles of Speech Communication* has a venerable heritage and a 50-year history of success for well over one million students, it has never stopped changing. To be sure, past users will find intact the features which probably attracted them to the book in the first place—Monroe's "motivated sequence"; the forms of supporting materials; the factors of attention; emphasis on speeches to inform, persuade, and actuate; types of imagery; and varied introductions, organizations or patterns, and conclusions. These features will be familiar to past users, and will please instructors new to the book as well.

And yet, the Ninth edition has kept pace with changing times, updating its vocabulary, exercises, organization, and applications. Many changes are almost invisible (more interesting prose, updated sample materials, and a clearer system of headings); others are more marked:

- a stronger stress on speech "skills" and criteria for assessing "communication competencies" necessary for effective speechmaking, reflecting the "back to basics" emphasis on skills as well as the importance of competency-based models of instruction
- a heavier stress on organizing informative, persuasive, and actuative speeches, reflecting current concern for organizational and outlining skills
- a devotion to communication careers and to public speaking as a prerequisite to achievement in any career, reflecting many programs' emphasis on service or training courses for students from many majors and with many different career aspirations
- a complete chapter on audience analysis, reflecting its importance in speech preparation, contemporary styles of professional audience analysis, and requests for more advice on how to use the results of audience analysis in the construction of speeches
- a new chapter on argument and public reasoning, reflecting the nationwide attention being paid to students' reasoning abilities
- a reorganization of the last chapters into a new Chapter 15, reflecting the current concern for business and professional communication skills in interviewing, group discussion, public panels or conferences, and question-and-answer sessions
- an entirely new appendix devoted to communication and careers reflecting today's interest in communication as an essential skill for living and working
- final appendix with sample speeches, including an employment interview, reflecting many instructors' desire to apply basic principles to a full range of public contexts

Principles of Speech Communication, Ninth Brief Edition, in summary, looks both back to its roots and forward to an evolving society, both to an articulation of fundamental principles and research findings as well as to application of those principles in varied ways, and both to the student wishing to construct better speeches and to the person hoping to become a more discerning consumer of public speech.

ACKNOWLEDGMENTS

A book such as this one, of course, is not the product of one professor and his predecessors. Because *Principles of Speech Communication* has been in the hands of so many instructors and students for half a century, it has been evaluated and reevaluated by several generations of users and experts. The Ninth Brief Edition has been built upon expert opinion acquired through a nationwide users' questionnaire graciously returned to us by the following speech instructors: Joann Bennette, Saddleback Community College; Stephen D. Boyd, Northern Kentucky University; Kay G. Brewer, Louisiana Tech University; Charles W. Castillo, Henry Rowe Schoolcraft College; Robert G. Chamberlain, Seattle Pacific University; Albert J. Croft, University of Wisconsin—Stevens Point; Barbara Ginader, Rio Hondo College; Robert A. Griffin, Southern Connecticut State College; Barbara Ann Harris, Penn Valley Community College; Marilyn J. Hoffs, Glendale Community College; Sandra Sarkela Hynes, University of Louisville; Emily J. Jennings, Manatee Junior College; Michael Jennings, Tennessee Temple University; Steven A. Jensen, Purdue University; Gary D. Keele, California State Polytechnic University—Pomona; Bill N. Morton, Lamar University; Emmett T. Long, California State University—Fullerton; Mary H. McLemore, Embry-Riddle Aeronautical University; Denise Mier, Baruch College; Michael Pearson, Villanova University; Mary Ruth Rang, University of Dayton; Betty Popper, City College of C.U.N.Y.; Roselyn Schiff, Loop College; Lois Self, Northern Illinois University; Fleur Steinhardt, Los Angeles City College; Robin Vagenas, University of Delaware; Barbara Weems, Wayne County Community College.

I am especially grateful for the advice and suggestions provided by the manuscript reviewers: Paul Batty, Parkland College; Roy M. Berko, Lorain County Community College; Stephen D. Boyd, Northern Kentucky University; Marilyn J. Hoffs, Glendale Community College; Keith T. Macksey, Manatee Junior College; Nancy Rooker, Brigham Young University; Dauphine Walker-Shivers, Wayne County Community College; and Lynn K. Wells, Saddleback Community College.

As an author, I also owe a great debt to Professor Linda Moore of the University of Akron, who took in hand four troublesome chapters and completely reworked them; her sense of directness, of student needs, and of the field in general shine through these chapters. As well, her manual, an Instructor's Guide to Using *Principles of Speech Communication,* Ninth Brief Edition is a combination of sound pedagogy, creative instructional strategies, practical exercises, and carefully developed test questions. My debt to other communication professionals also extends to Professors Nancy L. Harper and John Waite Bowers of the University of Iowa, who authored Appendix I. Both have been among this country's leading proponents of communication and career counseling.

Finally, I owe perhaps my greatest debts of all to Scott, Foresman and Company, for its extensive resources, talents, and investments in this project. The overall shape of the Ninth Brief Edition has been guided by Michael Anderson and Barbara Muller. Barbara also has been in charge of developing internal aspects of the book. The word-by-word preparation of the final manuscript has been in the able hands of Patricia Rossi. And my thanks extend to the Scott, Foresman personnel behind the scenes—the artists, the production people, and the marketing staff. Scott, Foresman's long experience in the development of speech communication textbooks shows through on every page of this book, and I am grateful for their commitment to the discipline. Without them, the words and ideas of three generations of authors—of Alan Monroe, Douglas Ehninger (1913–1979), and me—would remain buried away in cluttered minds and overflowing desks.

B.E.G.

CONTENTS

SPEECH COMMUNICATION MATERIALS FOR STUDY AND ANALYSIS

CHAPTER 1

The Speech Communication Process

What we call public address, public speaking, or speech communication is both a public act and an interrelated set of analytical and motor skills that advance the individual or collective interests of a society. The prefix *com-* (from the Latin *cum* meaning "with") and *munus* (referring to a service performed for the culture) are combined in our word *communication*—a word that in its broadest sense means sharing experience publicly for the common good. Communicating publicly, therefore, is part of most adults' lives. People are frequently called on to present oral messages of some length and complexity to large groups of listeners.

SPEECHMAKING IN SOCIETY

The Social Realm

Most of our talking is done in everyday social situations. Parents of young children discuss the closing of the local elementary school and attendant problems. Meetings with friends produce animated discussions of senior citizen housing, comparison shopping, and the upcoming local election. Members of special interest groups and church committees listen to reports in order to set up next year's projects and meeting dates.

Much of the "speechmaking" in your social life is informal. Nevertheless, the basics of public speaking are all present: introductions, bodies, and conclusions; central ideas or propositions along with supporting materials; the use of voice, face, gestures, and body for transmitting the messages from one person to others. Some of these special occasions will demand all the speaking skills you possess.

The Work Realm

For most people, the world of work is primarily a world of communication. The channels of oral communication bear much of this load—committee discussions, employment and appraisal interviews, instructions from supervisors to their subordinates, inquiries for information and advice, lunches and conferences with clients and colleagues. Indeed, a recent study found that, beyond a person's entry-level job, specialized college training was less important for success than general skills in interpersonal relations, oral and written communication, and business know-how.[1] And, in reference to oral communication skills specifically, another study found that speaking with others clearly and forcefully is important for almost all occupations of college graduates, and crucial for administrators, managers, sales personnel, allied health workers, educators, social workers, and counselors.[2] It is little wonder, therefore, that graduates of liberal arts programs as well as business schools, engineering colleges, and other professional programs list oral communication training as a determining factor in work-related success.[3] See Appendix I for an enlarged discussion of careers and communication.

Your nine to five environment, therefore, depends on "speeches." These speeches are somewhat more formal than the ones you offer to

[1]N. L. Ochsner and Lewis C. Solmon, *College Education and Employment—The Recent Graduates* (Bethlehem, Pa.: The College Placement Foundation, 1979). See also Carol A. Carmichael, "Most College Grads Satisfied with Jobs," *Chicago Tribune,* September 16, 1979.

[2]Ann Stouffer Bisconti and Lewis C. Solmon, *College Education on the Job—The Graduates' Viewpoint* (Bethlehem, Pa.: The College Placement Council Foundation, 1976), p. 43.

[3]Carol H. Pazandak, "Followup Survey of 1973 Graduates, College of Liberal Arts," Minneapolis: College of Liberal Arts, University of Minnesota, 1977 (multilith); Jack Landgrebe and Howard Baumgartel, "Results of the Graduation Requirement Questionnaire for College of Liberal Arts and Sciences Alumni," Lawrence: College of Liberal Arts and Sciences, University of Kansas (typescript); "Instruction in Communication at Colorado State University," Fort Collins: College of Engineering, Colorado State University, July 1979 (multilith); Edward Foster et al., "A Market Study for the College of Business Administration, University of Minnesota, Twin Cities," Minneapolis: College of Business Administration, University of Minnesota, November 1978 (multilith). These and other studies are reported in Samuel L. Becker and Leah R. V. Ekdom, "That Forgotten Basic Skill: Oral Communication," *Association for Communication Administration Bulletin,* #33 (August 1980).

friends, family, and neighbors. That is because (1) your purpose is often more specific than it is in social interaction, and (2) your audience's expectations are usually very concrete in most work situations. Work-related speeches tend to be more formalized, narrower, and more focused than those you give in social settings.

The Public Realm

The most formalized speechmaking generally occurs in the public realm—in political gatherings, lecture settings, ceremonial occasions, or religious groups. Here, the effective public communicator must have something to say and know how to say it within the customs and traditions governing the event or setting. Presidents, lecturers, orators, and preachers deliver weighty messages to their audiences, and are expected to "sound like" presidents, lecturers, orators, and preachers.[4] Their speeches must be both compelling and emotionally moving.

The points to remember as you begin this book and this course are: (1) Although your idea of a "speech" may be such that you cannot see yourself giving one, the facts are that you have talked and will talk publicly a good deal. Even in a day of mass media and computerized written messages, giving speeches remains a vital part of everyone's lives in social, work, and public arenas. (2) While you may think of "speeches" as highly structured and formal, they actually vary a good deal in terms of their seriousness, breadth, and complexity. Few of us will make our living as public servants and orators of renown, but all of us will address more public audiences than we probably realize. (3) Finally, even though settings and purposes vary a great deal, the event we call "making a speech" can be characterized by a limited set of core elements or skills.

WHY STUDY SPEECHMAKING?

Indeed, why study it in a classroom? After all, you have been communicating orally with others for all but the first few months of your life. And you probably already have several basic oral communication skills at your

---

[4]L. S. Harms, "Listener Judgments of Status Cues in Speech," *Quarterly Journal of Speech,* 47 (April 1961), 164–168; Robert Hopper and Frederick Williams, "Speech Characteristics and Employability," *Speech Monographs,* 40 (November 1973), 296–302; James D. Moe, "Listener Judgments of Status Cues in Speech: A Replication and Extension," *Speech Monographs,* 39 (November 1972), 144–47; Susan Milmoe et al., "The Doctor's Voice: Postdictor of Successful Referral of Alcoholic Patients," *Journal of Abnormal Psychology,* 72 (1968), 78–84.

In the American socio-political tradition, we assume that the public expression of views on public issues is both the right and the responsibility of every citizen. Historically and today, citizen communicative participation in the business of the society is epitomized by the New England town meeting, where the community gathers to make decisions.

disposal. Yet, there are several important reasons to study formally the communication process and the skills which comprise it.

1. *Much of our communicative behavior occurs "out of awareness"; learning to make conscious communicative decisions increases your effectiveness.* Anthropologist Edward Hall notes that all human beings learn their social roles and society's expected interaction patterns in three ways—informally, formally, and technically.[5] "Informal" learning involves imitation, watching others act, and then acting in the same way. As a child you learned informally how to play games, for example, by watching other children play "cops and robbers," "doctor," and "space invaders." You learned some of your communicative behavior in the same way, by listening to how others spoke. "Formal" learning involves admonition, being told "how-to-do-it" by a parent or other authoritative figure. Some of your communicative behavior was acquired formally, as when a parent said, "Say

[5]Edward T. Hall, *The Silent Language* (1959; rpt. New York: Fawcett World Library, 1966), Chapter 4, "The Major Triad," pp. 63–92.

'please' "; "Don't talk that way to your aunt"; "Don't say 'ain't' "; "Speak up!";
"Don't talk with your fingers in your mouth."

Informal and formal modes of learning, of course, have their place, and
have been important to your communicative development. But, to become
truly proficient—to solve communicative problems you face, to avoid
misunderstanding as much as possible, to maximize your effect on others—
you must learn about speech communication technically. "Technical" learning involves explanations, rationales for "why" one should do or believe or
value thus-and-so. One of the primary reasons you are in a public speaking
classroom is to hear someone trained in communications explain the "whys"
of the process.

2. *A speech classroom is a laboratory, and hence an ideal place for
personal communicative experimentation.* Most of us, when we speak
publicly, have a comparatively limited repertoire of communicative behaviors. We tend to talk in much the same way each time we speak, whether it's
a comparatively informal or formal situation, whether it's in a classroom,
political meeting, or church basement.

A key theme of this book will be *adaptation*—adapting your speeches to
your purposes, the audiences attending to your speech, and the occasions or
settings in which you are speaking. There is no better place, really, to
expand your communicative adaptability, to increase and refine your
speaking skills, and to enlarge your repertoire of communicative behaviors
than in a classroom.

3. *Studying oral communication not only allows you to increase your
repertoire of public speaking skills, but also makes you a more perceptive
consumer of oral messages.* You undoubtedly will spend more of your
communicative life listening than talking. In your lifetime, you will be
exposed to literally thousands of oral messages—among friends, at work, in
public, while listening to the radio or watching television. You will meet or
hear hundreds of people who will want some of your time and effort, your
money, your commitments to varied causes. Ours is a highly oral society,
even more so now that we are immersed in an electronic environment.

To protect yourself, to help you choose among all of the commitments
you could make, you need to be able to understand, interpret, and evaluate
the thousands of messages you'll hear.[6] To gain that kind of mastery, you

---

[6]Consumer-oriented skills are described and discussed in Bruce E. Gronbeck and
Douglas M. Trank, "Public Address," in *Education in the 80's: Speech Communication*, ed.
Gustav W. Friedrich and Joy H. McClintock (Washington, D.C.: National Education Associ-
ation, 1981), esp. pp. 113–114, 116–117. See Chapter 2 of this book as well.

need (a) "a rhetorical vocabulary," that is, a set of words and concepts which allows you to identify various sorts of techniques people are using when they speak, and (b) a set of "rhetorical principles," that is, generalizations and evaluative standards against which you can measure someone else's motives, performances, and effects.

Therefore, you will find this book loaded with "words"—with a relatively technical (but we hope comprehensible) vocabulary for talking about various aspects of speeches and speechmaking, with words for various sorts of introductions and conclusions, arrangement patterns, linguistic strategies, types of gestures, types of speeches and speech purposes, types of settings, and the like. Before you can understand and interpret anything in your environment, including others' speeches, you need a set of words for dissecting and talking about it. And, you'll also find in this book numerous rhetorical principles—generalized statements about such matters as communication rules, sources of personal credibility and ethics, the importance of gaining and holding attention, psychological models, and so on. These principles will allow you to order your thoughts and to develop measuring rods against which you can judge the speeches of others.

You are studying public speaking, therefore, to become more highly conscious of your own communicative behavior, to increase your communicative flexibility and range, and to learn more about ways to protect yourself as a listener. If you keep these three purposes in mind, you'll maximize your own learning in this class.

BASIC ELEMENTS IN THE SPEECH COMMUNICATION PROCESS

In spite of the many differences among speeches given in the social, work, and public realms, and in spite of the individualized communicative skills each of us possesses, there nevertheless exists a fundamental process of oral communication. Every time someone speaks to others, the same set of elements comes into play, interacting with each other to produce a communicative event. Because the event involves several people, each with unique needs and interests, and because a speech extends through time and space, it is useful first to examine each element separately, and then to put them together in an overview of the entire process or event. Because all of the elements interact dynamically—with each element in some significant way affecting all other elements—we may term the whole process a *speech transaction.* Let us begin, however, by examining the individual elements—the speaker, the message, the listeners, the channels, and the communicative situation.

The Speaker

Insofar as the speaker is concerned, all speech transactions are shaped by four factors: (1) *communicative purpose;* (2) *knowledge of subject and communication skills;* (3) *attitudes toward self, listeners, and subject;* and (4) *degree of credibility.*

Speaker's Purpose. *Every speaker has a purpose.* Except in the rarest of circumstances, you do not speak to others out of accident or whimsy. You speak to achieve some goal. Your purpose may be as simple as the wish to appear sociable, or, at the other extreme, as complex as the desire to alter cherished values or to advocate dangerous courses of public action. You may wish to provide entertainment, call attention to a problem, test an idea, refute an assertion, ward off a threat, establish or maintain status, or gain any number of other ends. The important point is this: Public speaking is a *purposive activity;* that purpose, in large measure, controls what you say and even how you say it.

Speaker's Knowledge. *In every speaking situation the speaker's knowledge of the subject and mastery of communication skills affect the character of the message and the effectiveness with which it is transmitted.* Occasionally, we all like to listen to certain speakers because of their personalities or because they are witty or entertaining; sometimes, we do not especially care what the speaker says. Usually, however, audiences demand something—something worth thinking about or doing. If you have only surface knowledge of the topic, listeners normally will feel cheated and the communication process will be short-circuited. In other words, your knowledge of the subject in some ways controls audience response. It also controls the actual shape of the speech—what is emphasized, what is used as supporting material, and how everything is organized into a coherent message.

Additionally, in order to succeed in the world of oral communication, you must acquire, refine, and integrate a series of fundamental skills. We will see as we work our way through this book that the term "communication skills" encompasses a wide variety of abilities—setting communicative goals, finding and assembling relevant information, organizing messages in coherent and compelling ways, illustrating them visually when necessary, and delivering them in a manner which clarifies and emphasizes key notions. You already possess many of the requisite skills; through practice, instruction, reading, and observation of other speakers, you will improve your command of the others.

Speaker's Attitudes. *In every speaking situation the speaker's attitudes toward self, listeners, and subject significantly affect what is said and* *how it is said.* All of us carry with us a picture of ourselves as persons—a self-concept or image of the kinds of individuals we are and of how others perceive us.[7] That image is complex; it is derived from numerous experiences in numerous settings, and it controls our self-evaluations and the ways we interact with others.

Your own *self-image* influences how you will behave in a given speaking situation. If you have little confidence in your abilities or are unsure of your opinions or knowledge, you tend to advance ideas hesitatingly. Your voice becomes weak and unsteady, your body stiffens, and your eyes watch the floor rather than audience. If you are overly confident, you may move in the other direction—adopting an overbearing manner, disregarding the need for facts and logical demonstrations, riding roughshod over the feelings and needs of listeners. Ideally, you should have enough self-confidence to believe firmly in your ability to communicate something worthwhile to others, and yet enough sensitivity to the audience's intelligence, needs, and integrity to keep them foremost in mind while you speak.

Equally important in speech transactions are your *attitudes toward listeners.* Each time we speak, we do so from a certain status or role position—as parent or child, instructor or student, supervisor or employee. These role positions, in turn, affect our power relationships with audiences, determining whether we are superiors, inferiors, or equals. And third, those power relationships often affect the actual ways we talk to others publicly.

If you perceive someone as intellectually inferior, you tend to use simple vocabulary, clear structure, and concrete ideas; if someone seems politically inferior, you may talk condescendingly, self-confidently, assured of your own status. Or, if you view your auditors as superior, you are likely to talk in a deferential or highly qualified manner, protecting your "self" and sometimes even distrusting your own thoughts. It becomes important, therefore, to think seriously about your perceptions of your relationships to your listeners, and to adjust your speaking style and even your speech content according to your attitudes toward those listeners.

Finally, our behavior as speakers inevitably is influenced to a greater or lesser degree by how *we feel about the subject* we are discussing. Do you really believe what you are saying? Do you find your subject matter

---

[7]For a discussion of interrelationships between self-concept and communication, see Gordon I. Zimmerman, James L. Owen, and David R. Seibert, *Speech Communication: A Contemporary Introduction,* 2nd ed. (St. Paul: West Pub. Co., 1977), esp. pp. 32–43; and Gail E. Myers and Michele Tolela Myers, *The Dynamics of Human Communication: A Laboratory Approach,* 3rd ed. (New York: McGraw-Hill Book Co., 1980), Chapter 3, "Self-Concept: Who Am I?" pp. 47–72.

interesting or boring? Is it crucial that your auditors know about it? Is it relevant to someone's needs? Your answers to these questions are reflected in how you use your voice and body, in the intensity of the language you use to communicate your ideas, and even in your selection of ideas.

In summary, as a speaker you convey—verbally and nonverbally—how you feel about yourself, your audience, and your subject matter, and you make many verbal and nonverbal decisions while preparing and delivering a speech based on those attitudes.

Speaker's Credibility. *In every speaking situation the speaker's success in winning agreement, inspiring confidence, or promoting ideas and action is significantly affected by the listeners' estimate of his or her credibility.* The term "credibility"—and its relatives, "image" or *"ethos"*—refer to the degree to which an audience finds a speaker to be a trustworthy, competent, sincere, attractive, and dynamic human being. Social scientific research has repeatedly demonstrated that if speakers can heighten an audience's estimate of these qualities, they will significantly increase the impact of a message. Although we do not have room to review all of the conclusions reached by researchers, the following generalizations are representative of ways in which the factors of credibility work in communicative interactions: (1) References to yourself and your own experience—provided they are not boasting or excessive—tend to increase your perceived trustworthiness and competence, and references to others (authorities) tend to increase your perceived trustworthiness and dynamism. (2) Using highly credible authorities increases your perceived fairness. (3) If you can demonstrate that you and your audience share common beliefs, attitudes, and values, your credibility will increase. (4) Well-organized speeches are more credible than poorly organized speeches. (5) The more sincere you appear to be, the better your chances of changing your listeners' attitudes.[8]

An audience's perception of the speaker's credibility, in other words, is affected by a broad range of behaviors and in turn can decisively affect the degree to which you are accepted and successful. Your ability to project yourself as a competent, trustworthy, sincere, attractive, and dynamic person may well determine the fate of your message. The message and the messenger are usually inseparable in the minds of listeners.

---

[8]These and other generalizations relative to source credibility are most usefully summarized in Stephen W. Littlejohn, "A Bibliography of Studies Related to Variables of Source Credibility," *Bibliographic Annual in Speech Communication: 1971*, ed. Ned A. Shearer (New York: Speech Communication Assoc., 1972), pp. 1–40; cf. Ronald L. Applebaum et al., *Fundamental Concepts in Human Communication* (San Francisco: Canfield Press, 1973), pp. 123–46.

The Message

In all speech communication transactions, the message which the speaker transmits is made up of the same three variables: content, structure, and style.

Content. That the messages we transmit to our listeners have a content—are about something we want them to be aware of—is obvious. What is less obvious, however, are the many different sorts of content which comprise a message. There are, of course, "ideas"—assertions about the state of the world, facts and figures, analogies and examples, generalizations as well as more specific statements. But the content of a speech also includes your feelings about those ideas, interpretations of ideas you wish your audience to accept, courses of action you want the listeners to pursue, beliefs you are attempting to challenge. Many different kinds of "meanings" make up the content of a speech.

Structure. Any message we transmit is of necessity structured or organized in some way, simply because we say some things first, others, second, and still others, third, fourth, and so on. Even if you seem to ramble on, auditors will look for a pattern which makes the message seem coherent. It is important, then, for a speaker to provide a pattern in order to guide the audience's search for coherence. That structure may be as simple as numbering points, ("First, I will discuss . . . , next I will . . . and finally, I will . . ."), or as complex as a full outline with points and subpoints. One way you control the clarity and force of your message, therefore, is by providing a recognizable pattern for it.

Style. The third variable in every spoken message is style. Just as you must select and arrange the ideas you wish to convey to audiences, so also must you select words, arrange them in sentences, and decide how to reveal your self-image to that group of hearers. Selecting and arranging words as well as revealing ourselves to be certain sorts of persons are matters of "style." Given the innumerable word-selection choices, the great varieties of sentence structures, and even the many sorts of self-images available to the speaker, a good many styles are possible. Styles can be "personal" or "impersonal," "literal" or "ironic," "plain" or "elevated," even "philosophical" or "poetic"; such labels refer to particular combinations of vocabulary, sentence syntax (arrangement), and images of the speaker. What we call style, therefore, really has nothing to do with "prettiness" or "stylishness";

rather, it includes those aspects of language use that convey impressions of speakers, details of the world, and emotional overtones.[9]

The Listeners

In all forms of speech, the listeners—like the speaker—have goals or purposes in mind. Moreover, the way a message is received and responded to varies according to the listener's (1) *purpose,* (2) *knowledge of and interest in the subject;* (3) *level of listening skill;* and (4) *attitude toward self, speaker, and the ideas presented.*

Listeners' Purpose. *Listeners always have one or more purposes they want to fulfill.* Listeners, no less than speakers, enter into the speech transaction in search of rewards. They may wish to be entertained or informed, advised or guided. These purposes form their expectations—expectations, as we shall see, which control to whom, how, and why they listen. Speakers who violate those expectations—turning an informative talk, say, into a political harangue—risk ineffectiveness or even failure.

Listeners' Knowledge of Subject. *In speech transactions, the listeners' knowledge of and interest in the subject significantly affect how the message will be received and responded to.* Speakers often are told to address listeners "where they are." "Where they are" is determined by two factors—their knowledge of the topic, and their personal interest in it. A knowledgeable audience is bored by an elementary speech, whereas one with little knowledge is confused by a technical description. Disinterested listeners may even go so far as to walk out on a speaker who has not made the topic relevant to their interests. An important aspect of what we shall be calling audience analysis, therefore, is a matter of (1) gauging listeners' prior knowledge so as to achieve an appropriate level of sophistication in the speech, and (2) finding ways to make the message relevant to the beliefs, desires, and motivational drives of the auditors.

Listeners' Command of Listening Skills. Speakers also must try to estimate the audience's listening skills. With relatively homogeneous audi-

---

[9]For a useful discussion of communication stylistic choices, see Gary Cronkhite, *Public Speaking and Critical Listening* (Menlo Park: The Benjamin-Cummings Pub. Co., Inc., 1978), esp. pp. 255–72.

ences, this may be easy to do. For example, you would expect a group of six-year-olds to have short attention spans, little ability to follow complex chains of reasoning, and a strong need to "see" ideas via visual aids and graphic descriptions. In contrast, you would expect graduate students to be able to sustain attention for long periods of time, to follow multi-stepped logical progressions, and to grasp easily abstract concepts. In other situations, however, it is difficult to predict the auditors' degree of listening sophistication. You then must constantly survey the listeners, looking for signs of understanding or puzzlement, acceptance or rejection. Those signs or cues are termed *feedback*—reactions "fed back" to speakers during the process of communication. "Reading feedback" is often your only way of determining a listener's skill of comprehension.

Listeners' Attitudes.   *In every speech encounter, the listeners' attitudes toward themselves, the speaker, and the subject significantly affect how they interpret and respond to the message.* Just as the speaker's communicative behavior is influenced by his or her attitude toward self, subject, and listener, so do these same factors affect the listeners' responses. Listeners with low self-esteem tend to be swayed more easily than those whose self-image is stronger. Listeners whose opinions seem to be confirmed by the views of the speaker are also susceptible to great influence. Moreover, as a rule, people seek out speakers whose positions they already agree with, and they retain longer and more vividly ideas which they strongly approve.[10] In other words, listeners' attitudes—which comprise another extremely important area for audience analysis—can be used (or, conversely, must be overcome) by speakers who wish to maximize their communicative effectiveness.

The Channels

All speech communication is affected to a greater or lesser extent by the channels through which the message is transmitted. The transaction between speakers and listeners occurs through several channels. The *verbal channel* carries the words, the culture's agreed-upon symbols for ideas. The *visual channel* transmits the gestures, facial expressions, bodily movements, and posture of the speaker; these tend to clarify, reinforce, or add emotional reactions to the words. At times the visual channel may be supplemented with a *pictorial channel*—so-called "visual aids," such as diagrams, charts,

---

[10]See the personality analysis of receivers in Michael Burgoon, *Approaching Speech Communication* (New York: Holt, Rinehart & Winston, Inc., 1974), pp. 64–69.

graphs, pictures, objects, and the like. The *aural channel*—also termed the paralinguistic medium—carries the tones of voice, variations in pitch and loudness, and other vocal modulations produced by the speaker's stream of sounds. Like the visual channel, the aural channel heightens some meanings and adds others. Because these four channels are heard and seen by listeners simultaneously, the "message" is really a combination of several messages flowing through all of these pathways. You should learn to control or shape the messages flowing through all four channels.

The Communicative Situation

All speech communication is affected by the physical setting and social context in which it occurs.

Physical Setting. The physical setting of the speech influences listeners' expectancies as well as their readiness to respond. People waiting in the quiet solemnity of a cathedral for the service to begin have quite different expectations than do theatergoers gathered to witness the opening of a new Broadway play. Listeners at an open-air political rally expect a different sort of message from those gathered to hear a scholarly lecture on political theory presented in a college classroom.

The furniture and decor of the physical space also make a difference. Comfortable chairs and soft-hued drapes tend to put discussion groups at ease and to promote a more productive exchange. The executive who talks to an employee from behind a large desk set in the middle of an impressively furnished office with the title "President" on the door gains a natural advantage not only because of a superior position but also because of the physical setting.

Social Context. Even more important than physical setting in determining how a message will be received is the social context in which it is presented. A "social context" is a particular combination of people, purposes, and places interacting communicatively: *People* are distinguished from each other by such factors as age, occupation, power, degree of intimacy, and knowledge. These factors in part determine how one "properly" communicates with others. You are expected to speak deferentially to your elders, your boss, a political leader with "clout," a stranger whose reactions you cannot immediately predict, or a sage. The degree to which people are superior to, equal with, or inferior to each other in part determines each one's communicative style. Certain *purposes* or goals are more or less appropriately communicated in different contexts as well. Thus, a memorial service is not a time for attacking a political opponent—a "meet the candidates" night is. In some contexts it is considered unreasonable to threaten someone before you have tried to find reasonable compromises. Some *places* are more conducive to certain kinds of communicative exchanges than others. Public officials are often more easily influenced in their offices than in public forums, where they tend to be more defensive; sensitive parents scold their children in private, never in front of their friends.

Another way of saying all this is to observe that societies are governed by customs, traditions, or what we now are calling *communication rules.* A "communication rule" is a guide to communicative behavior; it specifies, more or less precisely, what can be said to whom and in what circumstances. While communication rules are guides to communicating, they can, of course, be broken. Occasionally, rule breaking is inconsequential; sometimes, it determines success or failure; and always, it involves a certain amount of risk.[11]

In summary, the social context in which we speak determines an audience's judgment of *appropriateness* and *competency.* We learn to communicate appropriately and competently by learning and, usually, following the communication rules that govern our society. You have spent your lifetime learning those rules; we will cite many of the more explicit ones that govern public speaking throughout this book.

INTERACTION OF THE ELEMENTS IN PUBLIC COMMUNICATION TRANSACTIONS

All speech communication, thus, entails a complex pattern of interaction among the five primary elements: speaker, message, listeners, channels, and situations. A public speech can be considered an *interaction* of these elements because:

---

[11]Much research on physical setting and social context is summarized in Mark L. Knapp, *Essentials of Nonverbal Communication* (New York: Holt, Rinehart & Winston, 1980), Chapter 4, "The Effects of Territory and Personal Space," pp. 75–96. The determinative aspects of social expectations in human communication generally are discussed in such books as John J. Gumperz and Dell Hymes, eds., *Directions in Sociolinguistics: The Ethnography of Communication* (New York: Holt, Rinehart & Winston, 1972) and Peter Collett, ed., *Social Rules and Social Behavior* (Totowa, N.J.: Rowman and Littlefield, 1977). And, more specifically, the current state of our knowledge about "rules" and their importance in communication is documented in Susan B. Shimanoff, *Communication Rules: Theory and Research,* Sage Library of Social Research, No. 97 (Beverly Hills: Sage Pub., 1980).

▶ A change in one element usually produces changes in all others. So, for example, if a speaker's attitude toward the listeners is optimistic and enthusiastic, that attitude may be reciprocated by audience members who get caught up in the excitement. On the other hand, if a speaker adopts a highly formal style in building a message, the audience is likely to react with solemnity and seriousness.

▶ No single element controls the entire process. A speech is not "a thing," nor is the speaker the sole controlling mechanism. Undoubtedly, because "you" the speaker construct the message— with your ideas, feelings, and communicative capabilities— speeches are more or less extensions of that "you." But that message is modified by the way you use communicative channels, by audience expectations and listening skills, and even by the setting in which you present it. All five elements endlessly affect each other as a speech unfolds through time and space.

It also is useful to think about a speech as a *transaction.* Inherent in the notion of "transaction" is the idea of selective exchange:

▶ I prepare a speech to "give" to you, and you in turn give me your attention and even your reactions (called feedback).

▶ From among all of the things I *could* say about some subject, I *actually* select only a few, and tailor them to your interests, wants, and desires, as well as to limitations of time and space. You, in turn, from among all of the reactions you could have to my speech, select a few things to say about me, and about what I have said.

▶ As I assert my right to speak to fellow human beings, you assert your right to listen or not, to react as you see fit.

Even though, therefore, we tend to think about speeches as "one way" communication, actually the influences flow in two directions—from speaker to listener and from listener to speaker. The notion of selective transaction is crucial in understanding the speech-making process, for speakers and audiences modify each other's behaviors and thoughts. *Indeed, one of oral communication's primary advantages over other modes of communication—written and electronic—is that it is a transaction, a face-to-face process of mutual give-and-take.* It is a uniquely human mode of information sharing and decision making.

THE SKILLS AND COMPETENCIES NEEDED FOR SUCCESSFUL SPEECHMAKING

Because public speaking is an interactive process whereby people transact various kinds of information and business, one must possess or acquire certain skills to make the process work. Six basic qualities, in particular, merit attention in this brief overview: (1) *integrity*, (2) *knowledge*, (3) *sensitivity to listener needs*, (4) *sensitivity to speaking situations*, (5) *oral skills*, and (6) *self-confidence and control*.

Integrity

Your reputation for reliability and high motives is perhaps your single, most powerful means of exerting influence as a speaker. Especially in a day of electronic advertising and mass mailings—when every pressure group, cause, and special interest can worm its way into the public mind, often with conflicting analyses and recommendations for action—integrity becomes all important.

How do people sort out good from bad analyses, prudent from imprudent recommendations? Ultimately, most of us make our decisions—especially in areas where we have little firsthand experience—by deciding whom we should trust. If you have a reputation for being truthful, for careful support of your ideas, for fairness in treating opponents, and for a deep-felt commitment to the betterment of your peers, your effectiveness as a speaker will increase markedly.[12]

Knowledge

Expertise, as we noted when discussing credibility, is essential if you want to affect your listeners. As you acquire skills in research and analysis, you will employ your knowledge more and more successfully when speaking.

To broaden your knowledge and enhance your understanding of the world and the ideas and values of people in it, you must read widely and observe carefully. When carefully considered and supplemented by additional study, the background you already have will provide sufficient material for your practice speeches. Selecting and organizing that material will help you marshal and clarify your thinking. Indeed, you will do well to

---

[12]A fuller discussion of the role that personal integrity plays in successful public communication may be found in Otis M. Walter, *Speaking to Inform and Persuade* (New York: The Macmillan Co., 1966), Chapter 8, "The *Ethos* of the Speaker."

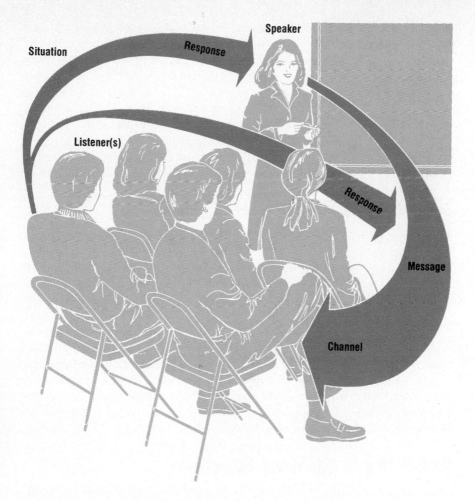

The Speech Communication Transaction

A SPEAKER, influenced by past conditioning, present
SITUATION, communicative purpose, level of knowledge
    and speaking skill, and attitudes toward self, subject, and listener(s), transmits a
MESSAGE which has content, structure, and style, over
CHANNELS which limit or shape the messages to one or more
LISTENER(S) whose reception of the message is, in turn, influenced by
    conditioning, purpose, situation, and attitudes toward self, subject,
    and speaker. They respond by sending feedback to the speaker in
    the form of visual or verbal signals.

begin in just this way—by talking about things that are vivid parts of your own personal experience. As you grow in skill and confidence, you will want to reach beyond immediate and familiar topics. You may wish to investigate and speak about ideas and developments relevant to your personal future— your job, your chosen career, or profession. Be careful also to acquire knowledge and develop interests *outside* your work, however. To become a well-rounded and interesting speaker, you must know about more than a single subject. Keep abreast of current happenings in your world, your country, your community by reading at least one daily newspaper, listening frequently to news broadcasts, and watching well-documented telecasts.

Sensitivity to Listener Needs

Sometimes we talk publicly simply to hear ourselves talk; occasionally we talk for purely *expressive* reasons. Usually, however, we speak for *instrumental* reasons—to give others information or ideas, to influence their thoughts or actions. The most successful public speakers are "other-directed," concerned with meeting their listeners' needs and solving their problems through oral communication.

To be an other-directed public communicator, you must be particularly sensitive to the desires, needs, and queries of your listeners. Generally, this means you must regard your auditors as intelligent, feeling creatures—as people "worth" taking into account as you prepare and deliver speeches. More specifically, this also means that you have to be willing to engage in audience analysis. Large portions of this textbook will be devoted to increasing your skills in audience analysis.

Sensitivity to Speaking Situations

As we suggested earlier, the physical setting and the social context surrounding a speech exert undeniable pressures on speakers (and their listeners). They create both a *set of expectations* and a *readiness to act* in certain ways.[13] Those expectations are often termed, as we suggested, the "customs" or the "rules" governing some group or setting, and readiness to act is usually discussed as "mind set" or "crowd mentality." Successful speakers

---

[13]The importance of context in determining interpretations of messages is treated well in Irving Biederman, "Perceiving Real-World Scenes," *Science,* 177 (July 7, 1972), 177–80. A book that makes expectations and their effect upon communicative reactions central is Bruce E. Gronbeck, *The Articulate Person: A Guide to Everyday Public Speaking,* 2nd ed. (Glenview, Ill.: Scott, Foresman and Co., 1983).

are adept at analyzing both conditions. That is, you must be willing to probe a group's customs or rules. Before you speak to a Rotary Club, for example, you should know what the members "want" from speakers, where you will fit into the program, how formal you are expected to be, to what degree they normally allow speakers to advocate courses of action or to defend causes. Before talking to a church or city council, you should find out how long people are allowed to speak in defending an idea, what level of emotional intensity is normal, what kinds of evidence (personal experience? statistical documentation?) are expected. Furthermore, you certainly will want to find out something about the homogeneity or diversity of the group members, the physical arrangements, and the like, so as to identify the usual "mind sets" or "response patterns" associated with particular situations. This kind of preparation will help ensure that your communication fits the group's customs and meets their expectations.

Oral Skills

Fluency, poise, control of the voice, and coordinated movements of the body mark the skillful public speaker. Combined with integrity, knowledge, and self-confidence, such skills can significantly increase your effectiveness by enabling you to communicate your ideas forcefully and attractively.

Skill in speaking is gained principally through practice. Practice, however, proceeds best when based on a knowledge of sound principles and carried on under the direction of a competent instructor. Moreover, care must be exercised that in practicing you do not develop distracting habits or acquire an unnatural or artificial manner of delivery. Good public speaking is animated, but it is also natural and conversational. It commands attention not through the use of tricks and techniques, but because of the speaker's earnest desire to communicate. Indeed, many successful public speakers seem merely to be *conversing* with their audiences. In the chapters that follow we shall extend our consideration of these and other communicative skills and suggest how you may develop, refine, and implement their use in practical speaking situations. Also, at the end of the chapters in this textbook we have provided some "Oral Activities" designed to encourage and guide your practice in mastering these necessary skills.

Self-Confidence and Control

The competent speaker has an appropriate measure of self-confidence and self-control. So central are self-confidence and control to effective public speaking that, in a sense, much of what we say in this book is aimed toward
(*text continues on page 21*)

Overcoming Speech Fright

I. *Take Precautions to Prevent Problems Ahead of Time:*
   1. Rehearse aloud, and be sure to try several different wordings for maximum flexibility.
   2. Use legible notes, well spaced for easy reference; number your pages.
   3. Be familiar with the setting—size of room, closeness of audience, amplification equipment—so you're not surprised.
   4. Even while practicing, constantly focus on your ideas—what you'll be saying first, second, third, etc.—rather than your fears of "how you're doing."
   5. As you practice, tell yourself what you're doing "right"—how well you've marshalled your facts, examples, statistics, etc.
   6. Visualize yourself doing well before the audience, psychologically "see" yourself impressing your listeners, getting a good response from them.

II. *Search and Destroy Your Hidden Fears:*
   1. *Information:* What's your shakiest piece of information or your least-supported claim? Can you improve it?
   2. *Audience:* Who's going to be there? Whom do you most dread facing? Why? Can you overcome that dread through better preparation? through convincing yourself that the dread is unfounded?
   3. *Questioning:* What's the one question you hope no one will ask? How will you answer it? (Remember that presidents of the United States prepare for press conferences by practicing answers to all the nasty questions the press corps is likely to ask.)
   4. *Appearances:* Are you worried about looking young? Inexperienced? Poorly or inappropriately dressed? Awkward? How can you compensate for those worries in what you do, wear, or say?
   5. *Disasters:* What's the worst thing that could go wrong during the speech? What can you do to prevent it?
   6. *End of Your Career:* What's the worst thing that could happen as a result of this speech? Will it happen? Is it really the end of the world? So what?

III. *Prepare Yourself Physically to Speak:*
   1. As your time to speak nears, take several deep breaths, hold them, and then slowly release them.
   2. If your mouth has a tendency to dry out (that's called "cottonmouth"), drink water before and even during your speech. Or use a mint or breath spray.
   3. Just before you rise to speak, tense the muscles in your legs, arms, chest, stomach, buttocks, and face (if you can without others seeing you). Tensed muscles will relax for a while after forced tension.
   4. Just before you utter your first word, take one last deep breath, and perhaps tense your hands and arms if you can do so unobtrusively.
   5. And remember, the act of speaking will drain off excess energy within a minute or two, especially if you remember to move during the introduction of your speech.

developing or strengthening this essential quality. The quality is attained primarily by overcoming a series of fears.[14]

What we term *speech fright* or *communication apprehension* is a complex psycho-physical condition that arises from psychological stress (fear of public failure, feelings of inadequacy) and physiological overloads (increased flow of adrenalin in times of expectancy or fear, increased heart rate and blood pressure, excessive muscular tension). Speech fright is a perfectly natural reaction to stress, something felt by 60 to 70 percent of Americans, according to surveys. Although the reaction varies a good deal from person to person, it tends to produce sweaty palms, throaty tension, body rigidity, and vocal hesitations ("ahms," "ahs," half-words, rephrasings).

Keep in mind, though, that for the vast majority of us, speech fright is simply a fear which must be overcome in ways we overcome most of our other fears. These include engaging in the activity often enough to discover it's not fatal, talking through our fear with others to see how they control it, and attacking it physically and psychologically through focused activities. See the outline, "Overcoming Speech Fright," for suggestions.

Keep in mind, too, another feature of communication apprehension: It can be *used positively* by most speakers. Speech fright tends to make you more alert, more energetic as you try to dissipate the extra adrenalin coursing through your veins and as you psyche yourself up for meeting the challenge of public address. This extra energy gives you an edge—like being "up" for a game. Ultimately, then, it gives you the self-confidence you need to speak effectively.

 ## GROUP PROJECTS

1. Interview a local booking agent for public lectures, the director of the campus speaker's bureau, or another individual in a similar position to determine which speech skills are most highly prized in "professional" speakers. Discuss the list of skills you obtain, comparing them with your own preferences and those of your classmates.

2. To get acquainted, divide into interest groups based on academic areas, special interests, political preferences, or some other broad factor suggested by your instructor. Select a representative from each group to report on why members became interested in the particular area and what plans they have for future involvement or participation in the area.

---

[14]"What Are Americans Afraid Of?" *The Bruskin Report*, 13, #53: "Surveys Reveal Students' Concern Over Jobs, Public-Speaking Anxiety," *Pitt News*, May 1978, p. 4.

INDIVIDUAL PROJECTS

1. After thoughtful analysis, prepare an inventory of your personal speech needs and your abilities as a speaker. (Your instructor may make this the first assignment in a Personal Communication Journal that you will maintain throughout the term.) The inventory, at minimum, should contain detailed responses to the following items:

I am _____   I can _____

I am not _____   I cannot _____

I want _____

2. To the extent that the physical facilities of the classroom permit, your instructor will ask members of the class to seat themselves in a large circle or in smaller groups around two or three separate tables. Informality should be the keynote in this particular activity. After the instructor has completed a brief self-introduction, each class member will provide a self-introduction based generally on the following pattern:

My name is _____

My major (or my major interest) is _____

I am enrolled in this college/university because _____

_____

In addition to a grade credit, what I hope to get from this course in speech communication is _____

3. Each student will work with another member of the class. You will introduce your partner to the class, and your partner will introduce you. In addition to getting acquainted with your classmates, this project will provide practice in obtaining, selecting, and ordering information.

SUGGESTIONS FOR FURTHER READING

Lloyd Bitzer, "The Rhetorical Situation," *Philosophy and Rhetoric*, 1 (January, 1968), 1–14.

Frank E. X. Dance and Carl E. Larson, *The Functions of Human Communication: A Theoretical Approach* (New York: Holt, Rinehart & Winston, 1976), "Part 1: A Theoretical Strategy," pp. 3–51.

Stephen W. Littlejohn, "A Bibliography of Studies Related to Variables of Source Credibility," *Bibliographic Annual in Speech Communication: 1971*, ed. Ned A. Shearer (New York: Speech Communication Association, 1972), pp. 1–40.

C. David Mortensen, *Communication: The Study of Human Interaction* (New York: McGraw-Hill Book Company, 1972), especially Chapter 2, "Communication Models," and Chapter 8, "Situational Geography."

Susan B. Shimanoff, *Communication Rules: Theory and Research*, Sage Library of Social Research, No. 97 (Beverly Hills: Sage Publications, Inc., 1980).

CHAPTER 2

Listening: Speaker-Audience Interaction

When was the last time you listened? It was probably just a few moments ago. Listening accounts for over 40 percent of all of your communication time; more time is spent listening than writing, reading, or speaking.[1] Listening serves important functions in our culture because through it we learn the rules and expectations of our society and how to assess the feelings and needs of others. Young children do most of their learning by listening— even now you depend on it for learning each time you go to class.

Listening is also vital in the public speaking setting. The listener is a key element in the communication process, because without a receiver for a message, the speaker would have little motivation for speaking. When preparing a speech, the speaker makes choices based on information about listeners' attitudes, backgrounds, and general frames of reference. If the listener does not understand the message, the communication event is not complete, not valid.

In this chapter, we will explore the listening process, give guidelines for more effective listening, and provide a checklist to help you listen more efficiently in the speech classroom. With this information, you should be better able to structure your speeches with the listener in mind and also begin to improve your own listening skills.

---

[1] See studies reviewed by Andrew Wolvin and Carolyn Coakley, *Listening* (Dubuque, Ia.: Wm. C. Brown Co., 1982), Chapter 1.

LISTENING BEHAVIOR

Hearing and Listening

To listen to a message, you must first hear it. Hearing is the physiological process whereby sound waves travel through the air and make impact on the tympanic membrane; listening is the process of attaching meaning to aural signals.[2] The following diagram illustrates the speaking-hearing process. Once the sound waves have been set to the brain, listening can begin. After the sound waves register in the brain, the receiver interprets them and places them in meaningful contexts. The way this meaning is assimilated is the heart of the listening process.

We often assume that a person who is hearing is also listening, but that may not be true. Because we are called on to do so much listening, we sometimes prefer not to understand what we hear. The public speaker should be aware that even though the sound waves may be transmitting a message to the audience, and even though the volume of the presentation is adequate, the audience may not be attaching meaning to what is being said. As a receiver of messages, you may recall a time when a speaker was sharing ideas, but you elected not to listen. You heard; you waited until the person quit transmitting sound. That was your cue that the speech was finished and that you were to applaud or respond in some way. You may not have comprehended anything that the speaker said—you were hearing but not listening. Getting an audience to actually listen, therefore, is one of the public speaker's primary goals.

The Listener-Speaker Relationship

Too often we assume that the speaker is responsible for successful communication. As described in Chapter 1, the communication process is circular, and the listener is a vital component. After processing the message, the listener is responsible for providing adequate feedback to the speaker to indicate that the message has been received and understood. A receiver who is not listening will not be able to provide the necessary feedback. If listener feedback indicates misunderstanding or doubt, the speaker then has the opportunity to rephrase or recast the idea using other symbols. As speakers,

---

[2]Thomas Lewis and Ralph Nichols, *Speaking and Listening* (Dubuque, Ia.: Wm. C. Brown Co., 1965), p. 6.

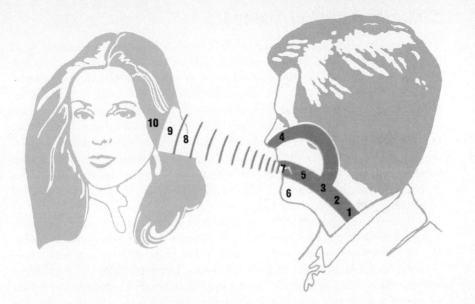

The Production and Reception of Human Sound

(1) *A stream of air* is sent from the lungs through the trachea to (2) the *vocal folds* ("voice box"), which in turn vibrate at various pitches, depending upon tension in the muscles. As the sound proceeds up the throat, it is shaped by (3) the *palate* and given resonance or additional tones by (4) the *nasal and sinus regions.* The sounds or phonemes which make up our language are formed primarily by (5) the *tongue,* (6) *jaw placement,* and (7) the *lips.* The formed sound, in "waves," travels through the air to an ear. It enters (8) the *outer ear* (concha), moves through (9) the *auditory canal* (external meatus), and strikes (10) the *tympanum* (eardrum). The eardrum "translates" the sound waves once more to physical vibrations, which, through the bones of the middle ear, send the vibrations via nerves to the brain.

we are continually searching for nonverbal and verbal cues which signal that our messages are being understood. As receivers, we are responsible for providing useful feedback to the speaker; and accurate feedback is dependent upon careful listening.

Communication, then, is a joint responsibility. A speaker who does not make every attempt to provide a clear, vital message cannot expect avid listeners; and receivers who do not take time and energy to listen and respond to the speaker cannot expect the speaker to try to meet particular needs of the audience. These dual responsibilities provide the critical interaction necessary for good communication.

Characteristics of Listeners

Successful, mutually rewarding speech transactions, therefore, depend upon joint efforts. Yet, a problem can arise: Few of us are good listeners. Although researchers vary in their assessments of the average listening comprehension rate, they agree that we do not utilize our listening potential.[3] Some studies indicate that we may be listening at only a 25 percent comprehension rate, that we may be understanding only one fourth of all of the information aurally transmitted. There are several reasons why people are poor listeners. As a speaker, it is important that you be aware of these so you can better adjust and adapt your messages. For the next few pages, imagine yourself as a listener. This will help you understand more clearly the challenges and obligations you will have as a speaker.

One of the reasons that we are poor listeners is that our complex minds can comprehend many more words per minute than speakers can produce. As listeners, we can mentally handle more than 400 spoken words per minute, yet the average speaker produces between 125–175 words per minute. Stated in a slightly different way, the listener needs only 15 seconds of every minute to comprehend what the speaker said. The time lag thus created in the listener's mind presents special problems. In the excess time, the listener begins to think about other things. Perhaps you can recall a situation where you started out listening to a speaker but soon found yourself thinking about an upcoming test or lunch or an important appointment. As you listened, other priorities gradually took more of your thinking time. Before long, you were not thinking about the speech at all. The multitude of "other things" listeners can think about often takes the attention that originally had been paid to listening. As listeners, we "drop in" and listen for a few seconds, then go back to our own thoughts. This tendency poses many problems for the speaker who is sincerely trying to convey an understandable message.

Furthermore, as listeners, we often bring into the communication setting our past, our feelings, our values, and our attitudes. Sometimes the speaker will present a thought or a word which triggers a past experience. At that point we start to think about that experience and soon forget the message being presented.

Our attitudes, values, and beliefs can cause us to give personalized interpretations and meanings to the spoken message. When we do not agree

---

[3]For a discussion see Carl Weaver, *Human Listening* (Indianapolis, Ind.: Bobbs-Merrill Publishers, 1972), Chapter 1, and Larry L. Barker, *Listening Behavior* (Englewood Cliffs, N.J.: Prentice-Hall, Inc., 1971), Chapter 3.

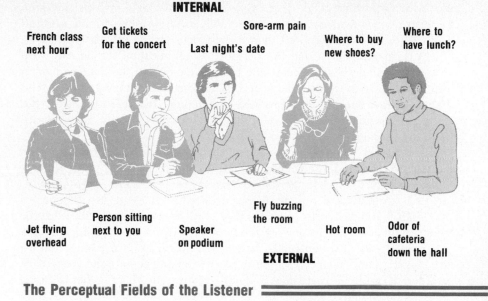

INTERNAL

French class next hour | Get tickets for the concert | Sore-arm pain | Last night's date | Where to buy new shoes? | Where to have lunch?

Jet flying overhead | Person sitting next to you | Speaker on podium | Fly buzzing the room | Hot room | Odor of cafeteria down the hall

EXTERNAL

The Perceptual Fields of the Listener

with the message, we spend mental time "debating" the ideas of the speaker instead of listening for the full development of those ideas. Much faulty listening can be attributed to the fact that as listeners we do not give the speaker the benefit of a full presentation before drawing conclusions about the "rightness" or "wrongness" of the ideas. At times, our feelings color our reception so much that we attribute ideas to the speaker that were not actually presented. This happens especially when we disagree with the speaker. Perhaps you can recall a time when you disagreed with the speaker—you convinced yourself through selective perception and filtering that the speech contained a particular message, when in fact, it may have been quite different. Many arguments begin because of this listening problem.

A second problem is passive listeners: Listening is an active process. It takes energy, and many of us are lazy listeners. Because it takes energy to focus mentally, we prefer to sit back and assume a passive role. Being passive is much easier than concentrating on the speaker's message, but, unfortunately, it leads to ineffective listening. Think back for a moment to the last time you enjoyed a good movie. When you left the theatre you may have felt tired even though you had nothing to do but watch and listen. Because you empathized with the actors, you were "living" the flow of events with the characters. This empathic response takes energy, the same type of energy you use when you are actively listening. It is easier to pretend to listen or to "fake attention" than it is to focus on the spoken message.

A third problem is that the physical communication setting can work against listening. Seats are hard; the room is too cold or too hot; the person next to you is coughing; the heater is making a distracting sound. The listening environment may produce distractions that compete with the speaker's message. Physical well-being and comfort usually take priority with the listener.

Fourth, the listener's own needs also may compete with the speaker's ideas. Perhaps you didn't sleep well, have a cold, or are hungry. All of these personal factors compete for your energy and focus. Again, your physical needs as an individual win out over your intellectual needs as a listener.

Fifth, because it takes mental and physical energy to deal with words or concepts that we don't know, it is easier to turn off the listening process when the speaker uses unfamiliar language. As listeners, we assume that we are unable to understand what the speaker is talking about if the vocabulary is different or the ideas are new. Unfamiliarity requires energy that listeners may not be willing to expend. Unless the listener is willing to take the time to attach meaning to the symbols, true listening is impossible.

And finally, preset ideas about the topic, the speaker, or the occasion also may interfere with adequate listening comprehension. If you have heard that Professor Smith is a boring lecturer, you will enter the class with that preset notion. Chances are that you will find that Professor Smith's lectures are boring, not because they are but because you allowed the reputation to interfere with the reality of the communication event. Many speakers are not given a fair hearing because the audience accepts conclusions about them or their topics beforehand. Again, it is easier to validate these claims through partial listening or no listening at all than it is to focus energy and then come to a legitimate conclusion. Perhaps Professor Smith is not a very good lecturer, but you should come to this conclusion based on a fair sample of lectures, not on the reputation that preceded your experience in class.

What, then, can you as speaker expect from a listening audience? You know they probably will have other things on their minds, things of more concern to them than the information you want to share. They may not be physically or mentally prepared to listen. Their preconceived biases about you, the topic, or the words and ideas you present may interfere with acceptance of your message. Lastly, you know that you, as speaker, will have to make some adjustments and adaptations for your listeners just because they are listeners. We will talk about those speaker responsibilities later in this chapter.

Purposes of Listening

Just as speakers have different motivations for speaking, so, too, listeners have different expectations and purposes for listening. Wolvin and Coakley identify five reasons or purposes for listening: listening for appreciation, discrimination, therapeutic value, comprehension, and critical analysis.[4]

The purpose of *appreciative listening* is to enjoy sensory stimulation. Although most appreciative listening is in response to stimuli such as musical scores or the reading of poetry, some may listen appreciatively to the pattern of speech used by the speaker or the softness or musical quality of the voice. Do you recall enjoying a speaker because of the way the voice sounded? How much do you remember about the content presented? Some speakers have voices or a sense of verbal style that invite appreciative listening.

In *discriminative listening*, the receiver draws conclusions about the spoken message based on an interpretation of the way the message is presented. Here the listener may be turning less attention to the content or meaning of the words than to the emotional coloring of the message. Listeners sense how the speaker feels about the message based on how the speaker delivers the speech. Think about a time when you knew your parents were angry with you, not so much by their words but more by the way they spoke them. You were discerning a particular feeling about what they were communicating. Public audiences use this same sense when interpreting what the speaker means; we listen to the words not only for meaning but also for sincerity or personal feeling. As you speak, then, some members of the audience may be listening to discriminate feelings rather than to understand the message.

Therapeutic listening occurs when the listener is acting as a "sounding board" for someone who needs to talk out a concern. Although all listening is empathic to some degree, therapeutic listening is more so. This purpose for listening is most often associated with interpersonal settings, but it occurs in public settings as well. An audience listening to a public confession of religious conversion or a public apology for improper conduct may be engaged in therapeutic listening.

Listening for comprehension occurs when the listener wants to gain additional information provided by the speaker. When we listen to radio or television for news or sports information, when we attend to directions on how to do something, when we listen "to learn in classrooms" we are listening for comprehension. When your audience is listening to comprehend, they will be more receptive to your message.

---

[4]The material on the purposes of listening were drawn from Wolvin and Coakley, Chapters 4–8.

In *critical listening* the receiver of the message must decide on the worth of the message. We practice this type of listening when we evaluate commercials or when we listen to persuasive political messages. In critical listening, we establish criteria by which to judge the value of the message. After applying these criteria, we decide to accept or reject, to act or delay action on the message.

When you speak, then, you should try to determine your audience's purposes for listening. However, in most cases, the audience will depend on you to tell them how they should be listening. When you begin the speech, include your purpose for speaking; clue your audience as to the type of listening they should be prepared to do. Of course, there will always be times when, even though you tell the audience what the speech purpose is, individual members of the audience will decide to listen for other reasons. While speakers always hope that the public speaking audience listens primarily for understanding and analysis, some members of the audience may only attend to the speaker's voice and emotional cueing. Knowing this should help you satisfy the variety of listening purposes that members of one audience may have.

GUIDELINES FOR EFFECTIVE LISTENING

As we noted earlier, both the speaker and the listener are vital components of the communication process. Both the sender and the receiver need to assume responsibility if the message is to be understood as intended. Their tasks are different but complementary.

Listener's Responsibilities

Although we all listen for different purposes in different communication settings, we will focus here on skills for comprehensive and critical listening since these two are most useful for public speaking audiences. In doing so, we will suggest ways of improving skills by listener analysis of self, speaker, and message.

Listener Analysis of Self.   To become a better listener in the public setting, you first must identify your listening patterns and preferences. Think carefully about the times when you are a very good listener, when listening is easy for you and when you remember most of the content of the message. What types of settings are those? What kinds of things do you do to keep your attention focused on the message and the speaker? Think also about those times when it is difficult for you to listen for comprehension and critical analysis. Why is it difficult to listen? Are you uninterested in the

Listening for appreciation, discrimination, therapy, comprehension, and critical analysis represents the five basic purposes for which people listen to others. On some occasions, one or another of these purposes will dominate in your mind. On other occasions—as in a classroom, for example—you often will shift your mental operations from purpose to purpose as the occasion progresses.

subject? Are you bored or tired? Taking stock of your listening habits will help you recognize your strong and weak listening qualities.

Think also about your listening preferences. Are there people to whom you prefer to listen? Are some classes especially exciting for you even though they are required lecture courses? What features of these people and classes cause you to think and listen with an eager ear? By quickly scanning your habits, patterns, and preferences for listening, you can begin to identify and reinforce positive aspects of your listening behavior.

In addition to reviewing your listening behavior you can begin to correct poor habits by preparing to listen. Before you actually enter the communication event or shortly after the speaker begins the message, ask yourself this series of questions:

1. *What is my purpose in listening?* Do I expect to gain information and understanding or to make a critical decision based on the speaker's presentation? Think about your listening behavior when a teacher announces "This material will be on the next test." You probably pay particular attention to that material, making sure that you understand it. By recognizing why you are listening, you can better analyze the message. If the message has personal importance, you will be more likely to give it your attention.

2. *Am I impartial about the topic being presented?* If you are not willing to let the speaker fully develop ideas before you draw conclusions, you may

be wasting the speaker's time and yours. Set aside your prior feelings until the speaker has had a chance to develop a position. That does not mean that you cannot disagree; every listener has the duty to question and evaluate the materials presented. But you should suspend judgment until all of the ideas have been developed.

3. *How much do I know about the topic?* If you still have a great deal to learn, you can better direct your attention to listening. If you know a lot about the topic, be prepared to compare the speaker's information to your knowledge. This may provide additional motivation for listening.

4. *What do I expect from this speech?* Be realistic. If a classmate is giving a speech about the stock market, you will be disappointed if you expect to learn the secret to small investments and quick return. If you expect only to increase your understanding of the way the stock market works, your expectations may be more easily satisfied. Don't burden the speaker with expectations that the person is not prepared to fulfill.

5. *What do I know about the speaking situation?* If you can anticipate the length of and the occasion for the speech, you can better focus your attention. In your class, you will be listening to a variety of speeches. You will know through the description of the assignment how long these speeches will be. Mentally prepare yourself to focus your attention on the speech for the expected period of time. Learning to listen is a skill that develops over time. If you can listen actively for shorter periods of time—for example the five minutes it may take for a classmate to give a speech, you gradually can increase the length of time that you will be able to listen.

6. *What can I expect from the listening environment?* Become aware of the physical environment. Note the temperature and sounds of the room. If you can deal with these and other possible distractions beforehand, you will be less likely to allow your attention to steal away after the speaker begins. Tell yourself that the room temperature and conditions will not interfere with your listening. A similar assessment should be made about the way you feel. If you are anxious about a test in your next class, deal with that mentally so that your concern will be less likely to disrupt your listening. Of course, you will not change the circumstances, but by mentally tabulating all of the conditions that could interfere with your skills, you can put these concerns into perspective.

7. *What "trigger" words or ideas cause me to stray from the listening situation?* As you listen, don't let past experiences distract you from the current communication event. Take note of special words that seem to pull you away from the speaker's message. After the listening situation is over,

try to think why those words caused your attention to be redirected. If they were unfamiliar, look them up in a dictionary. Building vocabulary will also help you prepare for the listening situation. By increasing your vocabulary, you will be less likely to be distracted by unfamiliar words.

Listener Analysis of Speaker.   Speaking does not occur in a vacuum. Both speaker and listener bring past experiences to the communication environment. In doing so, the listener attends not only to the message the speaker transmits but also considers the speaker's credibility. The following series of questions may help you decide how to view the speaker and what impact that perception will have on the message:

1. *What do I know about this speaker?* Rightly or wrongly, the reputation of the speaker will influence how you listen to the message. If your previous experience with the speaker has been favorable, you will be more likely to be receptive to the message. If you have had a disagreement with the person or if the person is someone you do not respect, you may allow that prior knowledge to filter and color the way you understand the message. We tend to do this when listening to political speakers, especially those we do not support. We assume that because we have not agreed with them before, we will not agree now; so instead of listening to the message, we mentally reinforce the reasons why we disagree. Without listening carefully, you may never consider worthwhile ideas which deserve your attention.

2. *How believable is the speaker?* We tend to answer this question based on previous experiences with the speaker or on information about the speaker. If you know that the speaker has misled another audience, you will probably assume that you are being subjected to the same treatment. You may adjust your listening to search out unfounded conclusions, assuming they are untrue. In doing so, you may be listening for detail and not for the main ideas presented. When you listen this way, you do remember the detail but have little reference to what the detail describes or modifies. You need to listen for the main ideas presented; the detail will follow. If you know that the speaker has reported false information, you should weigh that when considering and evaluating the message after it has been fully presented.

3. *Has the speaker prepared for the occasion by conducting adequate research and by considering relationships among ideas?* As listeners, we are more likely to accept messages that we perceive as carefully planned and researched. Yet just because a source has been cited by the speaker does not mean that careful research and planning has been conducted. You need to listen to the total presentation of ideas, noting the relationships between the

message and the supporting materials. Your opinion about the speaker's believability is based partially on his or her knowledge of the subject. Suppose you decided to buy a new car. You enter a showroom eager to find out about fuel efficiency and car durability. A resourceful salesperson volunteers to answer any questions you may have. Upon hearing your concerns, the salesperson begins a prepared speech about the new models, citing commendations from a driving magazine. Your interest will probably slacken because the person skirted the topics you were concerned about. If the salesperson had responded by answering your questions and then offering validation for the response, you would have been a more attentive listener.

4. *What is the speaker's attitude toward this presentation?* As listeners, we use our ears and our eyes to grasp meaning. We assess whether a message is worthy of our time in part by the attitudes the speaker projects. A speaker who appears flippant and uncaring creates an obstacle to productive listening. The speaker's manner of presentation may interfere with your listening skills. Some speakers have annoying habits that draw attention away from the message. Do you recall a speaker who paced back and forth while speaking or one who continually toyed with a paper clip or spoke so slowly that you couldn't follow the train of thought? As listeners, we must be careful that the speaker's mannerisms don't divert our attention from the message. If they are annoying, reconcile yourself to the situation and don't allow your concentration to be affected. Since we depend on nonverbal cues to enhance our understanding of the message, we must work to factor out distracting elements.

Listener Analysis of Message.   The message is the speaker's product. It gives information about the topic and expresses views. Therefore, the message should be the principal focus of the listener's energy. The receiver can better focus energy on the message by structuring listening behavior to answer three questions:

1. *What are the main ideas of the speech?* Try to discover the speaker's purpose for speaking and the ideas which contribute toward that purpose. Usually these can be found by determining the thesis of the speech and the statements that help the speaker explain the thesis. The main ideas serve as a skeleton on which the speaker builds the speech. The next time you listen to a commercial, listen for the main idea. What types of information does the person give to encourage you to accept the product? Listen the same way to a speech: By focusing on the main idea, we can better recall the message.

2. *How are the main ideas arranged?* By searching for the pattern of organization used by the speaker, the listener can see more easily the

relationships between and among the main ideas. If you know that the speaker is using a chronological pattern of development or a motivational sequence of ideas, it is easier to identify the main ideas and keep them ordered as the speech progresses.

3. *What sorts of supporting materials are used to develop the main ideas?* Consider the timeliness, the quality of the source, and the content of the supporting materials. Supporting materials are used to clarify, amplify, and strengthen the main ideas of the speech. Analyze these materials to help you evaluate the ideas presented. Check to make sure that the supporting materials, as well as the main ideas, make sense to you. If there is a discrepancy between your knowledge and the ideas presented by the speaker, find out why it exists. This should help you clarify the differences and reach a conclusion about the validity of the total message.

To focus your attention on the main ideas of the speech, on the pattern of development, and on the use of supporting materials, you should constantly *review, relate,* and *anticipate. Review* what the speaker has said. Take a few seconds to summarize the content of the message, to think about the way the materials have been developed. Mentally add to the summary review each time the speaker initiates a new topic for consideration. *Relate* the message to what you already know. Consider how important the message is to you and how you might use the information at some future time. *Anticipate* what the speaker might say next. Given the development of the materials to that point, what is the speaker likely to say next? Use the anticipation stage as a way of continuing to focus on the content of the message. It's not important if you are right or wrong—the important element is that you have directed your attention to the message. By reviewing, relating, and anticipating you can use up the extra time generated by the speech-thought lag and keep your attention focused on the message.

Speaker's Responsibilities

Even though it is the listener who finally judges the transmitted message, there are several steps that you as speaker can take to help the listener. These efforts are concentrated in three areas: preparing the speech, capturing and holding attention, and presenting the speech.

Preparing the Speech. When preparing the speech, keep in mind that it is often difficult for the listener to follow the structure of your presentation and to keep track of what's been said. Try to use an organizational pattern which is complementary to your purpose and is easy for the listener to follow. You may want to share the means of development with your audience with an initial summary or forecast early in the speech. This will help the listener follow your development. Guidelines in Chapters 11–12 will help you determine which organizational pattern is best for the types of speeches and audiences you will be addressing.

Careful planning and preparation will help guarantee that your message is clearly presented and is easy to follow. Researching the topic area to select the most appropriate forms of support will help you develop your ideas fully. The supporting materials make it easier for the listener to remember the main ideas of your speech. Poor planning makes the audience lose respect for the speaker; if your topic is worth speaking about, it is worth preparing.

When preparing your speech, anticipate points where your listeners will need special guidance. Forecasts and internal summaries will help the listeners focus on your ideas. Think about concepts that may be especially difficult for the listeners to understand. Try to present those concepts several times using different wording each time so that the listeners can better identify with the materials and ideas. Paraphrasing is a useful tool for the speaker.

During your planning, remember to keep your listeners in mind. If the audience is expecting a five-minute speech, try to tailor your presentation for that expectation. If you know that the environment is going to be uncomfortable for the audience, try to adapt your topic and length of speech to accommodate the physical situation. Your audience analysis may suggest other ways to adapt your message for easy comprehension.

Preparation also includes practice. While practicing your speech, you can work out awkward phrasing which might confuse the audience. Further, practice helps you feel more comfortable with your ideas. Your presentation will be easier to view, to listen to, and to accept if you are at ease and confident.

Using the Factors of Attention.   The speaker must recognize that the audience's listening behavior varies during the speech. It is important, then, to attack the problem of attention. If you can capture their attention and turn that attention into interest, the chances are that the listeners will be able to really *listen* to the whole message. It is important that every speaker, regardless of purpose, understand the relationship between interest and attention and be acquainted with those strategies which are specially designed to arouse and maintain interest in the message.

Interest and attention are closely related. People not only pay attention to what interests them, but—conversely—what they pay attention to over a period of time often tends to *become* interesting. Frequently, students begin a required course convinced that they are going to be thoroughly bored.

THE FACTORS OF ATTENTION

After a while, however, the course begins to interest them and may actually arouse them to the point that they continue to investigate the subject matter covered for many months or years. The important thing in a speech, therefore, is to capture the attention of the audience in the first place and to ensure that listeners give the message a fair hearing. When this is done—if the speaker is skillful and the message worthwhile—interest grows as the talk proceeds.

What is attention? For our purposes, it may be thought of as focus on one element in a given field, with the result that other elements in that field fade, become dim, and for all practical purposes momentarily cease to exist.[5] Consider, as an example, the baseball fan sitting in the bleachers. The home team is one run ahead in the ninth inning; the visiting team is at bat; the bases are loaded; there are two outs; and the count is three and two. The pitcher wraps his fingers around the ball, winds up, and curls a slider over the corner of the plate. The umpire bawls, "Strike three! You're out!" Only then does the fan lean back, take a long breath, and notice what has been going on around her: that she has dropped her sack of peanuts or thrown off her hat, that her neighbor has been thumping her on the back, that threatening clouds are gathering on the horizon. While all her faculties were focused on the crucial pitch—while, as we say, she was paying attention to it—she was largely unaware of her immediate surroundings. It is this focusing upon one source of stimuli to the greater or lesser exclusion of others that we call *attention*.

How can you as a speaker capture the attention of your listeners? How can you get them to focus on what you are saying rather than listen to the knocking radiator, study the hairstyle of the woman in the first row, or worry about tomorrow's dental appointment?

A great deal depends on how you deliver your speech—on the vigor and the variety of your gestures and bodily movements, on the flexibility and animation of your voice. Your reputation and prestige *(ethos)* also will help secure a degree of attention, and the color and impressiveness of your language or style will contribute, too. *Fundamentally, however, you will*

---

[5]Psychologist Floyd L. Ruch, University of Southern California, describes attention more precisely as "The process of psychological selectivity by which we select from a vast number of potential stimuli, only those which are related to present interests and needs." He explains: "From among the many stimuli which are within range physiologically, we select—and consciously react to—only those that are related to our present needs and interests. . . . Most psychologists regard attention as having three interrelated aspects, all of which are part of a single complex act. Attention is (1) an adjustment of the body and its sense organs, (2) clear and vivid consciousness, and (3) a set toward action." In *Psychology and Life*, 7th brief ed. (Glenview, Ill.: Scott, Foresman and Company, 1967), pp. 295, 572.

capture attention through the types of ideas you present to your hearers. As the experience of many speakers has shown, some types of ideas have greater attention value than others; people not only are attracted to them in the first place, but—upon listening to these ideas—their interest or concern is further aroused.

Those types of ideas which have high attention value are sometimes called the "factors of attention" and include the following:

1. Activity or Movement   4. Familiarity   7. Conflict
2. Reality   5. Novelty   8. Humor
3. Proximity   6. Suspense   9. The Vital

These terms, of course, overlap; and in an actual speech the qualities they represent often are combined. For purposes of explanation, however, we can consider them separately.

Activity. If you were at the theater and one actor was standing motionless while another was moving excitedly about the stage, which one would you look at? The moving one, more likely. Ideas that "move" likewise tend to attract attention. Narratives in which something happens or in which there are moments of uncertainty and crisis nearly always have attention value. Similarly, expository talks hold attention when, for instance, the parts of a machine are described as being in motion or when aspects of a process are introduced.

In addition, your speech as a whole should "move"—should, as someone has said, "march" or press forward. Nothing is so boring as a talk that seems to stand still. For this reason, it is important to make the progress of your speech apparent to your audience by indicating when you have finished one idea and are ready to tackle the next, or by previewing the ground yet to be covered. Instructions and demonstrations, particularly, demand orderly, systematic "marching." Do not spend too much time on any one point, and do not elaborate the obvious; constantly push ahead toward a clearly defined goal.

Reality. The earliest words a child learns are the names of "real" objects and of tangible acts related to them. This interest in reality—in the immediate, the concrete, the actual—persists throughout life. The proposition $2 + 2 = 4$ when unrelated to any specific events, persons, or circumstances isn't very interesting. Instead of talking in abstractions, talk of real-life people, places, and happenings. Use pictures, diagrams, and charts, especially in reports. Tell not what happened to "a certain prominent physician of this city," but to Dr. Clare Fitzgerald, who lives at 418 Paine Street. Make your descriptions specific and vivid. Remember always that actual cases are more real to a listener than general trends or broad classifications, particular names and places are more interesting than impersonalized, vague allusions.

Proximity. A direct reference to someone in the audience, to some object near at hand, to some incident that has just occurred, or to the immediate occasion on which the speech is being made usually will command attention. A reference to a remark of a preceding speaker or of the chairperson creates a similar effect. If attention lags, call a member of the audience by name or make him or her the central character in a hypothetical illustration. Not only will this awaken anyone who happens to be dozing (heaven forbid!), but it will also tend to increase the attention-level of the other members. As psychologists Floyd L. Ruch and Philip G. Zimbardo point out, "Individuating listeners is one of the most effective means of getting—and holding—attention. When you are talking to a single individual, looking him straight in the eye increases the likelihood that he will look back at you and listen to what you have to say."[6]

Familiarity. Many things are familiar to us because we meet them in our daily lives. Knives and forks, rain, automobiles, toothbrushes, classes, and a host of other common objects and events are closely built into our experiences. Because they are so much a part of us, these familiar things catch our attention. We say, "Ah, that is an old friend"; oral instructions almost always profit from references to the familiar. But, as with old acquaintances, we become bored if we see too much of them and nothing else. In a spoken message, the familiar holds attention primarily when the speaker introduces it in connection with something unfamiliar or when some fresh or unknown aspect of it is pointed out. Stories about Lincoln and Washington, for example, are interesting because we are familiar with their characters; but we don't like to hear the same old railsplitter or cherry-tree tales unless they are given a new twist or application.

Novelty. As an old newspaper adage has it, when a dog bites a man, it's an accident; when a man bites a dog, it's news. Perhaps we should marvel that airplanes make countless flights across the oceans every day, but we take this for granted. Even missile launchings and space travel command less attention than they did a few years ago. Routine occurrences are not news; only novel happenings, dramatic advances, or unusual developments attract wide notice.

Two special types of novelty are *size* and *contrast*. Insofar as *size* is concerned, especially large or especially small objects or amounts attract

---

[6]Floyd L. Ruch and Philip G. Zimbardo, *Psychology and Life*, 8th ed. (Glenview, Ill.: Scott, Foresman and Company, 1971), p. 268.

attention. Reference to a $8,000 automobile or to a $80,000 home would not stand out as unusual; but reference to a $30,000 automobile or to a $300,000 home would. In a speech on the high cost of national defense, a speaker caught the attention of his listeners with this sentence: "Considering that it costs more than $5,000 to equip an average soldier for combat, it is disquieting to learn that in a year his equipment will be 60 percent obsolete."[7]

Although attention-arousing in themselves, large and small figures become even more compelling when thrown into *contrast* with their opposites. Here is how Henry W. Grady, in an address at the University of Virginia, used novel or startling contrasts to focus attention on the gap between the rich and the poor:

> A home that cost three million dollars and a breakfast that cost five thousand are disquieting facts to the millions who live in a hut and dine on a crust. The fact that a man . . . has an income of twenty million dollars falls strangely on the ears of those who hear it as they sit empty-handed with children crying for bread.[8]

In utilizing the materials of novelty be careful, of course, not to inject elements that are so different or unusual that they are entirely unfamiliar. As we have emphasized, your listeners must at least know what you are talking about, or their attention will soon waver. They must be able to relate what you say to things they know and—preferably—have a degree of experience with. Best results are achieved by the proper combination of the new and the old, of the novel and the familiar. Note, too, that novelty may gain attention, but will not necessarily hold it.

Suspense.   A large part of the interest which people have in a mystery story arises from uncertainty about its outcome. When giving a speech, create uncertainty by pointing out results which have mysterious or unknown causes or by calling attention to forces which threaten uncertain effects. Introduce suspense into the stories you use to illustrate your ideas, especially in lectures or even in demonstrations. Mention valuable information you expect to divulge later in your talk but which requires an understanding of what you are now saying. Make full use of the factor of suspense; but in doing so, observe two cautions: (1) Do not make the information seem so difficult or mysterious that your listeners lose all hope of

---

[7]Neal Luker, "Our Defense Policy," a speech presented in a course in advanced public speaking at the University of Iowa.

[8]From an address by Henry W. Grady, presented to the Literary Societies of the University of Virginia, June 25, 1889.

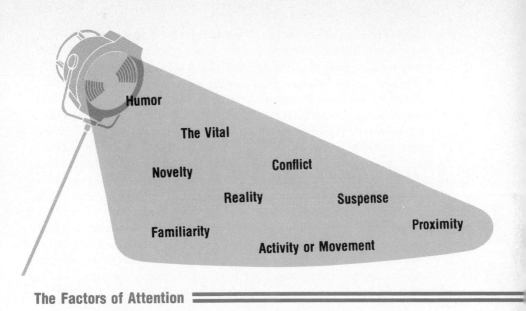

The Factors of Attention

comprehending it; and (2) make sure that the information, when it finally is revealed, is important enough to warrant the suspense you have created.

Conflict. The opposition of forces compels attention—especially if the listeners identify themselves with one of the contending sides. Often conflict, like suspense, suggests uncertainty; but even when there is little doubt of the outcome, the combat itself draws attention. Football games, election contests, the struggle against disease and the adverse elements of nature—all these have an element of conflict within them; and people become interested when the conflict is vividly described. For the same reason, controversy is more interesting than concurrence. A vigorous attack upon some antisocial force—be it organized crime, graft, or child abuse— will draw more immediate attention than an objective analysis of it, although the analysis might—in the long run—prove more effective or enduring. Describe a fight, show vividly the opposition between two factions, or launch a verbal attack on somebody or something, and people usually will listen to you. Be cautious, however, of sham battles. If you set up straw men and knock them down, the reality—and hence the effectiveness—of your message may be destroyed. Nevertheless, communicating a sense of conflict can vitalize a report or lecture, especially when you want listeners to visualize a decision they must make in the future.

Humor. Laughter indicates enjoyment, and people pay attention to that which they enjoy. Few things, in fact, will hold an audience as well as the speaker's judicious use of humor. It provides relaxation from the tension often created by other factors of attention—conflict and suspense, especially —and thus reduces fatigue while still exercising a measure of control over the perceptions of the listener. When using humor, however, remember that its attention-holding power is likely to be much stronger if you keep two guidelines in mind: (1) *Be relevant.* Beware of wandering from the point under discussion. Any joke or anecdote you may use must reinforce rather than detract from the central ideas of your speech. (2) *Use good taste.* Avoid humor on occasions where it would be out of place, and refrain from using those types of humor which might offend the sensitivities of your listeners.

The Vital.   Finally, people nearly always pay attention to matters that affect their health, reputation, property, or employment. If you can show your audience that what you are saying concerns them in one or more of these ways, the chances are good that they will consider your message vital and will listen to it closely. Pointing out how your subject concerns persons close to them also will command your listeners' attention because people tend to identify themselves with family, friends, and associates. If the other factors of attention are important, an appeal to the *vital* is indispensable.

The vital, humor, conflict, suspense, novelty, familiarity, proximity, reality, and *activity or movement*—these nine attention-attractors should be your constant guides when you are assembling, sorting out, and presenting ideas for a speech. (See "The Factors of Attention," p. 41.) The detail they provide a speech will help you achieve clarity and concreteness, and their psychological power to engage listeners' minds will help you relate what is new or unknown to experiences which are old or known.

Presenting the Speech.   The actual presentation of the speech can help the receiver be a better listener. See that your delivery style is appropriate for the audience, topic, and occasion. Be sure also that your nonverbal communication matches your verbalized thoughts and feelings so that you are not sending contradictory messages.

Interpreting audience feedback during the presentation will help you modify, adapt, or recast any ideas you see the audience is misunderstanding or doubting. If the listeners notice that you are sincerely making every effort to communicate your thoughts, they will tend to be more receptive and try harder to be good listeners. Your use of feedback is one way the audience assesses your desire to communicate effectively. If you look for nonverbal clues from the audience and determine that they are not understanding your message, quickly think back over what you have said and try to rephrase main points in simpler language. Include a brief internal summary of the points you have covered, and if the situation allows, ask for questions.

The speaker should project an appropriate attitude when speaking. If you are talking about a serious topic, make sure your approach and demeanor reflect that. Dealing with life-or-death issues in a humorous manner may be offensive, but on the other hand, some topics lend themselves to a lighter approach. The attitude that you project can help your audience better appreciate the ideas you are sharing with them.

Finally, as a speaker, remember how it feels to be a listener. Make a list of the positive and negative reactions you have to the ways that speakers present ideas. Try to avoid making some of the same errors that annoy you. Remember that good speakers are also good listeners. Review critiques of your speaking and try to correct any weaknesses before you speak again.

LISTENING IN THE SPEECH CLASSROOM

This course can make an important contribution by providing you with the opportunity to practice listening. Critical listening skills can be developed in several ways in this classroom as well as in others. You can (1) practice critiquing the speeches of other students, taking part in post-speech discussions; (2) listen critically to discussions, lectures, oral presentations, and student-teacher exchanges in your other classes, identifying effective and ineffective communicative techniques employed by a variety of people in several different contexts; (3) make an effort to listen to speakers outside of class, in the community, observing carefully their successes and failures and analyzing why they meet with certain reactions; and (4) read the sample speeches in this book, taking them apart systematically in order to isolate the communicative cues which might have facilitated comprehension and acceptance.

While you undoubtedly will become a more informed listener after you have studied this book and been part of classroom speaking assignments, you nevertheless can now start to become a more proficient listener. First, you can use the Speech Evaluation Form on page 44 as a checklist of listening concerns. Depending upon the particular assignment, the nature of the audience, and the demands of the occasion, some of the checkpoints on the form will be more significant and applicable than others. For now, use the form as a general guide, and then later, concentrate upon those aspects of it that are relevant to a specific speech assignment.

And second, participate regularly in post-speech evaluations, even of early classroom speaking assignments. Do not hesitate to provide direct feedback to your classmates, pointing out what was good, what worked and what didn't seem to work so well, what was clear and what remained cloudy.

Speech Evaluation Form

The Speaker
____ poised?

____ positive self-image?

____ apparently sincere?

____ apparently concerned about the topic?

____ apparently concerned about the audience?

____ apparently well prepared?

The Message
____ suitable topic?

____ clear general purpose?

____ sharply focused specific purpose?

____ well-phrased central idea or proposition?

____ adequately supported (enough, varied, trustworthy sources)?

____ supporting materials tailored to the audience?

____ introduced adequately?

____ concluded effectively?

____ major subdivisions clear, balanced?

____ use of notes and lectern unobtrusive?

Transmission
____ voice varied for emphasis?

____ voice conversational?

____ delivery speed controlled?

____ body alert and nondistracting?

____ gestures used effectively?

____ face expressive?

____ language clear (unambiguous, concrete)?

____ language forcible (vivid, intense)?

The Audience
____ all listeners addressed?

____ their presence recognized and complimented?

____ their attitudes toward subject and speaker taken into account?

The Speech as a Whole
Audience's expectations met?

_____

Short-range effects of the speech?

_____

Long-range effects?

_____

Possible improvements?

_____

Good, constructive classroom criticism is both positive and negative—but always supportive. Such oral commentary accomplishes two goals: it provides a beginning speaker with much-needed reaction, and it forces you, the listener, to verbalize your thoughts and recognize explicitly your standards and expectations. In this way, both you and the speaker gain: the speaker acquires a sense of the range of reactions being generated in an audience, and you gain a better sense of your own mind.

Listening, then, is a two-way street, a joint responsibility of speaker and listener. Only when both parties are sensitive to its points of breakdown and to techniques which can enhance it will oral communication be a successful transaction. Much of what we will have to say in later chapters will rest directly upon this process.

GROUP PROJECTS

1. As a check on listening abilities, participate in a class discussion on a highly controversial topic. Conduct the discussion with the rule that before anyone can speak, he or she must first summarize to the satisfaction of the previous speaker what that speaker said. As a result of this activity, what conclusions can you draw about:
   (a) people's ability to summarize accurately and satisfactorily, and
   (b) the manner in which good listening and feedback reduce the amount and intensity of disagreement.

2. Your instructor will play a tape of a five-to-ten-minute radio newscast. Listen carefully to the newscast, but do not take notes. Immediately after listening to the tape, try to list the news items mentioned. When your instructor plays the tape a second time, check your recall. Meet in a small group to discuss the accuracy of responses. How might you improve your listening? If you were watching a televised newscast, would there be a significant difference in recall? You may want to test the difference by watching a videotaped newscast and repeating the exercise.

INDIVIDUAL PROJECTS

1. Keep a "Listening Log." For three days, record for each communication interaction: who you were listening to, what the listening purpose was, and how effectively you listened. At the end of the three days, read over your entries. Focus on the listening patterns. Analyze your listening behaviors in the various experiences. How could these behaviors be changed to improve your listening skills?

2. Analyze your listening behavior. On the left-hand side of a sheet of paper, list all of the situations in which you are a good listener. In the right-hand column, indicate why you are a good listener in each of those situations. Turn the paper over. In the left-hand column, list the situations in which your listening skills are poor. Go back and review the situations that are favorable for listening. Then go back to the poor listening situations and indicate how you can change your poor behaviors.

3. Consider the following question: How can speakers objectively evaluate their own efforts? After a performance assignment, test your self-evaluation skills by completing the Speech Evaluation Form at the end of this chapter. When the instructor returns his or her written critique (and those of classmates who may also have evaluated the presentation), compare these responses to your own analysis. Try to account for any differences between your self-evaluation and the evaluations of others. What do the differences tell you about the speaker's need to consider the audience as listeners when preparing and presenting a speech?

4. Exercise good listening skills in your everyday communication with friends. The next time you and a friend engage in a serious conversation, avoid interrupting your friend's comments. Repeat in your own words what was said and ask your friend to correct any misconceptions.

5. List ideas that trigger your prejudices. Choose one of these as the subject for a two-to-four-minute speech. In your speech, concentrate on answering why you hold this feeling and how analyzing it will affect your listening skills the next time you encounter the idea.

 ## SUGGESTIONS FOR FURTHER READING

Larry L. Barker, *Listening Behavior* (Englewood Cliffs, N.J.: Prentice-Hall, Inc., 1971).

Baxter Geeting and Corinne Geeting, *Huh? How to Win Through Assertive Listening* (Sacramento, Ca.: Communications Design, Inc., 1976).

Lyman K. Steil, Larry L. Barker, and Kittie W. Watson, *Effective Listening* (Reading, Mass.: Addison-Wesley, 1983).

Carl Weaver, *Human Listening: Processes and Behavior* (Indianapolis: Bobbs-Merrill, Inc., 1972).

Andrew D. Wolvin and Carolyn G. Coakley, *Listening* (Dubuque, Ia.: Wm. C. Brown, 1982).

CHAPTER 3

Planning and Preparing the Speech

More than any other single factor, perhaps, a successful speech depends on careful planning. Planning ahead saves you time, keeps you from wandering aimlessly through the library and from sitting at your desk for hours waiting for inspiration. Once you have thought through the speech and made some initial decisions about what to say and how to put the speech together, it is a comparatively easy job to assemble materials and mold them into an effective piece of communication with an audience.

There is no magic formula for planning and preparing speeches; the task can be irksome and frustrating. There is, however, a generally accepted checklist of steps to guide your efforts and lessen your frustration. You may not always follow the steps in precisely the order suggested. Nevertheless, if you consider them all, you will find that they demystify and simplify the process of speech construction. We will discuss selecting and narrowing the subject, determining the purposes, analyzing the audience and occasion, gathering materials, arranging and outlining the points, and practicing the speech aloud; we also will offer some preliminary advice on delivering the speech, as the chapters treating delivery come later in the textbook.

SELECTING AND NARROWING THE SUBJECT

On many occasions, the subject of your speech will be determined—at least in part—by the group you are invited to address. If you are speaking at a public hearing on a proposed rezoning of your neighborhood, you need not select a topic, for it is already determined by your audience's concerns and interests. Yet, there are many speaking occasions in which you will have to exercise some choice. In a speech classroom, of course, you must do so. Or, if you are asked to deliver a lay sermon in church, you may have to decide, for example, whether to talk about religious duty or false religiosity or missionary efforts. If you are to speak to a Spanish Club, should you discuss employment opportunities for Spanish majors, Latin American tour packages, or the subtleties of Basque cuisine? When addressing a school-board meeting devoted to "back to basics" education, you may wish to urge the adoption of better elementary textbooks, teacher in-service training, or special reading programs.

When confronted with the task of choosing a subject, observe the following guidelines:

Select a subject about which you already know something and can find out more. Knowledge you already possess can guide your efforts to find a suitable focus, to tailor the discourse to the specific audience you face, to assess areas in which your knowledge is thin, and to know where to locate additional materials you will need for your talk.

Select a subject that is interesting to you. If you are excited about what you are talking about, you will find preparation an interesting and rewarding task, and more important, your message and your presentation will probably reflect your motivation and enthusiasm.

Select a subject that will interest your audience. The more interest your listeners have in the subject, the less you will have to worry about holding their attention when you speak. A subject may be interesting to an audience for one or more of the following reasons:

A. It concerns their health, happiness, prosperity, or security. (Thus, you might talk to a senior citizens group about Medicare.)
B. It offers a solution to a recognized problem. (You might suggest new ways your citizens' action group can raise needed money.)
C. It is new or timely. (You could talk to your local "Friends of the Library" about city libraries which are installing videotaping capabilities.)
D. It is a topic surrounded by controversy or conflict of opinion. (Almost any subject can be approached in this way.)

If your subject is interesting to you and (potentially) to your audience, your next task will be to narrow it down to a manageable size. Narrowing a subject involves three additional considerations:

Narrow your subject so that you can discuss it adequately in the time at your disposal. In a ten-minute speech, you would be unable to cover adequately "The Rise and Fall of Baseball as the Premier American Sport."

Instead, you might, for example, describe three or four changes baseball has made in response to television. Fit the "size" of your topic to time available.

Gauge your subject so that it is neither above nor below the comprehension level of your audience. If, for example, you want to talk about laser technology to an audience of beginning students, you might choose to describe only its most basic principles; to a group of physics majors, however, you probably would move on to explain in technical terms its various applications.

Narrow your subject to meet the specific expectations of your audience. An audience which comes to a meeting expecting to hear a discussion of gun safety will probably be distraught if, instead, you lecture on the need for stricter gun-control laws. People attending the inauguration of a president probably would be more than mystified if the president-elect launched a fifteen-minute comic monologue satirizing the whole affair. The announced purpose of a meeting, the demands of particular contexts, and other group traditions can affect an audience's expectations of what it is to hear. If you disregard them, you may seriously undermine the impact of your message.

In other words, selecting and narrowing a topic involves sorting through all of the things you *could* say in order to find one, two, or three points you can establish, clarify, and support in the time you have available. Perhaps an example can illustrate this idea. Suppose you decide to talk informatively about gardening. Within that subject are countless narrower topics, including:

—the growth of private or hobby gardening over the last decade (facts and figures on clubs, seed sales, the canning industry, etc.);

—methods for preserving homegrown vegetables (canning vs. freezing vs. drying vs. cold storage);

—soil enrichment (varieties of natural and artificial fertilizers, the strengths and weaknesses of each);

—factors to consider when selecting vegetables to plant (plot size, family eating habits, amount of time available for tending, cost of supermarket vegetables of each type);

—available strains of any given vegetable (selection of seeds based on geography, climate, soil characteristics, regional pests/bacteria, uses to which the vegetables will be put, germination and heartiness);

—literature on gardening (library books, TV programs, governmental pamphlets, magazines, seed catalogs, fertilizer company brochures);

—varieties of gardening tools (inexpensive hand tools, medium-cost hand-powered tools, more expensive power machinery);

—year-round gardening (window-box gardening, "grow" lights, cold
frames, hot frames, greenhouses).

Given this list of sub-topics, your procedure for selecting and narrowing
might run something like this:

1. *Subjects I know something about:*
   methods for preserving homegrown food
   soil enrichment
   literature on gardening
   varieties of gardening tools
   year-round gardening
2. *Subjects interesting to me:*
   all but soil enrichment
3. *Subjects interesting to my audience* (a 4-H club):
   methods for preserving homegrown food
   literature on gardening
   year-round gardening
4. *Topics I can talk about in the available time:* (note narrowing)
   one or *two* methods of preserving homegrown food
   two or *three* kinds of gardening literature
   one kind of year-round gardening
5. *Topics I can fit to the audience comprehension level:*
   Because 4-H club members are experienced gardeners,
       don't discuss home food preservation, as most of them already
           know a lot about this sub-topic
       don't discuss gardening literature, as few of these kids want to
           spend more time reading about gardening; in the past, they've
           found it easier to learn from other gardeners than from books
       they've shown interest before in the topic of year-round garden-
           ing (when Henry did a speech on "grow" lights, they followed
           him easily)
6. *Topics which will meet their expectations for a 4-H demonstration
   project:*
       year-round gardening, specifically, how to build an inexpensive
           homemade greenhouse

In other words, selecting and narrowing a topic involves: (1) probing
yourself and your experience for topics on which you are knowledgeable and
interested, (2) thinking seriously about your audience's interests and abilities, and (3) narrowing the topic according to the decision-criteria which
slowly but surely drive you to a particular sub-topic you can cover

adequately in the time available and in accordance with audience and situational expectations. All of this may seem like a complicated chore, yet if you attack it systematically, you often can easily move through this preparation step.

If you have trouble thinking about general topics, look at the checklist of "Subject Categories" inside the back cover of this book for suggestions.

DETERMINING THE PURPOSE

Once you know what you want to talk about, the next question you face is "why?" Why do *you* wish to discuss this subject? Why might an *audience* want to listen to you? You should approach these "whys" in three ways: first, think about *general purposes* (the reasons people generally have when they speak in public); next, consider the *specific purposes* (the concrete goals you wish to achieve in a particular speech); and finally, focus your thoughts on the *central idea* or *proposition* (the statement of the guiding thought you wish to communicate).

The General Purpose

In most public communication situations, you address your listeners in order to inform or to persuade them, thus:

GENERAL PURPOSE	AUDIENCE RESPONSE SOUGHT
To inform	Clear understanding or comprehension
To persuade or to actuate	Acceptance of ideas or recommended behaviors

Usually you are talking to others publicly because you possess some knowledge of potential relevance and benefit to them; or because you hope to influence their beliefs, attitudes, or actions. At times, of course, public communicators may have somewhat different general purposes—to entertain an audience, to help celebrate an event, to apologize for or justify some behavior, to pay tribute to a distinguished individual, and the like—but even these purposes can be translated into basically informative or persuasive goals. The entertainer normally is conveying information or views about the world in the process of bringing enjoyment to others; the celebrant is informatively orienting listeners to the significance of an event; the apologist is making his or her behavior more understandable and acceptable; and the eulogist is highlighting in an informative and appreciative manner the key achievements of the person in question. We will discuss some of these more

Gardening is a topic appropriate to many audiences and occasions. But it is too broad; it must be narrowed to fit time limits, your audience's background, and their expectations. When narrowing a topic, look for sub-topics (1) about which you already know something; (2) which are interesting to you personally; (3) which can be dealt with concretely and adequately in the time available for your speech; (4) which will not under- or over-estimate your audience's abilities; and (5) which they expect to hear discussed on this occasion.

specialized purposes (see Chapter 14, "Speaking on Special Occasions"), but for the most part we will concentrate on informative and persuasive oral discourse.

To Inform.   When your overall objective is to help the members of your audience understand an idea or comprehend a concept or a process, or when you seek to widen the range of their knowledge, the general purpose of your speech will be to inform. Such is the goal of scientists who report the results of their research to a group of colleagues, of college lecturers or work supervisors or public figures who address community groups on subjects in which they are acknowledged experts.

To evoke understanding, you must add to the information possessed by your audience. By providing examples, statistics, illustrations, and other instructive materials, you seek to expand or alter their reservoir of knowledge. That change alone, however, may not be enough to ensure a response of understanding. For not only must an informative speech provide raw data, but also its message and supporting data must be structured and integrated in such a way that listeners will clearly and quickly perceive the import of the whole. For example, an informative speech on how to build a stereo set not only must include the necessary information, but also must present that information in an orderly sequence of steps. Understanding in this instance will depend not only on learning *what* to do, but also on knowing *when* to do it and *why*. Many of your listeners may already be familiar with much of your information and still lack understanding. No one has ever "put it all together" for them; no one has shown them exactly how to proceed step by step in order to achieve the desired end.

In short, in order to communicate an informative message successfully, you must relate your ideas to the existing knowledge of the audience; you must organize them so they are easy to follow and remember; and you must present enough concrete examples and specific data to improve the audience's understanding of your topic.

To Persuade or to Actuate.   The purpose of a speech to persuade or to actuate is to influence listener belief or action. While it may be argued that all speeches are in some degree persuasive, there are many situations in which speakers have outright persuasion as their primary and most insistent purpose. Promoters and public relations experts try to make you believe in the superiority of certain products, personages, or institutions; lawyers seek to convince juries; social action group leaders exhort tenants to believe in the existence of landlord collusion; politicians debate campaign issues and strive to influence voters' thinking.

Usually, as a persuasive speaker you will seek only to influence the beliefs and attitudes of your listeners. Sometimes, however, you will want to go a step further and try to move them to *action*. You may want them, for instance, to contribute money, sign a petition, organize a parade, or participate in a demonstration. The distinguishing feature of an actuative speech is that instead of stopping with an appeal to their beliefs or attitudes, you ask your listeners to demonstrate their convictions and feelings by *behaving* or *acting* in a specified way.

Whether or not you seek immediate and overt action from the members of your audience, however, you invariably imply that what they believe should influence how they feel. Thus an attorney who wants a jury to believe that a client acted while insane also wants the jurors to feel a certain way about that client, to feel perhaps that the accused is deserving of pity or mercy. Conversely, a speaker who seeks to engender strong feelings about a subject also seeks to intensify listener beliefs and encourage certain kinds of behavior. For instance, in an acceptance speech a presidential candidate not only strives to arouse feelings of loyalty to person and party, but also seeks to reinforce our beliefs about our country's strengths and weaknesses, and to convince us to vote—preferably for him or her—as an act of patriotic behavior. Therefore, although listener acceptance of the speaker's ideas is the goal of a speech to persuade, the effective speaker will realize that to gain this response from listeners, their beliefs, attitudes, and inclinations to act must be changed in some significant way.

Because the speech to persuade or to actuate characteristically is designed to influence or alter the beliefs and action-tendencies of listeners, you should fill it with well-ordered arguments supported by facts, figures, and examples. In order to persuade successfully, however, you must do more than provide factual data: You must make your listeners *want* to believe or act as you propose. Therefore, in addition to evidence and arguments, you must also introduce strong motive appeals; you must show how the proposal you advocate is related to your listeners' interests—how it will satisfy certain of their basic drives, wishes, or desires. (This matter will be explored in detail in Chapter 12.)

To inform and to persuade or actuate are, then, the *general* purposes a speech may have. To speak without a more precise objective in mind, however, would be foolhardy. The broad, overall purpose of a talk must be narrowed and made more *specific* before you can hope to communicate successfully.

The Specific Purposes

A second important way to think about speech purposes is to consider specific purposes; that is, challenges related to a particular topic explored before an actual audience on a specific occasion by a real human being—you. Specific purposes represent actual goals you want to achieve. Though concrete in nature, specific purposes can be extremely wide-ranging. Some of them you may verbalize; for example, you may tell an audience what you want it to understand or do as a result of your speech. Some are private, known only by you; for example, you probably hope to make a good impression on an audience, hope it will approve of and even like you, although you probably would not say that aloud. Usually, a speech has short-term specific purposes (goals you hope to accomplish immediately) and occasionally it even has long-term purposes. So, for example, if you are speaking to the members of a local food cooperative on the virtues of baking their own bread, your short-term purpose might be to get people to go home that night and try out your recipe, while your long-term goal could be to have them change their food-buying and food-consuming habits.

Theoretically, therefore, you undoubtedly have any number of private and public, short-term and long-term specific purposes whenever you rise to speak. More practically, however, you will want to reduce that mass of goals to a dominant one. We may define *the* specific purpose of a speech as the *precise response* desired from the audience by the speaker. Formulated into a clear, concise statement, the specific purpose delineates exactly what you want the audience to do, feel, believe, understand, or enjoy.

The Central Idea or Proposition

Once you have settled upon the specific purpose, you are ready to cast into words a *central idea* or *proposition* (sometimes termed a "thesis statement") which will form the controlling thought of your speech. A central idea is a statement which captures the essence of the information or concept you are attempting to communicate to an audience. A proposition, or claim, is a statement which phrases the belief, attitude, or action you wish an audience to adopt. Central ideas, therefore, are characteristic of informative speeches, and propositions form the core of persuasive discourses. (In Chapter 13, we will discuss the various types of propositions, or claims, in persuasive speeches—claims of fact, claims of value, and claims of policy. See pages 269–272.)

The precise phrasing of central ideas and propositions is all-important because your wording captures the essence of your subject-matter and purpose and guides audience expectations. Assume, for example, that you were going to give the informative speech on building an inexpensive homemade greenhouse we referred to earlier. You might decide to phrase your central idea for that speech in at least three different ways:

Wording #1: "With only a minimum of carpentry skills, even a
 teenager can build a homemade greenhouse."
Wording #2: "With some creative searching around your home and
 neighborhood, anyone can build a homemade greenhouse for less
 than $150."
Wording #3: "Building an inexpensive homemade greenhouse will
 allow you to start garden plants early and grow some crops year
 around."

Note that in the first version, the stress is upon audience members' abilities to complete the technical aspects of the task; presumably, the speech would offer a step-by-step description of the construction process—preparing the bed, pouring cement for the foundation, erecting the superstructure, and covering that structure with transparent materials. The second version suggests quite a different speech, one focused on securing the materials. It might discuss places to find scrapped lumber, ways to get old storm windows to use as the greenhouse's glassed surface, areas in the neighborhood where one can get free sand for the cement, etc. And, in contrast, the third version would discuss the actual construction of the greenhouse only superficially (perhaps with a handout on the construction process), concentrating instead on interior design—which shelves to reserve for seedlings, and which shelves to prepare for year-round crops such as tomatoes, herbs, peppers, miniature fruit trees, and the like.

If anything, phrasing a proposition or thesis statement is an even more crucial preparatory act than phrasing a central idea, because the wording you select can control several different aspects of your relationship with your audience. Note the following examples:

▶ Varying the audience's perception of the speaker's intensity:

1. "Do not eat cured pork because it is *unhealthy.*"
2. "Do not eat cured pork because it is *carcinogenic.*"
3. "Do not eat cured pork because it will *kill you.*"

As you move from version one to version three, you are phrasing your own feelings in progressively more intense language; each successive version expresses the speaker's attitude in harsher language.

▶ Varying the reasons for taking some course of action:

1. "Make use of our school's Division of Career Planning because they can help you *plan your curriculum.*"
2. "Make use of our school's Division of Career Planning because they will help you *select a major.*"
3. "Make use of our school's Division of Career Planning because they will teach you how *to prepare resumes and to interview for jobs.*"
4. "Make use of our school's Division of Career Planning because they will put you *in touch with employers.*"

In these four examples, you are varying the rationales behind the actions you wish listeners to take. Presumably, one can take some course of action for any number of reasons; your proposition should be phrased in a way that captures what you think will be the most compelling reasons for this *particular audience.*

▶ Varying the evaluative criteria for judging something:

1. "The city's new landfill is an *eyesore* [aesthetic judgment]."
2. "The city's new landfill is a *health hazard* [personal-safety judgment]."
3. "The city's new landfill is a *political payoff to the rich companies which supported council members' campaigns* [political judgment]."

Each of these propositions is condemning a civic project, but in different ways. The first version judges the landfull negatively on aesthetic grounds, the second, on safety grounds, and the third, on political grounds. Were you to advocate the first version, you would have to demonstrate that (a) aesthetic qualities are important criteria for judging landfills, and (b) the landfill indeed will be visible to a significant number of community members. For the second version, you would have to argue successfully that health hazards are a matter of public concern, then that this particular landfill allows hazardous materials to be deposited. And, in defending the third version you would have to document (a) the campaign contributions and (b) the fact that major users or beneficiaries of the depository are the companies which gave the most money to the successful candidates. In each case, then, the selection of a particular evaluative criterion controls the main features of the speech.

We may put together, overall, what we have been saying about general purposes, specific purposes, and central ideas or propositions in the following manners:

Subject: Cardiopulmonary Resuscitation (CPR).
General purpose: To inform.
Specific purposes:

- ▶ to explain the three life-saving steps of CPR.
- ▶ to interest the auditors in signing up for a CPR course.
- ▶ to impress upon listeners their social responsibilities relevant to CPR.

Central idea: "Cardiopulmonary resuscitation—CPR—is a three-step, life-saving technique which anyone can learn for use in emergencies."

Subject: Accident insurance for students.
General purpose: To actuate.
Specific purposes:

- ▶ to get members of the student council to approve the group insurance policy offered by the ABC Insurance Company.
- ▶ to provide inexpensive accident insurance for students currently without such protection.
- ▶ to demonstrate that the ABC Insurance Company is the best one available for the money.
- ▶ to overcome opposition from student council members and to remind the council of its obligations to its constituency.

Proposition: "The student council should approve the purchase of the group accident policy offered by the ABC Insurance Company (because many students do not have access to accident insurance, because it is the duty of the student council to serve its constituency, and because ABC's policy is less expensive than others we have examined)."[1]

Carefully explore your general and specific purposes before you begin to construct a public message. A sensitivity to general purposes will guide your thinking about speech materials and their structure. And, a realization of your specific purposes will allow you to understand your own hopes and fears, the range of effects you will potentially have upon your audience, and the measures by which you may gauge the effects. Considering thoughtfully both general and specific purposes also enables you to define central ideas or propositions—thus capturing in your mind the primary thrust or aim of your speech. Once you have clarified your purposes, you are ready to consider more analytically the people who will make up your audience.

ANALYZING THE AUDIENCE

As we emphasized in both Chapters 1 and 2, the communication process involves a *listener* as well as a *speaker* and a *message*. Talking to hear your own voice may be pleasurable or may help you confirm your identity,[2] but it is not to be confused with communicating ideas or feelings to others. Often speakers forget this important fact. They become so engrossed in their own interests, so impressed by ideas that seem important to them, that they forget they are communicating with people whose interests and attitudes may be quite different from their own. It is a fairly safe assertion that more speeches fail for this reason than for any other.

The most important lesson you as a speaker can learn, therefore, is to see things from the standpoint of your listeners, to employ what is sometimes described as a "receiver orientation."[3] You must continually ask yourself, "How would I feel about this if I were in their place?" To answer this question accurately requires a thorough analysis of the audience and occasion because, obviously, an argument which would convince some people would leave others unmoved, and ideas that might be appropriate on one occasion would be inappropriate on another.

---

[1]Your proposition statement may or may not include the reasons—the "because" clauses —which justify its acceptance. You may be better able to specify them once you have gone on to the next step, analyzing the audience.

[2]See Charles T. Brown and Charles Van Riper, *Speech and Man* (Englewood Cliffs, N.J.: Prentice-Hall, Inc., 1966), pp. 35–36.

[3]In this connection, see especially David K. Berlo, *The Process of Communication* (New York: Holt, Rinehart & Winston, Inc., 1960), pp. 52, 62.

Audience analysis ultimately is a matter of finding out as much as you can about the people who compose the group—their age, gender, social-economic-political status, origins, backgrounds, prejudices, and fears. You also must try to find out how much they know about your subject, what they probably believe in and value, and what their probable attitudes are toward you and your subject. In your public speaking classroom, all this is easy enough to do—simply ask some people around the room. In other circumstances, you might have to become a bit more creative, and to work harder. For that reason, the next chapter will be devoted to ways in which you can analyze your audience. But, however you do it, audience analysis is perhaps *the* crucial step in speech preparation, for it is the primary determinant of success in speechmaking: After all, if you have not adapted your talk to your listeners, they won't listen and no transaction will take place.

ANALYZING THE SPEECH OCCASION

To this point, we have emphasized the necessity of analyzing the *audience* for whom your speech is designed. An equally important aspect of your preparation is an analysis of the *occasion* on which you will be speaking. (Indeed, aspects of the two are often inseparable.) In making such an analysis, you should consider the following key questions carefully:

What Are the Nature and Purpose of the Occasion?

Is yours a voluntary or a captive audience? A voluntary audience attends a speech primarily because they are interested in the speaker or the subject. A captive audience is required to attend, perhaps at the explicit instruction of the boss or under threat of a failing grade in a course. In general, the more "captive" your audience, the less initial interest they will show and the greater will be their resistance to accepting your information or point of view.

Are people interested in learning more about your subject, in taking some positive action concerning it, or have they perhaps come to the meeting for another reason? Are your subject and purpose in line with the reason for the meeting, or are you merely seizing the occasion to present some ideas which you think are important? Are you one in a series of speakers whom the audience has heard over a period of weeks or months? If so, how does your speech relate to those which have been previously presented? These also are important questions you will need to answer when you are analyzing the nature and purpose of the occasion.

What Rules or Customs Will Prevail?

Will there be a regular order of business or a fixed program into which your speech must fit? Is it the custom of the group to ask questions of the speaker after the address? Do the listeners expect a formal or informal speaking manner? Will you, as the speaker, be expected to extend complimentary remarks to some person or persons or to express respect for some traditional institution or concept? Knowing these facts will help you avoid feeling out of place and will prevent you from arousing antagonism by some inappropriate word or action.

What Will Precede and Follow Your Speech?

At what time of day or night will your speech be given? Immediately after a heavy meal or a long program, both of which may induce drowsiness and dampen listener interest? Just before the principal address or event of the evening? By whom and in what manner will you be introduced to the audience? What other items are on the program? What are their tone and character? All these factors will, of course, influence the interest the audience may have in your speech. In some instances, you will be able to use the other events on the program to increase interest or confidence in your own remarks; sometimes they will work against you. In any case, you must always consider the effect which the program as a whole may have on your speech.

What Will Be the Physical Conditions Affecting the Occasion?

Will your speech be given out-of-doors or in an auditorium? Is weather likely to be hot or cold? Will the audience be sitting or standing; and, if sitting, will the members be crowded together or scattered about? In how large a room will the speech be presented? Will an electronic public-address system be used? Will facilities be provided for the audiovisual reinforcements you will use, or must you bring your own? Will you be seen and heard easily? Are there likely to be disturbances—noise or interruptions from the outside? These and similar environmental factors have an effect on the temper of the audience, their span of attention, and the style of speaking you will have to employ to make adjustments to the environment or situation.

GATHERING THE SPEECH MATERIAL

Having carefully considered the subject and purpose of your speech and analyzed the audience and occasion, you are now ready to begin gathering material. Ordinarily you will start by drawing together what you already know about the subject and deciding roughly what ideas you want to include. Nearly always, however, you will find that what you already know is not enough. You will need to gather additional information—facts, illustrations, stories, and examples—with which you can develop your speech. Some of this information may be acquired through interviews and conversations with people who know something that you do not know about the subject. Other materials will be gathered from newspapers, magazines, books, and government documents, or will come from radio or television programs. In particular, such sources as the "News of the Week in Review" section of *The New York Times, U.S. News and World Report, Wall Street Journal, Harper's,* and *The Observer* should be consulted by a speaker who plans to deal with a current question of public interest. Many magazines of general interest are indexed in the *Readers' Guide to Periodical Literature;* numerous encyclopedias, yearbooks, government reports, almanacs, and other reference materials will be found in your college library. (See Chapter 5, pp. 95–118, for more detailed advice on gathering materials.)

MAKING AN OUTLINE

Early in your preparation you may want to make a rough sketch of the points you wish to include in your speech. A complete outline, however, cannot be drawn up until you have gathered all of the necessary material. When this material is at hand, set down in final order the principal points you expect to present, together with the subordinate ideas which will be necessary to explain or to prove these points.

In Chapter 6, you will find a number of specific patterns by which the ideas in a speech may be arranged. There, too, you will find the form which a complete outline should take. For the present, remember two simple but important rules: (1) arrange your ideas in a clear and systematic order, and (2) preserve the unity of your speech by making sure that each point is directly related to your specific purpose.

PRACTICING ALOUD

With your outline completed, you are ready for the final step in preparation: Practicing your speech for oral presentation. You probably will find that the best method is to talk through the outline aloud, following the planned sequence of ideas. Do this until you have learned this sequence thoroughly and until you can express each idea clearly and fluently. Then, putting the outline aside, think the speech through silently, point by point, to make certain that the ideas are fixed in your mind. Next, go through the speech aloud, but this time do not look at the outline at all. On your first oral trial you may inadvertently omit some points and interchange others, but do not let this worry you. Practice until all the ideas are expressed in their proper order and until the words flow easily. The more surely you command your material, the more poise and confidence you will have as you stand before the audience. The self-assurance every speaker desires comes in large measure from always knowing exactly what to say next. Many speech instructors suggest that the final stages of your speech rehearsal be done standing in front of a full-length mirror.

When you can go through the speech several times without forgetting any point or without hesitating unduly in putting your thoughts into words, your preparation is done. As you practice speaking from your outline, however, preserve a mental image of your listeners and project your speech as though you were actually talking to them. The good speaker talks *with* people, not *at* them.

DELIVERING THE SPEECH

Let's assume that you have prepared and practiced your speech, and that in this concluding and climactic step you now stand before your audience, ready and eager to communicate. "How," you ask, "should I deliver my message? What can I do that will help me communicate what I want to say while I am saying it?" Three simple rules should guide the delivery of your early speeches: (1) be yourself; (2) look at your audience; and (3) communicate with your body as well as your voice.

1. *Be yourself.* Act as you would if you were engaged in an animated conversation with a friend. Avoid an excessively rigid, oratorical, or aggressive posture; but don't lean on a lectern or table or a wall. When you speak, you want the minds of your listeners to be

7. Delivering the Speech

6. Practicing the Speech Aloud

5. Arranging and Outlining the Points

4. Gathering the Material

3. Analyzing the Audience and Occasion

2. Determining the Purpose

1. Selecting and Narrowing the Subject

Essential Steps in Planning, Preparing, and Presenting the Speech ══════

focused on the ideas you are expressing, not on your delivery of them.

2. *Look at your listeners.* As we continue to emphasize throughout, watch the faces of your listeners for clues to their reactions. You'll need this feedback to gauge the ongoing effectiveness of your speech—to know whether you are putting your message across or whether you should make some prompt adjustments. Moreover, people tend to mistrust anyone who does not look them in the eye. So, if you fail to so so, they are likely to misjudge you and undervalue your ideas. And, finally, they nearly always listen more attentively if you look at them while you are speaking.

3. *Communicate with your body as well as your voice.* Realize that as a speaker you are being seen as well as heard. Movements of the body, gestures of the arms and head, changes in facial expression and muscle tension—all can help clarify and reinforce your ideas.

Keep your hands at your sides, so that when you feel an impulse to gesture, you can easily do so. Let other movements of your body also respond as your feelings and message dictate. Do not force your actions, but do not hold them back when they seem natural and appropriate to what you are saying. Try earnestly to transmit your ideas to others, and sooner or later you will make bodily responses of some kind, for they are an integral part of the desire to communicate.

This chapter has stressed one key to success in speechmaking—the ability to ask and answer important questions *before* you stand up to speak. By asking pivotal questions concerning your subject matter, your purposes, your central idea or thesis, your audience, the occasion, the material that ought to be included in your speech, patterns that allow you to package your ideas effectively, and your own delivery habits, you can solve possible problems before they arise, clarify goals and desired responses, and prepare yourself psychologically and physically for oral communication. *The key to successful speechmaking is the ability to make conscious, strategically sound rhetorical choices.* If you are specifically conscious of *what* you are trying to do and *how* you are doing it, and if you have rationales—reasons—for *why* you are approaching the speech in the ways you are, your chances for effective communication improve immeasurably.

❝❞ A SAMPLE STUDENT SPEECH

The following speech by Russell Walker, a student at Murray State University, was prepared to fulfill an assignment in a basic public speaking course.

Mr. Walker chose to discuss "Reality 101" not only because it reflected a topic of current concern—the "back to basics" movement in education—but also because it met other requirements of a good speech: (1) the topic was something which vitally affected him as a person trying to use practically the skills he supposedly had been taught; (2) it was appropriate to an audience of students facing similar problems; and (3) it could be covered adequately in the time allotted. Notice the clear sense of purpose, the careful transitions built in to lead the listeners step by step, and the use of varied supporting materials (statistics, quotations, examples, restatement). The proposition governing this speech is, "The American educational system has failed to emphasize basic learning skills."

REALITY 101*
Russell Walker

Introduction

"Soap and education are not as sudden as a massacre, but in the long run they can be just as deadly."[1] In these words, Samuel Clemens—better known as American philosopher-humorist Mark Twain—expresses his opinion of two American institutions. We can only hope Twain was wrong about the lethal properties of soap. However, evidence is mounting that he may have been right about education.   /1

Former President Gerald Ford recently hailed the advent of a "new realism" in American education.[2] Unfortunately, few educators share his optimism, and many accuse the system of strangling real learning. The view of one Midwestern school-board member is typical: "In many schools," she said, "education exists in name only. Even in affluent, highly respected schools, there is a sense of desperation."[3] A four-month study by the Ford Foundation last spring concluded that "schools will continue to drift toward coma, as standards sink lower and lower."[4] Social critic Ivan Illich has even recommended "deschooling" society, saying that contemporary education has no real value.[5]   /2

These charges are supported by the cold hard numbers of students' scores on the Scholastic Aptitude Tests. The SATs, as they are called, are administered each spring to college-bound high-school juniors and seniors across the United States, and are designed to measure both verbal and mathematical skills. Average scores have taken a nosedive, and are now in their twelfth consecutive year of decline.[6]   /3

Unfortunately, the effect of the educational crisis is not limited to test scores on a computer printout; it touches the people, the 3.1 million high-school graduates who roll off the academic assembly-line each year. In Washington, D.C., one student graduated as valedictorian of his class, confidently applied to George Washington University, and then failed to make even half the minimum acceptable score on the admissions test. Joseph Ruth, GWU's Dean of Admissions, commented sadly, "My feeling about this kid is that he's been conned. He's been deluded into thinking he's gotten an education."[7]   /4

Proposition

A "new realism"? Hardly. In fact, just the opposite—a delusion, a fantasy of

---

*A speech given at Murray State University, spring term, 1978. Reprinted by permission of Mr. Walker and the Interstate Oratorical Association. Text supplied by Professor Robert Valentine.

education for millions of students. The system has failed, and failed tragically. The course is Reality 101, and American education is flunking out. /5

Specific Purpose
Let us examine the reasons for the failure of our schools, and a way to correct the catastrophe. /6

Body
Searching for the cause of the problem, many educators have seized upon an easy and readily available solution: lack of funds. Consequently, thus far, the nation's only response to the learning crisis has been to throw federal money at it and hope it will go away. In the 1960s and early 1970s approximately $10 billion in government funds were pumped into efforts to bolster education. The results? A Rand Corporation executive summed them up: "unexpected, temporary, uneven, and frustrating."[8] /7

Such simplistic solutions represent a Bayer Aspirin approach to the problem: Take two federal grants and call me in the morning. While more money may let schools do more of what they were already doing, dollars cannot help if the basic approach is wrong. The roots of the educational dilemma lie deep within the philosophy and goals of the system; specifically, in that system's failure to emphasize basic learning skills. /8

Minimum levels of competence in reading, writing, and simple arithmetic computation have a twofold importance. First, basic skills in these areas are essential for coping with the universe, regardless of occupation. Increasingly the information on which we all base life decisions pours down upon us in a deluge of letters and numbers. These are the symbols of an even more complex world, and students must learn to comprehend and use them well. /9

Secondly, a fundamental understanding of reading, writing, and elementary math forms the basis, for all later learning is built on this simple foundation. /10

Yet our schools are not providing many of their students with these basic skills. The U.S. Office of Education reported in 1976 that 11 percent of the 17-year-olds in those schools cannot read and comprehend an average newspaper page.[9] From CalTech to Harvard, college professors voice the familiar complaint: "Half the incoming freshmen can't write—and the other half can't even read!" True, many high schools now require seniors to pass a "minimum competence exam" before graduation, but most of these require performance at the ninth-grade level for fear of failing large numbers of students who cannot meet twelfth-grade expectations.[10] Meanwhile, colleges are forced to divert funds from academic programs to finance classes in remedial reading; military-training manuals are rewritten for a sixth-grade reading level, and a University of Texas study last summer finds that fully one out of five adult Americans is functionally illiterate.[11] As performance drops, standards are lowered to match in a self-perpetuating cycle of semi-literacy.   /11

The answer, then, to our educational quandary is to give the teaching of basic learning skills our top priority. The emphasis must begin early, with unpopular but effective rote memorization at the elementary level, and extend through secondary classes to maintain and upgrade students' abilities. We must test students frequently on the fundamentals throughout their educational careers, using meaningful, uncompromised standards of performance. Finally, we must institute at once remedial programs to salvage as many students as possible.   /12

Such a solution is supported by the findings of the Educational Council of the States, as reported in the June 1976 issue of *Science News* Magazine. The Council, in studying educational methods and results over the last six years, documented a definite trend away from rote memorization and repeated drill in the fundamentals, concomitant with the sharp drop in student performance. The laudable purpose of innovators has been to spare students repetitive exercises and allow them greater freedom for creative work; however, meaningful creativity can occur only after those standardized essential learning skills are well in hand. Spelling the same word five different ways is not originality, it is ignorance, and the real world beyond the classroom will treat it as such. Realizing this, the Council's final recommendation to schools was simple and direct: "Teach more basics."[12]   /13

Conclusion
This solution—shifting the emphasis and approach of education in the 16,200 school districts across the country—is not an easy one. Neither is the problem it must solve easy. We can do it—we can reform our schools to instill essential skills in our children—we can do it and we must. For only when we do will American education make a passing grade in Reality 101.   /14

Sources

[1]Samuel Clemens, *The Facts Concerning the Recent Resignation* (1867). [2]Fred M. Hechinger, "Murder in Academe: The Demise of Education," *Saturday Review* 3:16 (March 20, 1976). [3]S. N. Wellborn, "U.S. Education: A Drift Toward Coma," *U.S. News* 81:55 (October 18, 1976). [4]*Ibid.* [5]*Ibid.* [6]George F. Will, "D Is for Dodo," *Newsweek* 87:84 (February 9, 1976). [7]J. Egerton, "Back to Basics," *Progressive* 40:22 (September, 1976). [8]Merril Sheils, "Where Money Fouls," *Newsweek* 87:86 (March 29, 1976). [9]Associated Press Wire Story, June 12, 1976. [10]"Making Diplomas Count," *Newsweek* 87:50 (May 24, 1976). [11]Associated Press Wire Story, January 24, 1976. [12]"Rx Education: Back to Basics," *Science News* 109:391 (June 19, 1976).

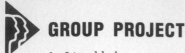

GROUP PROJECT

1. Listed below are groups of three statements about a single topic. Read each statement in the group, and write what you believe to be the central idea of the message. Compare your phrasing of the central ideas with those of members of your task group.

(a) Many prison facilities are inadequate.
(b) Low rates of pay result in frequent job turnovers in prisons.
(c) Prison employees need on-the-job training programs.

(a) There is a serious maldistribution of medical manpower and service.
(b) The present system of delivering medical service is excellent.
(c) Rural areas have a shortage of doctors.

INDIVIDUAL PROJECT

1. Rewrite each of the following poorly phrased statements to make it into a clear and concise central idea for a speech:

(a) "Today I would like to try and get you to see the way in which the body can communicate a whole lot of information."
(b) "The topic for my speech has to do with the high amount of taxes people have to pay."
(c) "A college education might be a really important thing for some people, so my talk is on a college education."

Now try your hand at rewriting the last two statements (b, c) as propositions. Be prepared to orally present your central idea and proposition statements.

SUGGESTIONS FOR FURTHER READING

Bruce E. Gronbeck, *The Articulate Person: A Guide to Everyday Public Speaking*, 2nd ed. (Glenview, Ill.: Scott, Foresman and Co., 1983), Chapters 2 and 4.

Jim D. Hughey and Arlee W. Johnson, *Speech Communication: Foundations and Challenges* (New York: Macmillan Publishing Company, Inc., 1975), Unit 5, "Communicative Purposes."

Robert C. Jeffrey and Owen Peterson, *Speech: A Text with Adapted Readings*, 3rd ed. (New York: Harper & Row, Publishers, 1980), Chapter 3, "The Speaker's Attitude and Purpose."

Brent D. Peterson, Noel D. White, and Eric G. Stephan, *Speak Easy: An Introduction to Public Speaking* (St. Paul: West Publishing Company, 1980), Chapter 3, "Selecting a Topic and Purpose."

Anita Taylor, *Speaking in Public* (Englewood Cliffs, N.J.: Prentice-Hall, Inc., 1979), Chapter 6, "Preparing: The Key to Successful Speeches."

CHAPTER 4

Understanding the Audience

Because public speaking is *audience-centered*, it is crucial that you understand the people you are addressing. Indeed, audience analysis is pivotal to the whole communicative enterprise. Selecting the topic, establishing your purpose, and narrowing the topic require consideration of the audience. And the remaining steps in speech preparation—finding and selecting supporting materials, arranging the materials, and casting introductions and conclusions —likewise will depend heavily upon audience analysis. Without adaptation to the audience, a speech can be "beautiful" but it will not necessarily be effective.

Traditionally, speakers have engaged in essentially two kinds of audience analysis: *demographic analysis* and *psychological profiling*. This is because human beings have been studied both as members of (demographic) groups and as self-sufficient (psychologically independent) individuals. That is, people exist in a series of easily identifiable *roles* (male or female, parent or child, banker or educator, rich or poor, Legionnaire or anarchist) and yet also exist as *individual beings* (who have unique personal experiences, beliefs, feelings, desires, attitudes).

This chapter, therefore, will help you systematically analyze your audiences, and show you how to adapt key portions of your speech to those people. One constant theme will be stressed: *The goal of audience analysis is to discover what facets of listeners' demographical and psychological backgrounds are relevant to your speech purposes and ideas, so that you can adapt your purposes and ideas to those relevant audience factors.* First, therefore, we will examine two ways—demographic and psychological analyses—to approach the goal; and then we will explore some ways you can use information you discover through analysis to actually adapt your speech purposes and ideas.

ANALYZING THE AUDIENCE DEMOGRAPHICALLY

Especially if an audience is composed of strangers, it may be easier to begin with a demographic or group-related analysis, because you often can directly observe demographic characteristics. You can identify gender, age, ethnic background (sometimes), group memberships (often), and the like. In doing a comparatively simple demographic analysis, you should ask such questions as:

Age.   Are there primarily young, middle-aged, or older people in the audience?

Gender.   Is the audience predominantly male or female?

Education.   Are many audience members likely to be well informed on my subject? And, do they have the educational background which should allow them to learn easily and quickly?

Group Membership.   Do these people represent or belong to groups that are known to possess certain kinds of information, particular sets of attitudes, or identifiable values?

Cultural and Ethnic Background.   Are audience members predominantly from particular cultural groups?

The importance of demographic analysis for the speaker is not simply the asking and answering of these and similar questions. Rather, *the key here is to decide how, if at all, any of these demographic factors will affect people's ability or willingness to accept and understand what you want to say.* Put more simply, the key is to figure out which, if any, of these factors is *relevant;* if any are, then you will want to adapt your message accordingly.

For example, if you are addressing a group of four-year-olds at a pre-school, you obviously must take *age* and *educational level* into consideration, perhaps by (1) talking simply, (2) using many clarifying examples, and (3) being sure you do not present too many ideas at once. Or, if you are addressing a group of *college-age females,* you would be more than foolhardy if you employed sexist language, called them "girls," and assumed they all planned on being "homemakers." *Cultural background* was important to then-President John F. Kennedy when he addressed a German audience gathered at the Berlin wall; he made sure he incorporated references to West Germany's struggle against Communism and used bits of German phraseology (especially "Ich bien ein Berliner") throughout the speech.

Group membership often is a particularly important factor. At least occasionally, you will address homogeneous groups—a local nurses' society, a church congregation, an Asian immigrants' support group. Under these circumstances, you often can assume that members of your audience will share several important beliefs, attitudes, and values, and that many of those tenets will affect their perception of and reaction to your message.

For example, suppose you are speaking for a Tenants' Union that would like financial support from your community's United Way campaign. The United Way Board of Directors is composed of people who, as a group, tend to think that (1) local programs deserve local financial support, (2) human services should be delivered as efficiently as possible, (3) unpaid volunteers help local organizations provide low-cost services, and (4) major support of an organization by prominent members of a community demonstrates that the organization is healthy and valuable. Knowing that the Board of Directors generally is committed to these tenets will help you select and phrase the arguments which comprise your plea for financial support. You will increase your chance for success if you are able to argue convincingly that your Tenants' Union is local and not a puppet of some national organization; that your overhead costs are low; that volunteers provide almost all the counseling and help for tenants in need; and that well-known law offices in the community are involved in helping your organization.

Demographic analysis, then, is one important analytical tool for the speaker, because it will help you select appeals or arguments and help you phrase your key ideas. More will be said about using demographic analysis once we examine the other main type of investigation.

ANALYZING THE AUDIENCE PSYCHOLOGICALLY

Social scientists and communication researchers have found it useful to divide people into psychological groups on the basis of fundamental beliefs, attitudes, and values. Because we will use these three terms throughout this book, we need to define them carefully, and discuss ways the concepts can be used by speakers who want to inform and persuade audiences.

Beliefs

A belief is a proposition thought by people holding it to accurately represent the state-of-affairs in the "real" world. A belief asserts something true or false in the world. It has been accepted by people based on their first-hand experience, evidence they have read or heard, authorities who have told them it is true, or even blind faith. So, you might believe that "Eating food hurriedly produces stomachaches" (first-hand experience); that "Iowa never has a killer frost after May 10" (something you read in an Iowa Extension Service pamphlet); that "Tax relief for corporations will create jobs" (something the President of the United States told you); or that "Treating people fairly will cause them to treat you with equal fairness" (something you hope is true).

Beliefs, therefore, are held by people for various reasons. They differ in other important ways as well. Some beliefs we call *facts*, others, *opinions;* and, some are *fixed,* and others, *variable.* Let us examine each of these sub-classes.

Facts and Opinions. We all hold beliefs with varying degrees of *certitude.* Those beliefs you hold strongly you are likely to call "facts." When you say, "It's a fact that John is six feet tall" or "It's a fact that cuts in government spending will reduce inflation," you are stating that you're very, very sure of those beliefs (even though the *actual* truth or falsity of those beliefs might be open to question). The beliefs you call "facts" are usually held with certainty because you are convinced that you have hard evidence backing them up. Thus, we may say that a *fact* is a belief held firmly by an individual and undergirded with strong evidence.

"Opinions," however, are a different matter. When you say "It's my opinion that . . . ," normally you are signaling to your listener that your belief is somewhat tentative, that is, held with something less than certainty. Or, when you use *tentative verbs* such as "I think that . . . ," and when you add *qualifiers* ("Perhaps it's true that . . .") or ("We probably could say that . . ."), you are letting your listeners know that the belief-statements being offered are opinions. You are "telling" them at least indirectly that your commitment to the statement is not especially strong and that you don't think you have incontrovertible evidence to support the belief-claim. Hence, we may say that an *opinion* is a belief held with low-to-moderate degrees of certitude and supported with something less than powerful or compelling evidence.[1]

---

[1]For an enlarged discussion of fixed and variable beliefs, see Milton M. Rokeach, *Beliefs, Attitudes, and Values: A Theory of Organization and Change* (San Francisco: Jossey-Bass, Inc., 1968), and his *The Nature of Human Values* (New York: Collier-Macmillan, Free Press, 1973).

Fixed and Variable Beliefs. A second way of classifying beliefs is to say that some are fixed and some are variable. "Fixed beliefs" are those which have been reinforced in your life and in your interaction with others over and over again. Obviously, many of your childhood beliefs are fixed (although some of them, such as "Parents are always right," tend to be less well fixed as you grow older). Other sorts of beliefs become fixed, or *anchored,* as well. Especially as you grow older, many political, economic, social, and religious beliefs harden in your mind. So, middle-aged and older people tend to vote political party lines election after election; tend to believe there are proper and improper ways to earn money; tend to believe that certain classes or types of people make better friends and associates than others; tend not to change churches or religions. Fixed beliefs, in a word, become habituated; they can even be called *stereotypes* because we often generalize our fixed beliefs (as when we say "All Democrats are . . . ," "If you want to get ahead in this world, you must . . . ," "People who go to fundamentalist churches are . . .").

In contrast, "variable beliefs" are less well anchored in our minds and experiences. You might enter college thinking you're very well suited by temperament and talent to be a chemist; then, after an instructor has praised your abilities in a composition class, you might see yourself as predestined to be a writer; next, you take a marketing class and find out you're very good at planning advertising campaigns. And so on, as you experience one class or department in college after another until you somehow come to select a major and degree program. In this case, your beliefs about your talents and ways you can best use them and satisfyingly change with your personal experiences and with testimony you heard from various (authoritative) instructors and counselors. Obviously, then, speakers usually need a clear sense about which of their audience's beliefs are fixed and therefore difficult-to-change, and which are variable and therefore more easily attacked.

Facts and opinions, fixed and variable beliefs—these related distinctions are important to you for two reasons: (1) Such assessments should help you outline some of the appeals you can make within your speech. If your investigations show you that the listeners hold some set of beliefs as factual, or accept certain beliefs as true, and if those "facts" and fixed beliefs support your central idea or proposition, you will certainly want to incorporate them into your speech. (2) And, these assessments also allow you to set *realistic expectations* as you plan your talk. Do not try to accomplish too much in a single speech if you know you will run into psychological resistance when you try to destroy too many facts and fixed beliefs; not all audience beliefs are equally amenable to change through speeches. Later in this chapter we will discuss further these questions of selecting belief-claims and setting speech goals.

Attitudes

Now, let us move to the second aspect of psychological profiling—attitudes. *Attitudes* may be defined as predispositions to respond positively or negatively to some person, object, or idea; they express preferences. Attitudes are expressed in such statements as "My dog's *better* than your dog," "Abortion is *wrong*," "I *hate* liars," "The Mona Lisa is a *beautiful* painting," "Public speaking is a *useful* course."

Because attitudinal statements express our preferences, predispositions, reactions, and basic judgments, they represent the core of our psychological life. They often control our behavior, because we tend to do things we like and avoid things we dislike. Also, we're only human, so most of us avoid even thinking about things (the suffering of others, death) we dislike or fear; we prefer instead to contemplate beautiful sights (a summer sunset), positive opinions (a sense of our own innate goodness), and preferred associates (a close friend). A speaker, therefore, is well-advised to attempt to assess the dominant attitudes of audiences. Especially relevant are the audience's attitudes toward the speaker, the subject, and the speech purpose.

The Audience's Attitude Toward the Speaker. The attitude of an audience toward you as a speaker will be based in part upon your known reputation and, in part, upon your behavior during the speech. Regarding your reputation, two factors are especially important: (1) the degree of your listeners' *friendliness* toward you, and (2) the degree of their *respect* for you and your knowledge of the subject. The potency of these factors may vary widely. A mother's affection for her small son, for instance, may be very strong; but her respect for her son's judgment may not be. On the other hand, the mother may have the greatest respect for the judgment of a neighbor even though she dislikes her as a person. Respect and friendliness are two different attitudes, but as a speaker you must attempt to take both into account.

As we noted in Chapter 1, when you begin to speak and throughout the entire time you are talking, the audience consciously or subconsciously assesses your credibility from many points of view. Among other things, they ask: (1) Are you a *competent* speaker? Do you give evidence of intelligence and expertise? (2) Are you *admirable?* Do you appear to be a good person? (3) Are you *trustworthy?* Do you seem honest, just, fair, and sincere? (4) Are you *dynamic?* Are you energetic, alert mentally? (5) Are you *courageous?* Do you seem to have strength and firmness? Collectively, these factors point up the need to know your subject thoroughly, to respect your audience, and to deliver your speech with sincerity and vigor.

The Audience's Attitude Toward the Subject. Sometimes people are *interested* in a subject; sometimes they are *apathetic* about it. In either case, the amount of interest they have will influence a great deal their perception of and response to a communication. Some researchers place *prior audience attitude* among the most crucial variables that determine speaking success.[2] If, for instance, the listeners are unfavorably disposed toward the speaker's subject or purpose, they may: (1) distort the substance of the message, (2) psychologically or physically leave the field, (3) discredit the communicator, or (4) use a host of similar defense mechanisms to avoid accurate perception of the speaker's intent and message-content.

An audience may be apathetic or neutral if its members see no connection between the speaker's subject and their own affairs. When your analysis indicates that your listeners will be apathetic, you need to show them how they are directly concerned with the problem you are discussing; or you need to arouse their curiosity about some novel aspect of the subject. Use all available means for holding and involving their attention. (See pages 36–42.) Even when the members of your audience are already interested, you cannot entirely neglect the problems of commanding and holding attention; but when your listeners are apathetic, you must make a special effort to arouse their interest.

Interest (or the lack of it) is only one aspect of an audience's attitude toward your subject. *Expectancy* is another. For example, as soon as we hear that a speech will be about the Gay Liberation movement, many of us begin to form favorable or unfavorable attitudes toward the speaker and the subject. As a general rule, the more the listeners know about your subject or the stronger the beliefs they hold concerning it, the more likely they are to have well-defined expectations. These expectations may be troublesome, for frequently they operate as listening barriers or as filters which distort the meanings that the audience assigns to your message. The introduction of your speech presents a special opportunity to create or to correct these audience expectations. All the time you are talking, however, you should bear in mind the problem of listener expectation, and make adaptations accordingly.

The Audience's Attitude Toward the Speech Purpose. If, with no preliminaries at all, you told the members of your audience the specific purpose of your speech, what would be their reaction or response? This

---

[2] See, for example, Muzafer Sherif and Carl L. Hovland, *Social Judgment* (New Haven, Conn.: Yale University Press, 1961).

"attitude toward speech purpose" is not the frame of mind you hope your audience will hold at the end of your speech; it is the one that exists *before you begin*. Since audience predisposition is seldom uniform, many different shades of attitude may be represented. It is best, therefore, to determine— by prior analysis—what attitude is *predominant* and to adapt your speech to that view while making allowances for variations in the character or intensity of listener belief.

When the general end of your speech is *to inform,* the attitude of your listeners toward the speech purpose will be governed largely by their attitude toward the subject, that is:

    (a) interested, or   *(b)* apathetic.

When your general purpose is *to persuade,* the listeners' attitude toward the speech purpose will be governed also by their attitude toward the specific belief or action which is urged; hence, their attitude will be one of the following:

    (a) favorable but not aroused;
    (b) apathetic to the situation;
    (c) interested in the situation but undecided what to do or think about it;
    (d) interested in the situation but hostile to the *proposed* attitude, belief, or action; or
    (e) hostile to any change from the present state of affairs.[3]

Determining the predominant attitude of your audience toward your subject and purpose should guide you in selecting your arguments and developing the structure and content of your message. If your listeners are apathetic, begin your speech on a point of compelling interest or startling vividness. Show them how your subject affects them. If they are hostile to the proposal, you may wish to introduce it more cautiously, emphasize some basic principle with which you know they agree, and relate your proposal to it. If they are interested but undecided, provide plenty of proof in the form of factual illustrations, testimony, and statistics. If they are favorable but not aroused, try to motivate them by using appeals that directly touch their desires for pleasure, independence, power, creativity, ego-satisfaction, and the like.

---

[3]Traditionally, it has been assumed that audiences who are hostile to the speaker's proposal or opposed to any change in the existing state of affairs are most difficult to persuade. For qualifications of this point of view, however, see Wayne N. Thompson, *Quantitative Studies in Public Address and Communication* (New York: Random House, Inc., 1967), pp. 38–39.

No analysis of an audience made prior to a speech is certain to be fully correct, and even if it is, audience attitudes may shift even while you are speaking.[4] Hence, you must watch listeners' reactions closely when your subject is announced and continue to do so throughout your entire speech. The way your hearers sit in their seats, the expressions on their faces, their audible reactions—laughter, applause, shifting about, whispering—all are clues to their attitude toward you, your subject, or your purpose. The conscientious communicator develops a keen awareness of these signs of *feedback* on the part of the audience and adapts his or her remarks accordingly.[5]

Values

A third important "content" of your mind is composed of values. Values may be defined as basic orientations to life—habitual ways of looking at the world or responding to problems. Values, in a sense, are psychologically "larger" than attitudes. Whereas attitudes represent particularized judgments about specific persons, objects, or ideas, values include broad categories into which many specific attitudes are grouped mentally. Thus, for example, a person may hold a specific attitude toward abortion:

Attitude: "Abortion is wrong."

That attitude probably is held, however, because of the way the person conceives of abortion, because of the valuative category into which the person psychologically "puts" abortion:

Values: Abortion is primarily . . .
     a medical question (*scientific* value).
     a moral question (*religious-philosophical* value).
     a question of a woman's right to control her own mind and
        body (*psychological* value).
     a matter of allowing groups in a society to make their own
        decisions without being dictated to by others (*sociological*
        value).

---

[4]Such changes during the course of a speech are often dramatic. See Robert D. Brooks and Thomas M. Scheidel, "Speech as Process: A Case Study," *Speech Monographs* 35 (March 1968), pp. 1–7.

[5]On adapting to feedback, see Paul D. Holtzman, *The Psychology of Speakers' Audiences* (Glenview, Ill.: Scott, Foresman and Co., 1970), pp. 33–36, 117.

something to be considered only in life-or-death situations
(*pragmatic* value).

something to be decided by a nationwide referendum (*political*
value).

Thus, a person's attitude, "Abortion is wrong," might be held because the
person values scientific evidence which suggests a fetus can survive as a
human being; because of religious authority which calls abortion murder;
because the person thinks sociological, psychological, or pragmatic questions
are irrelevant to abortion; or because, politically, most people in this country
may be opposed to abortion rights legislation.

Knowing, or trying to find out, what values members of your audience
habitually bring to bear on issues you are discussing, then, is a most
important part of audience analysis. Knowing, for example, that members of
the Board of Directors of United Way are strongly motivated by sociological
concerns (concerns for needy groups in the community) and by pragmatic
concerns (concerns for fiscal efficiency and responsibility) helped you
construct your speech in support of the Tenants' Union.

Values, then, are an individual's habitualized reasons for holding
particular attitudes. But, even more broadly, we can talk about *value
orientations*. These represent the positions relatively large groups of people
take toward life. Over the last three decades, for example, Americans have
read about the Puritan Ethic, the Establishment, the Silent Majority, the
Counterculture, Me-ism, Situational Ethics, Freaks, New Politics, the Old
Guard, Libbers, Moonies, Rednecks, the Moral Majority, and NeoLiberals.[6]

Value orientations are the broad, sweeping concepts (sometimes termed
ideologies) which members of groups or collectivities apply to basic questions in their lives. They can be thought of as clusters of more specific beliefs
and attitudes as well as the judgments groups habitually make toward events
in the world; they are response tendencies.

As a communicator who wants to understand listeners and to relate
harmoniously and productively with them, you need to be highly sensitive to

---

[6]For discussions of predominant value-orientations in American society, see Rokeach
(above, n. 1); Robin M. Williams, *American Society: A Sociological Interpretation*, 3rd ed.
(New York: Alfred A. Knopf, Inc., 1970), Chapter 11, as well as his "Changing Value
Orientations and Beliefs on the American Scene," in *The Character of Americans: A Book of
Readings*, rev. ed., ed. Michael McGiffert (Homewood, Ill.: Dorsey Press, 1970), pp.
212–30; and Frank E. Armbruster, *The Forgotten Americans: A Survey of the Values, Beliefs
and Concerns of the Majority* (New Rochelle, N.Y.: Arlington House, Inc., 1972). Also
remember that the Gallup and Harris polling organizations regularly issue reports on
attitudes and values in America; check with the Reference Desk at the library.

An "audience" is not a homogeneous mass; rather, it is a collection of individuals who belong to various demographic and psychological subgroups. Audience analysis is the key to speaking effectiveness, therefore, because it allows you to assess the degree to which demographic and psychological variables might affect an audience's perceptions of and reactions to your speech.

values and value orientations. Unless you recognize the differences that may exist between you and members of your audience, and take definite steps to bridge them, you cannot hope to cope effectively with the conflicts and controversies such cultural discrepancies are almost certain to generate. Unless you can discover *common ground*—common valuative ground—between and among them, you may well be in communicative trouble. A search for common ground represents a crucial step in audience analysis.

USING AUDIENCE ANALYSIS IN SPEECH PREPARATION

Neither demographic nor psychological analysis, of course, is an end in itself. Rather you are carrying out such analyses to discover what might affect the acceptance of you and your ideas. You are searching for *relevant* considerations. What you learn about your listeners through systematic investigation can conceivably affect every aspect of your speech—right down to the ways you phrase important ideas and deliver your sentiments. We will address such matters in Chapters 8, 9, and 10. For now, let us examine ways in which your analytical conclusions or findings ought to help you phrase your purposes and select your dominant appeals.

Audience Targeting: Setting Purposes Realistically

Few of us have difficulty determining our overall or general speech purposes—to inform, to persuade, to actuate. It becomes more difficult, however, to narrow down to specific purposes, and to phrase central ideas and propositions for particular speeches. After you have completed your audience analysis, however, you should be better able to *target your audience*, that is, to determine with some precision what you realistically can expect to accomplish with *this* audience in the time you have available. As you think about targeting an audience, four considerations should arise.

Specificity of Purpose.   Suppose you have a part-time job with your college's Career Planning and Placement Office; you know enough about its operations and have enough personal interest in it to want to speak about career planning and placement to different audiences. What you have discovered about different audiences should help you determine appropriate specific purposes for each audience. If you were to talk to a group of *incoming freshmen*, for example, you'd know that they probably:

1. know little or nothing about career planning and placement as a college office (i.e., have few beliefs, none of which are fixed);
2. are predisposed to look favorably upon career planning and placement (given job anxieties among college graduates);
3. are, at their particular stage of life and of educational development, more concerned with such pragmatic concerns as getting an adviser, getting registered, and learning about basic degree requirements than they are with longer-range matters like post-degree placement (and hence may not value your information without motivation);
4. are likely, however, to see you as an authoritative speaker and hence are willing at least to listen to you.

Given these audience considerations, you probably should keep your talk fairly general: Feed them basic, not detailed, information about career planning and placement; remind them that the office can relieve many of their later anxieties, as graduation nears; show them how thinking about possible careers will help them select majors and particular courses. You might phrase your specific purpose as follows: "To brief incoming freshmen on the range of services offered by the Career Planning and Placement Office." That orientation would include a basic description of each service and general exhortation to use the services to make some curricular decisions.

Were you, instead, to talk about this subject to an *incoming group of new faculty*, you'd probably assess the audience differently. You probably would discover that they:

1. know quite a bit about career planning and placement offices (having used them themselves and perhaps having worked with them in previous jobs);
2. have mixed feelings about career planning and placement (because some faculty think that too much emphasis upon careers turns colleges and universities into "trade" schools rather than centers of humane learning);
3. tend to value education "for its own sake," that is philosophically, rather than as a route to employment, that is pragmatically;
4. are likely to view you as a mere student, or as a mere college bureaucrat.

Given these factors, you'd probably have to get a good deal more specific in some areas. You'd want to describe the particular features of this office's operations rather than only its general duties; your listeners need to know "how," not "what," because they already know the "what." You'd have to reassure them that your office is an adjunct to the university's mission, that you realize not all course selections should be aimed solely at career choices. And, you probably would want to demonstrate your expertise by talking about career possibilities across a variety of fields (especially if you know what fields are represented in the group of incoming faculty). You might phrase your specific purpose like this: "To inform incoming faculty about Langford College's philosophy of career planning and placement, about ways faculty members in all fields can help their students use the Office, and about informational assistance the Office provides faculty members."

Audience analysis, therefore, will help you focus your specific purposes and determine which ones are appropriate to your listeners.

Areas of Audience Interest. Both demographic and psychological analyses are most useful to you in deciding what ideas will be of interest to your listeners. Suppose you know a good deal about laser technology. A group of industrial managers probably would be most interested in hearing a speech on lasers' manufacturing applications; a group of medical researchers, on its capabilities for improving surgical procedures; a group of physicists, on its theoretical principles; a general "public" audience, on ways lasers will transform their everyday lives.

In other words, you often are able to infer audience interests, at least potential interests, from knowing something about their demographic and psychological characters. This is not to say, of course, that you always must cater to them; sometimes, you will want to *create a new set of interests* in an audience. So, you might suppose that an audience of doctors always is interested in finding out something about the latest drugs for pain therapy, given their medical-scientific values; but yet, you might well want them to know more about the psychological effects of such drugs and to deal professionally with the ethical questions which surround the use of strong drugs with unstable patients. To achieve such a purpose, you'll have to create a new set of interests, especially by *tying the new interests to old ones*. So, for this speech, you might phrase your central idea as follows: "Knowing more about the psychological effects of the latest drugs available for pain therapy will make you a more humane as well as a more medically expert physician." Phrasing the central idea in this way explicitly ties the interests you are trying to create to ones the audience already has.

The Audience's Capacity to Act.   As a speaker, *limit your request to an action lying within your listeners' range of authority*. Do not ask them to do something they would be unable to do even if they wanted to. To demand of a group of students that they "abolish all required courses" would be foolish. They do not have the authority to take this action—the final word concerning course requirements belongs to a school's faculty. But, students do have the right and the capacity-for-action to bring pressure on the faculty toward this end. A more logical and positively framed proposition, there-fore, would be "Petition the faculty to make all courses elective."

You determine ranges of authority through analysis of the audience, especially of demographic factors. In the case of comparatively homoge-neous audiences (e.g., students), this is relatively easy to do. In the case of more heterogeneous groups, however, you may well have to take into consideration a broader range of capacities-to-act. So, in talking with a local school's PTA about instituting an after-school program of foreign language and culture instruction, you are addressing an audience comprised of school administrations (who can seek funding from the school board), teachers (who could be asked to volunteer some instructional time), and parents (who could petition the school board, convince their children to enroll, and volunteer their talents to help with the program). You thus would have to include among your specific purposes goals for each of these sub-groups of listeners.

Degrees of Change. Finally, your analyses of audiences, as we suggested earlier, should help you determine "how far" you can "move" an audience intellectually, emotionally, and actively. How much new material, new information, can you present to an audience in ten minutes? Your answer to that question will depend primarily upon your assessment of your listeners' age, degree of educational development, and previous stocks-of-knowledge. How intense, positively or negatively, can you get an audience to feel about some matter? If a group is adamantly opposed to, say, a new parking ramp for downtown, it is very unlikely that in a single speech you will be able to make them overwhelmingly in favor of one; an attempt to simply neutralize some of their objections would be better. How much can you expect people to do after your speech? If your pre-speech analyses indicates that this group of listeners strongly favors cycling as an activity, and is valuatively committed to governmental citizens' programs, then you probably can convince many of them to work long hours at mounting a public campaign for new bike paths in town and at convincing city council to commit the money for paths and urban bike lanes. If they are only moderately committed to cycling, however, you might rather appeal to civic pride, to questions of automobile-bicycle problems and of safety, and then ask them instead to make a small donation to the public campaign others are running.

Audience analysis, in other words, should help you determine how much you can change an audience and even what kinds of commitments you can expect from your listeners. You should phrase your specific purposes and central ideas or propositions accordingly.

Audience Segmentation: Selecting Dominant Ideas and Appeals

So far, we have been dealing with audience analysis as it helps you identify or target your audience, and then as it helps you phrase purposes, central ideas, and propositions. Keep in mind, however, that in reality there is no such animal as "an audience." Each person sitting in an auditorium is an individual; and no matter how people are crowded together, arranged in rows, or reached electronically by a message, they never completely lose that individuality. As we noted when discussing psychological profiling, your beliefs, attitudes, and values are, ultimately, yours—the products of your experiences, your own mental operations.

Ideally, of course, it would be nice if you could approach listeners one at a time. Indeed, often you can; that's called interpersonal communication.

But, because communicating with individuals is time-consuming and hence inefficient when dealing with matters of larger, public concern, speakers try to affect people in groups. There must be a middle ground between thinking of audiences as completely homogeneous masses and as solitary individuals. There is. Among advertisers, the approach is called audience segmentation. *Audience segmentation* is a matter of approaching a collection of listeners as a series of sub-groups, or "differentiated populations." Segmenting your audience into sub-groups will help you select your dominant appeals.

Avoiding Unnecessary Irritation.   The first way audience segmentation can help you select speech materials is by making you conscious of appeals to avoid. Were a speaker to say, "Because all you girls are interested in efficient cooking, today I want to talk about four ways a food processor will save you time in the kitchen," he or she probably would alienate two sub-groups in the audience: The females probably would be irritated with the stereotyped allusion to them as "girls," while the males who cooked would be offended by having been left out. The appeal would be better phrased: "Because everyone who cooks is interested in. . . ." Here, you are aiming the interest-appeal to the proper audience segment—the culinary masters. Similarly, unless you are sure there are no Roman Catholics in your audience, you probably will want to avoid blaming the Catholic religious hierarchy for the anti-abortion movement in this country; because so many people in this country identify with businesses and industries, you probably would not want to blame "the business establishment" alone for inflation; and, you probably would be foolhardy to refer to "dumb jocks," "artsy-craftsy theatre majors," and "computer fanatics" in a speech on the goals of college education to your speech class.

This is *not* to say, of course, that you never confront directly beliefs, attitudes, and values of sub-groups represented in your audience—that you always and only say what people "want" to hear. Obviously, in some areas of this country, the Catholic Church was active in the anti-abortion movement; some business practices have been responsible for part of the inflation problem; and, it perhaps is possible to distinguish between "essential" and "secondary" goals of education. You can find ways to talk about those sorts of things; only be sure that you avoid stereotyped references to people and groups, that you avoid blanket condemnation of groups of people, and that, when possible, you work around touchy subjects, and cite ample and unbiased evidence when you must attack a group's beliefs, attitudes, and sacred values.

Selecting Relevant Belief- and Attitude-Statements.   More positively, audience analysis and segmentation should help you select belief- and attitude-statements for inclusion in your speech. Suppose you were to give a speech to a local Rotary Club about the establishment of a community hospice—a team of medical personnel, psychologists, social workers, and other volunteers who work with terminally-ill people and their families. Suppose in this speech you are trying to raise money to set up the hospice. As a group, a Rotary Club normally is composed of business people, medical professionals, educators, social service personnel, lawyers, bankers, and the like. By thinking of the Rotary audience as segmented into such sub-groups, you should be in a position to offer each sub-group some reasons to support the community hospice, for example:

Proposition: A community hospice should be supported by all segments in our town because:

1. For doctors, nurses, and hospital workers, a hospice provides help for the dying, and therefore is a complement to your work to save the living.
2. For those of you working in social services, a hospice works with a social-team concept, and therefore gives you a way to work with needy people in a way you can't now.
3. For those of you in education, a hospice provides unequalled opportunities for on-the-job training for many different kinds of students, simply because it uses volunteers.
4. And, for those of you from the banks and businesses of this community, a hospice is a vital local resource, something which can be used by your employees and their families and which sets this community apart from all the others around our area.

Each of these appeals, of course, would be expanded in an actual speech, but perhaps you can see how each one of the four is based upon beliefs and attitudes you assume are important to segments of the audience. In our example, there is implicit reference to medical beliefs and attitudes ("Medical personnel provide services for the living," "Our job of providing medical services to the living is good"); to the beliefs and attitudes of social service personnel ("In our work, psychologists treat individuals' problems, social workers treat family problems," and "It would be a good idea to provide certain kinds of help to others in a team"); to educators' beliefs and attitudes ("Schools must find all ways possible to educate their students," "On-the-job training is a useful educational tool"); and to business beliefs and attitudes ("Businesses take care of all aspects of their employees' lives," "Our city might grow if we increase our social services and hence make it more attractive," "We will be more competitive if we improve our community"). Thus, *audience analysis, in combination with audience segmentation, is an invaluable tool for selecting your main lines of appeal and argument.*

Choosing Among Valuative Appeals.   And finally, as you might guess, audience segmentation will help select a valuative vocabulary for your speeches. Even informative speeches, as we will discuss them more fully later, need to contain appeals to audience interests; you can use a valuative vocabulary to motivate different segments of the audience to listen to and accept your information. So, for a class demonstration speech, you might say: "Today, I want to teach you three basic techniques of Oriental cooking—cutting meats and vegetables, using spices, and quick-cooking your food in a wok. If you learn these techniques, you'll expand your range of expertise in the kitchen (*personal value*), you'll save money on your food and energy bills (*economic value*), you'll prepare more than satisfying meals for your friends (*social value*), and you'll prepare nutritious, healthful meals for everyone" (*pragmatic value*). With that statement, you will have given your audience four different reasons for listening, and hence will have a good chance of appealing to everyone in your speech. (If that's not enough, tell them the meals will be beautiful, too, and thereby add an *aesthetic value!*)

Usually, however, valuative appeals are even more important to persuasive and actuative speeches. Because these speeches are attempts to alter people's beliefs, attitudes, and behaviors, and because, as we noted, values are a body of beliefs and attitudes, valuative appeals are absolutely crucial for persuasive and actuative communications. For example:

Proposition: The United States should take immediate, concrete steps to improve its relationships with the People's Republic of China. Why?

1. *Politically,* better relations with China will reduce international tensions and allow us to head off potential conflicts before they explode.
2. *Economically,* China represents the world's largest market for U.S. agricultural and industrial goods.
3. *Sociologically,* it's desirable for two cultures as different as ours and theirs to better understand each other, for in understanding lies intercultural cooperation.
4. *Culturally* (i.e., aesthetically), China and the United States have varied artistic traditions, so both worlds will be richer if we can increase cultural exchanges.
5. *Psychologically,* the levels of anxiety and distrust existing among citizens of both countries can be reduced through expanded people-to-people exchanges.

While we have not used every conceivable value-term in this segmentation-of-appeals, perhaps the procedure is clear: (1) Think through possible reasons people might accept your proposition in valuative terms. (2) And then, use a valuative vocabulary in phrasing your actual appeals-for-acceptance.

In conclusion, understanding your audience is certainly the most crucial step of speech preparation. The competent speaker makes many decisions about topic, specific purposes, phrasings for central ideas and propositions, dominant appeals, and even phraseology based upon demographical and psychological profiles of audience members. To help yourself with these tasks, you'll want to (1) think through your personal experiences with identifiable groups in the audience, (2) talk with program chairpersons and others who can tell you "who" is in the audience and something about their interests, (3) ask speakers who've addressed these and similar audiences what to expect, and (4) even interview some people who'll be there, to find out more about their beliefs, attitudes, and values—their range of concerns.

All these are not especially easy tasks, for most of us don't have available the resources of public opinion polling firms and extensive social-psychological target group profiles. You probably will be unable to precisely identify all possible facets of listeners' minds and habits. If you learn all you can about them, however, and if you use that knowledge to help make some key pre-speech decisions by discovering *relevant* considerations, you will significantly—maybe even determinatively—improve your chances for communicative success.

A SAMPLE ANALYSIS OF AN AUDIENCE

In this chapter we have surveyed an array of choices you must make as you analyze your audience and occasion. Those choices, however, will sort themselves out if you work systematically, trying to make them one step at a time. Observe how one student analyzed her audience as she prepared a speech on behalf of facilities for a women's intercollegiate athletic program.

AUDIENCE ANALYSIS:
FACILITIES FOR WOMEN'S ATHLETICS AT STATE UNIVERSITY

I. *BASIC SPEAKING SITUATION*
   1. *Title:* "A Sound Mind in a Sound Body in a Sound Building: Athletic Facilities for State University's Women"
   2. *Subject:* Training and sports facilities for women athletes.
   3. *General Purpose:* To actuate.
   4. *Specific Purpose:* To convince the Board in Charge of Athletics to

request from the regents and the state legislature money for a women's athletic facility.

5. *Specific Audience:* The Board in Charge of Athletics consists of the Director of Athletics, the Assistant Director of Athletics, Director of Men's Intramural Sports, Director of Women's Intramural Sports, six coaches of men's varsity sports, three coaches of women's varsity sports, two elected faculty members, and five elected student representatives. Eight of these people are women. Also in attendance as spectators are approximately two dozen interested women athletes (secondary audience).

6. *Proposition:* "The Board in Charge of Athletics should ask the regents to request from the state legislature money to construct a women's athletic facility."

II. *AUDIENCE ANALYSIS*
   A. *Demographic Analysis*
      1. *Age:* Of the twenty Board members, five are 18–22, and fifteen are between 30 and 55. The spectators are all 18–22. Except for appeals to future growth and school reputation, age will not be an important factor.
      2. *Gender:* On the Board, twelve males and eight females; the spectators are all female. Given the topic and proposition, gender will be a concern for audience members.
      3. *Education:* One third were physical education majors in college, most with advanced degrees; one third of the Board members are undergraduates; one third are Ph.D.'s in arts or sciences. Most of the spectators are physical education majors. All audience members are conscious of the importance of education for both careers and life in general.
      4. *Group Membership:* All members of the Board also belong to the general academic community. The place of athletics in a learning environment will be on their minds during the speech.
      5. *Cultural and Ethnic Background:* Two Board members are black, and two are Hispanic, but ethnic background should not be a factor here.
   B. *Psychological Analysis*
      1. *Beliefs:*
         a. *Accepted Facts and Beliefs:* Most are familiar with federal guidelines for male and female athletics, and were on the Board three years ago when it instituted intercollegiate competition for female athletes. All know the financial straits binding the college, the regents, and the state. Most know that the school recently has had trouble recruiting superior women athletes.
         b. *Fixed Beliefs:* All believe that physical development and talents are as important to life as mental and social development. All but

the two intramural directors believe that interscholastic competition is a most important college commitment.

   c. *Variable Beliefs:* Most probably believe, though, that male interscholastic competition is more important to the school than female competition; some may even think that competition in general is more important for males than for females. There may well be some subtle sexism which must be addressed gently in this speech. Also, most members of the Board probably think that the regents and legislature will not listen to a proposal for a building program—a belief which will have to be changed by this speech.

  2. *Attitudes:*

   a. *Audience Attitude Toward Speaker:* The Board probably is suspicious, even uneasy, about this request to address it; it probably also thinks that "outside" students are naive and idealistic when it comes to money and interaction with the regents and the legislature.

   b. *Audience Attitude Toward Subject:* The Board probably has considerable interest in it, although it is uncertain about the exact proposal that will be made.

   c. *Audience Attitude Toward Purpose:* Most Board members probably are undecided; a couple may be hostile, given statements they have made to the campus newspaper; the spectators probably hope the speaker can steamroller the idea through the Board. This is unlikely.

  3. *Values:*

   a. *Predominating Values:* Among the spectators, especially, the political value of "equality" is paramount, although it may be dangerous in this situation to stress it. Among Board members there is probably valuative commitment to physical achievement in general, to pride in the school's general reputation, and to pride in themselves as overseers of the physical education program. There also, however, is probably a fear of "politics"—of maneuvering through the regents and legislature—as a process which could jeopardize the school's general athletic budget.

   b. *Relevant Value Orientation:* Ideologically, all Board members generally are committed to athletic competition (intramural and intercollegiate) for all students as an ultimate value, even as a hallmark of the American way of life. You should be able to fit your speech purpose within this general outlook nicely.

III. *ADAPTIVE STRATEGIES*

  A. *Audience Targeting*

   1. *Specificity of Purpose:* To defuse one set of suspicions, make it clear that you're not simply crusading for feminist causes blindly.

While you will of course recognize the importance of women's athletics, put your stress on physical culture—the need for athletic facilities to improve recruitment, training, and competition within the college's general mission.

2. *Areas of Audience Interests:* Make sure you use Board members' fixed and accepted beliefs and values to advance your own goals; stress the members' commitments—and previous actions—which demonstrate their belief in "a sound mind in a sound body" as a goal of college education. Make them feel pride in an effort to improve the physical education program and the school's general reputation. In other words, show them it is in their self-interest, as well as the interests of student athletes, to push for the new facility.

3. *Audience's Capacity to Act:* Stress the desirability of action on this matter, but also work hard to show how it might be done. Suggest ways to approach the regents reasonably; indicate how you and the student athletes in attendance will help mount a lobbying campaign on the legislature. Point out examples of other schools which have convinced legislatures, even in times of financial trouble, to allow schools to let bonds for such facilities. "Feasibility" and "practicality" should punctuate this speech.

4. *Degrees of Change:* Don't demand a sports complex as large as that available for male athletes. Push instead for a "first phase" building with training rooms and general space.

B. *Audience Segmentation*

1. *Avoiding Irritation:* De-emphasize the feminist aspects of the issue. (That might well play nicely with the spectators, but it would only strengthen and energize Board resistance.)

2. *Relevant Belief- and Attitude-Statements:* Do recognize the spectators' commitments to women's athletics, and their firm resolve to do what is necessary to see that the college improves its facilities. (They have taken the trouble to come, and their commitments should be recognized.) But, aim the bulk of your speech at the Board itself—its commitments, its responsibilities, and its capacities to act. Be sure, too, to undermine some potentially negative beliefs and values: Make them understand you are a reasonable, sensible, understanding advocate; tell them about other schools which have made important strides in recruitment and general reputation by expanding women's athletics, and which even are getting decent gate receipts from women's competitions; stress the importance of competitive athletics to women as well as men, perhaps with examples of females who have moved into professional athletic lives.

3. *Relevant Valuative Appeals:* Underscore the virtues of physical achievement, pride in the school's reputation, pride in the Board itself for courageous action, and the Board's capacity to act

positively with the regents and legislature in this situation. Stress,
too, the importance of physical environment for both athletes and
spectators for athletic competition.

With this much hard pre-speech analysis completed, the student
preparing this speech found out what she should do next. The analysis
pointed particularly to kinds of *supporting materials* she needed to find:

1. Look up federal guidelines (Government Documents Office in the
   library) on comparable facilities for men's and women's sports.
2. Read the campus newspaper articles carefully to see if the two
   Board members really are hostile; also check the paper from three
   years ago (Newspaper Office) for statements some of the current
   Board members made in support of women's athletics when the
   program was instituted.
3. Regarding presumed resistance from the regents and the legislature, find examples from State University's past (Office of Facilities
   Planning) when those groups went along with school requests for
   bonding authority to build facilities.
4. Interview the women's athletic coaches (Fieldhouse Offices) concerning the names of specific athletes State University recruited
   but then lost to schools with superior facilities.
5. Search out quotations (Education Library, with help from Reference Desk) from educational experts regarding the importance of
   physical training and competition in college education. Also check
   the University charter and Athletic Department Mission Statement
   (Main Library, with help from Reference Desk) for statements
   requiring physical training and competition.
6. Prepare a list of schools similar to State University which have
   recently upgraded their women's athletics facilities (from women's
   athletic coaches). Prepare a brief survey which can be sent to their
   Women's Athletic Directors; ask on the survey (briefly!) for information on types of facilities, building and equipment costs, methods of financing, role (if any) of student body in the legislative
   campaign, alumni reactions, and gate receipts for specific sports.
7. Prepare a list of State University and other collegiate women
   athletes (see coaches of individual sports) who have completed
   undergraduate degrees here and elsewhere, and then gone on to
   professional sporting careers. Also find statements (Main Library)
   from female athletes regarding the importance of intercollegiate
   competition for postcollege, nonathletic careers.

8. Check (Campus Legal Services) on state laws regarding bonding authority for public buildings.
9. Work out a plan for students, faculty, and alumni cooperation (check with Student Government, Faculty Senate, and Alumni Office) in mounting a facilities campaign to convince the legislature. Also check with the Alumni Office regarding names of legislators who are State University graduates.

In addition to these kinds of guides to necessary supporting materials—the topic of this book's next chapter—the speaker has received a good deal of help in other areas of speech preparation: She knows generally what motive and valuative appeals to focus on, which to avoid; she has a sense for how she should present herself, her role and her ethos, so as to maximize her chances for success; she knows what beliefs she can count on to work in her favor, and what beliefs she has to change if she is to get the Board to take the first important steps. These are valuable kinds of knowledge—knowledge which should make her more confident and more effective.

Audience analysis is hard work, and even involves some guessing. Yet, it pays off in later stages of preparation, in the presentation, and in results. You won't regret it.

 ## GROUP PROJECTS

1. In a class discussion, talk about the speaking situation in your classroom. What are the prevailing rules and customs you must follow? What physical conditions affect the auditors' receptivity? Is age a factor? How? How about gender, level of education, and cultural-ethnic backgrounds? What does the presence of a high-authority figure—a teacher—do to the atmosphere? What, then, must speakers do to adapt any speech to these general conditions?

2. As a class, select some speech topic, then divide the class into five groups. Each group should frame a specific purpose statement: Group 1, for an audience that is favorable, but not aroused; Group 2, an audience that is interested, but undecided; Group 3, an audience that is apathetic; Group 4, an audience that is hostile toward the proposition or recommendation; and Group 5, an audience that is opposed to any change from the present situation. Then, write the five purpose statements on the chalkboard and compare them. What principles of audience analysis are exhibited in those five purpose statements?

3. Immediately after a round of speeches, each member of the class should note audience reactions to him- or herself *during the course of the speech.* Did they seem

attentive? Were there points in the speech when individuals thought they "lost" the audience? How did they know that? Did anyone look bored or distracted? How did the speakers know? In general, were individual speakers able to "read" feedback? How? Share your reactions as speakers in a general class discussion of feedback.

INDIVIDUAL PROJECTS

1. After your instructor has divided the class into four-person groups, meet with the other members of your group and discuss with them the next round of speeches to be presented: the actual topic you intend to use, your general and specific purpose, development of your idea or proposition, your speech plan or outline, useful kinds of supporting materials. Criticize each other's plans and preparation, offering suggestions for changes and more specific adaptations to this particular classroom audience. After discussing and evaluating the potential of your speech with a portion of your audience, you should be able subsequently to develop and present a better and more effectively adapted message to the class as a whole.

2. As a student of speech communication, you can learn something about the principles of audience analysis by observing how such public-opinion pollsters as Dr. George Gallup analyze "the great American audience" to derive the samples on which they base their predictions. Together with several other members of your class (as your instructor may designate), investigate these methods as described in books, magazine articles, and newspaper surveys, and report on them orally, either in individual presentations or in an informal discussion with the class as a whole.

3. Gather some advertisements (not want ads) and bring them to class. In groups, share your advertisements and see if you can determine the audiences for which they were intended. What attitudes are the advertisers trying to engage? Are they trying to create beliefs? What tactics do they use? How effective do you think these tactics are?

SUGGESTIONS FOR FURTHER READING

R. P. Abelson et al., eds., *Theories of Cognitive Consistency: A Sourcebook* (Chicago: Rand McNally, 1968).

Daryl Bem, *Beliefs, Attitudes, and Human Affairs* (Belmont, Calif.: Brooks/Cole Publishing Co., 1970).

Gary L. Cronkhite, "Perception and Meaning," in *Handbook of Rhetorical and Communication Theory*, ed. Carroll C. Arnold and John Waite Bowers (Boston: Allyn and Bacon, Inc., 1984).

Bruce E. Gronbeck, *The Articulate Person: A Guide to Everyday Public Speaking,* 2nd ed. (Glenview, Ill.: Scott, Foresman and Company), 1983, Chapter 8, "Changing Attitudes."

Gerald R. Miller, Michael Burgoon, and Judee Burgoon, "The Functions of Communication in Changing Attitudes and Gaining Compliance," in *Handbook of Rhetorical and Communication Theory,* ed. Carroll C. Arnold and John Waite Bowers (Boston: Allyn and Bacon, Inc., 1984).

CHAPTER 5

Finding and Using Supporting Materials

Every day each of us is asked to accept others' ideas. Sometimes acceptance comes in the form of understanding, sometimes in the form of action. Each time we listen to a lecture we are being asked indirectly to accept as true and relevant the ideas the speaker presents. Each time we purchase a product we do so because we believe the product will work; we have accepted the idea that the product is usable, of high quality, and right for us. When we prepare and present a speech, we are also asking for a kind of acceptance—acceptance of a central idea or proposition. Although we cannot control the audience, we can do some things to make it easier for the audience to accept our ideas.

Several of the steps in speech preparation noted in Chapter 3 involve identifying and developing the central idea or proposition of the speech. The speaker must review all of the materials appropriate to the subject and decide what major and subordinate points are needed to develop the main idea. The major and subordinate points represent the skeleton or frame of the speech. These points alone probably will not lead the audience to acceptance; each major and subordinate point must be clarified, amplified, or strengthened for the audience. If listeners are able to understand and accept these points, they will be more likely to accept the central idea. The items used to clarify, amplify, and strengthen the major and subordinate points are called *supporting materials*. The supporting materials give the speech substance. They provide a type of proof or rationale for the acceptance of the central idea or proposition and help the listening audience make the decision to accept.

After we have considered the forms and locations of supporting materials, we will illustrate their uses in speaking situations.

FORMS OF SUPPORTING MATERIALS

Supporting materials can help you create acceptance for ideas in the speech by clarifying them and by presenting information that simplifies or makes the point clearer to the audience. Sometimes amplifying—extending or making the point larger so the audience can better examine the idea—is effective. Still other times acceptance is attained when you present supporting materials that strengthen the point by lending others' credibility to the idea, making it more believable. Some points or ideas can best be developed by doing all three: clarifying, amplifying, and strengthening.

The verbal supporting materials used to clarify, amplify, and strengthen the central idea or proposition can be divided into six categories: (1) explanation, (2) comparison or contrast, (3) illustration (hypothetical or factual), (4) specific instance, (5) statistics, and (6) testimony.

Explanation

An explanation is a description or expository passage which serves to make a term, concept, process, or proposal clear or acceptable. Explanations tell what, how, or why, and are useful in showing the relationship between a whole and its parts. They may also give meaning to a difficult-to-envision concept.

Ernest Lefever's speech entitled "A Specter that Haunts the World" is about international terrorism. To make sure that the audience understood the meaning of "terrorism," Mr. Lefever offered the following explanation:

> Terrorism is the use of violence or the threat of violence against a person or group to achieve political objectives. Terrorism seeks to shock or intimidate a far wider group than its immediate victims. Terrorists murder, kidnap, torture, hijack, and bomb, or threaten to do so. Their targets are "the enemy" or innocent civilians.
>
> International terrorism refers to acts of violence across state borders. The international character of the act may derive from its objective, the citizenship

of the terrorist, the place he or she was trained, or the source of weapons or logistical support.[1]

Although explanation is a good way to begin to make an idea clear, be careful not to make your explanations too long or involved. Many audiences have been put to sleep by long-winded expositions and descriptions full of minute details. Keep your explanations simple, brief, and accurate, and combine them with other forms of support when necessary.

Comparison and Contrast

Comparisons point out similarities between something that is familiar to the audience and something that is not. Contrasts, on the other hand, clarify or support an idea by emphasizing differences.

Comparison. When used alone, comparisons are really analogies connecting something already known or believed with an idea a speaker wishes to have understood or accepted. When, during the darkest days of the Civil War, critics attacked the administration's policies, Lincoln answered them by comparing the plight of the government with that of Blondin, a famous tightrope walker, attempting to cross the Niagara River:

> Gentlemen, I want you to suppose a case for a moment. Suppose that all the property you were worth was in gold, and you had put it in the hands of Blondin, the famous rope-walker, to carry across the Niagara Falls on a tightrope. Would you shake the rope while he was passing over it, or keep shouting to him, "Blondin, stoop a little more! Go a little faster!" No, I am sure you would not. You would hold your breath as well as your tongue, and keep your hands off until he was safely over. Now the government is in the same situation. It is carrying an immense weight across a stormy ocean. Untold treasures are in its hands. It is doing the best it can. Don't badger it! Just keep still, and it will get you safely over.

Contrast. Contrasts help clarify complex situations and processes by focusing on differences. A speaker explaining Australian football might want to contrast it with the rules governing football as it is played in the United States. To clarify Japanese Kabuki theatre, a speaker may call upon a system of theatre more familiar to the audience. Contrasts, further, can be used not only to clarify unfamiliar or complex problems, but also to strengthen

---

[1]From "A Specter that Haunts the World" by Ernest W. Lefever, from *Vital Speeches of the Day*, Volume XLVIII, January 1, 1982. Reprinted by permission of Vital Speeches of the Day.

arguments you wish to advance. Contrasts used as supporting material for propositions often employ examples, as in the case of a speech by George A. Biesel of Coe College. He was concerned about "orphan drugs," that is, drugs which have the potential to treat "small population diseases" but which are not manufactured by pharmaceutical companies because of low profitability. Contrasts helped him make his case:

> Why then aren't drug companies producing orphan drugs? The answer is simple—profit. Take for example this scenario. A doctor from the National Institute of Health has found a cure for a killer disease and is looking for a company to market that cure. The offer is presented to a pharmaceutical company, which is told that only 25,000 people suffer from the disease. Immediately the door is closed, the request denied. The drug company is not interested in making a drug that will only be consumed by a limited number of people. To a pharmaceutical company, Valium, which can be consumed by 30 million people, is much more appealing than the haloperidol which would only be consumed by 10,000. The lack of profit creates more orphan drugs and leaves victims suffering. [2]

Comparison and Contrast Used in Combination.   And finally, you may employ comparisons and contrasts together so as to make statements about both of the contrasting ideas. For example, former U.S. Secretary of Health, Education, and Welfare Joseph A. Califano, Jr., traveled the country, addressing audiences composed of both smokers and nonsmokers. By combining comparisons and contrasts, he warned the smokers and psychologically reinforced the nonsmokers, in this fashion:

> The tragic consequences of [smoking] are dramatically evident if we compare the later health consequences of smoking for two sixteen-year-olds: one who smokes a pack a day and one who does not. According to one estimate, the sixteen-year-old smoker has one chance in ten of developing a serious lung disease: lung cancer, emphysema, or chronic bronchitis, for example— providing he or she manages to avoid a crippling or killing heart attack. By contrast, the nonsmoker will have one chance in one hundred of contracting a serious lung disease, and will have only half the risk of the smoker of suffering a heart attack. [3]

---

[2] From "The Unknown Orphan" by George A. Biesel. Reprinted from *Winning Orations* 1982 by special arrangement with the Interstate Oratorical Association, Larry Schnoor, Executive Secretary, Mankato State College, Mankato, Minnesota.

[3] From "Adolescents: Their Needs and Problems" by Joseph A. Califano, Jr., from *Vital Speeches of the Day*, Volume XLIV, August 15, 1978. Reprinted by permission of Vital Speeches of the Day.

ILLUSTRATION   **99**

Whatever form of comparison or contrast used, at least one of the items should be familiar to the audience and distinct enough from the other that the difference is clear.

Illustration

A detailed narrative example of the idea or statement you wish to support is called an illustration. Sometimes an illustration describes or exemplifies a concept, condition, or circumstance; sometimes it shows or demonstrates the results of adopting a plan or proposal. Always, however, an illustration is an extended example presented in narrative form which has some striking or memorable quality.

There are two principal types of illustrations: the hypothetical and the factual. The first tells a story which could have happened or probably will happen; the second tells what actually has happened.

Hypothetical Illustration.   A hypothetical illustration, although it is imaginary, must seem believable to the audience. It must seem real enough to have happened. In the following hypothetical illustration, the speaker is focusing on one aspect of crime on campuses:

> Suppose, like most of us, you put off completing a major term paper. At the last minute, you realize that you need several paper clips to combine segments of the paper but that neither you nor your roommate have any. "No problem," you think. "I'll stop by the bookstore on the way to class. I'll have plenty of time to clip the portions together before class starts." Once in the bookstore, you quickly locate a box of paper clips and hurry to the check-out counter only to find one cashier on duty and eight other people in line ahead of you. In a split second, you make a decision that may affect you for the rest of your life! You slip the box of clips into your pocket and head for the exit. You have just committed a crime. Obviously this story is ficticious, but it illustrates a very real problem on our campus: shoplifting.[4]

Because in a hypothetical illustration aspects of the situation can be manipulated at will, this form of support is an especially valuable means of clarifying an idea or of stimulating interest. Also, it provides a good way to explain a complicated process. As proof, however, the hypothetical illustration is weak. The very fact that the details can be manipulated by the speaker may justifiably cause the audience to withhold acceptance. When using

---

[4]From a speech by Lee Morrison at the University of Akron, spring term, 1982. Reprinted with the permission of Ms. Morrison.

hypothetical illustration, you should be sure to let the audience know that, in fact, the illustration is ficticious. Hypothetical illustration should be used with other forms of support.

Factual Illustration. A factual illustration is a narrative that describes in detail a situation or incident that has actually occurred. Because details are brought into the story and because the incident actually happened, the illustration frequently has high persuasive value.

In a speech noting dangerous conditions of some American bridges, David Gregory of Vanderbilt University shared this factual illustration:

> As he drove onto the Yadkin River Bridge on a foggy, February evening in 1975, James Venable of Siloam, North Carolina, was stunned when his car was inexplicably thrown into the right-hand railing of the bridge. As he returned to the driver's lane, his car was suddenly thrown into the left-hand railing of the bridge. Through the dashboard window, he could see the overlying tresses of the bridge lean and sway as if with a life of their own. As the bridge began to topple, Venable lost consciousness. He awoke to find himself lying chest deep in the icy waters of the Yadkin River. Around him lay the twisted remains of what had been the Yadkin River Bridge, until its sudden collapse. Atop the trunk of his car lay a white Mustang which had plunged from the newly exposed bridge piers. As Venable climbed to the safety of his car roof, he watched in horror as five more cars soared from the jagged highway into the murky water thirty feet below. Before help could arrive that evening, sixteen people had been injured. Four had died.
>
> The rather dramatic scenario of the collapse of the Yadkin River Bridge is unfortunately a true one and one whose occurrence has been repeated elsewhere in our country at a rate far too frequent for our comfort.[5]

Guidelines for Choosing Illustrations. Three considerations should be kept in mind when selecting illustrations, hypothetical or factual. *Is it clearly related to the idea it is intended to support?* If the connection is difficult to show, the illustration may not accomplish the goal. *Is it a fair example?* An audience is quick to notice unusual circumstances in an illustration; if you have focused on the exceptional case, your illustration will not be convincing. *Is it vivid and impressive in detail?* If this quality is absent, the advantage of using an illustration is lost. Be sure, then, that your illustrations are pointed, fair, and vivid.

---

[5]From "All Our Bridges Falling Down: The Crisis on America's Highways" by David Gregory. Reprinted from *Winning Orations,* 1981, by special arrangement of the Interstate Oratorical Association, Larry Schnoor, Executive Secretary, Mankato State College, Mankato, Minnesota.

Specific Instance

A specific instance is an *undeveloped* illustration or example. Instead of describing a situation in detail, it merely mentions the person or event in question. Speakers use specific instances to clarify ideas. You might use specific instance by saying, "You are all familiar with the machine in the university game room. The fun you have watching the yellow glob devour the dots or the losers hold off the invaders suggests the topic of my speech today: The impact computers have had on American leisure time." Or you can use a series of specific instances to help establish a point. U.S. Representative John LaFalce used several specific instances to clarify how sloganeering has become a part of our political language:

> If image-creating were left to soap, this speech would have no thesis. However, we find that sloganeering is also a fixture of political life. Here are just a few of the slogans, buzzwords, and euphemisms of our political day:
>
> Get the government off our backs and out of our pockets
> A rising tide lifts all boats
> Across the board tax cut
> Preserve the social safety net
> The All Savers' Certificate
> A window of vulnerability
> Revenue enhancements
> Let's make the dollar as good as gold
>
> This is not new. The use of slogans in the battles over national policies has always existed. This nation rallied around the cry "Remember the Maine" as we sent our young men to fight the Spanish-American War. Why did we fight World War I? Clearly, to "make the world safe for democracy."[6]

If the names, events, or situations you cite are well-known to your listeners, specific instances can aid comprehension or generate support for an idea. On subjects with which the listeners are not familiar, or on which there are marked differences of opinion, specific instances must be supplemented with other forms of support.

---

[6]From "The Packaging of Public Policy" by John J. La Falce, from *Vital Speeches of the Day*, Volume XLVIII, February 1, 1982. Reprinted by permission of Vital Speeches of the Day.

102

Statistics

Not all figures are statistics; some figures are used merely for counting. Statistics are figures that show relationships among phenomena; they emphasize largeness or smallness (magnitudes), describe subclasses or parts (segments), or establish trends. Because statistics reduce great masses of information into general categories, they are useful both in making clear the nature of a situation and in substantiating a potentially disputable claim.[7]

Magnitudes. Statistics can be used to describe the seriousness of a problem in a relatively brief space. Statistical description helps the audience grasp the dimensions of a problem more clearly. Tommya Cosco, a student at Eastern New Mexico University, highlighted the magnitude of the problem of chemical proliferation and waste by combining several numerical relationships:

> According to *Time* magazine September 22, 1980, in the United States alone chemists concoct some 1,000 new brews each year. Of the 50,000 chemicals available on the market, the EPA rates some 35,000 as either hazardous or potentially hazardous. These figures fail to account for the production of waste materials. In the April, 1980 issue of *Fortune* magazine it is noted that we produce some 125 billion pounds of toxic waste each year. This chemical heap is expected to double in size by the year 2000. In a recent study done by the EPA it was found that 93 percent of these wastes are being disposed of incorrectly. This problem is now affecting the entire nation. In *Laying Waste: the Poisoning of America by Toxic Chemicals,* Michael Brown notes that only 6 of the 50 states are even relatively safe: The other 44 are ranged from alarmingly toxic to potentially troublesome.[8]

Segments. Statistics can be used to isolate the parts into which a problem can be subdivided or to show aspects of a problem caused by discrete factors. This approach is especially helpful when you wish to break down a complex topic into its component parts. In discussing sources of income for a college or university, for example, you could segment the income by indicating what percentage comes from tuition and fees, how much from state and federal money, how much from gifts and contributions, and how much from miscellaneous sources. Then both you and your

---

[7]For a technical, yet rewarding, introduction to statistical analysis, see Frederick Williams, *Reasoning With Statistics* (New York: Holt, Rinehart & Winston, Inc., 1968).

[8]From "Chemically Produced Nightmare" by Tommya Cosco. Reprinted from *Winning Orations,* 1981, by special arrangement of the Interstate Oratorical Association, Larry Schnoor, Executive Secretary, Mankato State College, Mankato, Minnesota.

audience would be in a position to discuss alternatives to tuition hikes. Speakers also use statistical segments, as they use statistical magnitudes, to indicate the seriousness or lack thereof of some problem. For example, in a speech before a Public Affairs Council, Federal Elections Commissioner Joan Aiken sought to de-emphasize the importance of political action committees (so-called PACs) in the campaigns of individuals. As support for her position, she segmented PACs' contributions in terms of both dollars and percentages:

> In the 1980 election, there were 2,266 candidates running for the Senate and House. They raised a combined total of $240.1 million, $37.6 million of which came from non-party PAC sources. Corporate-sponsored PACs contributed 4.9 percent of the money received by Democratic candidates and 6.4 percent of the money received by Republican candidates. Organized labor gave 9.62 percent of the money received by Democratic candidates and only 0.65 percent of the money received by Republican candidates. Obviously, the overwhelming majority of the money raised for House and Senate candidates came from individuals.[9]

Trends.   Finally, statistics often are employed to describe trends, which are indications of where we have been and where we are going. Michael Raoul-Duval, Senior Vice President of the Mead Corporation, used trend analysis to depict the changing age of the middle class:

> The postwar "baby boom" with its increased birth rate from 1946 to 1965 and subsequent decline in births from 1966 to 1973 has created a demographic tidal wave that will dramatically influence our political and economic landscape as it rolls through the remainder of this century. While the total U.S. population growth rate will continue to slow in the next two decades, the decline among young people will be very dramatic—in fact, there will be six million less teenagers than there were in the 1970's. The 18 to 64-year-old working age group will drop from a current yearly growth rate of 1.5 percent to below one percent by 1984 and to less than a half of a percent in the middle 1990's. The traditional household forming ages of 25 to 34 will outgrow other groups during the early 1980's at a rate of around 1.5 percent. However, by the 1990's this rate will decline precipitously to minus two percent.[10]

In using statistics to indicate magnitude, divide phenomena into

---

[9]From "Working with the Federal Election Commission" by Joan D. Aiken, from *Vital Speeches of the Day*, Volume XLVII, February, 1981. Reprinted by permission of Vital Speeches of the Day.

[10]From "The New Middle Class" by Michael Raoul-Duval, from *Vital Speeches of the Day*, Volume XLVIII, April 1, 1982. Reprinted by permission of Vital Speeches of the Day.

segments, or describe trends, keep the following cautions in mind: (1) Translate difficult-to-comprehend numbers into more immediately understandable terms. In a speech on the mounting problem of solid waste, Carl Hall pictured the immensity of 130,000,000 tons of garbage by indicating that trucks loaded with that amount would extend from coast to coast.[11] (2) Don't be afraid to round off complicated numbers. "Nearly 400,000" is easier for listeners to comprehend than "396,456"; "over 33 percent" is usually preferable to "33.4 percent" and "over one third" probably is better than either of them. (3) Whenever possible, use visual materials to clarify complicated statistical trends or summaries. Hand out a mimeographed sheet of numbers; draw graphs on the chalkboard; prepare a chart in advance. In this way, you can concentrate on explaining the significance of the numbers, and not spend all of your time merely trying to report them. (4) Use statistics fairly. Arguing that professional women's salaries increased 12.4 percent last year may sound impressive to listeners—until they realize that women still are generally paid almost a quarter less than men for equivalent work. In other words, be sure to provide fair contexts for your numerical data and comparisons.

Testimony

When speakers cite the opinions or conclusions expressed by others, they are using *testimony*. Sometimes the purpose of testimony is merely to add weight or impressiveness to an idea; at other times it is intended to lend credibility or believeability to an assertion. Leland Miles' concern for the potential of nuclear weapons is underscored by the use of testimony:

> Most especially, the world has been shrunken by the potential of nuclear holocaust. . . .
>
> We've come a long way from the battlefield at Crecy, that notable battle where the crossbows of the English yeomen defeated the French knights. Those crossbows couldn't shoot their arrows much farther than a couple hundred yards, if that far. But now we have a Trident missile (mounted on a submarine) which can straddle the globe, which can strike a Soviet city thousands of miles away. Sakharov, the noted Soviet scientist, has put it bluntly when he said in

---

[11]From "A Heap of Trouble" by Carl Hall. Reprinted from *Winning Orations*, by special arrangement with the Interstate Oratorical Association, Larry Schnoor, Executive Secretary, Mankato State College, Mankato, Minnesota.

1975, "The unchecked growth of the thermonuclear arsenals threatens mankind with physical annihilation."[12]

Another example of testimony used as support for an assertion comes from a speech by Anne Manlove of North Dakota State University. To gain credibility for her assertion that the extinction of the whale related directly to her audience, she cited noted biologist Paul Ehrlich:

> . . . Many of us live inland and have never seen a whale and probably never will unless it's a killer whale at Sea Land or a Beluga Whale at the new zoo and that just isn't relevant. Well, it is relevant to every single one of us here.
> Paul R. Ehrlich, Stanford biologist in *USA Today* said, "The public must come to understand that every time a population or species or other organism goes extinct, the tenure of Homo Sapiens on this planet become a little less secure. When the bell tolls for the snail darter, it may also be tolling for us." Ehrlich went on to note—"Humanity's fate is inextricably bound up with the fate of the great whales . . . and other endangered species."[13]

Tests of Authority. All testimony should meet the twin tests of pertinence and audience acceptability. When used to strengthen a statement, rather than merely to amplify or to clarify, testimony also should satisfy four more specific criteria:

1. The person quoted should be qualified by training and experience as an authority. He or she should be an expert in the field to which the testimony relates.
2. Whenever possible, the statement of the authority should be based on firsthand knowledge.
3. The judgment expressed should not be unduly influenced by personal interest. An authority with a strong vested interest is suspect.
4. The hearers should realize that the person quoted actually *is* an authority. They should respect his or her opinion.

When citing testimony, don't use big names simply because they are

---

[12]From "Universities for Peace" by Leland Miles, from *Vital Speeches of the Day*, Volume XLVIII, March 1, 1982. Reprinted by permission of Vital Speeches of the Day.

[13]From "We Can't Afford to Lose Them" by Anne Manlove. Reprinted from *Winning Orations*, 1981, by special arrangement with the Interstate Oratorical Association, Larry Schnoor, Executive Secretary, Mankato State College, Mankato, Minnesota. Quotation by Paul R. Ehrlich in *USA Today*. Reprinted by permission of the author.

well known. A movie star's opinion on the nutritive value of a breakfast food is less reliable than the opinion of a registered dietician. The best testimony always comes from subject-matter experts whose qualifications your listeners recognize. Of course, always acknowledge the source of the testimony.

Explanation, comparison and contrast, illustration, specific instance, statistics and testimony—these, then, are the common forms of verbal supporting materials. Fill your speeches with them. Avoid abstract, unsupported statements—amplify your ideas, illuminate them, and make them concrete.

SOURCES OF SUPPORTING MATERIALS

For most speeches, you will have to do some research to get sufficient supporting materials. When this is the case, several sources are available to you: interviews with experts, letters and questionnaires, publications of all kinds, and radio and television broadcasts. Let us consider how each of these sources can be used to best advantage to accumulate substantive materials for your speeches.

Interviews

Beginning speakers often fail to recognize that vast amounts of useful and authoritative information may be gathered merely by asking questions of the right people. If, for example, you expect to talk about interplanetary navigation, what better-informed and more convenient source of information could there be than a member of your college's astronomy department? Or, if you are interested in the growth of and diversity within the T-shirt industry, why not talk with the proprietor of a local shop? Brief interviews, properly arranged and scheduled, frequently yield invaluable factual data and authoritative interpretations and opinions.

To set up such an interview, select an interviewee who you think will approach the subject with reasonable objectivity and knowledge. Make an appointment in advance, stating your purpose and explaining why you think he or she can be of help. Acquaint yourself with the informant's background —current position, previous jobs, books or articles written, etc.—to help you frame pertinent and penetrating questions and evaluate the responses you receive. And carefully develop an interview plan—goals you want to achieve, specific questions which will help you reach those goals—so that you do not wander through the conversation unsure of yourself and of the precise information you are seeking.

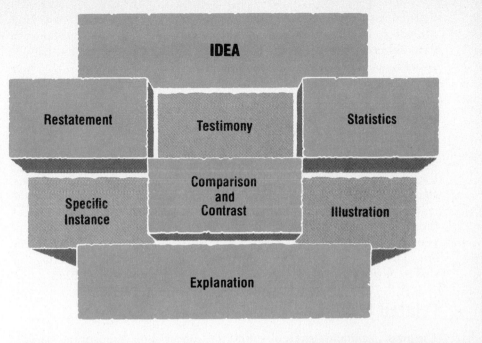

Materials for Verbally Supporting an Idea

When actually conducting the interview, be on time, restate your purpose, keep the interview moving at a lively pace, and carefully record the information and opinions you receive. A tape recorder, if you have one, will be a valuable aid, although be sure you have permission from the interviewee before turning it on. Finally, do not overstay your welcome. Respect the person's time, and leave graciously. Throughout, avoid arguing or disagreeing with the interviewee (you can do that later in your speech!) and don't parade your own knowledge. Rather, use the interview for what it is—a way of acquiring supporting materials to clarify, amplify, or strengthen a point in your speech.

Letters and Questionnaires

If you are unable to talk with an expert directly, you can sometimes obtain the information you need through correspondence. You might wish, for example, to write your senator for information regarding a pending bill in the legislature, or to a cereal company for data on the amounts of various sorts of sugars in its products. When you use this method, however, be sure that you make clear exactly what information you want and why you want it. Moreover, be reasonable—do not expect a busy person to spend hours or days gathering facts for you. Above all, do not ask for information that you yourself could find if you searched for it.

On other occasions, you may wish to discover what a group of people knows or thinks about a subject. If, for example, you wanted to give a speech on a proposed nuclear power plant, you could sample public opinion in the vicinity with a questionnaire. You might wish to send it to people randomly chosen from the town's phone directory, circulate it through a dorm or classroom, or even administer it in person to passersby on a street corner. In this way, you could construct your own statistical segments and magnitudes, right out of your own school and community. When developing a questionnaire, be sure it has an introduction which explains the exact purpose and the procedures to be followed in answering the questions. Keep it short, or people will throw it away. If you mail it, include a self-addressed, stamped envelope to help guarantee returns to you. And, when conducting the survey in person, be polite and ask for only a small amount of time.

Printed Materials

The most common source of supporting materials is the printed word—newspapers, magazines, pamphlets, and books. Through the careful use of a library—and with the help of reference librarians—you can discover an almost overwhelming amount of materials relevant to your speech subject and purpose.

Newspapers.   Newspapers obviously are a useful source of information about events of current interest. Moreover, their feature stories and accounts of unusual happenings provide a storehouse of interesting illustrations and examples. You must be careful, of course, not to accept as true everything printed in a newspaper, for the haste with which news sometimes must be gathered makes complete accuracy difficult. Your school or city library undoubtedly keeps on file copies of one or two highly reliable papers such as *The New York Times, The Observer, The Wall Street Journal,* or the *Christian Science Monitor,* and probably also a selection from among the leading newspapers of your state or region. If your library has *The New York Times,* it is likely to have the published index to that paper. By using this resource, you can locate accounts of people and events from 1913 to the present. Yet another useful and well-indexed source of information on current happenings is *Facts on File,* issued weekly since 1940.

Magazines.   An average-sized university library subscribes annually to hundreds of magazines and journals. Some—such as *Time, Newsweek,* and

Given the explosion of information in this country and the new technologies which now help us keep track of those data, finding supporting materials is both easier and more difficult than it once was. It is more difficult because so many more sources must be consulted, yet it is easier because technological aids— e.g. computers and (in this picture) micro-readers—can help in the search.

U.S. News and World Report—summarize weekly events. *The Atlantic* and *Harper's* are representative of a group of monthly publications which cover a wide range of subjects of both passing and permanent importance. Such magazines as *The Nation, Vital Speeches of the Day, Fortune, Washington Monthly,* and *The New Republic* contain comment on current political, social, and economic questions. For more specialized areas, there are such magazines as *Popular Science, Scientific American, Sports Illustrated, Field and Stream, Ms., Better Homes and Gardens, Today's Health, National Geographic,* and *American Heritage.*

This list is, of course, merely suggestive of the wide range of materials to be found in periodicals. When you are looking for a specific kind of information, use the *Readers' Guide to Periodical Literature,* which indexes most of the magazines you will want to refer to in preparing a speech. Or, if you wish more sophisticated material, consult the *Social Science Index* and the *Humanities Index.* Similar indexes also are available for technical journals, publications from professional societies, and the like; a reference librarian can show you how to use them.

Yearbooks and Encyclopedias. The most reliable source of comprehensive data is the *Statistical Abstracts of the United States,* which covers a wide variety of subjects ranging from weather records and birth rates to steel production and election results. More unusual data on Academy Award winners, world records in various areas, the "bests" and "worsts" of almost anything, etc., can be found in the *World Almanac, The People's Almanac,*

109

The Guinness Book of World Records, The Book of Lists, and *Information Please.* Encyclopedias such as the *Encyclopaedia Britannica* and *Americana Encyclopedia,* which attempt to cover the entire field of human knowledge, are valuable chiefly as an initial reference source or for background reading. Refer to them for important scientific, geographical, literary, or historical facts, for bibliographies of authoritative books on a subject, and for ideas you will not develop completely in your speech.

Documents and Reports.   Various governmental agencies—state, national, and international—as well as many independent organizations publish reports on special subjects. Among governmental publications, those most frequently consulted are the hearings and recommendations of congressional committees or those of the United States Departments of Health, Education, and Welfare, and of Commerce. Reports on issues related to agriculture, business, government, engineering, and scientific experimentation are published by many state universities. Such endowed groups as the Carnegie, Rockefeller, and Ford Foundations, and such special interest groups as the Foreign Policy Association, the Brookings Institution, the League of Women Voters, Common Cause, and the United States Chamber of Commerce also publish reports and pamphlets. Though by no means a complete list of all such pamphlets and reports, *The Vertical File Index* does offer you a guide to some of these materials.

Books.   There are few subjects suitable for a speech upon which someone has not written a book. As a guide to these books, use the subject-matter headings in the card catalog of your libraries. Generally, you will find authoritative books in your school library, and more popularized treatments in your city's public library.

Biographies.   *The Dictionary of National Biography* (deceased Britishers), the *Dictionary of American Biography* (deceased Americans), *Who's Who* (living Britishers), *Who's Who in America, Current Biography,* and more specialized works organized by field contain biographical sketches especially useful in locating facts about famous people and in documenting the qualifications of authorities whose testimony you may quote.

Computers.   The computer also can serve as an efficient source for finding supporting materials. Computer searches can provide both bibliographic and nonbibliographic information. By requesting a list of articles, books, or other printed materials that carry the key word or subject of your speech, you can generate an instant bibliography. Some computer systems let you retrieve content as well. More than 400 commercially available data bases can provide a variety of informational services. Some of these include: bibliographic searches, current awareness searches, numerical data retrieval, fact retrieval, question response, library references, resource location, and news announcements.[14] Most colleges and universities that have library computer access subscribe to online bibliographic utilities such as OCLC, Inc., Research Libraries Information Network (RLIN), or Washington Library Network (WLN). Computers are easy to use and can save you research time. Check with your school library about the computer facilities available to you.

Radio and Television Broadcasts

Lectures, discussions, and the formal public addresses of leaders in government, business, education, and religion are frequently broadcast over radio or television. Many of these talks later are mimeographed or printed by the stations or by the organizations that sponsor them. Usually, as in the case of CBS's *Meet the Press* or National Public Radio's *All Things Considered,* copies may be obtained for a small fee. If no manuscript is available, you may want to audiotape the program (as long as you make no public use of that tape) or to take careful notes. When taking notes, listen with particular care in order to get an exact record of the speaker's words or meaning. Just as you must quote items from printed sources accurately and honestly, so you are obligated to respect the remarks someone has made on a radio or television program and to give that person full credit.

Obviously, you will not have to investigate all of the foregoing sources for every speech you make. Usually, however, a well-conducted search turns up materials that will make your speech more authoritative and interesting than it otherwise would be. Learn how to skim rapidly through a mass of information to pick out the important facts and ideas.

RECORDING INFORMATION

When you find the information you have been looking for, either make a photocopy of it or take notes on the material. Whether you keep your notes on 4 x 6 note cards or in a notebook, it is helpful to have an accurate and legible record of the facts you wish to retain for your speech. An incomplete source citation may make it impossible to locate the source again; hurried scribbles may be difficult to decipher at a later time. Note cards are easier to use than a notebook because they can be classified as to topic area or type of

---

[14]For more information on computer library services refer to Ryan Hoover, *The Library and Information Manager's Guide to Online Services* (White Plains, N.Y.: Knowledge Industry Publications, Inc. 1980).

Specific Information	General Subject
Sources of Revenue for Colleges	Corporate Giving

Business corporations increased their gifts to higher education by 10.7 percent in 1981, despite a decline of 4.2 percent in their profits, according to the Council for Financial Aid to Education.

Corporate Contributions to Education
1979 $ 890,000,000.00
1980 $1,030,000,000.00
1981 $1,140,000,000.00

Source "Despite Falling Profits, Corporations Increase Gifts to Higher Education," The Chronicle of Higher Education, January 5, 1983, p. 14.

Sample Note Cards

support. However, if you are using a notebook, try to record each item on half of each page. Since most of your items of information will not fill a page, this will save paper; cutting the sheets in half will make it easier to sort your data or adopt a classification scheme and record information in accordance with particular themes or subpoints of your speech. When preparing the card, place the appropriate subject headings at the top of the card and the complete source citation at the bottom. This way, the card can be classified by general subject (top right heading) and by specific information presented (top left heading). Also, if you need to return to the same article or document, the complete citation will enable you to find the material with ease. You can avoid losing "just perfect" information by taking the time to record the material on the spot and by carefully noting the source of the data.

USING SUPPORTING MATERIALS

Once you have searched out potential materials for your speech, next you must decide when to use them and which types to employ.

Generally, supporting materials should be used when listeners will not accept an idea just because it is presented. Listeners reject what they don't understand or accept. You should ask yourself if each idea needs to be clarified, amplified, or strengthened before listeners will accept it. If your answer is "yes," you need to use supporting materials. Sometimes two or more types of support are combined as when statistics are used to develop an illustration or when the testimony of an authority is given to strengthen or verify an explanation. At other times they may be used singly. Remember that if the audience will not accept supportive ideas, they will reject the central idea or proposition of your speech. Rather than risk rejection, use support materials for each main statement.

Which form of support to use depends on the complexity of the idea and on the kind of audience you're addressing. Any of the forms of support may be used to clarify, to amplify, or to strengthen. However, some forms tend to accomplish those purposes better than others and are more effective with particular audiences.

Explanation, comparison, contrast, specific instance, and segment statistics are especially helpful in clarifying an idea. These materials allow the speaker to present information that simplifies an idea for the audience, and are useful when listeners have little background or knowledge about the topic or when the subject matter is complex.

Explanation, comparison, contrast, hypothetical and factual illustration, and magnitude and trend statistics may help the speaker amplify an idea, making it larger so the audience can better examine the concept. These forms of support may be especially useful when the audience has but a passing knowledge of the concept.

To strengthen or lend credibility to a point, you may want to use factual illustration, specific instances, statistics, and testimony. These forms strengthen the idea by making it vivid and believable. These techniques are beneficial when the audience is hostile or when acceptance of a particular idea is critical to the overall purpose of the speech.

Finally, be sure that the forms of support you select do *support* the ideas. If the materials used as supports do not clarify, amplify, or strengthen, they may not be applicable to the point being developed. Test out the relevancy of each supporting unit to be sure it contributes to the acceptance of the idea being developed.

Following are two outlines that illustrate how supporting materials can be used. In the first outline, note how the speaker has combined verbal and visual material to establish and develop the main point. In this speech, the supportive materials are used to amplify the idea.

"" A SAMPLE OUTLINE FOR AN INFORMATIVE SPEECH

HOW WE BREATHE

Explanation

I. The human breathing mechanism may be likened to a bellows which expands to admit air and contracts to expel it.
   A. When we inhale, two things happen.
      1. Muscles attached to the collarbone and shoulder bones pull upward and slightly outward.
      2. Muscles in the abdominal wall relax, allowing the diaphragm—a sheet of muscle and tendon lying immediately below the lungs—to fall.
   B. This permits the spongy, porous material of which the lungs consist to expand.
      1. A vacuum is created.
      2. Air rushes in.
   C. When we exhale, two things happen also.
      1. Gravity causes the rib cage to move downward.
      2. Muscles in the abdominal wall contract, squeezing the diaphragm upward.
   D. The space available to the lungs is thus reduced.
      1. The lungs are squeezed.
      2. Air is emitted.

Comparison

   E. The similarity between the breathing mechanism and a bellows is represented in this diagram:

Visual Aid

                    Show "How We Breathe" Diagram

*Restatement
of main
idea*

   F. In summary, then, to remember how the human breathing mechanism works, think of a bellows.
      1. Just as increasing the size of the bellows bag allows air to rush in, so increasing the space available to the lungs allows them to admit air.
      2. Just as squeezing the bellows bag forces air out, so contracting the space the lungs can occupy forces air to be emitted.

Study the following outline. Notice that the supporting materials are used to strengthen each of the points in the speech. The audience would be unlikely to accept these ideas without further development. Although the proof of a single point may not require the use of supportive materials as numerous or varied as those used in this outline, they are presented here to show how a number of different forms may be combined.

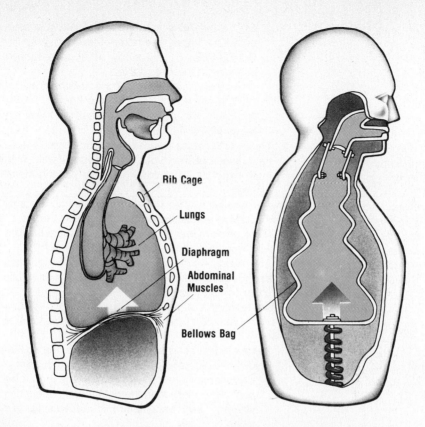

Rib Cage

Lungs

Diaphragm

Abdominal Muscles

Bellows Bag

A SAMPLE OUTLINE FOR A PERSUASIVE SPEECH

CABLE TELEVISION—AT YOUR SERVICE!

Proposition
First Supporting
Statement:
Hypothetical
Illustration
Specific Instances
Within the
Illustration

I. Cable television soon will revolutionize your everyday life.
   A. Suppose, on a rainy day a few years from now, you decide to "run" your errands from your living room.
      1. You turn on your two-way communication unit, and begin your round of errands:
         a. On Channel 37, your bank's computer verifies the amount of a recent withdrawal.
         b. On Channel 26, you ask the telephone company to review last month's long-distance charges.

c. On Channel 94, a supermarket lets you scan products, prices, and home-delivery hours.

d. On Channel 5, you study a list of proposed changes in the city charter.
  (1) You can "call in" for further information.
  (2) You can vote from your own home.

e. Channel 106 gives you access to resource personnel at the public library.

Restatement of Supporting Statement

2. Thus—with "cable television at your service"—you have accomplished your day's errands with minimum expenditure of time, gas, and parking-meter money.

Second Supporting Statement Specific Instances

B. These possibilities, once thought of only as dreams, are becoming actualities across the United States.

1. Most cities have "public-access" channels filled with local talent and ethnic programming.

2. Ann Arbor, Michigan, and Columbus, Ohio, have been leasing channels to private firms and public utility companies.

Third Supporting Statement Comparison

C. Cable television soon will be available to virtually every household in the United States at a reasonable cost.

1. Because the cost is shared by licensee and householder alike, no one bears an excessive burden.

Statistics

a. Commercial users find that leasing a channel costs little more than their computer-accounting systems and print/electronic advertising services.

b. Studio facilities for the public-access channels are made available at cost in most cable television contracts—normally about $30 per hour.

c. Current installation charges range from $15 to $50.

d. Monthly rental fees per household seldom exceed $10 for basic cable service.

Explanation Combined with Specific Instances

2. The technical characteristics of cable television render it inexpensive.

a. Some existent telephone lines and equipment can be used.

b. The conversion box mounts easily on a regular television set.

c. Studio costs are minimal.
  (1) Relatively inexpensive 1/2″ videotape and broadcasting equipment can be used.
  (2) Engineering and production personnel need minimal training for cable systems.

Restatement of Proposition	D. Given actual and potential uses, plus the positive cost-benefit ratio, cable television will revolutionize your daily life.
Comparison	1. Just as the wheel extended our legs and the computer our central nervous system, so will cable television extend our communicative capabilities.
Testimony Used as Restatement of Main Idea	2. In the words of Wendy Lee, communication consultant to new cable-television franchises: "We soon will be a nation wired fully for sight and sound. We will rid ourselves of the need for short shopping trips; we will cut the lines in doctors' offices; and we will put the consumer and the constituent into the front offices of his or her corporate suppliers and political servants. The telephone and the motor car will become obsolete."

GROUP PROJECT

1. Arrange to meet in the Reference Room of your college library. Work in groups of five. Each member will locate two of the items in the left-hand column of the following list. First, determine which of the sources listed in the right-hand column contains the material you need. When you locate your items, show your group the source and indicate where the source is shelved.

(a) Weekly summary of current national news	*Congressional Record* *Time*
(b) Brief sketch of the accomplishments of Henry Ford	*Vital Speeches* *Book Review Digest*
(c) Description of a specific traffic accident	*Oxford English Dictionary* local newspaper
(d) Explanation of major Indian tribes	*Who's Who* Statistical Abstracts
(e) Text of Ronald Reagan's last State of the Union Address	*Encyclopedia Americana* *New York Times*

INDIVIDUAL PROJECTS

1. The following list contains the names of people who may be considered authorities in their respective fields. Plan a hypothetical interview with one of these experts to obtain information for a speech that you might give in an area related to their expertise. Prepare a set of questions for the interview which are keyed to the information you wish to obtain.

Paul Ehrlich	Jessica Savitch	Erma Bombeck
Miles Davis	Tennessee Williams	Alvin Toffler
James Brady	William Proxmire	Judy Blume
Tom Hayden	Robert Michel	Jane Wyman
Neil Diamond	Bess Myerson	F. Lee Bailey
Garry Trudeau	Betty Friedan	Sandra Day O'Connor
Pelé	Jesse Jackson	Christiaan Barnard
James Watt	Coretta Scott King	Martha Graham

2. Choose one of the publications listed below with which you are not acquainted. Spend some time browsing through two or three issues. Prepare a two-to-three-minute report discussing the nature of the periodical. Mention how frequently it is published and where it is indexed. In addition, indicate its potential value to the public speaker.

Quarterly Journal of Speech	*Vital Speeches of the Day*
Mother Jones	*U. S. News and World Report*
Scientific American	*Commentary*
Psychology Today	*Washington Monthly*
Consumer Reports	*The New Yorker*
Punch	*Science*
The Futurist	*The Wilson Quarterly*

 # SUGGESTIONS FOR FURTHER READING

Nicholas Capaldi, *The Art of Deception* (Buffalo, N.Y.: Prometheus Books, 1974), Chapter 1, "Presenting Your Case."

Gary Cronkhite, *Public Speaking and Critical Listening* (Menlo Park, Ca.: The Benjamin/Cummings Publishing Co., 1978), Chapter 8, "Search and Research."

William R. Dresser, "The Impact of Evidence on Decision Making," in *Concepts in Communication,* ed. Jimmie D. Trent et al. (Boston: Allyn and Bacon, Inc., 1973), pp. 159–66.

Thomas Harte, "The Effects of Evidence in Persuasive Communication," *Central States Speech Journal* 27, (Spring 1976), 42–46.

Richard D. Rieke and Malcolm O. Sillars, *Argumentation and the Decision Making Process,* 2nd ed. (Glenview, Ill.: Scott, Foresman and Company, 1984), Chapter 5, "Support: Evidence."

CHAPTER 6

Arranging and Outlining Related Points

If a speech, whatever its type or purpose, is to communicate your thoughts effectively, it must satisfy at least three general criteria: (1) *The plan of the speech as a whole must be easy for the audience to grasp and remember.* If listeners have difficulty seeing how your ideas fit together or if the ideas are joined in ways that do not immediately make sense, attention will be distracted from your ideas and will be focused instead on untangling your remarks. (2) *The pattern must provide for a full and balanced coverage of the subject under consideration.* If you ignore or slight essential aspects of the topic, not only will the audience's understanding of the subject be incomplete, but you will be open to the charge of having presented an unfair or biased discussion. (3) *The speech must move forward steadily toward a complete and satisfying termination.* If you repeatedly backtrack to mention again points made earlier or if after a time you begin to run down or ramble, whatever punch you may have injected earlier will be lost; and the members of your audience, instead of listening as they should, will be impatient for you to end.

TYPES OF ARRANGEMENT

Bearing in mind these three criteria, let us consider some of the options available to you as you begin to think about packaging your ideas for your listeners. Generally, these options fall into four categories: (1) *sequential patterns*, (2) *causal patterns*, (3) *topical patterns*, and (4) *special patterns*.

Sequential Patterns

Sequential patterns adhere to the order in which events actually occurred, or they trace the physical relationships existing among the parts of a whole. In the first case, the sequence is called *chronological;* in the second case, *spatial*.

Chronological Sequence. When employing the chronological sequence, you begin at a certain period or date and move forward—or backward—in a systematic way. For example, you might describe last year's weather by considering conditions as they existed in the spring, summer, fall, and winter, respectively; methods for refining petroleum by tracing the development of the refining process from the earliest attempts down to the present time; the manufacture of an automobile by following the assembly-line process from beginning to end. Here is an example of an outline for a speech developed according to the *chronological* or *time sequence:*

THESIS STATEMENT: To appreciate our art department's collection of historical photographs, you must know something about the history of photographic technology.

I. In 1839 the French painter Daguerre introduced the Daguerrotype.

II. In 1851 Frederick Archer discovered the wet-plate process.

III. The modern era of dry-plate photography began in 1878.

IV. Roll-film first came on the market in 1883.

Spatial Sequence. In the spatial sequence the major points of a speech are arranged in terms of their *physical proximity* to one another. Comparative densities of population, for instance, may be discussed by referring in order to contiguous areas of the country; the layout of a new suburb may be explained by proceeding from east to west or north to south. Different aspects of a public service building also may sometimes be discussed according to this *spatial* or *geographical* method. For example:

THESIS STATEMENT: Knowing how our library is arranged floor by floor will help you gain access to its primary services.

I. As you enter the main doors, you will find the check-out counter.

II. Immediately past that counter you will find displays of newly acquired books, to help you keep up on publications of interest to you.

III. In the next room you will find the information desk, the serials department, the card catalog, and the reference room, so you can obtain the information you need to find what you are looking for.

IV. On the second floor you will discover three more specialized functions—the reserved book reading room, the newspaper collection, and the magazine and journal collection.

V. On the third and fourth floors you will find the book collection.

Causal Patterns

As their name implies, causal patterns of speech organization move either (1) from an analysis of present causes to a consideration of future effects, or (2) from a description of present conditions to an analysis of the causes which appear to have produced them. When employing the cause-effect arrangement, you might, for instance, first point out that a community's zoning ordinances are outdated or ineffective, and then predict that as a result of this situation fast-food chain establishments and gas stations will soon invade prime residential areas. Or, reasoning in the other direction, you could argue that the continued spread of fast-food chain establishments and gas stations into prime residential areas is the result of outmoded or ineffective zoning ordinances. Compare the following outlines:

THESIS STATEMENT: Inflation [*cause*] is so perilous because it affects many other aspects of our economy [*effects*].

I. Each year the cost of manufacturing goods goes up.
   A. Labor costs rise an average of nine percent annually.
   B. Raw material prices advance five to twelve percent each year.
   C. Transportation fees increase five to seven percent yearly.

II. The effects upon an economy can be disastrous—increased consumer prices, soaring interest rates, and double-digit inflation.

THESIS STATEMENT: Inflation [*effect*] is a complex economic phenomenon because so many interrelated factors can produce it [*causes*].

I. We all know that hamburger prices rose forty percent a pound more this year than last—but why?
   A. Open-range land for grazing has decreased.
   B. The cost of feed for pen-fed stock has increased dramatically because of export markets and because of last spring's drought.

    C. Costs for butchering, storage, and shipping have risen along with everything else.

  II. The resulting inflation, therefore, must be attributed to widely diversified causes which must be dealt with separately.

Note a characteristic of both these outlines: each starts with the aspect of the situation *better known* to audience members, and then proceeds to develop the *lesser known* facets of the problem. You will find a cause-effect pattern useful if the causes are more familiar to the listeners than the effects, and an effect-cause sequence preferable if the opposite is true.

Topical Patterns

Some speeches on familiar topics are best organized in terms of subject-matter divisions which over a period of time have become more or less standardized. For example, financial reports customarily are divided into assets and liabilities; discussions of government, into legislative, executive, and judicial functions; and comparisons of different kinds of telescopes, into celestial and terrestrial models. Topical patterns, thus, are most useful for speeches that *enumerate* aspects of persons, places, things, or processes. Occasionally, a speaker tries to discuss all the aspects of a subject, as in a speech on the three branches of government. More often, however, a partial enumeration of the possible topics or areas is sufficient. For example, a speech on where to read about starting a garden probably would deal with only a few sources of information.

READING UP ON GARDENING

THESIS STATEMENT: Anyone can become a gardener by reading three inexpensive, even free, types of materials.

  I. Although there are innumerable printed materials on starting a garden, let me tell you about three sources that are inexpensive and readily available.
    A. Pamphlets put out by seed and fertilizer manufacturers provide you with important information on seed characteristics, hardiness, yield, and cost.
    B. Pamphlets put out by the federal and state governments provide you with simple step-by-step directions for planting and caring.
    C. Magazines such as *Better Homes and Gardens* and *Organic Gardening* allow even beginners to specialize in particular kinds of gardening.

Topical patterns certainly are among the most popular and the easiest to use. Only take care, especially when doing a partial enumeration of topics, that you justify to your audience members the aspects of the situation or problem you choose to discuss. If someone asks, "But why didn't you talk about X?" then perhaps you have not made your range of topics seem coherent and commonsensical.

The types of speech organization thus far discussed, though they don't disregard the audience, are shaped principally by the nature of the subject matter that you as a speaker wish to communicate. Some subjects, such as the historical development of a nation or region, or a person's rise from obscurity to prominence, lend themselves more or less readily to the chronological pattern. Subjects of a geographical nature—discussions of the world's stock of natural resources or of its chronic famine areas—fit more easily into the spatial structure. Still other matters—the reasons for the success of a given economic policy or an account of recent rule changes in football—call, respectively, for the causal or special topical plan.

Special Patterns

At times, however, rather than employing any of these subject-oriented speech structures, you may decide that, for psychological or rhetorical reasons, it would be better to impose some special or more strongly audience-oriented pattern upon your material. Many such special patterns are possible and have been successfully employed by resourceful speakers. Four of them, however, are so generally useful that they warrant special mention here. We shall call them (1) *familiarity-acceptance order*, (2) *inquiry order*, (3) *question-answer order*, and (4) *elimination order*.

Familiarity-Acceptance Order. When using this order in giving an informative-type speech, you work from the familiar to the unfamiliar—from that which the audience already knows or understands to that which is new or strange. Similarly, if your aim is to persuade or to actuate, you take as a base the facts or values the listeners already accept, and you show how the beliefs or actions being urged follow logically from them.

Relating new or unfamiliar material to what is already known or understood has long been recognized by teachers as one of the most effective methods of classroom instruction. Indeed, it has often been argued that all of our knowledge is derived "analogically" in the sense that we learn not by adding unrelated bits of information or understanding to things previously known, but by comparing or contrasting the new with the old. Provided you appraise the audience's existing state of knowledge correctly and do not move on to new matters too rapidly, an informative speech structured on this principle usually has a better-than-average chance of success.

Persuasive speeches which use as their starting point facts or values the audience already accepts and then demonstrate how the matters to be established follow from them are often especially suited to doubting or hostile audiences. Of course, your reasoning must be valid and your conclusion must not exceed the evidence. When you meet these standards, your claim can be denied only if the listener is willing to be recognized as inconsistent. Here is an example of an outline of a persuasive-type speech employing the pattern just described:

THESIS STATEMENT: Mary Campagna embodies the values our party stands for, and therefore should be our nominee.

I. We all agree, I am sure, that experience, ability, and integrity are prime requisites for a holder of high public office.

II. Mary Campagna has these qualities.
   A. She has experience.
      1. She has served two terms as mayor of one of our largest cities.
      2. She has been in the State Senate for twelve years.
   B. She has ability.
      1. She has successfully reorganized the cumbersome administrative machinery of our city government.
      2. She has become a recognized leader in the Senate.
   C. She has integrity.
      1. She has never been suspected of any sort of corruption.
      2. Her word is as good as her bond.

III. Because Mary Campagna clearly has the qualities we demand of the holder of high public office, she deserves our support in her bid to be elected governor of this state.

Inquiry Order.   When using inquiry order, you retrace step by step the way in which you yourself acquired the knowledge or arrived at the proposal which you are now communicating to the audience. You may, for example, show listeners how to grow prize-winning dahlias by describing how the success and failure of your own experiments with various kinds of seeds, fertilizers, and garden locations eventually led to the recommendations now being offered. Or, if the purpose of your speech is to persuade or to actuate, you may recount how you first became aware of the existence of a problem and then searched for its causes and weighed possible solutions until the one now being advocated emerged as the best.

An arrangement of this kind, many speakers believe, has a double advantage. First, it enables listeners to judge more accurately the worth of the information or policy being presented; and, second, because all facts and possibilities are laid out for critical examination, it results in a more complete understanding or a firmer conviction than that produced by other methods.

Question-Answer Order. When following question-answer order in a speech, you determine in advance the questions most likely to arise in the listeners' minds about your subject or proposal, and then you deal with these questions in a way that favors your conclusion. Often, for example, upon first hearing of a new development in medical science, people will immediately want to know how it relates to their own health problems or to the needs of their loved ones; or upon first being told of a pending piece of legislation, they will wonder how it will affect their taxes or whether it will curb their freedom. By skillfully structuring your material so you address these questions early in the speech, you will be assured of a high degree of audience interest and will pave the way for the rest of the material to be presented.

Elimination Order. Whereas the sequential, causal, and topical patterns of organization are applicable to both informative- and persuasive-type speeches, elimination order is best suited to speeches designed to influence belief or secure action.

In this order, you first survey all of the available solutions to a recognized problem or all of the courses of action which could reasonably be pursued in a given situation. Then, proceeding systematically, you show that all of the possibilities except one would be unworkable, excessively costly, or in some other way undesirable. By these means, you lead the audience, in effect, to agree with the belief of behavior you advocate.

If elimination order is to be used effectively, two requirements are important. First, your survey must be all-inclusive. If one or more options are overlooked, the logic of the process will be defective and the listeners will not be obliged to accept the conclusion you desire. (See a discussion of "false division," page 279.) And second, the possibilities must be mutually exclusive; for, unless this is the case, one or more of the characteristics which render a rejected possibility impracticable or undesirable also may be present in the preferred point of view. Consider this example:

THESIS STATEMENT: Increasing bus ridership is the only way to effectively relieve downtown traffic congestion.

   I. There are really only three ways in which the congested traffic in our business district could be relieved.
     A. We could ban automobiles from the area.
     B. We could widen the streets.
     C. We could get more people to ride the buses.

  II. Banning automobiles would be impracticable.
     A. The citizens would object strongly.

    B. The city would lose the revenue from existing parking lots.

  III. Widening the streets would be impracticable.
    A. The cost would be prohibitive.
    B. The inconvenience to the business community would be great.

  IV. Therefore, the only acceptable solution is to get more people to ride the buses.
    A. Bus service could be more frequent.
    B. Our present buses could be overhauled and new ones purchased.
      1. The federal government would supply some of the necessary funds.
      2. A modest increase in fares would help offset the cost.

CONSISTENCY OF ARRANGEMENT

Sometimes you may want to choose one method of arrangement for the main points of your message and another method for the subordinate ideas. On no condition, however, should you shift from one method to another in the presentation of the main points themselves, because it would confuse your listeners. The following outline illustrates how space, special topical, and time sequences might be combined in a talk on the major cities of India.

THESIS STATEMENTS: The complexities of Indian culture are nowhere more evident than in India's cities.

  I. The major cities of *western* India include Bombay and Ahmadabad.
    A. Bombay
      1. Early history
      2. Development under the British
      3. Condition today
    B. Ahmadabad
      1, 2, 3 *(Develop as above)*

  II. The major cities of *central* India include Delhi and Hyderabad.
    A. Delhi
      1. Early history
      2. Development under the British
      3. Condition today
    B. Hyderabad
      1, 2, 3 *(Develop as above)*

  III. The major cities of *eastern* India include Calcutta and Madras.
    A. Calcutta
      1. Early history

      2. Development under the British
      3. Condition today
   B. Madras
      1, 2, 3 *(Develop as above)*

Note that in this outline space sequence is used for the main points, special topical sequence for subpoints A and B, and time sequence for sub-subpoints 1, 2, and 3.

PHRASING THE MAIN POINTS

For reasons of emphasis as well as of clarity, you should word the main points of your speech carefully. While illustrations, explanations, quotations, and the like comprise the bulk of any talk, the main points tie these supporting details together and, therefore, most directly convey the message you wish to communicate. In order to achieve maximum effectiveness in the statement of your main points, keep in mind these four characteristics of good phrasing: (1) *conciseness*, (2) *vividness*, (3) *immediacy*, and (4) *parallelism*.

Conciseness

State your main points as briefly as you can without distorting their meaning. A simple, straightforward declaration is easy to grasp; a long and complex statement tends to be vague and confusing. Avoid clumsy modifying phrases and distracting subordinate clauses. State the essence of your idea in a short sentence which can be modified or elaborated as you subsequently present the supporting material. Say, "Our state taxes are too high," not "Taxes in this state, with the exception of those on automobiles, motor boats, and trucking lines, are higher than is justified by existing economic conditions." The second statement may express your idea more completely than the first, but it contains nothing that your supporting material could not clarify, and its greater complexity makes it less crisp and emphatic.

Vividness

Whenever possible, state the main points of your speech in attention-provoking words and phrases. If your principal ideas are drab and colorless, they will not stand out from the supporting materials which surround them, nor will they be easy to remember. Because they are your main points, you should make them the punch lines of your speech. Notice how much more

Arranging and outlining may seem like unnecessary chores. Yet, if you want your speeches to be easy to grasp and remember, to provide balanced coverage of your subjects, and to develop smoothly from be-ginning to end, you'll find that planning sound speech structures will pay off. And, you'll be able to work comfortably and directly from a speaking outline.

vivid it is to say, "We must cut costs!" than to say, "We must reduce our current operating expenditures." Vivid phrasing should not, of course, be overdone or used to distort the truth; nor should the sort of language suitable for a pep rally or political meeting be used on a more dignified occasion. Within these limits, however, vividness of phrasing is desirable. (Note: The quality of vividness—and other matters pertaining to the wording of the speech—will be examined more extensively in Chapter 8.)

Immediacy

Try to word your main points so they will appeal directly to the immediate interests and concerns of your listeners. Remember that you are speaking not merely *about* something, but *to* somebody. Instead of saying "Chemical research has helped to improve medical treatment," say "Modern chemistry helps the doctor make you well." Rather than saying "Air travel is fast," say "Air travel saves you time." (Review in this connection the discussion of audience interests and desires, pages 81–87.)

Parallelism

Whenever possible, use a uniform type of sentence structure and similar phraseology in stating your main points. Since these points represent coordinate units of your speech, word them so they sound that way. Avoid unnecessary shifts from active to passive voice or from questions to assertions. Use prepositions, connectives, and verb forms which permit a similar balance, rhythm, and direction of thought. *Avoid* this kind of wording for a series of main points:

I. The amount of your income tax depends on the amount you earn.

II. You pay sales taxes in proportion to the amount you buy.

III. Property tax is assessed on the value of what you own.

Instead phrase the main points like this:

I. The amount of money you earn determines your income tax.

II. The amount of goods you buy determines your sales tax.

III. The amount of property you own determines your property tax.

Observe that in this series a part of each statement ("The amount of . . . you . . . determines your . . . tax.") is repeated, whereas the remainder of the statement is changed from point to point. Such repetition of key words may help your listeners remember the major ideas in your message.

ARRANGING SUBORDINATE IDEAS AND SUPPORTING MATERIALS

When you have selected, arranged, and phrased the main points of your speech, you are ready to organize your subordinate ideas and supporting materials in a way which will give substance and orderliness to the whole message.

Subordinating the Subordinate Ideas

A "string-of-beads discussion," in which everything seems to have equal weight—tied together as it usually is by *and-uh, and next, and then, and so*—not only lacks purposive form, but also obscures meaning. Because everything receives equal emphasis, nothing seems important; and the speech soon becomes tiresome. Regardless of how well you have chosen, arranged, and worded the main points, they will not stand out unless your lesser ideas are properly subordinated. Avoid giving the subpoints the emphasis due only to your principal thoughts, and avoid listing under such main thoughts ideas that are not subordinate to them.

Types of Subordinate Ideas

Subordinate ideas commonly fall into one of five classes: (1) *parts of a whole*, (2) *lists of functions*, (3) *series of causes or results*, (4) *items of logical proof*, and (5) *illustrative examples*. While other types might also be listed, these five are certainly among the most important.

Parts of a Whole.   If a main point concerns an object or a process that has a number of parts or refers to a total composed of many items, the subpoints then identify and treat those parts or items. For example, the grip, shaft, and head are the parts you would discuss in describing the manufacture of a golf club; or the number of television stations in England, Scotland, Northern Ireland, and Wales are the subtotals you would refer to when showing that the number of television stations in the British Isles has increased.

Lists of Functions.   If a main point suggests the purpose of some mechanism, organization, or procedure, the subordinate ideas may list the specific functions it performs. The purpose of a municipal police department, for example, may be made clear by discussing its responsibilities for traffic control, crime detection, and safety education.

Series of Causes or Results.   If a main point states that a cause has several effects, or that an effect results from a number of causes, the various effects or causes may be listed as subordinate ideas. For example, the causes of crop failure may be enumerated as drought, frost, and blight; or its effects as high food prices, deprivation, and possible riots.

Items of Logical Proof.   In a speech designed to influence belief, the subordinate ideas under a main point may consist of a group of separate but related arguments or of the successive steps in a single, coordinated line of reasoning. In either case, you should be able to relate the subordinate ideas to the main point by the word *because* (i.e., the main point is true because the subordinate ideas are true). You might support a plea for a new high school in your community with this series of separate but related arguments: "We need a new high school *(a)* because our present building is too small, *(b)* because our present building lacks essential laboratory and shop facilities, and *(c)* because the growth of our city has made it difficult for many students to get to our present building." Conversely, you should be able to proceed from the subpoints to the main point by using the word *therefore*. For example: "Our present high-school building *(a)* is too small, *(b)* lacks necessary facilities, and *(c)* is not centrally located; *therefore*, we should construct a new building." (The use of sound reasoning will be discussed in more detail in Chapter 13.)

Illustrative Examples. If a main point consists of a generalized concept or assertion, the subordinate ideas may illustrate it with specific cases or examples. You may use this method in both exposition and argument, the examples providing clarification in the first case, and proof in the second. For instance, you may explain the theory of reciprocal trade agreements by showing your listeners how such agreements work in actual cases involving specific goods and products; or you may, by citing the results obtained in certain communities which have added fluorine to their water supply, support the contention that fluorine in a community's drinking water helps in the prevention or the reduction of tooth decay.

Coordinating the Subordinate Ideas

Subordinate ideas not only should be directly related to the main point under which they fall, but they should also be coordinate with each other—that is, they should be equal in scope or importance. To list poor teachers, the lack of adequate textbooks, and a broken Coke machine as the reasons for poor scholarship among the students in a large high school would indicate that your analysis of your subject is in some way faulty: you are treating as equal three items which obviously are not equal in importance. Either the broken Coke machine is symptomatic of a greater evil—careless administration, a dilapidated school building, etc.—and therefore should be placed *under* this head, or it is irrelevant and should be eliminated from the speech altogether. To treat it as a factor equal to poor teaching and the lack of textbooks is to confuse a less important idea with more important ones and to create an unconvincing and incongruous effect.

Arranging the Subordinate Ideas

Subordinate ideas, no less than main points, must be arranged in an orderly and purposeful fashion. Parts of a whole, functions, or causes—even items of proof or illustrative examples—often can be listed according to the patterns already discussed for ordering the main headings. You can put your subordinate ideas in a sequential, causal, or topical arrangement—whichever pattern seems most appropriate. You may want to use one pattern for the items under one main point and a different pattern for those under another; do not, however, alter the pattern of the subordinate ideas *within* the same coordinate series, for this may seriously confuse your listeners. Above all, be sure to employ some systematic order; do not crowd the subordinate ideas in haphazardly just because they are subordinate. Moreover, be careful not to let the process of subordination become too intricate or involved, or your listeners will not be able to follow you; but however far you go, keep your subordination consistent and logical.

Supporting the Subordinate Ideas

The important role that supporting materials play in making a speech effective was discussed in Chapter 5. The general rule should be: *Never make a statement in a speech without presenting some facts or reasoning to clarify, illustrate, or substantiate it.* Too often speakers think that if they divide every main point into two or three subordinate ideas, they have done enough. In reality, however, such divisions add only to the skeleton of the speech. They do not supply the supporting materials upon which understanding or belief ultimately depends. The real *substance* of any talk lies in explanations, statistics, illustrations, instances, comparisons, and testimony. Within reasonable limits, the more of these materials you have, the stronger your speech will be.

We have now considered the principles that should govern the arrangement of ideas within a speech and have surveyed several patterns by which the main points may be ordered and by which the subordinate points may be coordinated. Even with a thorough grasp of these principles and patterns, however, you probably will be unable to work out all of the details of a speech entirely in your mind. To develop a tangible, overall view of the structure as well as the content of a talk, you will find it necessary to follow some kind of orderly procedure for setting ideas and facts down on paper. For this purpose, most speakers find it best to prepare an outline.

REQUIREMENTS OF GOOD OUTLINE FORM

The amount of detail you include in an outline will depend on your subject, on the speaking situation, and on your previous experience in speech composition. But regardless of these factors, any good outline should meet the following basic requirements:

Each unit in the outline should contain only one idea.   If two or three ideas are run together under one symbol, the relationships they bear to one another and to other ideas in the outline will not stand out clearly. Notice the difference between the following examples:

Wrong

I. You should ride a bicycle because bicycling is an ideal form of convenient and inexpensive transportation and because it is also an excellent form of healthful recreation and is fun.

Right

I. You should ride a bicycle.
   A. Bicycling is an ideal form of transportation.
      1. It is convenient.
      2. It is inexpensive.
   B. Bicycling is an excellent form of recreation.
      1. It is healthful.
      2. It is fun.

Less important ideas in the outline should be subordinate to more important ones.   Because a subordinate idea is a subdivision of the larger heading under which it falls, it should rank *below* that heading in scope and importance. It should also directly support or amplify the statement made in the superior heading.

Wrong

I. The cost of medical care has skyrocketed.
   A. Operating-room fees may be as much as $800 or $900.
      1. Hospital charges are high.
      2. A private room may cost as much as $450 a day.
   B. X rays and laboratory tests are extra.
   C. Complicated operations may cost several thousand dollars.
      1. Doctors' charges constantly go up.
         a. Office calls usually cost between $15 and $25.
      2. Drugs are expensive.
      3. Most antibiotics cost $1.25 per dose.
   D. The cost of non-prescription drugs has mounted.

Right

I. The cost of medical care has skyrocketed.
   A. Hospital charges are high.
      1. A private room may cost as much as $450 a day.
      2. Operating-room fees may be as much as $800 or $900.
      3. X rays and laboratory tests are extra.

    B. Doctors' charges constantly go up.
      1. Complicated operations may cost several thousand dollars.
      2. Office calls usually cost between $15 and $25.
    C. Drugs are expensive.
      1. Most antibiotics cost $1.25 per dose.
      2. The cost of non-prescription drugs has mounted.

The logical relationship between units of the outline should be shown by proper indentation.   Normally, your main points will be the most general as well as the most important statements in your speech. As such, they should be placed nearest the left-hand margin of your outline, with less important statements ranged beneath and to the right of them in the order of increasing specificity. In your finished outline, therefore, the broadest and most central statements will lie farthest to the left; the narrowest and most particular ones will lie farthest to the right. If a statement is more than one line in length, the second line should be aligned with the first. (For example, see item I., B. in the following full-content outline.)

A consistent set of symbols should be used throughout the outline.   An acceptable set of symbols is exemplified in the outlines printed in this chapter. But whether you use this system or some other, be consistent. Items comparable in importance or scope always should be assigned the same type of symbol.

The four requirements just named apply to any outline you may make. An additional requirement, however, applies to the final draft of a complete, formal outline: *All the main points and subordinate ideas in such an outline should be written out as full sentences.* Especially as you prepare outlines for your classroom speeches, you will find that putting the items of the outline into sentence form will help clarify in your mind the meaning of each point and will show its exact relation to the other points. You will also find that a carefully framed statement of each point and a recognition of its place in the overall structure of your speech are invaluable aids in helping you remember what you want to say when it is time to speak.

STEPS IN PREPARING AN OUTLINE

An outline, like the speech it represents, should be developed gradually through a series of stages. While the process of preparing an outline may vary from person to person and occasion to occasion, certain steps should always be taken: (1) first, you should develope a *rough outline*, one which identifies your topic, your purpose, and aspects of the topic you will treat. (2) Next, you will want to prepare a *technical outline*, in order to arrange all of your materials and to evaluate the sufficiency of your speech-building effort. (3) Finally, you should recast that material into a *speaking outline*, that is, into a form you will actually use when delivering your speech.

Developing a Rough Outline

Suppose that your instructor has asked you to prepare an informative speech on a subject in which you are interested. You decide that you will talk about Cardiopulmonary Resuscitation—or CPR—because you recently have gone through the training program and because you think everyone can profit from knowledge of these lifesaving techniques. Your broad topic area, therefore, is:

Cardiopulmonary Resuscitation

In the eight to ten minutes you have to speak, however, you obviously will not be able to cover everything you might say about this subject, nor could you possibly teach your audience how to use CPR techniques. Therefore, recalling what you learned in Chapter 4 about adapting your material to your listeners and to time-limits, you decide to focus your discussion on some background on lifesaving and CPR and on a brief description of the procedures and techniques involved. Consequently, you limit your topic as indicated below:

CARDIOPULMONARY RESUSCITATION
(A brief description of where the techniques came from
and what they involve.)

In determining the limits of your subject, you already have made a preliminary selection of some of the principal ideas to be dealt with in your speech. Now you jot these points down to see how they may be modified and fitted into a suitable sequence. Your list may look something like this:

Kinds of accident victims
Previous methods of lifesaving
Organizations which support CPR training
Sources of CPR training
Costs of CPR training
Steps in using CPR techniques

This list covers a number of points you may want to be sure to include, but the order appears random. As you think about organizing these items, you successively review various arrangement patterns: A chronological pattern will enable you to organize the history of CPR and the steps involved in administering it to someone, but it really would not give the speech as a whole a sense of coherence. Either of the causal patterns might work well for a persuasive speech, but, since this is primarily an informative discourse, you do not really want to spend time on describing how CPR as a "cause" affects the operations of the human body. Among the special patterns, an inquiry order could work, although you discard it because you do not really know enough about audience members' questions to employ it effectively. So, you settle upon a *topical* order, because you really want to bring to your listeners two kinds of information—the background of CPR and a description of CPR techniques:

> *Background of CPR*—previous methods of lifesaving, and organiza-
> tions which support and sponsor CPR training;
> *Description*—steps in using CPR techniques.

As you think about this pattern, another thought occurs to you: you could announce these two subtopics, and then further subdivide each of them chronologically, in this manner:

I. Background of CPR
   A. Previous methods of lifesaving
   B. Organizations which supported its development
   C. Organizations which currently provide training

II. Steps in using CPR techniques
   A. Clear the airways of a victim
   B. Restore breathing for a victim
   C. Restore circulation for the victim

You now have prepared a *rough outline*. You have identified your topic, clarified your purpose, considered various subtopics and settled upon a reasonable number of them, and decided on a coherent method for organizing and developing your speech. Notice in the resulting rough outline that the main points of the speech follow one method of arrangement (topical) and the subordinate ideas follow another, parallel pattern (each main point being developed via chronology). As we mentioned previously, this combination is perfectly acceptable. When mixing patterns as we have done here, however, be sure one predominates and that the other is clearly presented as well.

When you have thus chosen and arranged the major points, or "heads," of your speech, proceed to phrase them more precisely, then to place under each major head the subordinate ideas by which it is to be explained and amplified. This additional development enables you to sketch in the necessary supporting materials in the form of examples, statistics, comparisons, and the like.

Developing a Technical Outline

You now are ready to assemble a full-content outline. This normally is done in two steps: First, you draft the speech as completely as possible, using standard outline form. You may have to combine or rearrange certain points as they appear in your rough draft, or perhaps even drop several of them because of overdevelopment or time pressures. Cast all of the items as complete sentences—sentences which convey your meaning clearly and exactly. Arrange the sentences so that they adhere to the following principles of good outline form:

(a) each unit in the outline contains only one idea;
(b) less important ideas are subordinated to the more important ones;
(c) logical relationships between units are illustrated through proper indentation; and
(d) a consistent set of symbols is used throughout the outline.

Each of these outlining principles is illustrated in the outline which follows.

In analyzing the completed outline to discover possible gaps or weaknesses, it frequently is helpful to work out a *technical plot* of your speech. To make such a plot, lay the completed outline beside a blank sheet of paper; and on this sheet, set down opposite each unit a statement of the materials or devices used in developing it. Where you have used statistics in the outline, write the word *statistics* in the technical plot, together with a brief statement of their function. In like manner, indicate all of the forms of support and methods of development you have employed.

Used as a testing device, a technical plot can help you determine whether your speech is structurally sound, whether there is adequate supporting material, whether you have overused one or two forms of support, and whether the appeals you plan are adapted to the audience and occasion. Many speeches, of course, do not need to be tested this thoroughly; and experienced speakers often can make an adequate analysis without drafting a complete technical plot. For the beginner, however, there is no more effective way of checking the structure of a speech and testing the methods used to develop it.

A SAMPLE FULL-CONTENT OUTLINE

The following example shows, then, both the complete content of an outline and its technical plot. For illustrative purposes, all items in the outline are stated as complete sentences. Such completeness of detail may be desirable if the occasion is an especially important one or if you sometimes have difficulty framing thoughts extemporaneously. Usually, however, it may be sufficient to write out only the main ideas as complete sentences and to state the subordinate ideas and supporting materials as key phrases.

THE A-B-C'S OF CPR[1]

(The introduction and conclusion for this speech will be developed in some detail in Chapter 7, "Beginning and Ending the Speech," pp. 145–160.)

TECHNICAL PLOT	FULL-CONTENT OUTLINE
First topic: background *[Optional topic: develop only if there is time]*	I. To understand the importance of CPR techniques, one needs to know something about its background. A. Let's review some of the ancient methods of resuscitation—flagellation and heat in the Middle Ages; fumigation, inversion, and the barrel methods of the 18th century; the Russian and trotting-horse methods of the 19th century; and artificial respiration as taught in the 20th century.
Beginning of the idea	B. In 1966, the National Academy of Sciences—National Research Council sponsored a Conference on Cardiopulmonary Resuscitation.
Details on recommendations	1. It recommended that medical, paramedical, and allied health personnel be trained in CPR. 2. Its recommendations resulted in widespread professional acceptance of CPR and related training programs.
Second phase	C. That conference was followed, in 1973, by the National Conference on Standards for CPR and Emergency Cardiac Care sponsored by the American Heart Association and the National Academy of Sciences-National Research Council.
Authoritative testimony	1. Participating in the 1973 conference were over thirty-five national medical, governmental, and service organizations; American Heart Association chapters from thirty-seven states; and representatives from thirty medical schools.

---

[1]"Standards for Cardiopulmonary Resuscitation (CPR) and Emergency Cardiac Care (ECC)" from Supplement to *Journal of The American Medical Association*, August 1, 1980, Vol. 244, No. 5. Copyright © 1980 by the American Medical Association. Reprinted with permission from the American Heart Association.

TECHNICAL PLOT	FULL-CONTENT OUTLINE

Details on spreading the idea

2. In part, the 1973 conference urged that:
   a. Professional and public educational programs to increase awareness of heart attack symptoms and emergency treatment be opened immediately;
   b. The public, particulary, become more involved in basic life-support training; and,
   c. Communities integrate emergency cardiac care as part of a comprehensive medical services program, making them available throughout entire communities.

Details on how the idea was phased into the country

3. To carry out the recommendations, the 1973 conference argued that:
   a. Professionals such as police, firefighters, lifeguards, and the like be trained in CPR immediately;
   b. High-risk industry workers and families of cardiac patients be trained next; and,
   c. Then, the training be extended to school children and the general public.

Transition

D. And, that's where I—and I hope you—come in.

Second topic: steps in CPR technique

II. What, then, *is* CPR?

Explanation— what

A. Technically, CPR is a series of actions for basic life support, wherein one recognizes airway obstruction, respiratory arrest, and cardiac arrest, and then properly applies—singly or with another person—a series of measures for alleviating those problems.

Comparison (analogy)

B. CPR can be compared to procedures used by traffic controllers when they are faced with a blocked interstate highway.
   1. First, they must open sideroads or remove vehicles blocking the highway.
   2. Second, they must signal the stopped vehicles to get moving.
   3. Third, they must bring in rescue or tow trucks to restore cars which have become disabled during the stoppage.

Use of a mnemonic device to aid recall

C. Likewise, CPR is as simple as A-B-C.
   1. "A" stands for "airways."
      a. If you come upon a collapsed person, first shake the person, shouting, "Are you all right?"

<table>
<tr><td>

**TECHNICAL
PLOT**

</td><td>

FULL-CONTENT OUTLINE

</td></tr>
</table>

<table>
<tr><td valign="top">

*Develop the
details
in chronological
order, offering an
explanation—how*

</td><td valign="top">

  b. If there is no answer, put the person on his or
     her back.
  c. Then, lift the neck or chin to open the airway,
     looking for chest and stomach movement, lis-
     tening for sounds of breathing, and feeling for
     breath on your cheek.
 2. "B" stands for "breathing."
  a. If opening the airway does not start spontane-
     ous breathing, you must provide rescue breath-
     ing.

</td></tr>
<tr><td valign="top">

*(Generally
demonstrate these
techniques)*

</td><td valign="top">

  b. The best method is the mouth-to-mouth tech-
     nique.
    (1) Pinch off the nose with one hand, holding
        the head in a tilted position with the other.
    (2) Immediately give four quick, full breaths in
        rapid succession.
  c. Then check for a pulse along the carotid artery.
 3. "C" stands for "cardiac compression."
  a. Pressing on the person's chest in the right place
     will start to provide artificial circulation.
  b. To force the heart to pump, you must set up a
     rhythmical, rocking motion to ensure the proper
     amount of pressure and relaxation.

</td></tr>
<tr><td valign="top">

*(Hold up card—it
saves you a lot of
technical
description)*

</td><td valign="top">

  c. You then begin a procedure whereby you alter-
     nate chest compressions and mouth-to-mouth
     breaths, in ratios which you will find on the card
     I have given you.

</td></tr>
</table>

TECHNICAL PLOT	FULL-CONTENT OUTLINE

                                     4. Continue these techniques until help comes, until you are exhausted, or until there are unmistakable signs that the person will not recover.

Restatement and reinforcement with visual aid   III. I have outlined the basic A-B-C's: A—open airways; B—start rescue breathing; C—initiate cardiac compression. This poster should help you remember them. These comprise the CPR techniques to use when coming upon a victim.

Warning   A. Remember, though, that there are variations in techniques when dealing with a child rather than an adult, a drowning or electrical shock victim, or someone with a fractured neck.

Reiteration of speech purpose   B. My job today is *not* to teach you CPR; that can only be done in an authorized CPR training class. My job is, rather, to tell you what it is, to let you know it can and ought to be learned by everyone in this room.

DEVELOPING A SPEAKING OUTLINE

In Chapter 7 we will complete the technical outline by adding introductory and concluding materials: statistics, appeals to the audience's interests and curiosity, and the like. But enough details have been offered thus far to indicate the virtues of full, technical outlines.

As you probably realize, however, the outline just built would be difficult to work from were you to actually deliver a speech on CPR. Because it is a full-sentence outline, it is "too dense" to be manageable from a lectern. Moreover, because all of the details are included, you probably would be tempted simply to read it to your auditors. If you did that, you would lose vital audience contact.

Normally, therefore, you must compress the technical outline into a form more convenient for use during the presentation of the message. This may involve rewording the main heads in phrase or key-word form on a sheet or notecard, putting statistics or quotations on other notecards, and the like. The actual method you use, of course, will depend upon your personal habits; some people like to work from sheets of paper, others, from notecards. Whatever your preferences are in these matters, your actual speaking outline should serve two functions while you are addressing the audience: (1) it should provide you with reminders of the direction of your speech—main points, subordinate ideas, etc.; and (2) it should record material of a technical or specific nature which must be carefully or precisely worded. A key-word speaking outline might look like this:

THE A-B-C'S OF CPR

I. Background
   —ancient methods of lifesaving
      Middle Ages: flagellation, heat
      18th: fumigation, inversion, barrel
      19th: Russian, trotting-horse
      20th: back, front, mouth-to-mouth
   —move to CPR
      1966: National Academy of Sciences/
            National Research Council Conference on CPR
            —recommended training for pros
            —fostered general acceptance
      1973: American Heart Association and NAS/NRC Conference on
            Standards for CPR and Emergency Cardiac Care
            —35 med., gov't., service organizations
            —AHA chapters from 37 states
            —reps from 30 med. schools
              1. rec. pro and public ed programs
              2. rec. public involvement
              3. rec. development of community programs
            —to carry out recs.:
              1. train pros immediately
              2. then industry workers, families
              3. next into schools and public

II. CPR = ABC's
   Technically, CPR is a series of actions for basic life support, wherein one recognizes airway obstruction, respiratory arrest, and cardiac arrest, and properly applies—singly or with another person—a series of measures for alleviating those problems.
   —like unblocking traffic (open roadways, signal traffic, bring in rescue trucks)
   A = "airways"
   —first shout
   —then on back
   —look/listen/feel
   B = "breathing"
   —start rescue breathing
   —mouth-to-mouth
      —pinch nose
      —4 quick full breaths

—check pulse
C = "cardiac compression"
—press on chest
—rhythmical motion to start heart
—alternate chest/mouth-to-mouth

III. Summarize A-B-C's (SHOW POSTER!)
   —warning: *don't* forget it varies with age (adult/child), and state (drowning, electrical shock, fractured neck)
   —my job: tell you what it is

Notice four characteristics of this speaking outline: (1) Most points are noted only with a key word or phrase. If you have practiced the speech from the full, technical outline, a word or two should be enough to trigger your memory at these points. (2) Use a full sentence when you want to say something in a precise way, as illustrated in the formal definition of "cardiopulmonary resuscitation." (3) You even may wish to include some directions to yourself, as we have done here with the reference to "SHOW POSTER!" (4) Emphasis can be indicated in any number of ways—all capital letters, underlining, indentation patterns, etc. Find a method of emphasis which will catch your eye easily, and which will help you remember what is subordinated and/or related to what.

In summary, arranging and outlining may seem to some to involve only a lot of useless busywork. In some situations, that undoubtedly is true. In the case of impromptu speeches, for example, you probably will do no more than jot a few near-unintelligible notes on a scrap of paper. Yet, in the case of longer speeches, arranging the points carefully will allow you to structure your discourse clearly and vividly, and outlining the entire speech will force you to assess its soundness. Arranging and outlining, therefore, helps you check on your speech's *form*, its *coverage* of the subject, and its *suitability* to your purposes and the needs of the audience.

GROUP PROJECT

1. For each of the topics listed below suggest two ways that materials might be ordered. Discuss which of the two ways, in general, would be more effective.
   (*a*) Directions for driving in snow
   (*b*) An explanation why foreign students in the U.S. are demonstrating against the leadership in their home country
   (*c*) A rationale for including women in any revised draft system
   (*d*) The effect that the influx of tourists from the West will have on China
   (*e*) A description of the proposed route for a highway bypass

▶ INDIVIDUAL PROJECT

1. For a speech entitled "The Investigator as Resource," discussing why a lawyer may want to hire a private detective on a case-by-case basis, rearrange the following points and subpoints in proper outline form:

(a) Investigative services can save the lawyer time.

(b) Investigative reports indicate areas where the lawyer should concentrate in building a case.

(c) It's advantageous for a lawyer to employ an investigator on a case-by-case basis.

(d) The investigator performs two basic services.

(e) Known witnesses must be interviewed and other witnesses sought out.

(f) The detective examines reports from the FBI or other governmental and private agencies and evaluates them for reliability and to determine what has to be done.

(g) The investigator examines, collects, preserves, and analyzes physical evidence.

(h) The investigator compiles information in an effort to reconstruct an incident.

(i) Lawyers may need only occasional detective assistance on especially critical cases.

(j) Investigative reports can be used in out-of-court settlements.

▶ SUGGESTIONS FOR FURTHER READING

Loren J. Anderson, "A Summary of Research on Order Effects in Communication," in *Concepts of Communication,* ed. Jimmie D. Trent et al. (Boston: Allyn & Bacon, Inc., 1973), pp. 128–138.

Donald C. Bryant, Karl R. Wallace, and Michael C. McGee, *Oral Communication: A Short Course in Speaking,* 5th ed. (Englewood Cliffs, N.J.: Prentice-Hall, Inc., 1982), Chapter 7, "Structure and Movement: Outline, Introduction, Conclusion," pp. 95–123.

James Gibson, *Speech Organization: A Programmed Approach* (New York: Holt, Rinehart & Winston, Inc., 1971).

Michael Osborn, *Speaking in Public* (Boston: Houghton Mifflin Company, 1982), Chapter 10, "Outlining the Informative Speech," Chapter 13, "Developing, Outlining, and Wording the Persuasive Speech," pp. 217–236, 289–320.

Roger P. Wilcox, "Characteristics and Organization of the Oral Technical Report," in *Communicating Through Behavior,* ed. William E. Arnold and Robert O. Hirsch (St. Paul: West Publishing Company, 1977), pp. 201–206.

CHAPTER 7

Beginning and Ending the Speech

Every speech, whether long or short, needs a beginning and an end. Often speakers spend considerable time working on the development of the body of the speech, carefully researching materials, arranging ideas, and inserting supporting materials, but neglect the equally important task of planning how to begin and end the speech. Preparing the main ideas of the speech is important but you must realize that the introduction and conclusion to the speech help you gain acceptance for your ideas. The impact of the speech will be greater if you have planned how to direct the listeners' attention to the subject at the outset and how to tie together your ideas in a firm and vigorous conclusion. In this chapter we will first discuss the aims of an effective introduction and suggest various ways in which these aims may be achieved. Then we will consider the requirements of a suitable ending and review several specific methods by which the conclusion may be developed. Finally, we will discuss how to integrate the introduction and conclusion into the body of the speech.

BEGINNING THE SPEECH

If the beginning of the speech is to complement the main idea or proposition, the introduction has to: (1) gain listeners' attention, (2) secure good will and respect for the speaker, and (3) prepare the audience for the discussion that is to follow.

Gaining Attention.   As a speaker you want the listeners to attend to all of your speech, but you must first gain their attention. You must capture their attention during the first few moments of the speech—unless they're prepared to attend to what you say, your most interesting and useful information and most persuasive appeals will be wasted. By demonstrating the vitality of the topic and showing how important that topic may be for the audience, you can begin to turn the attention of the audience into a more developed interest. (You may want to review the Factors of Attention, pp. 35–42.)

Securing Goodwill.   In many respects, the audience will begin to form opinions about you and your topic even before you begin to speak. If your speech is to be successful, the audience should have a good opinion of you. You must try to enhance that opinion during the first few moments of the speech. The confidence you have in your topic and your general presence on the platform may serve as nonverbal cues for the audience. In many situations, your own reputation or the chairperson's introduction will help generate goodwill. However, there may be times when the audience is outwardly opposed to you or your topic. In these instances, it is important for you to deal with opposition openly so that your topic will receive a fair hearing. By commenting on the differences that exist between your view of the topic and the views of the listeners, you can let them know that you are aware of the lack of agreement but are seeking to find areas of consensus. When confronted by indifference, distrust, or skepticism, you must take steps to change these attitudes. These issues must be handled early in the speech so that your position will be received openly.

Preparing the Audience.   Finally, you should lead the thinking of your listeners naturally into the speech subject. You must prepare the audience to receive the speech by giving the purpose early in the presentation; audiences that must guess the thrust and purpose of the speech soon lose interest.

By gaining attention and developing interest, securing goodwill and respect, and preparing the audience, the introduction can better complement the central idea or proposition of the speech. To help you achieve these ends, there are a number of established means for developing the introduction of the speech:

1. Referring to the subject or occasion
2. Using a personal reference or greeting
3. Asking a rhetorical question
4. Making a startling statement of fact or opinion
5. Using a quotation
6. Telling a humorous anecdote
7. Using an illustration

Referring to the Subject or Occasion

If the audience already has a vital interest in the subject you are to discuss, you may only need to state that subject before presenting your first main point. The very speed and directness of this approach suggest alertness and eagerness to address your topic. Professor Russell J. Love used this approach when discussing rights for people with severe communication problems:

> My talk tonight is concerned with the rights of the handicapped—particularly those people with severe communication disabilities. I will be presenting what I call a bill of rights for the severely communicatively disabled.[1]

Although such brevity and forthrightness may strike exactly the right note on some occasions, you should not begin all speeches in this way. To a skeptical audience, a direct beginning may sound immodest and tactless; to an apathetic audience, it may sound dull or uninteresting. When listeners are receptive and friendly, however, reference to the subject often produces a businesslike and forceful opening.

Sometimes, instead of referring to the subject to be discussed, you may want to refer to the occasion which has brought the audience together or to the surroundings in which your talk is being presented. Professor Love elected to use reference to the occasion in an address "The Barriers Come Tumbling Down":

> It is certainly a distinct privilege and pleasure for me to make some remarks at this 1981 Commencement at Harris-Hillman School. I'm sure that most of us are filled with a mixture of feelings on this day. The graduating seniors no doubt have a feeling of accomplishment and a feeling of excitement about the future. Parents and friends feel pride and joy. Faculty have a feeling of a job well done and also a strong sense of the passage of time as another class moves on. At first thought, some of you may regard this ceremony as just a routine ritual, just one more graduation ceremony, not unlike thousands of similar ceremonies that are being held in elementary schools, high schools, colleges, and universities all

---

[1] Russel J. Love, "A Bill of Rights for the Severely Communicatively Disabled," given at a Speech, Hearing and Deafness Awareness Dinner, May 14, 1981.

across this vast land. If you think this about the present graduation, I'm going to ask you to pause and think again. I submit to you—seniors, parents, relatives, friends, and faculty—that this specific commencement is a very special event. Why is it so special? In a nutshell, it is special because the graduates themselves are special people.[2]

Using a Personal Reference or Greeting

At times, a warm personal salutation from the speaker or a pleasurably recalled earlier association with the audience or the scene serves as an excellent starting point. This is particularly the case if the speaker occupies a high-status position and has considerable prestige in the eyes of the audience. President Gerald Ford took advantage of this situation in opening his remarks before the House of Representatives on August 21, 1974:

> *Mr. Speaker and my former colleagues of the House of Representatives:* You do not know how much it means to me to come back and see all of you and to be so warmly welcomed. It makes one's political life a great, great experience to know that, after all of the disagreements we have had and all of the problems we have worked on, there are friends such as you. It is a thing that in my opinion makes politics worthwhile. I am proud of politics, and I am most grateful for my friends.[3]

The way in which a personal-reference type of introduction may sometimes be used to gain a hearing from a hostile or skeptical audience is shown by Anson Mount, Manager of Public Affairs for *Playboy* magazine, in a talk presented to the Christian Life Commission of the Southern Baptist Convention:

> I am sure we are all aware of the seeming incongruity of a representative of *Playboy* magazine speaking to an assemblage of representatives of the Southern Baptist Convention. I was intrigued by the invitation when it came last fall, though I was not surprised. I am grateful for your genuine and warm hospitality, and I am flattered (though again not surprised) by the implication that I would have something to say that could have meaning to you people. Both *Playboy* and the Baptists have indeed been considering many of the same issues and ethical problems; and even if we have not arrived at the same conclusions, I am impressed and gratified by your openness and willingness to listen to our views.[4]

---

[2]From "The Barriers Come Tumbling Down" by Russell J. Love. Given at the Harris-Hillman School Commencement, May 21, 1981. Reprinted by permission of Russell J. Love.

[3]Excerpt from speech before House of Representatives on August 21, 1974, by President Gerald Ford, from *Public Papers of the President.* Washington, D.C.: U.S. Government Printing Office, 1975, p. 39.

[4]Excerpt from a speech presented to the Christian Life Commission of Southern Baptist Convention by Anson Mount, Manager of Public Affairs for *Playboy* magazine, from *Contemporary American Speeches,* 3rd ed.

If the personal reference or greeting used in the introduction is modest and sincere, it may establish goodwill as well as gain attention. Effusiveness and hollow compliments, however, should be avoided. Audiences are quick to sense a lack of genuineness on the part of the speaker, and they always react unfavorably toward feigned or falsified sentiments. At the other extreme, avoid apologizing. Do not say, "I don't know why I was picked to talk on this subject when others could have done it so much better," or "Unaccustomed as I am to public speaking . . ." Apologetic beginnings suggest that you speech is not worth listening to. Be cordial, sincere, and modest, but do not apologize.

Asking a Rhetorical Question

A third way to open a speech is to ask a question or a series of questions to start the audience thinking about your subject. Jacqueline Jackson, a student at Regis College, used this approach to introduce a speech on "Why Johnny Can't Read":

> Johnny can't read. Johnny can't write. Johnny doesn't know how to spell. Johnny's not good with numbers. Johnny has a hard time remembering. Johnny lost the football game. Maybe Johnny's retarded and we're not doing enough for him. Maybe Johnny's gifted and we're holding him back. Johnny can't get along with others; Johnny can't get along with his teachers either. Johnny can't seem to do anything right. But why can't Johnny read, write, spell, play football, or get along with others? Could it be the fault of the schools? That seems to be the answer that the mass media have been promoting for years. Is the American school system responsible for the unbalanced, semi-literate children of today? Should the school system be responsible to educate every unbalanced semi-literate? Are schools being asked to do too much? Are schools being asked to do the right things?[5]

Making a Startling Statement

On certain occasions you may open a speech with what some writers have referred to as the "shock technique," making a startling statement of fact or opinion. This approach is especially useful when listeners are distracted or apathetic. The following shows how a speech on weight control might be introduced:

> There's a disease sweeping our country. None of us is immune. There are no

---

[5]From "Why Johnny Can't Read" by Jacqueline Jackson. Reprinted from *Winning Orations*, 1981, by special arrangement with the Interstate Oratorical Association, Larry Schnoor, Executive Secretary, Mankato State College, Mankato, Minnesota.

miracle drugs to combat it, although Americans spend millions of dollars each year to try to deal with the illness. The disease can affect all ages, all economic classes, all ethnic groups. It can cause permanent bodily damage, shorten life span, and may even cause death. Some of you may already be affected; most of you will in some way be touched by this disease. The disease is obesity; the cure, you. Today I will examine some of the causes of obesity and suggest some preventative measures.

Using a Quotation

If judiciously chosen and presented, a quotation may be an excellent means of introducing a speech, because it can both focus the auditors' thinking and set a proper emotional tone. A student at the University of Iowa, Alicia Becker, began a speech on crises in higher education in this way:

> "It was the best of times, it was the worst of times; it was the age of foolishness, it was the age of reason; it was the epoch of belief, it was the epoch of incredulity; it was the season of light, it was the season of darkness; it was the spring of hope, it was the winter of despair." With those words Charles Dickens described the era of the French Revolution, nearly 200 years ago. But he could just as well have been talking about today and tomorrow. We live in a similar age of contradiction and turbulence, in an atmosphere which threatens to destroy every institution, including this school. Today, I would like to discuss with you some ways in which contradictory forces from the government, the people of this state, the faculty of the university, and the students who attend it are threatening the basic purposes of your education.[6]

Telling a Humorous Anecdote

At times you may begin a speech by telling a funny story or relating a humorous experience. But be sure that the story or experience you recount will amuse the audience and that you can tell it well. If your opening remarks fail to arouse interest or to put the audience in a receptive frame of mind, your speech will be off to a poor start. Also be sure that the anecdote contributes to the central purpose of your talk. A joke or story that is unrelated to your subject not only wastes valuable time but channels the thinking of your listeners in the wrong direction. Finally, be sure that what you say is in good taste. Not only do doubtful or "off-color" stories violate the accepted standards of social behavior, but they may also seriously undermine the respect which the members of the audience should have for you as a speaker.

---

[6]From a speech given at the University of Iowa, spring, 1978, by Alicia Becker.

Consistent with the requirements we have just described, Hanna Gray introduced the Commencement Address at Duke University in May, 1982:

There is a famous story, famous at any rate in the Connecticut River Valley, which has to do with a crusty and patriotic old Vermonter who lived on an island in the Connecticut River through which ran the boundary separating New Hampshire and Vermont. One year, a team was sent out to survey that boundary and its members discovered, quite unexpectedly, that the old man lived not as had always been thought in Vermont but on the New Hampshire side of the line. In a state of some anxiety and trepidation, they went to confront him with the news that he lived in New Hampshire, and to their astonishment he replied, "Well, thank the good Lord. I was beginning to think I'd never be able to tolerate another one of them damn Vermont winters." Members of the graduating class: yours is the exact analogue to the old man's position. The boundary that separates you from another Durham winter has been drawn. You have been surveyed, found to be BAs, BSs, MAs, MBAs, MSs, JDs, MDs—I could go on—but in any case, you have been surveyed and found to be all those good things and therefore also citizens of some state which is popularly known as "the real world." Yet, tomorrow your spiritual terrain will be roughly the same as today, and so will you: quite undramatically unchanged, yet perhaps somewhat gratified to have survived into your new citizenship.[7]

Using an Illustration

One or more real-life incidents, a story taken from literature, or a series of hypothetical illustrations also may be used to get a speech underway. As in the case of the humorous anecdote, however, any illustration you use should not only be interesting to the audience in its own right, but should also be closely connected with the central idea you want to communicate. Kathy Winegar, a student at Concordia College, used this technique to introduce a speech concerning fetal alcohol syndrome:

Shelly is 18 months old, but her size and development are equivalent to that of a normal 7 month old child. When Shelly's mother delivered her in the hospital, she weighed only 4 pounds 12 ounces, she had bilateral hip dislocations, an abnormally small sized head, narrow eyes, and smelled of alcohol. At 2 months, she was admitted to the hospital again, only this time it was with congenital heart failure. At 18 months she was diagnosed as mentally retarded. John is newborn. He weighs a mere 2 pounds 5 ounces. Narrow eyes, a misshapened nose, a small head, only one functioning kidney and a severely deformed arm characterize the visible signs of mental retardation in this life. What do Shelly

---

[7]From Commencement Speech by Hanna H. Gray. Given at Duke University, May 9, 1982. Reprinted by permission.

and John have in common? Is it their physical condition? Is it their mental retardation? Yes and no. Shelly and John are innocent victims of what has been termed as Fetal Alcohol Syndrome.[8]

These, then, are seven useful ways of opening a speech: *a reference to the subject or occasion, a personal reference or greeting, a rhetorical question, a startling statement, an appropriate quotation, a humorous anecdote*, and *a striking illustration.* Sometimes one approach may be used alone; at other times, two or more of them may be combined. Whether used singly or in combination, however, the materials comprising your introduction always should be aimed at the same objective: arousing the attention and winning the goodwill and respect of your listeners. Moreover, those materials should be relevant to the purpose of your speech and should lead naturally into the first of the major ideas you wish to present. That is, the introduction should be an integral part of the speech. It should not be, for example, a "funny story" told merely to make an audience laugh, but rather should be thematically and tonally tied into the body of the speech. Many speakers will use a *forecast*—"In this speech, I will first . . . , and then will . . ."—in order to complete the task of orienting an audience before moving on to the substance of the discourse. A forecast is a relatively easy and yet effective way to make the transition from introductory notions to your main concerns.

To establish a common ground of interest and understanding and to point the audience toward the conclusion you ultimately hope to reach— these are the functions your introductory remarks always should serve.

ENDING THE SPEECH

Just as the introduction to the speech accomplishes specific purposes, so too does the ending or conclusion. A suitable conclusion should: (1) focus the thought of your audience, (2) establish a concluding mood, and (3) convey a sense of finality.

Focusing. The principal function of the ending or conclusion of a speech is to *focus the thought of the audience on your central theme and purpose.* If your speech has one dominant theme or idea, you will usually restate that point at the end in a manner that makes your meaning clear and forceful. If your speech is more complex, you may bring its most important

---

[8]From "Fetal Alcohol Syndrome" by Kathy Winegar. Reprinted from *Winning Orations*, 1981, by special arrangement with the Interstate Oratorical Association, Larry Schnoor, Executive Secretary, Mankato State College, Mankato, Minnesota.

points together in a condensed and uniform way; or you may spell out the action or belief which these points suggest.

Establishing mood.   In addition to bringing the substance of the speech into final focus, your conclusion should *aim at leaving the audience in the proper mood.* If you want your listeners to express vigorous enthusiasm, you should stimulate that feeling in your closing remarks. If you want them to reflect thoughtfully on what you have said, you should encourage a calm, judicious attitude. Therefore, you should decide whether the response you seek requires a mood of serious determination or lighthearted levity, of warm sympathy or utter disgust, of thoughtful consideration or vigorous desire for action; then you should plan to end your speech in a way which will create that mood.

Conveying finality.   Finally, a good ending should *convey a sense of completeness and finality.* Listeners grow restless and annoyed when they are given reason to feel that the speaker has finished, only to hear him or her ramble on. Therefore, avoid false endings. Tie the threads of thought together so that the pattern of your speech is brought clearly to completion.

Some of the means most frequently used to conclude speeches are:

1. Issuing a challenge or appeal
2. Summarizing
3. Using a quotation
4. Using an illustration
5. Supplying an additional inducement to belief or action
6. Stating a personal intention

Issuing a Challenge or Appeal

When using this method, the speaker openly appeals for support or action, or reminds the listeners of their responsibilities in furthering a desirable end. Such an appeal must be vivid and compelling and should contain within it a suggestion of the principal ideas or arguments presented in the speech. Leland Miles, President of the University of Bridgeport, selected this method when urging university presidents to seek peace studies for their campuses:

> Peace is not something that you pick up off the ground and say, oh look, peace! I found peace. Peace you've got to work at, peace you've got to create, peace you've got to make, peace you've got to produce. And the only way I know to produce it is through education, which is our business. Rodrigo Carazo, the president of Costa Rica, has said, "If you want peace, educate for peace." I agree. He has also said, "War begins in the minds of men and women. It is therefore in the minds of men and women that we must construct the defenses

Introductions and conclusions complete speeches. Introductions should gain attention, secure goodwill, and prepare audiences for the main remarks. Conclusions should focus audience members' thoughts on your ideas, establish appropriate moods, and convey feelings of finality. All this should be done coherently, with materials relevant to you, the occasion, the subject, and the audience.

of peace." I say let all of us join in building those defenses. Let all of us in our own ways attempt to build on our respective campuses constituencies for peace. We have constituencies for fraternities, constituencies for drugs, constituencies for better jazz concerts, why not constituencies for peace? Let's all transform our institutions into universities for peace, by requiring some kind of internationalized curriculum for all our students. Let's not leave the critical task of survival to Costa Rica alone.[9]

Summarizing

A summary conclusion reviews the main ideas that have been presented and draws whatever inferences may be implicit in the speech as a whole. In a speech to inform, a summary ending is nearly always appropriate because it restates and helps impress upon the listeners the points you especially want remembered. In a speech to persuade, a summary conclusion provides a final opportunity to reiterate your principal arguments and appeals. Richard

[9]From "Universities for Peace" by Leland Miles, from *Vital Speeches of the Day*, Volume XLVIII, March 1, 1982. Reprinted by permission of Vital Speeches of the Day.

Heckert used this approach when concluding his speech "The Human Side
of Managing Complexity":

> As you can see, I have now come full circle in this discussion of the individual,
> the organization, and the society, and of how all three can combine to make
> complexity work—or to let it overcome us. I have moved from small to large:
> person to organization to society. I have started with the importance of early
> education and training, followed individuals so trained into the organization and
> discussed some basic organizational principles, and then looked at a few
> somewhat-philosophical questions involved in the relationship of the organiza-
> tion with government and the large society. Throughout, the stress has been on
> the individual. Successful management of complexity depends on him or her.
> Successful management of complexity in the future will depend on many of you
> in this audience. I truly wish you well.[10]

Using a Quotation

A quotation, either in poetry or prose, may be used to end a speech if it
bears directly on the central idea you have been trying to communicate, or if
it strongly suggests the attitude or action you wish your listeners to take.
Some poetry, for instance, may provide in figurative, climactic language the
theme or essence of your message. A few words of quoted prose may
encapsulate your speech purpose and lend color and authority to your
conclusion. Pierre S. Du Pont IV, Governor of Delaware, employed a
quotation from a famous statesman to lend credibility to the thesis of his
presentation "The Proper Role of the Federal Judiciary":

> It is time we try to save the courts from themselves. Law professors and law
> students, indeed the profession as a whole, must play a vital role in this effort. It
> is your place to criticize, join the dialogue, emphasize the tradition of restraint
> in articles and books, in legal brief and oral arguments. Time is running short.
> Winston Churchill once remarked that "Democracy is the worst form of
> government; except for all the others." It is incumbent upon each of us who are
> accountable to the people in our democracy to remind our own undemocratic
> institution, the judiciary, that this role in perpetuating the truth of Churchill's
> remark is to remain accountable to the Constitution and the law, and to no
> other.[11]

---

[10]From "The Human Side of Managing Complexity" by Richard E. Heckert, from *Vital
Speeches of the Day*, Volume XLVIII, May 1, 1982. Reprinted by permission of Vital
Speeches of the Day.

[11]From "The Proper Role of the Federal Judiciary" by Pierre S. Du Pont IV, from *Vital
Speeches of the Day*, volume XLVIII, January 1, 1982. Reprinted by permission of Vital
Speeches of the Day.

Using an Illustration

Just as an illustration which captures your leading ideas may be used to begin a speech, so may it be used to close your discourse. A speech-ending illustration should be both *inclusive* and *conclusive:* inclusive of the main focus or thrust of your speech, conclusive in tone and impact.

> There is an old story about James Russell Lowell when he was the American Ambassador to the Court of St. James during the late nineteenth century. The French Ambassador of the time—who was himself a historian as well as a diplomat—approached Lowell with a question: "Mr. Ambassador, how long will the American republic endure?" The American Ambassador replied: "As long as the ideals of the Nation's Founding Fathers." This administration intends to use every resource at its disposal to ensure that this government reflects the ideals of the Founding Fathers. Those principles have long enabled our Nation both to endure and to prosper. In the furtherance of those principles, however, we will not ourselves seek short-term successes at the expense of basic principles. We will demand of ourselves that same adherence to sound constitutional principles that we intend to demand of the other branches of government.[12]

Supplying an Additional Inducement to Belief or Action

Sometimes a speech may be concluded by quickly reviewing the leading ideas presented in the body of the talk and then supplying one or more additional reasons for endorsing the belief or taking the action proposed.

> All in all, you will find an annual checkup by a competent physician to be a wise investment, no matter what your age or how well you may feel at the moment. As I have pointed out, in their early stages a number of potentially serious diseases have no symptoms of which the victim is in any way aware. Many other ills if caught in time can be eliminated or brought under control. Finally, the time and money a good checkup will cost you are only a tiny fraction of the time and expense a serious illness entails.
>
> Here, as in other aspects of life, be guided by the old but still pertinent adage, "A stitch in time saves nine." Remember that even though you may be foolish enough to take chances with your own well-being, you owe it to your loved ones and to those dependent on you to take no chances with the most precious of all things—your own good health. Make an appointment for a checkup today!

---

[12]From "The Federal Legal Council" by William French Smith, from *Vital Speeches of the Day*, Volume XLVIII, January 15, 1982. Reprinted by permission of Vital Speeches of the Day.

Stating a Personal Intention

A statement of the speaker's intention to act as his or her speech recommends is particularly valuable when the speechmaker's prestige with the audience is high, or when a concrete proposal needing immediate action has been offered. If the speaker can indicate an intention to take immediate action, that lends credibility both to the speaker and to the ideas presented. When asking the audience to give blood, the following conclusion might be appropriate:

> Today I have illustrated how important healthy blood is to human survival and how bloodbanks work to insure the possibility and availability of blood for each of us. It is not a coincidence that I spoke on this vital topic on the same day that the local Red Cross Bloodmobile is visiting campus. I want to urge each of you to ensure your future and mine by stopping at the Student Center today or tomorrow to make your donation. The few minutes that it takes may add up to a lifetime for a person in need. To illustrate how firmly I believe in this opportunity to help, I'm going to the Student Center to give my donation as soon as this class is over. I invite any of you who feel this strongly to join me.

Regardless of the means you choose—whether you close your speech with a *challenge or appeal*, or with a *summary, quotation, illustration, added inducement, or statement of personal intention*—remember that your conclusion should focus the thought of your listeners on the central theme you have developed. In addition, a good conclusion should be consistent with the mood or tenor of your speech and should convey a sense of completeness and finality.

FITTING THE BEGINNING AND ENDING TO THE BODY OF THE SPEECH

In Chapter 6 we considered various patterns for developing the body or substance of a speech and the principles to be followed in outlining that part of it. When the introduction and conclusion are added to the outline the completed structure should look something like this:

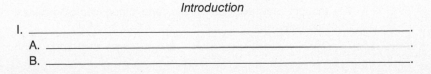

Introduction

I. _____.
   A. _____.
   B. _____.

Body

I. _____.
   A. _____.
   B. _____.
      1. _____.
      2. etc._____.
II. _____.
III. _____.

Conclusion

I. _____.
   A. _____.
   B. _____.

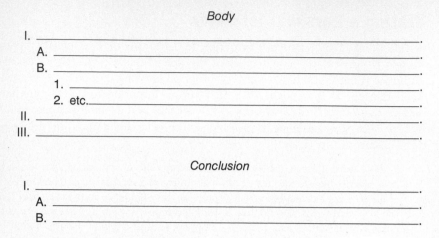

A SAMPLE OUTLINE
FOR AN INTRODUCTION AND A CONCLUSION

An introduction and conclusion for a classroom speech on cardiopulmonary resuscitation, as outlined in Chapter 6 (pages 138–141), might take the following form:

THE A-B-C'S OF CPR

Introduction

I. About 1,000,000 persons in the United States experience acute heart attacks each year.
   A. More than 650,000 die annually.
   B. About 350,000 of these deaths occur outside a hospital, usually within two hours of the onset of symptoms.
II. The real tragedy is that a large number of these deaths could have been prevented by prompt, adequate, on-the-spot treatment—treatment most of us have not learned how to give.
   A. Most of us are ignorant of basic first aid appropriate for heart attack, drowning, electrocution, suffocation, or drug intoxication victims.
   B. I don't know about you, but I used to fear that I would be involved in an emergency situation and not know what to do.
      1. I thought only doctors, nurses, and other medical professionals could help.

2. That's when I heard about CPR—Cardiopulmonary Resuscitation —and the half-day training sessions anyone could attend.
III. I went through a CPR workshop last spring, and I want to tell you about it.
   A. For only a dollar, the cost of materials, I gained the knowledge necessary to save a life.
   B. With only a couple of hours of reading and a four-hour training session, you, too, can gain the skills—and the confidence needed to put your skills into action.
IV. [Thesis Statement] Cardiopulmonary Resuscitation—CPR—is a three-step, life-saving technique which anyone can learn for use in emergencies.
V. For you to clearly understand what CPR is, I'll first offer a bit of background on the phenomenal growth of this technique over the last decade. Then, I will discuss some primary facts about it—what I call the ABC's of CPR. And finally, I'll tell you how, for only a small investment of time and effort, you can gain the satisfaction of knowing you can be better prepared to help your fellow human beings.

[Body]

Conclusion

I. Almost every community in America, through the American Red Cross, school programs, YMCAs, clubs, hospitals, and other groups, has CPR training available.
   A. It usually involves only a few pennies for the materials, a few hours of preparation, and about four hours of training.
   B. Periodic refresher courses, of shorter length, are available for those who are afraid they will forget it; and cards such as this one [holds up the card] can be carried around as reminders.
II. The ABC's of CPR, especially when they become integrated within community-wide emergency cardiac care programs involving mobile cardiac units and special area facilities, undoubtedly will significantly reduce those three quarters of a million deaths each year.
   A. With heart attacks still the number one killer in this country, everyone must get involved.
   B. You can, of course, try to buy off your conscience with a few dollars to the yearly Heart Fund drives, but you also can overcome some of your fear and hesitation by seeking training for yourself as well.
   C. On that card I gave you is the name of the nearest CPR workshop center in this area. Now that you know what CPR is, contact the center and attend the next training session.
   D. If my life is ever in the balance, I want *you* trained!

GROUP PROJECT

1. In a small group in class, decide what might be the best way for these people to open the following speeches.

SPEAKER	SITUATION
(a) Phyllis Schlafly	Opening session of a Pro-Life conference
(b) Roger Staubach	Banquet sponsored by Fellowship of Christian Athletes
(c) Jimmy Carter	Seminar relating to peace in the Middle East
(d) Ralph Nader	Keynote for National Association of Business conference

INDIVIDUAL PROJECT

1. After listening to one or more of the following types of speeches, evaluate the introduction and conclusion which the speaker used in (a) a classroom lecture; (b) a sermon; (c) an open hearing at a meeting of the city council; (d) remarks made at a fraternity, sorority, or dormitory council meeting; and (e) a formal address, "live" or televised, made by a political candidate. In orally reporting your evaluation, supply sufficient information about the speaker and speaking situation so that someone who was not present could understand why you evaluated a particular beginning or ending as you did.

SUGGESTIONS FOR FURTHER READING

Bert E. Bradley, *Fundamentals of Speech Communication: The Credibility of Ideas*, 2nd ed. (Dubuque, Ia.: Wm. C. Brown Company, Publishers, 1978), Chapter 9, "Beginning and Ending the Speech."

Donald C. Bryant and Karl R. Wallace, *Fundamentals of Public Speaking*, 5th ed. (Englewood Cliffs, N.J.: Prentice-Hall, Inc., 1976), pp. 277–287, "Introductions" and "Conclusions."

Edwin Cohen, *Speaking the Speech*, 2nd ed. (New York: Holt, Rinehart & Winston, 1983), Chapter 8, "Introducing Your Speech" and Chapter 9, "Concluding Your Speech."

Gary T. Hunt, *Public Speaking* (Englewood Cliffs, N.J.: Prentice-Hall, Inc., 1981), Chapter 7, "Building Introductions and Conclusions."

Herbert W. Simons, *Persuasion: Understanding, Practice, and Analysis* (Reading, Mass.: Addison-Wesley Publishing Company, 1976), Chapter 10, "Orienting Receivers."

CHAPTER 8

Wording the Speech

So far, we have focused on the process of creating speeches: preparing, organizing, and adapting messages to their intended audiences. We now shall turn our attention for the next three chapters to the *modes of creating (encoding) and interpreting (decoding) messages*. These modes—language, visual aids, and bodily and vocal behaviors—are the means by which public speakers communicate ideas, attitudes, feelings, and values to listeners.

We will begin the discussion of modes by examining language—the choices of wording and style that you as a speaker make when you put your ideas and feelings into language. First, we will suggest the essential features of effective speaking styles, that is, language styles, which improve listeners' chances for understanding what you want to say. And then, we will review several language strategies you may wish to employ on various speaking occasions, especially when you are trying to affect an audience's beliefs, attitudes, and values.

ESSENTIALS OF EFFECTIVE SPEAKING STYLES

Communicating with precision and clarity is not always easy. Yet, rhetorical and communication theorists for centuries have known that speakers increase listener *comprehension* and *retention* of ideas if certain virtues of oral style are kept in mind. The virtues of *accuracy, simplicity, coherence,* and *appropriateness* are widely recognized as the primary features of effective speaking styles.

Accuracy

Careful word choice is an essential ingredient in transmitting your meaning to an audience. The man who tells a hardware store clerk that he has "broken the hickey on my hootenanny and needs a thingamajig to fix it" had better have the hootenanny in his hand to procure the right thingamajig. The ambiguity of his message is no greater, however, than that of the orator who proclaims that "we must follow along the path of true Americanism." The sentiment being expressed may be a noble one, but it is cast in lofty generalities which not only are trite but have different meanings for different people.

When you speak, your goal should be precision. Leave no doubt as to your meaning. Words are symbols that stand for the concepts or objects they represent; thus, your listener may attach to a symbol a meaning quite different from the one you intend to convey. *Democracy,* for example, does not mean the same thing to a citizen of the United States as it does to a citizen of the Soviet Union, or, in fact, to one American citizen and another. The term *democracy* will elicit different meanings in those belonging to the Moral Majority and those belonging to the American Communist Party.

It is also imprecise to discuss people or objects in a particular class as though they were no different from other members of the same class. Asian-American A differs from Asian-Americans B and C; one Oldsmobile may be an excellent car and another may be a lemon. Students of General Semantics continually warn us that many errors in thinking and communication arise from treating words as if they were the actual conditions, processes, or objects and—as such—were fixed and timeless in meaning. From their perspective, the phrase "once a thief, always a thief" is an imprecise and inaccurate reference to apply to all persons convicted of theft; a person is more than a label.[1]

To avoid vagueness in definition and elsewhere, choose words that express the exact shade of meaning you wish to communicate. Although dictionary definitions are not infallible guides, they do represent commonly accepted usages stated as precisely as possible. Observe, for example, the

---

[1]For more extended treatments of this subject, see Doris B. Garey, *Putting Words in Their Places* (Glenview, Ill.: Scott, Foresman and Company, 1957), and Roger Brown, *Words and Things* (Glenview, Ill.: Scott, Foresman and Company, 1968).

distinctions a good dictionary makes among related words, such as *languor, lassitude, lethargy, stupor,* and *torpor.* In a synonym dictionary or a thesaurus the words listed for the verb *shine* are *glow, glitter, glisten, gleam, flare, blaze, glare, shimmer, glimmer, flicker, sparkle, flash, beam.* The English language is rich in subtle variations. To increase the precision of your expression, make use of this range of meaning in your choice of words.

Simplicity

"Speak," said Lincoln, "so that the most lowly can understand you, and the rest will have no difficulty." This advice is as valid today as when Lincoln offered it; and because modern audiences as created by the electronic media are vaster and more varied than any Lincoln dreamed of, there is even more reason for contemporary speakers to follow it. Say "learn" rather than "ascertain," "try" rather than "endeavor," "use" rather than "utilize," "help" rather than "facilitate." Never use a longer or less familiar word when a simpler one is just as clear and accurate. Billy Sunday, the famous evangelist, gave this example:

> If a man were to take a piece of meat and smell it and look disgusted, and his little boy were to say, "What's the matter with it, Pop?" and he were to say, "It is undergoing a process of decomposition in the formation of new chemical compounds," the boy would be all in. But if the father were to say, "It's rotten," then the boy would understand and hold his nose. "Rotten" is a good Anglo-Saxon word, and you do not have to go to the dictionary to find out what it means.[2]

Simplicity does not mean that your language must be simplistic or that you should "talk down" to your audience; it does suggest that you consider the advantages of short, easily understandable words that convey precise, concrete, specific meanings. The able speaker, regardless of experience, pays close attention to these qualities because they contribute vividness and interest to the speech.

Coherence

Transmitting ideas orally requires attention to the perceived *coherence* of your message. Audiences do not have the luxury of going back over your points as they do in reading an essay; nor do they have punctuation marks to

---

[2]Quoted in John R. Pelsma, *Essentials of Speech* (New York: Crowell, Collier, and Macmillan, Inc., 1934), p. 193.

help them distinguish one idea from another. Hence, speakers use *signposts* in the form of carefully worded phrases and sentences to enable listeners to follow the movement of ideas within a speech and to perceive the overall message structure.

Summaries are useful signposts in ensuring that your audience is able to see the overall structure: *preliminary* and *final summaries* are especially helpful in laying out or pulling together the major divisions or points of the speech:

Preliminary Summaries	*Final Summaries*
Today I am going to talk about three aspects of . . .	I have talked about three aspects of . . .
There are four major points to be covered in . . .	These four major points—(restate them)—are the . . .
The history of the issue can be divided into two periods . . .	The two periods just covered—(restate them)—represent the significant . . .

In addition to these summarizing strategies, signposts may be *connectives* which move an audience from one idea to another within the speech. The following are typical *transition* statements you might employ:

In the first place . . . The second point is . . .
In addition to . . . notice that . . .
Now look at it from a different angle . . .
You must keep these three things in mind in order to understand the importance of the fourth . . .
What was the result? . . .
Turning now . . .

The preceding signposts are *neutral*—they tell the audience that another idea is coming, but do not indicate the more subtle relationships that exist between the points being made. You can improve the clarity and coherence of your message by being precise about such relationships as *parallel/hierarchical*, *similar/different*, and *coordinate/subordinate*. Expressing these relationships requires *connectives* or *transitions* such as:

Not only . . . but also . . . [*parallel*]
More important than these . . . [*hierarchical*]
In contrast . . . [*different*]
Similar to this . . . [*similar*]
One must consider X, Y, and Z . . . [*coordinated*]
On the next level is . . . [*subordinated*]

The use of preliminary or final summarizing statements to capture the holistic structure of your speech, and more specific signposts to distinguish ideas and indicate their relationship to each other will help ensure that your message is perceived as a coherent whole by the audience.

Appropriateness

Besides being accurate and clear, your language should be appropriate to the topic and to the situation. Serious or solemn occasions call for diction that is restrained and dignified; light or joyful occasions, for diction that is informal and lively. Just as you would never use slang in remarks at a funeral service or in a speech dedicating a church or memorial, so you should never phrase a humorous after-dinner speech in a heavy or elevated style. Suit your language to the spirit and tone of the occasion; be dignified and formal when formality is expected, and light and casual when informality is called for. Be sure, also, that your language is appropriate to the audience you are addressing—that the terms you employ and the allusions you make are within the realm of the listeners' understanding.

 A SAMPLE SPEECH OF TRIBUTE

The qualities of linguistic *accuracy, simplicity, coherence,* and *appropriateness* are well illustrated in the following brief, but vividly phrased, tribute to the memory of Wernher von Braun, renowned scientist and space pioneer. Written and presented by social observer Eric Sevareid on the *CBS Evening News,* June 17, 1977, the speech pays tribute to von Braun's accomplishments and dreams. A sense of linguistic accuracy is achieved through Sevareid's exacting selection of words which capture his sense precisely—for example, *"new-fashioned* rockets," *"moral* balance sheet," *"plodding* earth," *"fratricidal* war." A feeling of simplicity is apparent in his avoidance of technical space-age jargon and in his deceptively simple grammatical constructions. A sense of coherence is created by time references ("A generation ago" vs. "yesterday," "Charles Lindbergh, as a young man" vs. "now," "now" vs. "once"); these techniques bind past and present together, pointing to the future. And, most important, throughout there is a tone of appropriateness. America in 1977 was doubting its future in the face of the atomic weaponry von Braun was in part responsible for. Yet, Sevareid was able to overcome negative judgments some might make about this scientist by concentrating upon his sense of adventure and moral commitment. The resulting speech was thus appropriate to the man being honored, the man presenting it, and the audience for whom it was intended.

EULOGY FOR WERNHER VON BRAUN[3]
Eric Sevareid

A generation ago, the Allied military, using the old-fashioned airplane, did their best to kill the German, his associates, and their new-fashioned rockets, which were killing the people in London. Yesterday, Wernher von Braun, American citizen, died peacefully in George Washington's hometown of Alexandria, Virginia.

Without this man, Hitler would not have held out as long as he did; without him, Americans would not have got to the moon as soon as they did.

Counting up the moral balance sheet for this man's life would be a difficult exercise. The same could be said for the Wright brothers. Perhaps the exercise is meaningless. Airplanes would have come anyway from someone, somewhere, and so would modern rockets. And what was done with these instruments would have been equally beyond the control of the individuals who first made them work.

There's always a dream to begin with, and the dream is always benign. Charles Lindbergh, as a young man, saw the airplane, not only as an instrument to liberate man from the plodding earth, but as a force for peacefully uniting the human race through faster communication and the common adventure. Now its benefits are measured against its role in returning warfare to the savagery of the Middle Ages, burning whole cities with their occupants.

And rockets are now the easiest instrument for sending the ultimate atomic weapon against any spot on the globe. They've also put men into space; and von Braun, like Lindbergh with the upper atmosphere, saw goodness in that. He said once, when men manning an orbital station can view our planet as a planet among planets, on that day fratricidal war will be banished from the star on which we live.

Lindbergh was wrong about aircraft in the atmosphere; there's no reason to believe that von Braun was right about spacecraft in space.

Everything in space, von Braun said, obeys the laws of physics. If you know these laws and obey them, space will treat you kindly. The difficulty is that man brings the laws of his own nature into space. The issue is how man treats man. The problem does not lie in outer space, but where it's always been: on terra firma in inner man.

---

[3]"Eulogy for Werner von Braun" by Eric Sevareid. Copyright 1977 by CBS, Inc. Reprinted by permission of the Harold Matson Company, Inc.

LANGUAGE STRATEGIES

Following the dictates of effective language styles will help listeners comprehend and retain what you are saying, but you will often have speaking goals which extend beyond comprehension. Sometimes, ideas will be so new to some listeners that mere accuracy and simplicity will not be enough; at other times, "how you want them to feel" will be even more important than "what you want them to think." In these situations, you will want to use particular language strategies which often can forward your communicative goals as convincingly as solid supporting materials. After all, as social beings, we live in a "web of words"—in "mental pictures" of not only what the world "looks like" but even how it feels to live in it. Our beliefs, attitudes, and values are rooted not only in our direct experiences but also in our images.

There are countless language strategies available to speakers. We will review five of the most common and discuss ways they are used by effective speakers. These categories are: *definitions, restatements, imagery, language intensity,* and *metaphor.*

Definitions

In most speaking situations, audience members need fundamental definitions of concepts. You cannot expect them to understand ideas if the words are unfamiliar *or* if you're using words in a manner different from their generally accepted definition. Eight sorts of definitions are useful to speakers:

Defining from dictionaries. A dictionary definition is a *reportive* definition, one which indicates how people in general use a word. Dictionary definitions put an object or concept in a category and specify its characteristics: "An orange is a *fruit* [category] which is *round, orange* in color, and a member of the *citrus family* [characteristics]." Dictionary definitions sometimes help you learn an unfamiliar or technical word, but they are seldom helpful to speakers because they only use large categories and the most general characteristics in the defining clauses. So, dictionary definitions can provide you and your audience with a general orientation to an idea and its dimensions, but normally must be followed by other kinds of definitions that more precisely clarify a concept.

Defining in your own words. Occasionally, a word has so many meanings that speakers have to indicate which one they wish to use. In that case, you must use a *stipulative definition*—one that stipulates the way you will use a word: "By speech I mean the act of offering a series of ideas and arguments to a group of hearers in a face-to-face situation." Such a definition orients the audience to your subject matter. Furthermore, if you think an audience respects an authority or expert, you can use that person's stipulative definition (an *authoritative definition*): "Hyman Smith, president of this school, defines a *liberal arts education* as one in which students are taught, not merely technical operations and job-related skills, but rather ways of thinking and reasoning. Today, I want to explore that definition and what it means to you in your four years here."

Defining negatively.   Further clarity can be added by telling an audience how you are *not* going to use a term or concept—by using a *negative definition*. Along with the stipulative definition of speech, for example, we could have said: "By *speech* I do not mean to refer to the production of the 'correct' sounds and words of the English language, even though that is a common meaning of the word; rather, I will mean. . . ." Defining negatively can clear away possible misconceptions. Using a negative definition along with a stipulative definition is a technique that is especially useful when you are trying to treat a familiar concept in a novel or different way.

Defining from original sources.   Sometimes, you can reinforce a series of feelings or attitudes you wish an audience to have about a concept by telling them where the word came from: "*Sincere* comes from two Latin words, *sine* meaning 'without,' and *ceres* meaning 'wax.' In early Rome, a superior statue was one in which the artisan did not have to cover his mistakes by putting wax into flaws. That statue was said to be *sine ceres*—'without wax.' Today, the term, a 'sincere person,' carries some of that same meaning. . . ." This is called an *etymological definition* when you trace a word's meaning back into its original language. It's termed a *genetic definition* when you explain where the idea rather than the word comes from. You could, for instance, explain the American concept of "freedom of speech" by looking at important discussions of that idea in eighteenth-century England, and then showing how the American doctrine took its shape from our ancestors' British experiences. Defining from original sources, either of the word or of the idea, gives an audience a sense of continuity and at times explains certain nuances of meaning we cannot explain in any other way.

Defining by examples.   Particularly if a notion is unfamiliar or technical, one of the best ways to define is an *exemplar definition*—one that simply points to a familiar example: "Each day, most of you stroll past Old Capitol on your way to classes. That building is a perfect example of what I want to talk about today—Georgian architecture." Be careful only to pick defining examples that your audience members will be familiar with.

Defining by context.   You also can define a word or concept by putting it in its usual context—through a *contextual definition*. This can be done verbally, as when a speaker says: "The difference between the words *imply* and *infer* is best understood in this way: The person generating a message *implies* a meaning; an observer *infers* an interpretation. Thus, *you* imply some idea or feeling in what you say, while *I* draw inferences about what you meant." A contextual definition also can go beyond such verbal descriptions, and, like a definition which uses examples, can point to a "real" context: "While there are many possible meanings to the word *revolution*, today I want to use it to describe the kinds of events which produced the American Revolution." You then would go on to specify those sorts of events. Defining by context gives an audience a sense of meaningfulness, and is a good tactic for making certain kinds of concepts concrete.

Defining by analogy.   Still another means for making technical or abstract notions easier to understand is the *analogical definition*. An analogy compares a process or event that is unfamiliar or unknown with something that is familiar or known: "Perhaps you can better understand this school's registration procedure if you think of it as an assembly line. First, raw materials (student identification cards, registration forms, lists of available classes and times) are brought into the plant (our fieldhouse). Then, those materials are shaped by skilled craftsmen (advisors, departmental representatives, and you). Next the needed adjustments are put together to make the product (your schedule). And finally, the completed product is checked by quality control people (representatives of the dean's office). Let's go through these steps one at a time." By relying upon a familiar concept or process, the analogical definition can make the unfamiliar idea much easier to grasp. Be sure, however, that the essential features of the two compared objects or processes are more similar than different. Don't confuse an audience with an analogy that doesn't fit.

Defining by describing operations.   Some words or concepts are best defined by reviewing the operations or procedures used in making or measuring something—by offering an *operational definition*. For example, we have no good way of defining *intelligence* with words. Rather, we usually define it in terms of how it is measured: "*Intelligence quotient* is a person's score on the Wechsler-Bellevue Intelligence Test compared with the scores of other members of the population." Along with exemplar and analogical definitions, operational definitions are especially good for making an audience "see" an idea or process.

Restatement

Were accuracy and simplicity your only criteria as an oral communicator wishing to convey meanings clearly, messages might resemble the famous bulletin of World War II: "Sighted sub, sank same." But because you are working with your listeners face-to-face, in oral and not written language, another criterion becomes important. Restatement, as we use the term, is intentional repetition of two kinds: (1) *rephrasing* of ideas or concepts in more than one set of words or sentences, and (2) *reiteration* of ideas or concepts from more than one point of view. Because words literally disappear into the atmosphere as soon as you speak them, as an oral communicator you do not have the writer's advantage when transmitting ideas to others. Instead, you must rely heavily upon rephrasing and re-examination.

Rephrasing.   The effect of skillful rephrasing to clarify a message and make it more specific can be seen in the following passage from John F. Kennedy's inaugural address:

> Let the word go forth from this time and place, to friend and foe alike, that the torch has been passed to a new generation of Americans—born in this century, tempered by war, disciplined by a hard and bitter peace, proud of our ancient heritage—and unwilling to witness or permit the slow undoing of those human rights to which this nation has always been committed, and to which we are committed today at home and around the world.
>
> Let every nation know, whether it wishes us well or ill, that we shall pay any price, bear any burden, meet any hardship, support any friend, oppose any foe to assure the survival and the success of liberty.[4]

Reiteration.   Reiterating an idea from a number of perspectives usually can be done by reformulating the elements that make it up or by redefining the basic concept. You can see this principle of reiteration at work in the following excerpt from a student speech. Note how the speaker defines and redefines "political image" in a variety of ways, thereby providing metaphorical, psychological, and sociological perspectives:

> A "politician's image" is really a set of characteristics attributed to that politician by an electorate [*formal perspective*]. A political image, like any image which comes off a mirror, is made up of attributes which reflect the audience's concerns [*metaphorical perspective*]. An image is composed of bits and pieces of information and feelings which an audience brings to a politician [*psychological perspective*], and therefore it represents judgments made by the electorate

---

[4]From *Public Papers of the Presidents of the United States: John F. Kennedy.* Washington, D.C.: U.S. Government Printing Office, 1961.

on the bases of a great many different verbal and nonverbal acts a politician has engaged in [*sociological perspective*]. Therefore, if you think of a political image only in terms of manipulation, you are looking only at the mirror. Step back and examine the beholder, too, and you will find ways of discovering what a "good" image is for a politician.

If carefully handled, restatement in the form of rephrasing or reiteration may help you clarify ideas and help your listeners remember these ideas more readily. Be careful, however, of mindless repetition—too many restatements, especially restatements of ideas already clear to any alert member of your audience, are sure to be boring.

Imagery

We receive our impressions of the world around us through sensations of sight, smell, hearing, taste, and touch. If your listeners are to experience the object or state of affairs you are describing, you must, therefore, appeal to their senses. But you cannot punch them in the nose, scatter exotic perfume for them to smell, or let them taste foods which are not present. The primary senses through which you as a speaker can reach your listeners *directly* are the visual and the auditory: they can see you, your movements, your facial expressions, and objects you use as "visual aids"; and they can hear what you say.

Despite this limitation, however, you can *indirectly* stimulate all of the senses of your listeners by using language that has the power to produce imagined sensations, or which causes them to recall images they have previously experienced. Through image-evoking language, you can help your hearers create many of the sensory "pictures" and "events" that you yourself have experienced or encountered. Through vivid words, you can project the desired image swiftly into the "mind's eye" of your listeners. The language of imagery is divided into seven classes, or types, each related to the particular sensation that it seeks to evoke. They are:

1. Visual *(sight)*
2. Auditory *(hearing)*
3. Gustatory *(taste)*
4. Olfactory *(smell)*
5. Tactual *(touch)*
   a. Texture and shape
   b. Pressure
   c. Heat and cold
6. Kinesthetic *(muscle strain)*
7. Organic *(internal sensations)*

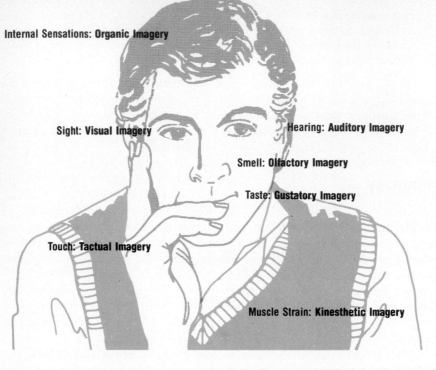

Internal Sensations: **Organic Imagery**

Sight: **Visual Imagery**

Hearing: **Auditory Imagery**

Smell: **Olfactory Imagery**

Taste: **Gustatory Imagery**

Touch: **Tactual Imagery**

Muscle Strain: **Kinesthetic Imagery**

Types of Imagery: "Doorways to the Mind"

Visual Imagery. Try to make your audience actually "see" the objects or situations you are describing. Mention *size, shape, color,* and *movement*. Recount events in vivid visual language. For example, in a time of "cold war" between the United States and Russia, General of the Army Douglas MacArthur knew he had to steel the cadets of the United States Military Academy for their uncertain future. His central theme—"duty, honor, and country"—was a refrain through the speech. To give that theme life, however, General MacArthur relied upon a variety of visual images in his view of the dedicated soldier stressing size, shape, color, and movement:

> In twenty campaigns, on a hundred battlefields, around a thousand campfires, I have witnessed that enduring fortitude, that patriotic self-abnegation, and that invincible determination which have carved his statue in the hearts of his people.
>
> From one end of the world to the other, he has drained deep the chalice of courage. As I listened to those songs in memory's eye I could see those

staggering columns of the First World War, bending under soggy packs on many a weary march, from dripping dusk to drizzly dawn, slogging ankle deep through mire of shell-pocked roads; to form grimly for the attack, blue-lipped, covered with sludge and mud, chilled by the wind and rain, driving home to their objective, and for many, to the judgment seat of God.

. . . Always for them: Duty, honor, country. Always their blood, and sweat and tears, as they saw the way and the light. And twenty years after, on the other side of the globe, again the filth of dirty foxholes, the stench of ghostly trenches, the slime of dripping dugouts, those boiling suns of relentless heat, those torrential rains of devastating storms, the loneliness and utter desolation of jungle trails, the bitterness of long separation of those they loved and cherished, the deadly pestilence of tropical disease, the horror of stricken areas of war.

Their resolute and determined defense, their swift and sure attack, their indomitable purpose, their complete and decisive victory, always through the bloody haze of their last reverberating shot, the vision of gaunt, ghastly men, reverently following your password of duty, honor, country.[5]

Auditory Imagery.   Through auditory imagery, speakers use words which help their listeners actually "hear" what they are describing. Auditory imagery may be used to project an audience into a scene, as Tom Wolfe does in the following example, where he is describing the opening of a "demolition derby":

Then the entire crowd, about 4,000, started chanting a countdown, "Ten, nine, eight, seven, six, five, four, three, two," but it was impossible to hear the rest, because right after "two" half the crowd went into a strange whinnying wail. The starter's flag went up, and the 25 cars took off, roaring into second gear with no mufflers, all headed toward that same point in the center of the infield, converging nose on nose.

The effect was exactly what one expects that many simultaneous crashes to produce: the unmistakable tympany of automobiles colliding and cheap-gauge sheet metal buckling.[6]

Gustatory Imagery.   Sometimes you may even be able to help your audience imagine the *taste* of what you are describing. Mention its saltiness, sweetness, sourness, or its spicy flavor. Observe how Jane Bochman, a

---

[5]Excerpts from "Duty, Honor and Country" by Douglas MacArthur in *The Dolphin Book of Speeches*, edited by George W. Hibbitt. Copyright © 1965 by George W. Hibbitt. Reprinted by permission of Doubleday & Company, Inc.

[6]A selection from *The Kandy-Kolored Tangerine-Flake Streamline Baby* by Tom Wolfe. Copyright © 1963, 1965 by Thomas K. Wolfe, Jr. Copyright © 1963 by New York Herald Tribune, Inc. Reprinted with the permission of Farrar, Straus & Giroux, Inc. and International Creative Management.

student at the University of Iowa, describes the taste of granola not only to stimulate the imagination of her listeners, but also to appeal to their aesthetic values:

> Few people forget their first taste of homemade granola. Unlike the commercial varieties, which are so heavily sugar-coated that they are almost indistinguishable from the usual Kellogg's products, homemade granola provides you with confusing sensations. The sweetness of honey is mixed with the saltiness of nuts. The rolled oats have a mealiness which contrasts sharply with the firmness of whole grain wheat. Your tongue bravely battles both stringy coconut and small, firm flax seeds. Overall, the first impression of sweet treats is followed by a lingering sourness. Your system as well as your taste buds are pleasantly awakened as you do early morning encounter with nature's best. If you have not had these experiences, then you obviously have not been making use of the health food store down the street.[7]

Olfactory Imagery.   Help your audience smell the odors connected with the situation you describe. Do this not only by mentioning the odor itself, but also by describing the object that has the odor or by comparing it with more familiar ones, as shown in this example:

> As he opened the door of the old apothecary's shop, he breathed the odor of medicines, musty, perhaps, and pungent from too close confinement in so small a place, but free from the sickening smell of stale candy and cheap perfume.

Such associations also allow your audience to make positive or negative judgments about the experience.

Tactual Imagery.   Tactual imagery is based upon the various types of sensation that we get through physical contact with an object. Particularly it gives us sensations of *texture* and *shape, pressure,* and *heat* and *cold.*

Texture and shape.   Enable your audience to feel how rough or smooth, dry or wet, or sharp, slimy, or sticky a thing is.

Pressure.   Phrase appropriate portions of your speech in such a way that your auditors sense the pressure of physical force upon their bodies: The weight of a heavy trunk borne upon their backs, the pinching of shoes that are too tight, the incessant drive of the high wind on their faces.

Heat and cold.   These sensations are aroused by what is sometimes called "thermal" imagery.

Review the excerpt from Douglas MacArthur's speech on page 172 for some vivid examples of tactual imagery.

---

[7]From a speech given at the University of Iowa, winter term, 1982. Reprinted with the permission of Ms. Bochman.

Kinesthetic Imagery.   Kinesthetic imagery describes the sensations associated with muscle strain and neuromuscular movement. Phrase suitable portions of your speech in such a way that your listeners may feel for themselves the stretching, tightening, and jerking of muscles and tendons, the creaking of their joints.

Jason Elliot, a student at the University of Iowa, makes skillful use of kinesthetic imagery to describe the experience of jogging:

> Even if you've gone through a brief warmup, early morning jogging can be a jolt to both mind and body. As you start, you first notice tiny cramps in your lower legs. Then, small, shooting pains begin to work their way upward, and you soon realize your knee sockets are literally pounding with each step. The muscles in your thighs complain bitterly about having to bear the brunt of the effort. Just when you think you're starting to get your legs under control, you notice that your chest is not happy about the whole affair, either. You feel like you have two cement blocks resting squarely on it; the arteries leading from your heart threaten to burst; your lungs seem to search in vain for a little more oxygen. Your breathing comes in gulps and gasps. But then almost magically, something happens: your legs feel like they could keep going forever, and your breathing becomes regular and painless. Serenity and tranquility set in, and you finally can occupy your mind with the landscape, the sunrise, the day's activities. You remember why you started jogging in the first place.[8]

Organic Imagery.   Hunger, dizziness, nausea—these are a few of the feelings organic imagery calls forth. There are times when an image is not complete without the inclusion of specific details likely to evoke these inner feelings in listeners. Be careful, however, not to offend your audience by making the picture too revolting. Develop the sensitivity required to measure the detail necessary for creating vividness without making the resultant image so gruesome that it becomes either disgusting or grotesque. Observe how H. G. Wells has made use of organic imagery to create a desired effect:

> That climb seemed interminable to me. With the last twenty or thirty feet of it a deadly nausea came upon me. I had the greatest difficulty in keeping my hold. The last few yards was a frightful struggle against this faintness. Several times my head swam, and I felt all the sensations of falling. At last, however, I got over the well-mouth somehow and staggered out of the ruin into the blinding sunlight.[9]

---

[8]From a speech given at the University of Iowa, fall term, 1981. Reprinted with the permission of Mr. Elliot.

[9]H. G. Wells, "The Time Machine," *The Complete Short Stories of H. G. Wells* (London: Ernest Benn, Ltd., 1927), p. 59.

The seven types of imagery we have considered—*visual, auditory, gustatory, olfactory, tactual, kinesthetic,* and *organic*—may be referred to as "doorways to the mind."[10] They function to open the audience to new levels of awareness in understanding and believing speakers and acting on their messages. Because people differ in their degrees of sensitivity to different types of imagery, you should try to build into your messages as many appeals to their senses of these perceptual "doorways" as possible.

In the following example, note how the speaker has *combined* various sensory appeals to arouse listener interest and reaction:

> The strangler struck in Donora, Pennsylvania, in October of 1948. A thick fog billowed through the streets enveloping everything in thick sheets of dirty moisture and a greasy black coating. As Tuesday faded into Saturday, the fumes from the big steel mills shrouded the outlines of the landscape. One could barely see across the narrow streets. Traffic stopped. Men lost their way returning from the mills. Walking through the streets, even for a few moments, caused eyes to water and burn. The thick fumes grabbed at the throat and created a choking sensation. The air acquired a sickening bittersweet smell, nearly a taste. Death was in the air.[11]

In this example, college student Charles Schaillol uses vivid, descriptive phrases to affect the senses of his listeners: *visual*—"thick sheets of dirty moisture"; *organic*—"eyes to water and burn"; *olfactory, gustatory*—"sickening bittersweet smell, nearly a taste."

To be effective, such illustrations must appear *plausible:* the language must convey an impression that what is being described did or could happen in the way the speaker chooses to tell about it. The "strangler" that struck Donora offers a plausible account of the event. More importantly, it does so in a fashion that arouses feelings. Audiences would not be as likely to share the experience if the speaker had simply said, "Air pollution was the cause of death in Donora."

Language Intensity

As a speaker, your word choice is determined partially by the way you feel about the object you are describing and the strength or *intensity* of that feeling. That is, by word or phrase you often communicate your *attitude*

---

[10]Victor Alvin Ketcham, "The Seven Doorways to the Mind," in *Business Speeches by Business Men,* ed. William P. Sandford and W. Hayes Yeager (New York: McGraw-Hill Book Company, 1930).

[11]From "The Strangler" by Charles Schaillol. Reprinted from *Winning Orations* by special arrangement with the Interstate Oratorical Association, Larry Schnoor, Executive Secretary, Mankato State College, Mankato, Minnesota.

Word choices reflect our feelings about objects, events, or persons, and express our attitudes toward them. Our vocabularies, thus, reflect our experiences and reactions to those experiences. To some who've had negative experiences, a policeman is "a pig"; to others with more or less neutral experiences, "a public official"; and to others who've had positive experiences, "a nice person who helped."

toward it. Consider, for example, the following "attitudinally weighted" terms:

Relatively Positive
{
"officers of the law"
"safety officials"
"men in blue"
}

Relatively Neutral
{
"traffic officials"
"police personnel"
"cops"
}

Relatively Negative
{
"the brass"
"the fuzz"
"pigs"
}

These nine terms are roughly rank-ordered according to their intensity, ranging from the highly positive "officers of the law" to the highly negative "pigs." These are examples of attitudinally weighted statements with highly positive, relatively neutral, or highly negative language intensity. Such language choices signal the intensity of your attitude toward a subject to your listeners.

How intense should your language be? This will depend on the issue position of your listeners. Professor John Waite Bowers has suggested a useful rule of thumb: Let your language be, roughly, one step more intense than the position or attitude of your audience.[12] If your audience seems generally neutral toward your idea or proposal, make your key pieces of language slightly positive or slightly negative in the degree of intensity you employ. If your audience already is committed, say, to your positive position on reform, then you can afford to make your language quite intense. In general, audiences that are hostile to your proposal will reject highly intense language; audiences sympathetic to your views will not be negatively affected by your use of "loaded" language.

Metaphor

The images created by appealing to the various senses often use *metaphors*—words which suggest a comparison between two dissimilar things. Charles Schaillol's "fog . . . thick sheets" is one example of a metaphor used to illuminate the image he wished to create of the fog's effect. To be successful, as Michael Osborn notes, the metaphor should "result in an intuitive flash of recognition that surprises or fascinates the hearer."[13] Furthermore, good metaphors should extend our knowledge or increase our awareness of a person, object, or event. A reference to a table's "legs" may illuminate the object, but it lacks any fascination. When they are fresh or vivid, metaphors can be powerful aids to the evoking of feelings in listeners (e.g., "balanced on four obese toothpicks, the antique table swayed under the heavy load"). Their potency cannot be discounted, nor can their prevalence as descriptive labels for people or events be ignored.

While vividness and freshness can make metaphors highly appealing to audiences, on other occasions you will want to employ metaphors drawn from everyday or common experiences. In almost every public speech he delivered, for example, Martin Luther King, Jr., appealed to our experiences of lightness and darkness, as he did in the following quotation:

With this faith in the future, with this determined struggle, we will be able to

[12]John Waite Bowers, "Language and Argument," in *Perspectives on Argumentation,* ed. G. R. Miller and T. R. Nilsen (Glenview, Ill.: Scott, Foresman and Company, 1966), esp. pp. 168–172.

[13]Michael Osborn, *Orientations to Rhetorical Style* (Chicago: Science Research Associates, 1976), p. 10.

emerge from the bleak and desolate midnight of man's inhumanity to man, into the bright and glittering daybreak of freedom and justice.[14]

This simple light-dark metaphor was important to King's thinking and speechmaking because it allowed him to suggest (1) sharp contrasts between inhumanity and freedom, and (2) the inevitability of social progress (as "daybreak" always follows "midnight"). In other words, the metaphor "worked"—it worked in communicating King's beliefs about justice and injustice, and in urging a course of action upon his followers.

In summary, words are not neutral conduits-for-thought. Words not only reflect the "real" world outside your mind, but they also, as rhetorical critic Kenneth Burke suggests, help to *shape* our perceptions of people, events, and social contexts. It is clear that language has a potent effect on people's willingness to believe, to feel, and to act. Wording the speech, therefore, for you becomes a matter of both adopting a linguistic style appropriate to the demands of oral communication, so as to increase accuracy, simplicity, coherence, and an audience's sense of "rightness"; and of employing such language strategies as definitions, restatements, imagery, varied language intensity, and metaphors to recreate within audiences the understandings and feelings you yourself have.

GROUP PROJECTS

1. For practice in conveying material accurately, yet with simplicity, you and the members of your task group should rewrite a complicated message (e.g., an insurance policy, agreement for a credit card or loan, income tax form).

2. Hold a small-group discussion on the use and/or abuse of language. Choose from these related topics:

(*a*) discussions concerning death   (*c*) terminology of sports announcers
(*b*) computer language   (*d*) "lines" used to seduce

3. Can a change in the use of language influence a change in attitudes? In developing an answer to this question, consider such examples as the feminists' emphasis on using non-sexist terms, the "black is beautiful" aspect of modern black nationalism, the use of positive labels for describing employment ("sanitary engineer" for the person picking up the trash, "public relations counsel" for an individual getting favorable publicity for a client).

---

[14]From "Love, Law and Civil Disobedience" by Martin Luther King, Jr. Copyright © 1961, 1963 by Martin Luther King, Jr. Reprinted by permission of Joan Daves.

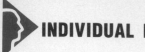

INDIVIDUAL PROJECTS

1. Construct a two- to three-minute story utilizing as many clichés and mixed metaphors and as much slang as you can. Derive your topic for this exaggerated narrative from the category of animal, vegetable, or mineral. Read your narrative to the class, and do not be surprised if your classmates can think of even more overused and misused expressions relating to your topic.

2. What connective phrase might you use to join (a) a major idea with a subordinate one, (b) a less important idea with a more important one, (c) two ideas of equal importance, (d) ideas comparable in meaning, and (e) contrasting or opposing ideas? If, in the next outline you develop, you encounter any of these five structures (a–e), use the connectives you have just proposed. How effective are the connective phrases in these instances? Would other words/phrases appear to work better?

3. Write a three- to four-minute speech narrating your feelings about a particular location. For instance, you might describe the town in which you grew up, a building you always dreamed of seeing, or a place made famous by one of your favorite authors. Present the speech from manuscript. Carefully revise your manuscript to take advantage of the suggestions made in this chapter. In particular, make generous use of varied and vivid imagery, appropriate words with connotative effect, and clear and graceful connective phrases.

SUGGESTIONS FOR FURTHER READING

Kenneth Boulding, "Introduction to 'The Image,'" in *Dimensions in Communication: Readings*, 2nd ed., eds. James H. Campbell and Hal W. Hepler (Belmont, Ca.: Wadsworth Publishing Company, Inc., 1970), pp. 26–35.

Gary L. Cronkhite, *Public Speaking and Critical Listening* (Menlo Park, Ca.: The Benjamin-Cummings Publishing Co., Inc., 1978), Chapter 10, "Language and Style."

Abne M. Eisenberg, *Living Communication* (Englewood Cliffs, N.J.: Prentice-Hall, Inc., 1975), pp. 149–180.

Dan P. Millar and Frank E. Millar, *Messages and Myths: Understanding Interpersonal Communication* (Port Washington, N.Y.: Alfred Publishing Co., Inc., 1976), Chapter 6, "Openness and Self-Disclosure."

Michael Osborn, *Orientation to Rhetorical Style* (Chicago: SRA, 1976).

CHAPTER 9

Visually Illustrating the Speech

In the mid-1960s, when Marshall McLuhan asserted that American culture was returning to a tribal state, he was recognizing the power of electronic visual communication to bring together diverse peoples and ideas.[1] Humanity, we can safely assume, invented visual art long before it concocted the arbitrary system of signs we call language; and human beings, we are discovering through careful observation, are capable of effective visual communication long before they begin to communicate verbally.

Visual communication, indeed, is fast becoming a well-developed and important area of scholarly and practical study. The Gestalt psychologists in the 1930s and 1940s offered us our first systematic theories concerning how people learn to perceive and interpret visual media; and the growth of the visual-media industries (film, television, and photographic reproduction) spurred studies of psychological and social conditions which maximize visual

---

[1] Marshall McLuhan, *Understanding Media: The Extensions of Man* (New York: McGraw-Hill Book Company, 1965).

learning and information-intake.[2] Such ongoing research is of vital importance to a world in which computers can reproduce information spatially and
in which copying machines put faithful duplicates of originals in the hands of
consumers almost instantly.

The study of visual communication is especially important to the public
speaker because it relates to oral communication in two significant ways. (1)
As we will discuss, the human body itself is a visual message, one which is
"read" by an information-seeking audience; and (2) as a speaker you are
frequently faced with questions concerning visual aids or visual supporting
materials: Should I employ visual aids? If so, what kind? How big? When
should I introduce a picture, a bar graph, or a working model? Should I as a
speaker look at the chalkboard or the audience? These are eminently
practical questions about everyday speechmaking. Systematic research has
not offered answers to all such questions, but it is far enough along to show
you that the visual portions of your speech deserve as much of your time,
effort, and skill as the verbal portions.

THE FUNCTIONS OF VISUAL MATERIALS

Visual materials serve the speaker in two important ways: (1) they aid
listener comprehension and memory; (2) they add persuasive impact to a
message.

Comprehension and Memory

Well-executed visuals can significantly aid your auditors' comprehension of
your message. If a picture is worth a thousand words, then it is useful
principally because it adds important information that is more easily

---

[2]The general theories of Gestalt psychology are clearly reviewed in Ernest R. Hilgard,
Theories of Learning, 4th ed. (Englewood Cliffs, N.J.: Prentice-Hall, Inc., 1975). Their
applications in areas of visual communication can be found, among other places, in Rudolph
Arnheim, *Visual Thinking* (Berkeley: University of California Press, 1969); John M. Kenne-
dy, *A Psychology of Picture Perception* (San Francisco: Jossey-Bass, Inc., Publishers, 1973);
Leonard Zusne, *Visual Perception of Form* (New York: Academic Press, Inc., 1976);
E. Heidt, *Instructional Media and the Individual Learner* (New York: Nichols, 1976);
Carolyn M. Bloomer, *Principles of Visual Perception* (New York: Van Nostrand Reinhold
Co., 1976); Vernon S. Gerlach and Donald P. Ely, *Teaching and Media: A Systematic
Approach*, 2nd ed. (Englewood Cliffs, N.J.: Prentice-Hall, Inc., 1980); Les Satterthwaite,
Graphics: Skills, Media and Materials, 4th ed. (Dubuque, Ia.: Kendall/Hunt, 1980); and
Gavriel Salomon, *Interaction of Media, Cognition, and Learning* (San Francisco: Jossey-Bass,
Inc. 1979).

understood visually than aurally. Visual research has demonstrated that bar graphs, especially, make statistical information more accessible to an audience, that simple (as opposed to complicated) drawings enhance recall, and that charts and even "human interest" visuals (especially photographs) help an audience retain data. Indeed, in some cases, the ideas you are talking about may be essentially "visual" ideas, for example, brush strokes used by painters, the topography of Tibet, or the spectral—color—analysis of gases on faraway planets. In these situations, mere words would not suffice to let your listeners understand your message.

Persuasiveness

A growing body of literature supports the notion that visual aids, in addition to enhancing comprehension and memory, may actually heighten the persuasive effects of speeches. Undeniably, a speaker's credibility—the audience's perception of the speaker's good sense, trustworthiness, and dynamism—is positively affected by appropriate visuals. Moreover, certain types of messages—especially those which can be supported by facts, figures, and examples—are strengthened by visual support.[3]

In other words, whereas we normally think of "supporting materials" (see Chapter 5) as verbal constructs or ideas, it is also advantageous to consider visual aids as useful, even necessary, supporting materials. That is, they add more than entertaining or aesthetically pleasing qualities to a speech. With care, they can be so integrated into a public presentation as to play a major role in oral instruction and persuasion. Ours is a culture which often wants to be "shown." Visual materials, then, often are crucial means by which speakers can achieve their purposes.[4]

---

[3]For more specific studies of the effects of various sorts of visual materials, see F. M. Dwyer, "Exploratory Studies in the Effectiveness of Visual Illustrations," *AV Communication Review*, 18 (1970), 235–240; G. D. Feliciano, R. D. Powers, and B. E. Kearle, "The Presentation of Statistical Information," *AV Communication Review*, 11 (1963), 32–39; William J. Seiler, "The Effects of Visual Materials on Attitudes, Credibility, and Retention," *Speech* [Communication] *Monographs*, 38 (November 1971), 331–334; M. D. Vernon, "Presenting Information in Diagrams," *AV Communication Review*, 1 (1953), 147–158; L. V. Peterson and Wilbur Schramm, "How Accurately Are Different Kinds of Graphs Read?", *AV Communication Review*, 2 (1955), 178–189; Alan G. Chute, "Effect of Color and Monochrome Versions of a Film on Incidental and Task-Relevant Learning," *Educational Communication and Technology Journal*, 26 (1980), 10–18; and Marilyn J. Haring and Maurine A. Fry, "Effect of Pictures on Children's Comprehension of Written Text," *Educational Communication and Technology Journal*, 27 (1979), 185–90.

[4]For clear explorations of the relationships between ideas and visuals, see Sol Worth, "Pictures Can't Say Ain't," *Versus*, 12 (1975), 85–108; and Edgar B. Wycoff, "Why Visuals?", *AV Communications*, 11 (1977), 39, 59.

THE SELECTION AND USE
OF VISUAL MATERIALS

Given the fact that as a resourceful speaker you can employ a number of different types of visuals, you must make some careful choices. These choices usually should be based on four factors: (1) *your own personality and purposes*, (2) *the communicative potential of each type of visual material*, (3) *proper integration of verbal and visual materials*, and (4) *the nature of the audience and the occasion.*

Start with Your Self

Visual materials may contribute in important ways to your audience's perception of you as a person—your concerns, your values, your feelings, and your ideas. A speech on scrimshawing, with examples of objects that you have carved from whalebones, not only tells an audience that you have certain skills and hobbies, but also indicates your attitudes toward the preservation of folk culture. The bar graphs you utilize in a speech on inflation not only demonstrate support for your proposition, but also represent your attitudes toward concrete, summary data. Visual aids, especially those you prepare in color and detail, communicate both your forethought (you cared enough for your audience to make something for them) and, perhaps, a measure of your ingenuity and flair for the artistic. Because visual supporting materials are presented as a *part* of the total communication process, you reveal much about yourself by what you show an audience. They express *you* while, at the same time, help you express and support your ideas.

Consider the Communicative Potential
of Various Visual Materials

Keep in mind, of course, that each type of visual material has certain potentials for communicating particular kinds of information and feelings, and that each type interacts with your *spoken* presentation as well as your audience's state of mind. In preparing speech materials of this kind, remember that often pictorial or photographic visuals can make an audience feel the way you do. Aids such as slides, movies, sketches, and photographs can be used effectively to accompany travelogs or reports of personal experiences because they evoke in others the kinds of *feelings* you experienced in another place, situation, or time.

Visuals containing descriptive or verbal materials, on the other hand, can help an audience *think* the way you do. In contrast to pictorial materials, such aids as cutaways, models, diagrams, charts, and dittoed summaries of statistical data frequently add *rational support* to propositions you are trying to defend. The nature of your topic and your communicative purpose, therefore, play a large role in determining the kinds of visuals you ought to employ in a given circumstance. A speech informing listeners of your experiences in Indonesia should probably be accompanied by slides or films and even some household artifacts. A speech to persuade your listeners that the United States ought to sever all association with the North Atlantic Treaty Organization probably should be supported by maps, charts, and chalkboard drawings.

Integrate Verbal and Visual Materials Effectively

As you make your decisions about the visual elements you will use to support and illustrate your speech, *choose only those objects and materials which are relevant to your speech topic and communicative purpose.* In other words, be sure that your visual materials will work *for*, and not *against*, you. Some visuals, if not selected carefully, may distract, frustrate, or actually anger an audience. You can guard against such negative and unintended effects by making sure you:

1. *Painstakingly prepare all of your visual aids well in advance of your speech.* Carefully think through your aids using familiar shapes (for example, the pie) and contrasting colors (red on white, blue on yellow, etc.), and make sure that the image, concept, steps, or other constituent elements—the things you really wish to emphasize—are immediately and strikingly visible.

2. *Keep charts, diagrams, and other graphic aids clear and simple.* Research has demonstrated that plain bar graphs—probably because they offer not only numbers but also a visualization of numbers through the use of "bars"—are the single most effective method for displaying statistical comparisons.[5] Let simplicity be your watchword in the preparation of all visual aids. Cut away extraneous information, however interesting, and display your material in clear simple form—bars, pies, and pictures.

3. *Make your visuals—especially those with materials which must be read or scrutinized closely—large enough to be seen clearly and easily.* Listeners—especially those in the back rows—get frustrated when, in the

text continues on page 188

---

[5]See especially the Vernon and the Peterson and Schram articles (n. 3) for further advice.

TYPES OF VISUAL SUPPORT

The Object Itself: If it is portable and intricate, the object itself may be brought to the podium. The correct use of an optical microscope could hardly be explained without having an actual instrument at hand. The adjustment of focus, of the eyepiece, and of the illumination sources would not be clear unless the audience could clearly see how to do it. Furthermore, the object creates a level of interest often impossible to generate with words alone. And, audience participation can be fostered if you hand out pieces of paper for a speech on origami, or samples of "chocolate" chip cookies made from carob chips.

The Use of Your Self: Many topics provide subjects for physical demonstrations. Speeches on yoga positions, ballet steps, or tennis strokes gain concreteness and vitality from speakers who illustrate their subjects personally.

Models: If an object is too large to bring into the room or too small to be seen easily, you will want to use a model. Small-scale models of geodesic domes, for example, could illustrate the home of the future for certain audiences; large-scale models of molecules could add specificity to something normally invisible.

Slides: Even though they require projection equipment and darkened rooms, slide projectors or overhead projectors give many speakers the added advantage of showing shape, color, texture, and relationships. It would be almost impossible to communicate a painter's or a sculptor's style without such aids.

Films: Films add other dimensions to a talk—moving, changing relationships or vivid illustrations. A speech on the disintegration of families would gain considerable force if you showed a clip from *The Failing Marriage;* a discussion of creativity would profit immeasurably from showing a segment of *Why Man Creates.*

Chalkboard Drawings: By now, you have been conditioned to "reading the board" in school. Chalkboards are often substituted for more permanent illustrators by lazy speakers, but, more important, they are especially valuable when you wish to "unfold" an idea, step-by-step, before an audience, or when you suddenly feel the need to depict an idea or process you thought would be clearly understood merely through words. So, supervisors often lay out next month's sales campaign step-by-step on the board, and a football coach occasionally discovers that the breakdown in trap blocking must be sketched out.

Graphs: Graphs take several different forms. *Bar* graphs show the relationship of two or more sets of figures. Figures comparing the income of various professionals, for example, are well illustrated with bar graphs. *Line* graphs show relations between two or more variable facts. Economists are fond of showing the disparities between "real" and "actual" income by plotting across time average real and actual incomes of consumers. *Pie* graphs show percentages of a circle divided proportionately; for example, a charitable organization uses a pie graph to point out how it spends its contributions (wages/salaries/campaigns/target projects, each being a "wedge" in the pie). And, *pictorial* graphs show relative amounts by size or number of symbols. A nutritionist will, for example, make concrete the amount of meat consumed per capita in various countries with a chart containing a "small" cow for India, a larger one for Sweden, and a still larger beast for the United States.

Diagrams: To avoid the problems of drawing on chalkboards, many speakers will prepare flipcharts or tagboard diagrams before delivering the speech. A *cutaway* diagram of an object—say, a four-cycle engine—can display the inner workings of an automobile. A *three-dimensional* diagram can illustrate complex relationships otherwise difficult to comprehend; posters available at your local planetarium are often of this variety.

Organizational Charts or Tables of Organization: Business executives and governmental representatives virtually make their living by preparing and talking from organizational charts. In these days of highly complex organizations, businesses, and bureaus, we all profit from the visualization of power and personal relationships in this way.

Mimeographed, Dittoed, Photocopied, or Printed Information: You certainly can hand out statistical information, suggestions for later actions, addresses of organizations or persons who should be written to, or stages in an intricate process. Such materials can be studied later, used to jog memories, and employed in follow-up actions. They are especially important when you want your audience to remember the seven danger signs of cancer, to write their congressional representatives, or to vote on a specific resolution or motion.

For illustrations of some of these types of nonverbal supporting materials, see pages 188 and 189.

middle of the speech, they suddenly notice that they are having to lean forward and squint in order to see a detail on a sketch or diagram. Make your figures and lettering large enough so that, as John Hancock noted in connection with the Declaration of Independence in 1776, they "can be seen by the King of England without his glasses."

4. *In preparing to present visually the details of an object, device, or process, decide well in advance whether to bring in the object or device itself or a model of it.* This is especially pertinent to the so-called "demonstration" speech. For instance, if you have practiced a particular craft or mastered a certain skill and wish to communicate the details or steps in the creative process, you probably will want to show a working sample or product of that process. This can be effective; but when you elect to do it, keep in mind throughout the demonstration speech that the *object* or *process model* is "communicating" at the same time and very possibly as much as you are. It is telling the audience: "Here's what it is." "Here's why it's worth your while," etc. Take pains to ensure, therefore, that everyone in your audience can

The message you communicate to others is actually made up of multiple messages presented via many channels of communication. This means that speakers must (1) make all of those messages say the same or complementary things, and (2) use all available channels to improve communicative effectiveness.

Visual materials may compete with you for the audience's attention. Therefore, especially when using filmed and projected visual materials, (1) talk a bit more loudly, (2) increase your movement, and/or (3) alternate "telling" and "showing."

clearly see the object or device—perhaps even handle it. This latter possibility gives rise to a fifth precaution.

5. *Be prepared to compensate orally for any distraction your visual aid may inadvertently create among your audience.* If you do pass around a sample of your work—a purse you have beaded or a shirt you have embroidered—remember that an actual object or a detailed model is a complex, potent visual stimulus. This makes it a "message-maker" in its own right; and in a very real sense, you must compete with it for the listeners' attention. Carefully tell your audience what aspects of it to examine closely, and which ones they may ignore. If, despite your precautions, the actual object or full-scale model is likely to prove unavoidably distracting, build enough reiteration into your speech to make reasonably certain your hearers can follow your train of thought even while they are studying the object and passing it around. As added insurance, you might also provide a schematic diagram or sketch of it on the chalkboard, visually reinforcing the verbal message you are trying to communicate.

6. *When using slides, films, overhead projectors, or videotapes, be prepared to make the verbal and physical adjustments necessary to coordinate the visual materials with the spoken materials.* When employing such visual aids, you often darken the room, thereby compelling your audience to concentrate upon a source of light: the "silver screen" in the case of slides and films, the 21-inch screen in the case of a TV set. At such times, you—the *oral* communicator—must compete with the *machine* or *electronic* communicator. If, as often happens, your audience begins to concentrate harder upon the flow of light than upon the flow of words, you defeat your own purpose. Therefore, when using projected materials as visual support, either (1) talk more loudly and move more vigorously when communicating simultaneously with the machine, or (2) refuse to compete with it at all. That is, show the film or the slides either *before* or *after* you comment on their contents. Whatever strategy you use, however, make sure that the projected visual materials are well integrated into the rest of your presentation.

When using overhead projectors, consider your three options: With an *opaque projector,* you can show audiences a printed page, photographs, and anything you can reproduce on a sheet of paper; with a standard *overhead projector* (which projects only "see-through" materials), you either can write notes on a heavy plastic sheet which can be rolled past the light source, or you can project pre-made transparencies (either purchased or made yourself). An opaque projector is fine for last-minute visuals taken from books, etc., although keep in mind that an audience has difficulty reading a book page, and that an opaque projector not only distorts an image but also is difficult to see more than twenty to thirty feet from the screen. It also is heavy and noisy. If possible, therefore, use a regular overhead projector and make transparencies ahead of time. Or, if you'd rather draw visual aids on the roll of plastic, work neatly, use colors ("magic" markers work nicely), and print large enough for your work to be seen from the back of the room. Finally, turn on the opaque or overhead projectors only when you want the visual showing; otherwise, it will distract the audience's attention from you.

7. *Hand to your listeners a copy of those materials you wish them to think back on or carry away from your speech.* If, for example, you are making recommendations to a student council, you may provide copies of a proposal for the council's subsequent action. Or, if you are reporting on the results of a survey, the most pertinent statistics will be more easily comprehended (and remembered later) if you give each listener a duplicate copy. Few people can recall the "seven warning signs" for cancer, but they could keep a list of them in a handy place if you presented each member of

your audience with a notecard on which such a list appears. Remember that we are referring here only to speech material that is legitimately *visual*. Obviously, you will not put everything you have to say on a ditto. Select only those elements or items which bear on the information you have introduced in your speech, especially those having future or lasting value.

The foregoing suggestions should enable you—with some prespeech thought and planning—to take good advantage of visual materials' communicative potential. By judiciously selecting, preparing, and handling diagrams, charts, models, slides, and similar graphic aids, the conscientious speaker can increase listeners' comprehension. In sum, good visual material is not distracting. It "fits," it is essential to the verbal messages, and it leaves an audience with a feeling of completeness.

Consider the Audience and Occasion

In choosing the type and content of the visual supporting material you will use, your common sense will tell you that you must also take into consideration the *status* of the subject in the minds of your audience. Ask yourself: Do I need to bring a map of the United States to an audience of American college students when discussing the westward movement of population in this country? Or, if I'm going to discuss offensive and defensive formations employed by a football team, should I or should I not bring in a "play book" showing such formations? And, can I really expect an audience to understand the administrative structure of the federal bureaucracy without an organizational chart?

How much an audience *already knows, needs to know*, and *expects to find out* about you and your subject are clearly determinants which must weigh heavily when you are faced with a choice as to the types and numbers of visual supports you will use in a speech. How readily that audience can comprehend *aurally* what you have to say is another. Granted, it is not always easy to assess any of these conditions or capabilities. It may be exceedingly difficult, in fact, to decide how much an audience of college freshmen and sophomores knows about college or governmental structures; and, certainly, you cannot judge easily how well acquainted a canoeing club audience is with football plays. That being the case, probably the next-best thing you can do is to check out your speculations by "asking around" among your probable listeners well ahead of the time you are scheduled to deliver your speech. In other words, before making any final decisions about visual supporting materials, *do as much audience research and analysis as you possibly can.*

As a part of your advance planning for the use of visuals, also take into account the nature of the *occasion* or the uniqueness of the *circumstances* in which you will be speaking. You will find that certain kinds of occasions seemingly cry out for certain types of graphic supporting materials. The corporate executive who presents a projective report to the board of directors without a photocopied or printed handout and without diagrams and pictures probably would be drummed out of the firm. The military adviser who calls for governmental expenditure for new weapons without offering simultaneously pictures or drawings of the proposed weapons and printed technical data on their operations is not likely to be viewed as a convincing advocate. At halftime, an athletic coach without a chalkboard may succeed only in confusing team members—not helping them. In classroom settings, students who give demonstration speeches without visuals frequently feel inadequate, even helpless—especially when they realize that most of the other speakers are well fortified with such supports. In short, if you are to speak in a situation which literally demands certain kinds of visual media, plan ahead and adapt your message to take full advantage of them. If the speech occasion does not appear to require visual supports, analyze it further for possibilities anyway. Use your imagination. Be innovative. *Do not overlook opportunities to make your speech more meaningful, more exciting, and more attention-holding in the eyes of your listeners.*

THE IMPORTANCE OF PRACTICE

Future research on the effects of visual communicative efforts undoubtedly will expand this advice on the use of visual aids. In time, we undoubtedly will learn much more about visual literacy, about ways in which people "read" objects, sketches, diagrams, and drawings. For the present, in a basic speech communication course you can at least practice integrating visual and verbal communication carefully and smoothly. You can gain experience using a flipchart with ease, writing legibly on a chalkboard, and drawing a graph which helps rather than hinders the transmitting of messages. With practice, you will discover that the pictorial channel, like the other channels of communicating meaning, can become a useful—even an exciting—part of your public speechmaking. Making your words, your voice, your bodily movement, and your visual materials *all communicate the same message* to an audience may well provide you with one of the most potent challenges you will encounter in the basic college speech communication course.

GROUP PROJECTS

1. Participate in a class discussion on the topic "Proper and Improper Uses of the Chalkboard." Consider how some of your current and former teachers have used it. The following questions may be useful in guiding the group's considerations: What communicative functions are best served by the chalkboard? What communicative functions could be better served by slides, overhead projectors, or dittoed handouts? Are there special problems with the use of visuals when audience members are taking notes while listening?

2. Work in small groups to develop at least two different types of visual aids for the following topics. A representative of each group will report to the class as a whole and will either tell about or show the projected visual aids.

  (a) How to play a musical instrument
  (b) How to splint a broken arm or leg
  (c) How to construct something
  (d) How to do the drownproof swimming technique
  (e) How to visit an art museum
  (f) How to cut your utility bill

INDIVIDUAL PROJECTS

1. Nonverbal supporting materials capture appropriate moods, clarify potentially complex subjects, and sometimes carry the thrust of a persuasive message. Look around you; examine magazine advertisements, "how-to-do-it" articles in magazines, store windows, special displays in museums or libraries, and slide-projection lectures in some of your other college classes. *(a)* Using the *types* considered in this chapter, classify the nonverbal supporting materials you have encountered. *(b)* Assess the *purposes* these materials serve—clarification, persuasion, attention-focusing, mood-setting, and others you may wish to cite. *(c)* Evaluate the *effectiveness* with which each of the nonverbal supporting materials you have examined is doing its job. *(d)* Prepare a class report or a paper on the results of your experiences and observations.

2. Prepare a short speech explaining or demonstrating a complex process. Use two different types of visual materials. Ask the class to evaluate which of these aids was most effective.

3. You and another classmate might be assigned to explain a complicated process. Working together, develop two or more visual aids to enhance your joint presentation. Plan a performance in which the two of you share the delivery responsibilities. When one speaker talks, the other may be in charge of displaying visual aids. How effective are these duet performances? How does having a thoroughly initiated partner increase the speaking options?

SUGGESTIONS FOR FURTHER READING

Doris A. Dondis, *A Primer of Visual Literacy* (Cambridge, Ma.: The M.I.T. Press, 1974).

George F. Horn, *Visual Communication: Bulletin Boards, Exhibits, Visual Aids* (Worcester, Ma.: Davis Publications, Inc., 1973).

Irving J. Rein, *The Public Speaking Book* (Glenview, Ill.: Scott, Foresman and Company, 1981), pp. 83–86.

Les Satterthwaite, *Graphics; Skills, Media and Materials*, 4th ed. (Dubuque, Ia.: Kendall/Hunt, 1980).

Walter A. Wittich and Charles F. Schuller, *Instructional Technology: Its Nature and Use*, 5th ed. (New York: Harper & Row, Publishers, 1973).

CHAPTER 10

Delivering the Speech

The effectiveness of a speech depends on several factors. Careful preparation, research, and organization are primary determinants of success, but the way you present your ideas is equally important. You want to make sure that the actual presentation of the speech promotes the acceptance of the ideas you so carefully developed. To help ensure that acceptance, you must use the channels of communication effectively.

The speaker must be aware of all of the channels of communication: The *verbal and pictorial channels* usually carry the substance of your ideas, while the *aural and visual channels*—your voice and bodily movements—help transmit your feelings and attitudes toward yourself, your audience, and your topic. Your speech will gain strength and vitality if you choose an appropriate manner of presentation. To help you better understand this capstone of the speech preparation process, we will discuss here three important aspects of presentation: selecting the method of presentation, using your voice to communicate, and using your body to communicate.

SELECTING THE METHOD OF PRESENTATION

What method should you use when presenting your speech? The method you select should be based on several criteria, including the type of speaking occasion, the seriousness and purpose of your speech, audience analysis, and your own strengths and weaknesses as a speaker. Attention to these considerations will help you decide whether your method of presentation should be: (1) impromptu, (2) memorized, (3) read from a manuscript, or (4) extemporized.

The Impromptu Speech

An impromptu speech is one delivered on the spur of the moment. No specific preparation is made; the speaker relies entirely on previous knowledge and skill. The ability to speak impromptu is useful in an emergency, but you should limit your use of this method to situations in which you are unable to anticipate the need to speak. Too often the "moment" arrives without the "spur." When using this method, try to focus on the central idea, carefully relating all significant detail to it. This strategy will help you avoid the rambling, incoherent "remarks" that the impromptu method often produces.

The Memorized Speech

As its name implies, this type of speech is written out word for word and committed to memory. Although a few speakers are able to use this method effectively, it presents certain problems. Usually memorization results in a stilted, inflexible presentation; the speaker may be either excessively formal and oratorical, or may tend to hurry through the speech—pouring out words with no thought as to their meaning. Using the memorized speech makes it difficult for the speaker to take advantage of audience feedback to adapt and adjust ideas as the speech progresses. If you memorize your speech, you first should write it out to help with recall. Remember that you tend to use more formal language when writing than you do when speaking. Be sure that your speech doesn't sound like a written essay.

The Read Speech

Like the memorized speech, the read speech is written out, but in this method the speaker reads from a manuscript. If extremely careful wording is required—as in the President's messages to Congress, where a slip of the tongue could undermine domestic or foreign policies, or in the presentation of scholarly reports, where exact, concise exposition is required—the read speech is appropriate. Many radio and television speeches also are read from manuscript because of the strict time limits imposed by broadcasting schedules. The ability to read a speech effectively is valuable in certain situations. But this method should not be employed when it is neither useful nor necessary. No matter how experienced you may be, when you read your message, you will inevitably sacrifice some of the freshness and spontaneity necessary for authentic communication. Again, as with the memorized speech, it is difficult to react to audience feedback. Also, the speech may sound somewhat stilted because you used more formal written language. If you use this method, "talk through" the speech as you are writing it to ensure a sense of oral style.

The Extemporaneous Speech

Representing a middle course between the memorized or read speech and the speech that is delivered impromptu, the extemporaneous speech requires careful planning and a detailed outline. Working from an outline, practice the speech aloud, expressing the ideas somewhat differently each time you go through it. Use the outline to fix the order of ideas in your mind, and practice various wordings to develop accuracy, conciseness, and flexibility of expression. If the extemporaneous method is used carelessly, the result will resemble an impromptu speech—a fact which sometimes leads to a confusion of these two terms. A proper use of the method, however, will produce a speech which is nearly as polished as a memorized one and certainly more vigorous, flexible, and spontaneous. (Refer back to Chapter 6 for guidelines to help you phrase the main points of the speech.) With few exceptions the speeches you deliver will probably be extemporaneous. For that reason, most of the advice in this textbook is geared to that method.

USING YOUR VOICE TO COMMUNICATE

Regardless of your method of presentation, the effectiveness of your speech will depend in large measure on your voice. Your voice is the instrument that helps convey the meaning of your message. The way your voice transfers language can affect how the listener perceives and interprets the meaning of that language.[1] A good voice enables a speaker to make a message clearer

---

[1] For examples as to how the listener uses voice to judge the speaker, see David W. Addington, "The Relationship of Selected Vocal Characteristics to Personality Perception," *Speech Monographs* 35 (November 1968), 492–503; L. S. Harms, "Listener Judgments of Status Cues in Speech," *Quarterly Journal of Speech* 47 (April 1961), 164–168; Robert Hopper and Frederick Williams, "Speech Characteristics and Employability," *Speech Monographs* 40 (November 1973), 296–302; James D. Moe, "Listener Judgments of Status Cues in Speech: A Replication and Extension," *Speech Monographs* 39 (November 1972), 144–147.

and more interesting. Listen to a child at a church or school program rattle off a poem or speak lines in a play. Even though every word may be clearly audible, the child's vocal expression often is so drab and monotonous that the author's ideas are imperfectly conveyed. On the other hand, recall a play-by-play account of a football or baseball game broadcast by skilled sports announcers. Did not the vividness of their descriptions depend in large measure upon the way they used their voices?

Currently, our culture seems to prize one essential vocal quality above all others—a sense of "conversationality." The most successful speakers of our time have cultivated the ability to make the members of an audience feel they are being directly, even intimately, addressed. There is no trick for learning the art of conversationality. It comes, primarily, from the realization that you are speaking "with" not "at" an audience, that you are addressing a group of living, breathing human beings who want to be talked to as such. Your principal concern, then, as you consider the vocal channel of public speaking, should be mental rather than physical.

As far as the use of your vocal mechanism is concerned, however, there are some physical aspects of voice worth thinking about. Because voice is so important in conveying impressions of yourself, in getting clear concepts across to an audience, and in emotionally coloring your thoughts, we will review some general characteristics of an effective voice, and consider ways it can be adapted to particular speaking situations.

A flexible speaking voice has intelligibility, variety, and understandable stress patterns. These vocal attributes comprise the "meanings" public speakers convey to audiences via their use of the vocal fundamentals of communication. Furthermore, *the successful speaker is able to employ the voice to emotionally color the ideas captured in the words.*

The Effective Speaking Voice

Intelligibility. "Speak clearly!" "Speak up!" "Slow down!" Each of us has been subjected to commands such as these throughout most of our lives. People who make such remarks are essentially asking that our speech be more intelligible, more understandable. In normal, person-to-person conversation, we all tend to articulate sloppily, and to speak more rapidly and more softly that we would in public speaking situations. We can usually do so with no ill effects because we know the persons we are talking to and because we are probably only three to five feet apart. But in public speaking, you often are addressing people you do not know, and you will frequently be twenty-five feet or more away from your auditors. In such situations, it is more difficult for you to be understood. To ensure maximum intelligibility while speaking publicly, you must consider four independent but related factors: (1) *the overall level of loudness at which you speak;* (2) *the rate at which you speak;* (3) *the care with which you enunciate important words;* and (4) *the standard of pronunciation you observe.*

Adusting the Loudness Level.   Probably the most important single factor in intelligibility is the loudness level at which you speak as related to the *distance* between you and your listeners and the amount of *noise* that is present.[2] Obviously, the farther away your listeners are, the louder you must talk for them to hear you well. Most of us make this loudness-level adjustment unconsciously when projecting our voices over extended distances. What we often forget is that a corresponding adjustment is required when the listeners are only a few feet away. You must realize also that your own voice will always sound louder to you than to your listeners because your own ears are closer to your mouth than theirs are.

In addition to distance, the amount of surrounding noise with which you must compete has an effect on the required loudness level. Even in normal circumstances some noise always is present. For example, the noise level of rustling leaves in the quiet solitude of a country lane (10 decibels) is louder than a whisper six feet away. The noise in empty theaters averages 25 decibels, but with a "quiet" audience it rises to 42. In the average factory, a constant noise of about 80 decibels is characteristic. This is just about the same level as very loud speaking at a close range.

How can you determine the proper strength of voice to use in order to achieve sufficient loudness for the distance and noise conditions of a particular speech situation? You can always use your eyes to see if your auditors appear to be hearing you; or, even better, you can *ask* them. Get your instructor's advice on this point. Ask your friends to report on the loudness of your voice as you talk in rooms of various sizes and under varying noise conditions. Listen to the sound of your voice so that you can begin to correlate your own vocal production with their reports. You will soon learn to gauge the volume you must use in order to be heard.

Controlling the Rate.   In animated conversation, you may well jabber along at 200–250 words per minute. This rate is especially characteristic of

---

[2]The term *loudness* is here used synonymously with *intensity* because the former term is clearer to most people. Technically, of course, loudness—a distinct function in the science of acoustics—is not strictly synonymous with intensity. To explain the exact relationships between the two terms is beyond the scope of this book because the explanation involves many complicated psychophysical relationships. For a full discussion of these relationships, see Stanley S. Stevens and Hallowell Davis, *Hearing: Its Psychology and Physiology* (New York: John Wiley & Sons, Inc., 1938), pp. 110ff.

people raised in the North, Midwest, Southwest, or West. As words tumble out of your mouth in informal conversational situations, they usually are intelligible because the distance they must travel is short. In large auditoriums or outdoors, however, rapid delivery can impede intelligibility. Echoes can often distort or destroy sounds in rooms, and in outdoor situations words often seem to drift and vanish into the open air.

When addressing larger audiences, then, most of us must slow down to an average of 120–150 words per minute. Obviously, you do not go around timing your speaking rate, but you can remind yourself of potential rate problems as you rise to speak, and, again, you certainly can get feedback from your instructors and your classmates regarding their perceptions of your speaking rate.

All of this is not to say, of course, that you never should speak rapidly. Undoubtedly, there are temperamentally excitable persons who tend to talk rapidly most of the time, and there certainly are situations when a quickened delivery will help you stir and intensify the emotions of your auditors. If you are such a person and if you talk in emotion-charged situations, you will have to learn to compensate. As your rate increases, for example, you must often adjust your volume and almost always you should take more care in your enunciation of sounds and words.

Enunciating Clearly.   Enunciation refers to the crispness and precision with which we form words vocally. Most of us are "lip lazy" in normal conversation: we tend to slur sounds, drop out syllables from words, skip over beginnings and endings of words. Careless enunciation may not inhibit communication between intimate friends, but it can seriously undermine a speaker's intelligibility in front of an audience.

When speaking publicly, you may have to force yourself to say "go*ing*" instead of "go-*in*," "j*u*st" instead of "j*i*st" (which can aurally be mistaken for "gist"), gov*ern*-ment instead of "g*u*v-ment," etc. Physiologically, this means opening your mouth a bit more widely than usual, forcing your tongue to move around your mouth, and forming the consonants of English firmly with your lips and tongue. If you are having trouble making your vocal mechanism enunciate well, ask your instructor for some exercises to improve your performance.

Meeting Standards of Pronunciation.   Related to questions of enunciation or articulation are those of pronunciation and dialect. To be intelligible, not only must you form sounds carefully, but you also must meet audience expectations regarding acceptable pronunciation. If you fail to pronounce words acceptably, your listeners will not be able to grasp easily and quickly the meaning or significance of what you say. And, even if your words are recognized, any peculiarity of pronunciation is almost sure to be noticed by some of the people who hear you. Such a mistake not only may distract their attention from your line of thought, but may also discredit your knowledge and authority as a speaker.

Standards of pronunciation, of course, differ from region to region. These differences we term *dialects*. A dialect is "a variety of language that is used by one group of persons and has features of vocabulary, grammar, and pronunciation distinguishing it from other varieties used by other groups."[3] Thus, your pronunciation of words, together with the ways in which you arrange them grammatically or syntactically, determines your dialect: a British or German "accent," a white Southern or black Northern dialect, a Detroit vernacular, a New England "twang," etc. Any given dialect has its own rules for pronunciation which may be quite different from the rules of another dialect. When a Midwestern American ear tries to interpret the sounds emitted by a cockney English mouth, noncommunicative confusion may result.

Unfortunately, dialects may produce not only misunderstandings between speakers and listeners, but often they may also produce *negative judgments*—judgments which may seriously affect some auditors' perceptions of the speaker's credibility, education, reliability, responsibility, and capabilities for leadership.[4] This happens because dialects and even professional jargon contribute heavily to what paralinguists call "vocal stereotypes."[5] This means that, as a speaker, you have to make some serious decisions regarding your accent: Should you learn to talk in the grammar, vocabulary, and vocal patterns of "middle America" when addressing such audiences? Many speakers of dialects are forced to become "bilingual," using the vocal patterns of their own background when talking with local audiences, and patterns we call Midwestern American when facing more varied audiences.

---

[3]By permission. From *Webster's Third New International Dictionary* © 1981 by Merriam-Webster® Inc., Publishers of the Merriam-Webster Dictionaries.

[4]In support of these ideas see Mark L. Knapp, *Essentials of Nonverbal Communication* (New York: Holt, Rinehart & Winston, 1980).

[5]Studies of vocal stereotyping may be found in W. E. Lambert, H. Frankel, and G. R. Tucker, "Judging Personality Through Speech: A French-Canadian Example," *Journal of Communication* 16 (1966), 312–313; David W. Addington, "The Relationship of Selected Vocal Characteristics to Personality Perception," *Speech Monographs* 35 (1968), 492–503; W. J. Weaver and R. J. Anderson, "Voice and Personality Interrelationships," *Southern Speech Communication Journal* 38 (1973), 275–278; and B. L. Brown, W. J. Strong, and A. C. Rencher, "The Effects of Simultaneous Manipulations of Rate, Mean Fundamental Frequency, and Variance of Fundamental Frequency on Ratings of Personality From Speech," *Journal of the Acoustical Society of America* 55 (1974), 313–318. (The last study is particularly interesting because it offers advice on ways of altering vocal stereotypes.)

Variety.   As you move from intimate conversation to the enlarged context of public speaking, you may find that you tend to lull an audience with the sameness of your vocal style. You may also discover that many listeners will accuse you of monotony—especially a monotonous pitch or rate. When speaking in a large public setting, you should compensate for the greater distance sounds travel by varying characteristics of your voice. You must learn to vary *rate, pitch, force,* and *pauses.*

Varying the Rate.   Earlier we discussed the overall rate at which one normally speaks. Consider ways to alter your speaking rate in accordance with the ideas you are expressing. The emotional character of your subject matter likewise should affect variations in rate. So, you should consider slowing down to add emphasis to a particular point, or to indicate your own thoughtfulness. And, you probably will want to quicken the pace when you are offering general background material or when your ideas are emotionally charged. Observe, for example, how a sports announcer varies speaking rate from play to play, or how an evangelist changes pace regularly. A variable rate helps keep an audience's attention riveted on the speech.

Changing the Pitch.   As a public speaker you should concern yourself with three aspects of pitch (the musical "notes" in your speaking voice): (1) *pitch level*—whether your pitch is habitually in the soprano, alto, tenor, baritone, or bass range; (2) *pitch range*—the number of "notes" you actually use while speaking; and (3) *pitch variety*—how often you change the pitch level of your voice. Let us examine each of these aspects separately.

We all have a *habitual pitch level*, which would be charted on a musical score. This you can consider your normal speaking level, and it forms the heart of your vocal communication. Unless you are doing impressions or seeking a job as a low-voiced FM radio announcer, you probably should not tamper with it. You need to think about your habitual pitch level only when you practice to extend your pitch range, our second concern.

People unaccustomed to speaking publicly often employ too limited a *pitch range.* In normal conversation, you may use only a few notes—even less than an octave—and get away with it. If you try to talk in a limited range from a podium, however, you may seem monotonous. Given the distances sounds must travel between speaker and audience and the length of time speakers talk, you have to exaggerate, have to employ a larger than normal range. Your pitch "highs" must become higher and your "lows" must become lower. Only in this way will you be employing an effective variety and using vocal tones appropriate to the emotional content of your speech. Obviously, you can get carried away. Just as a narrow pitch range communicates boredom or a lack of involvement, an extremely wide pitch range can communicate overenthusiasm, artificiality, or uncontrolled excitement or fear.

The key to successful control of pitch, ultimately, depends on understanding the importance of *pitch variation*. Pitch variations should be conditioned by two considerations: (1) As a general rule, employ higher pitches to communicate excitement, and lower pitches to create a sense of control or solemnity. Use different parts of your range, in other words, for different kinds of emotions. (2) And, as a second rule, let the sense of any particular sentence control pitch variations. So, move your voice up at the end of a question; change to higher or lower notes to add emphasis within a particular sentence. An abrupt change in pitch is called a *step*. When a more gradual or continuous pitch inflection accompanies the production of the sound, it is termed a *slide*. Both of these techniques are illustrated in the following line:

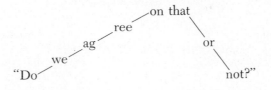

Here, the speaker successively steps his voice up until he reaches a high pitch level on the word "that," which is emphasized; then he slides down the scale on the phrase "or not." Such vocal steps and slides are primarily useful in communicating thought content. By mastering their use, you will be able to make your meaning clearer and more precise.

Stress.   A third significant aspect of vocal behavior is stress—the ways in which sounds, syllables, and words are accented. Without vocal stress, everything in a speech would sound the same, and the resulting message would be both incomprehensible and emotionless. Without vocal stress, you would sound like a computer. Vocal stress is achieved in two ways—through vocal emphasis and through the judicious use of pauses.

Adding Emphasis.   Emphasis refers to the points in a sentence where, principally through increased vocal energy (loudness), changes in intonation (pitch), or variations in speed (rate), one vocally makes certain words or phrases stand out. By emphasis, we mean the way you accent or "attack" words. Emphasis is most often achieved through changes in loudness or energy; variations in loudness can affect the meanings of the sentences you utter. Consider a simple sentence, "Our friends are in the living room." Notice how the meaning varies with the word being emphasized:

1. OUR friends are in the living room. (not *their* friends)
2. Our FRIENDS are in the living room. (not our enemies)

3. Our friends ARE in the living room. (even though you do not think so)
4. Our friends are in THE living room. (the one you and I agree is a special place)
5. Our friends are in the LIVING ROOM. (and not the bedroom, etc.)

Without careful control of vocal force, a speaker is liable to utter messages subject to a great many possible meanings. A lack of vocal stress, therefore, not only creates an impression of boredom, but also can cause needless misunderstandings.

Emphasis also is fostered through changes in pitch and rate. Relatively simple changes in pitch, for example, can be used to "tell" an audience where you are in an outline, as when a speaker says,

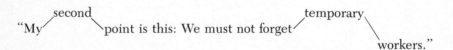

In this sentence, the audience can hear that the speaker has completed one idea and moved on to the next, and that temporary workers will be the principal concern of that section. Variations in rate can operate in the same way. Consider the following sentence:

"We are a country faced with . . . [moderate rate] balance of payments deficits, racial tensions, an energy crunch, a crisis of morality, unemployment, government waste . . . [fast rate] and-a-stif-ling-na-tion-al-debt." [slow rate]

This speaker has built a vocal freight train. The ideas pick up speed through the accelerating list of problems, and then come to an emphatic halt when the speaker's main concern—the national debt—is mentioned. Such variations in rate essentially communicate to an audience what is and what is not especially important to the speech. Emphasis has been achieved through the control of speaking rate.

Emphasis is an important characteristic of the flexible speaking voice. When talking informally to a friend on the street, we all emphasize "naturally," the way our culture has taught us to communicate. Many people, however, become so stiff when talking from a podium that they retreat to vocal patterns characterized by little force, a single pitch, and a steady rate. They become monotonous, especially when they try to read from a full manuscript. Remember that conversationality is your goal when standing before an audience. In that way, you probably will return to your normal emphasis patterns.

Employing Helpful Pauses.   Pauses are intervals of silence between or within words, phrases, or sentences. Pauses punctuate thought by separating groups of spoken words into meaningful units. When placed immediately before a key idea or the climax of a story, they can create suspense; when placed immediately after a major point or central idea, they add emphasis. Introduced at the proper moment, a dramatic pause may express your feeling more forcefully than words. Clearly, silence can be a highly effective communicative tool *if* used intelligently and sparingly, and if not embarrassingly prolonged.

Not all pauses, of course, are silent. Sometimes, speakers fill gaps in their discourse with sounds—"umms," "ahs," "ers," "well-uhs," "you knows," etc. No doubt, you have heard speakers say, "Today, ah, er, I would like, you know, to speak to you, umm, about a pressing, well-uh, like, a pressing problem facing this, uh, campus." Such vocal intrusions destroy any chance the speaker has of getting a firm, convincing message through to an audience. You should make a concerted effort to remove them from your speaking behavior.

Don't be afraid of a little silence. Pauses allow you to achieve stress for important ideas, as the audience awaits the outcome of a story, the key concept toward which you have been building, or the poignant identification of the person you have been describing. Too many pauses, of course, can make you appear manipulative. But, strategic silence is an important weapon in the effective oral communicator's arsenal.

Controlling the Emotional Quality

A listener's judgment of a speaker's personality and emotional commitment often centers on that person's vocal quality—the fullness or thinness of the tones, whether or not it is harsh, husky, mellow, nasal, breathy, resonant, etc. Depending upon your vocal quality, an audience may judge you as being angry, happy, confident, fearful, sincere, sad, and the like.

Fundamental to an audience's reaction to your vocal quality are what G. L. Trager calls *emotional characterizers*—a sense of laughing, crying, whispering, inhaling or exhaling, etc.[6] Physiologically, such characterizers are produced by highly complex adjustments of your vocal mechanism—lips, jaw, tongue, hard and soft palates, throat, and vocal folds. Psychologically, what is important about them is that they combine in various ways with the

[6]For an analysis of emotional or vocal characterizers, see George L. Trager, "Paralanguage: A First Approximation," *Studies in Linguistics* 13 (1958), 1–13.

words you speak to communicate different shades of meanings to a listener. Consider, for a moment, a few of the many ways you can say the following sentence:

"Tom's going for pizza tonight with Jane."

First, say it as though you were only *reporting* the fact to a mutual friend. Now say it as though *you cannot believe* Tom is going with Jane. Or, again, as though it is *impossible* Jane would go with Tom. Then indicate that you wish *you were going* instead of Tom or Jane. Next, say it as though you cannot believe Tom is *actually spending money* on pizza when he could be purchasing something less expensive. Finally, say it as though you are *expressing doubts* about Tom's motive—indicate that you think he is after more than pizza on this trip.

As you said that sentence over and over, you not only varied your pitch and loudness, but probably also made some strange and complicated changes in your emotional characterizers. Such changes are important determiners of how a message should be taken or interpreted by listeners, who want to know how you feel (angry, sad) and how they should "take" the message (literally, ironically, satirically, honestly). In brief, the characterizing aspects of voice, or what David Crystal defines as "a single impression of a voice existing throughout the whole of a normal utterance,"[7] are of prime importance in determining the overall or general impression you make on an audience.

While, of course, you cannot completely control such vocal qualities, you can be alert to the effects they are likely to produce in listeners and make adjustments in your voice consistent with the demands of your spoken messages—as you have just done in repeating the simple statement about Tom, Jane, and pizza. We are not urging that you experiment over and over again with every sentence in a speech so as to achieve the desired emotional overtone. We are saying, however, that key ideas—and more especially, key evaluations and expressions of your attitudes—will be interpreted more accurately by your audience if you give consideration to such characterizers. Keep your repertoire of vocal qualities in the forefront of your mind as you decide whether to yell at, cry with, sneer at, plead with, harp upon, or humble yourself before an audience.

---

[7]David Crystal, *Prosodic Systems and Intonation in English* (Cambridge: University Press, 1959), p. 123.

Practicing Vocal Control

Do not assume that you will be able to master in a day or a week all of the vocal skills that have been described. Take time to review and digest the ideas presented. And above all, *practice*. Ask your instructor to provide exercises designed to make your vocal apparatus more flexible—breathing, phonation, resonance, articulation, and control of rate, pause, and inflection. When you are able to control your vocal mechanism, to make it respond to your desires, then you will be able to achieve vocal intelligibility, variety, and stress. Then you will be able to add the emotional coloring the well-tuned vocal instrument is capable of generating. Remember that any vocal skill, before it can be natural and effective with listeners, must be so much a habit that it will work for you with little conscious effort when you begin to speak and will continue to do so throughout the course of your oral message.

Once your voice can respond as you want it to in the enlarged context of public speaking, you will be able to achieve the sense of *conversationality* so highly valued in our society.

USING YOUR BODY TO COMMUNICATE

Just as your voice gives meaning to your message through the aural channel, your physical behavior carries meaning through the visual channel. While the audience is using the aural channel to grasp your ideas, it is simultaneously using the visual message you send to add clarity. You can use the two complementary channels to help create a better understanding of your presentation.[8] To help you explore ways of enhancing the use of the visual channel, we will examine the speaker's physical behavior on the platform.

[8]See, for example, Haig Bosmajian, ed., *The Rhetoric of Nonverbal Communication* (Glenview, Ill.: Scott, Foresman and Company, 1971), Paul Ekman, "Differential Communication of Affect by Head and Body Cues," *Journal of Personality and Social Psychology* 2 (November 1965), 726–735; Julius Fast, *Body Language* (New York: M. Evans & Co., Inc., 1970), Edward T. Hall, *The Silent Language* (New York: Doubleday & Company, Inc., 1973); Mark L. Knapp, *Nonverbal Communication in Human Interaction*, 2nd ed. (New York: Holt, Rinehart & Winston, Inc., 1978), Albert Mehrabian, "Communication Without Words," *Psychology Today* 2 (September 1968), 52–55; B. G. Rosenberg and Jonas Langer, "A Study of Postural-Gestural Communication." *Journal of Personality and Social Psychology* 2 (October 1965): 593–597.

Dimensions of Nonverbal Communication

In recent years a growing body of research has emphasized anew the important roles that physical or nonverbal behaviors play in effective oral communication.[9] Basically, those roles can be reduced to three generalizations: (1) Speakers reveal and reflect their emotional states by their nonverbal behaviors in front of audiences. Your listeners read your feelings toward yourself, your topic, and your audience from your facial expressions, from the way you stand and walk, from what you do with your head, arms, shoulders, and hands. Summarizing a good deal of research into nonverbal communication processes, communications scholar Dale G. Leathers has noted: "Feelings and emotions are more accurately exchanged by nonverbal than verbal means. . . . The nonverbal portion of communication conveys meanings and intentions that are relatively free of deception, distortion, and confusion."[10] (2) The nonverbal cues which emanate from a speaker can enrich or elaborate the message which comes through words. A solemn face can reinforce the dignity of a funeral eulogy. The words, "Either you can do this or you can do that," can be illustrated with appropriate arm-and-hand gestures. Taking a few steps to the left or right "tells" an audience that you are moving from one argument to another. (3) And, as we noted in Chapter 2, nonverbal messages can be sent from the audience back to the speaker, providing useful feedback in the form of frowns, smiles, nervous shifting, etc.

In other words, nonverbal communication is a two-way street, with messages sent both from speaker to listener and from listener back to speaker. Because we already have discussed feedback in Chapters 2 and 3, we will concentrate here upon the speaker's control of "body language." Such language can usefully be discussed under four heads: (1) *proxemics* (the use of space), (2) *movement and stance*, (3) *facial expressions*, and (4) *gestures*.

Proxemics.   One of the most important but perhaps least recognized aspects of nonverbal communication is proxemics, or the use of space by

---

[9]Most of this research is summarized in three books: Randall P. Harrison, *Beyond Words: An Introduction to Nonverbal Communication* (Englewood Cliffs, N.J.: Prentice-Hall, Inc., 1974); Mark L. Knapp, *Nonverbal Communication in Human Interaction*, 2nd ed. (New York: Holt, Rinehart & Winston, Inc. 1978); and Dale G. Leathers, *Nonverbal Communication Systems* (Boston: Allyn & Bacon, Inc., 1976).

[10]Dale G. Leathers, *Nonverbal Communication Systems* (Boston: Allyn & Bacon, Inc. 1976), pp. 4–5.

human beings. Two components of proxemics are especially relevant to public speakers:

1. *Physical Arrangements*—the layout of the room in which you are speaking, including the presence or absence of a podium, the seating plan, location of chalkboards and similar aids, and physical barriers between you and your audience.

2. *Distance*—the extent or degree of separation between you and your audience.[11]

Each of these components has a bearing on how you communicate publicly. Most public speaking situations include an audience seated or standing, a podium or table, and a speaker facing the audience. Objects in the physical space—the podium, table, flags, etc.—tend to set the speaker apart from the listeners. This "setting apart," one must remember, is both *physical and psychological*. Literally as well as figuratively, objects can stand in the way of open and free communicative exchange. As a result, especially if you are trying to create a relatively informal and direct atmosphere, you will want to reduce those barriers. Some speakers talk from beside a lectern instead of behind it. Others stand in front of it, or even sit on the front edge of a table while talking. There is no single rule for using space. Rather, consider the formality of the occasion (working from behind a lectern is more formal and therefore is better suited to lectures, presentations, prepared reports, etc.); the nature of the material you are offering (you may need a lectern to read from if you are dealing with statistics or extensively quoted material); and your personal characteristics (some speakers need the "protection" provided by a lectern, while others feel much more comfortable speaking beside or in front of it). Your instructor can give you further advice.

The distance component of proxemics adds a second set of considerations. Speakers in most situations are talking over what Edward T. Hall has termed a "public distance"—twelve feet or more away from their listeners.[12] To communicate with people at that distance, you obviously cannot rely on your normal speaking voice, minute changes in posture or muscle tone, etc.

---

[11]For a fuller discussion of each of these components, see Leathers, pp. 52–59.

[12]Hall divides interhuman communication distances into four segments: *intimate distance*—up to 1-½ feet apart; *personal distance*—1-½ to 4 feet; *social distance*—4 to 12 feet; and *public distance*—12 feet or more. On the basis of these distinctions he has carefully noted how people's eye contact, tone of voice, and ability to touch and observe, change from one distance to another. See Edward T. Hall, *The Hidden Dimension* (New York: Doubleday & Company, Inc., 1969), Chapter X, "Distances in Man."

Common Stances of the Public Speaker

Some situations call for authoritarian, formal relationships between speakers and audiences; many visiting lecturers, diplomats, politicians, and religious leaders speak from behind lecterns, often with manuscript speech texts.

At other times, speakers wish to reduce the physical and psychological distance between themselves and audiences by moving in front of lecterns and tables; team leaders, classroom instructors, and communicators offering demonstrations or exhibits, for example, often employ this sort of stance.

Instead, you must *compensate* for the distance by employing larger gestures, broader shifts of your body from place to place, and increased vocal energy. Perhaps the necessity to communicate in larger terms, with bigger-than-usual movements, is one of the qualities which makes public speaking such a new and strange experience to some people. With practice, however, you can acquire and refine the techniques of effective nonverbal delivery, and can overcome these fears and feelings of strangeness.

Movement and Stance.   How you move and stand provides a second set of nonverbal cues for your audience. *Movement* includes shifts you make from one spot to another during the delivery of a speech; *posture* refers to the relative relaxation or rigidity of your body, as well as to your overall stance (erect, slightly bent forward or backward, or slumping).

Purposive movements can, in a very real sense, communicate ideas about yourself to an audience. The speaker who stands stiffly and erectly may, without uttering a word, be saying either (*a*) "This is a formal occasion" or (*b*) "I am tense, even afraid, of this audience." The speaker who leans forward, physically reaching out to the audience, is saying silently but

And, some speakers wish to directly encourage oral feedback from auditors or to "tell" listeners that the situation is highly informal; counselors, discussion leaders, group resource people, for example, often talk in close contact with their audiences.

eloquently: "I am interested in you. I want you to understand and accept my ideas." Sitting casually on the front edge of a table and assuming a relaxed posture communicate informality and a readiness to engage in a dialogue with your listeners.

Movements and postural adjustments *regulate* communication. As a public speaker, you may, for instance, move from one end of a table to the other to indicate a change in topic; or you may accomplish the same purpose simply by changing your posture. At other times, you may move toward your audience when making an especially important point. In each case, you are using your body to signal to your audience that you are making a change or transition in the subject matter of the speech, or are dealing with a matter of special concern.

Along with all this, an equally important point to remember is that your posture and movements can not only work for you, but also against you. Aimless and continuous pacing back and forth is distracting. A nervous bouncing up and down or swaying from side to side will make the audience tense and uneasy. If you adopt an excessively erect stance, you may lose rapport with your listeners. Your movements, in other words, should be *purposive*. Only then will stance and movement help your communicative effort and produce the sense of self-assurance and control you want to exhibit.[13]

Facial Expressions.   Your face is another important nonverbal message channel. When you speak, your facial expressions function in a number of ways: First, they communicate much about yourself and your feelings. What Paul Ekman and Wallace V. Friesen call *affect displays* are given to an audience via your face. That is, an audience scans your face to see how you feel about yourself and how you feel about them.[14] Second, facial details provide listeners with cues that help them *interpret the contents* of your message: Are you being ironic or satirical? How sure are you of some conclusion you have stated? Is this a harsh or a pleasant message? Psychologist Albert Mehrabian has devised a formula to account for the emotional impact of a speaker's message. Words, he says, contribute 7 percent, vocal elements 38 percent, and facial expressions 55 percent.[15] And third, the "display" elements of your face—your eyes especially—establish a *visual bonding* between you and your hearers. The speaker who looks down at the floor instead of at listeners, who reads excessively from notes or a manuscript, or who delivers a speech to the back wall has severed visual bonding. Our culture has come to expect eye-to-eye contact from speakers who are deemed "earnest," "sincere," "forthright," "self-assured," etc. In other words, it is in part through regular eye contact with individuals in your audience that you establish your *credibility*, that you convince your audience that you are a trustworthy, sincere, dynamic human being.[16]

Of course, you cannot control your face completely, which is probably why listeners search it so carefully for clues to your feelings, but you can make sure that your facial messages do not belie your verbal ones. In

---

[13]See F. Deutsch, "Analysis of Postural Behavior," *Psychoanalytic Quarterly* 16 (1947), 195–213; W. James, "A Study of the Expression of Bodily Posture," *Journal of General Psychology* 7 (1932), 405–436; Albert Mehrabian, "Significance of Posture and Position in the Communication of Attitude and Status Relationships," *Psychological Bulletin* 71 (1969), 359–372.

[14]An excellent review of research on facial communication can be found in Leathers, Chapter 2. Those wishing a larger treatment should see Paul Ekman, Wallace V. Friesen, and P. Ellsworth, *Emotion in the Human Face: Guidelines for Research and an Integration of Findings* (New York: Pergamon Press, Inc., 1972).

[15]"How to Read Body Language," by Flora Davis. *Glamour Magazine,* September 1969.

[16]For a difficult but rewarding essay on the management of demeanor, see Erving Goffman, *Interaction Ritual: Essays on Face-to-Face Behavior* (New York: Doubleday & Company, Inc., 1967), "On Face-Work," pp. 5–46.

practical terms this means that when you are uttering angry words, your face should be communicating anger; when you are sincerely pleading with your listeners, your eyes should be looking at them intently. In short, use your face to maximum communicative advantage.

Gestures. Gestures include purposeful movements of the head, shoulders, arms, hands, or some other part of the body. Fidgeting with your clothing or aimlessly rearranging notecards on the podium are not gestures because they are not purposeful, and they distract from, rather than support or illustrate, the ideas you are expressing. The public speaker commonly employs three kinds of gestures:

1. *Conventional Gestures*—signs or symbols which have had specific meanings assigned to them by custom or convention. The raised-hand "stop" gesture of the policeman directing traffic, the hand-and-finger language of deaf persons, and the arm signals of football referees are examples of conventional gestures.

2. *Descriptive Gestures*—signs or symbols which depict or describe more or less directly the idea to be communicated. Speakers, for example, often describe the size, shape, or location of an object by movements of hands and arms. They may extend an upraised arm to indicate the height of a stranger. They may make hand-and-finger motions to help describe what a punch press looks like or to demonstrate the successive steps in its use.

3. *Indicators*—movements of the hands, arms, or other parts of the body which represent feelings. Thus, speakers may throw up their arms when disgusted, pound the podium when angry, shrug their shoulders when puzzled, or point a threatening finger when issuing a warning. In using such indicators or signs, speakers are in a sense trying to transmit their own feelings directly to their listeners.[17]

In sum, then, gestures can function in three important ways to aid the speaker: (1) *Pictorialization*. Gestures can be used to "draw pictures" for your audience, especially to indicate sizes, shapes, and relationships between objects. Such pictures depend primarily upon what we have called descriptive gestures. (2) *Condensation*. Gestures, particularly conventional gestures, may take the place of words in many instances. They can be shorthand movements for things it would take many words to describe fully. (3) *Arousal*. Gestures often work in concert with facial expressions to communicate your state of mind to the audience. Indicators are especially important in this regard because an audience usually reads not only your face

---

[17]For a more complete system for classifying gestures, see Paul Ekman and Wallace V. Friesen, "Hand Movements," *Journal of Communication* 22 (December 1972), 360.

Public speakers commonly employ three kinds of gestures: *Conventional gestures* are physical signs or symbols which have meanings assigned to them by customary group or cultural usage. *Descriptive gestures* depict or describe the size, shape, or location of some object or person. *Indicators* are gestural movements which represent such personal feelings as disgust, anger, puzzlement, joy, or concern.

but also the rest of your body for cues concerning how your message is to be interpreted.

Characteristics of Effective Gestures. Although you can perfect your gestures only through practice, you will obtain better results if, as you practice, you keep in mind three characteristics of effective gestures: (1) *relaxation,* (2) *vigor and definiteness,* and (3) *proper timing.*

When your muscles are strained or tense, you have difficulty expressing yourself naturally, and awkward gestures result. One of the best ways to relax is to move about. "Warm up" by taking a few easy steps or by unobtrusively arranging your notes or papers. To avoid stiffness and awkwardness, make a conscious effort to relax your muscles before you start to speak.

Good gestures are lively, vigorous, and definite. Put enough force into them to make them convincing. A languid shaking of the fist is a poor way to support a threat or issue a challenge; an aimless or hesitant movement of the arm confuses rather than clarifies. Do not pound the table or saw the air constantly; exaggeration of minor points is ludicrous. Vary the nature of your gestures as the ideas in your speech demand; but alway make them vigorous enough to show your conviction and enthusiasm.

Timing is crucial to effective gestures. Try making a gesture after the word or phrase it was intended to reinforce has already been spoken, and observe the ridiculous result. The stroke of a gesture—that is, the shake of the fist, the movement of the finger, or the break of the wrist—should fall exactly on, or should slightly precede, the point the gesture is used to emphasize. If you practice making gestures until they have become habitual and then use them spontaneously as the impulse arises, you will have no trouble on this score. Poor timing is often the result of an attempt to use "canned" or preplanned gestures.

Adapting Nonverbal Behavior to Your Presentations

Although you never can completely control your "body language," you can gain skill in orchestrating your gestures and other movements. You can consciously make *some* decisions about how you will use your body to communicate.

Start with your "self."   Know what kind of person you are—whether, for example, you are basically quiet and reticent or excitable and extroverted; whether you are prone to vigorous physical activity or like to "take things easy and relax"; whether you talk easily and well on your feet or prefer to sit while talking. Once you think through the kind of person you are, then you can work more purposefully. Find ways to stimulate and activate yourself during the delivery of your message, for if you do not move, an audience will notice and judge you as apathetic, indifferent, or listless. Choose the mode of self-motivation that is best for you.

Plan a proxemic relationship with your audience which reflects your own needs and attitudes toward your subject and your listeners.   If you feel more at home behind a lectern, plan to have it placed accordingly. If you want your whole body to be visible to the audience, yet feel the need to have notes at eye level, stand beside the lectern and arrange your notecards on it. If you want to relax your body (and are sure you can compensate for the resulting loss of action by increasing your vocal volume) sit behind a table or desk. If you feel free physically and want to be wholly "open" to your audience, stand in front of a table or desk.

The farther you are from your listeners, the more important it is for them to have a clear view of you.   The speaker who crouches behind a lectern in an auditorium of three hundred people soon loses contact with them. The farther away your audience is, the harder you must work to project your words, and the broader your physical movements must be. Review in your own mind large lecture classes you have attended, sermons you have heard in large churches, or political rallies you have attended.

Recall the behaviors and techniques of speakers who worked effectively in such situations, choosing and adapting those that might also work for you.

Insofar as practical, adapt the physical setting to your communicative needs and desires.   If you are going to use such visual aids as a chalkboard, flipchart, working model, or process diagram, remove the tables, chairs, and other objects which obstruct the listeners' view and therefore impair their understanding of your message.

Adapt the size of your gestures and amount of your movement to the size of the audience.   Keeping in mind what Edward Hall noted about public distance in communication (pages 209–210), you should realize that subtle changes of facial expression or small movements of the fingers cannot be seen clearly when you are twenty-five feet or more from your listeners. Although a great many of the auditoriums in this country have a raised platform and a slanted floor to allow a speaker to be seen more clearly, you should, nevertheless, adjust by making your movements and gestures larger.

Continuously scan your audience from side to side and from front to back, looking specific individuals in the eyes.   This does not mean, of course, that your head is to be in a constant state of motion; "continuously" does not imply rhythmical, nonstop bobbing. Rather, it implies that you must be aware—and must let an audience know you are aware—of the entire group of human beings in front of you. Take them all into your field of vision periodically; establish firm visual bonds with them occasionally. Such bonds enhance your credibility, and keep auditors' attention from wandering.

Use your body to communicate your feelings about what you are saying.   When you are angry, do not be afraid to gesture vigorously. When you are expressing tenderness, let that message come across your face. In other words, when you are communicating publicly, employ the same emotional indicators you do when you are talking to another individual on a one-to-one basis.

Use your body to regulate the pace of your presentation and to control transitions.   Shift your weight as you move from one idea to another. Move more when you are speaking more rapidly. When you are slowing down to emphasize particular ideas, decrease bodily and gestural action accordingly. Because arbitrarily, preplanned movements aren't usually effective, avoid them; but do give careful thought to pacing and regulating by nonverbal means those portions of your speech that could well benefit from these considerations.

Finally, use your full repertoire of descriptive and regulative gestures while talking publicly.   You probably do this in everyday conversation without even thinking about it; so recreate that same attitude when addressing an audience. Here, physical readiness is the key concern. Keep your hands and arms free and loose enough so that you can call them into action easily, quickly, and naturally. Let your hands be comfortably at your sides, relaxed, but in readiness. Occasionally, rest them on the lectern. Then, as you unfold the ideas of your speech, use descriptive gestures to indicate size, shape, or relationship, making sure the movements are large enough to be seen in the back row. Use conventional gestures also to give visual dimension to your spoken ideas. Keep in mind, of course, that there are no "right" number of gestures that you ought to use. However, during the preparation of your talk, you can think of the kinds of bodily and gestural actions that would most appropriately and effectively complement your delivery.

Selecting the appropriate method of presentation and using your voice and body productively to communicate will enhance the chances of gaining support for your ideas. The key to the effective use of these elements is *practice*. Through practice, you can better judge your choice of method of presentation. You will also have a better opportunity to see how your voice and body complement or detract from your ideas. The more confident you feel about presenting the speech, the more comfortable you will be, and confidence is built through careful preparation and practice. Remember that the nonverbal channel of communication also creates meaning for your audience.

 GROUP PROJECTS

1. Divide the class into teams and play "charades." (Those needing rules for classroom games should read David Jauner, "Charades as a Teaching Device," *Speech Teacher* 20 [November 1971], 302). A game of charades not only will loosen you up psychologically but should help sensitize you to the variety of small but perceptible cues you "read" when interpreting messages.

2. Meet briefly in task groups to determine which of the four methods of speaking would be most appropriate in each of the following situations. Choose a reporter to convey the group's justification for selections to the class.

(*a*) A college president addressing her faculty on the goals of the college for 'the school year.

(*b*) A student's response to his speech professor when asked what he hoped to learn in the course.

(*c*) A president of a large company reporting to all administrative personnel on the success/failure of the company for the past year.

(*d*) A student participating in the National Oratorical contest.

(e) An alumna of a local high school attending a reunion and being asked to comment on the adequacy of her high-school training for college.

(f) A sales representative attempting to get the board of directors of a business chain to use his advertising agency.

INDIVIDUAL PROJECTS

1. During the next few days observe a speaker whom you would consider particularly unexciting. Take notes on the speaker's use of proxemics, bodily movement and stance, facial expression, and gestures. Prepare a synopsis of your findings for presentation to the class.

2. Spend at least thirty minutes observing nonverbal communication in a high-noise area such as a factory or a low-noise area such as a library. Prepare a brief report for the class in which you describe the types of nonverbal cues you observed and their apparent effectiveness.

3. Conduct an experiment to gauge people's reactions to "invasions" of their personal space or territory. In at least three different and relatively uncrowded locations (e.g., the library, a classroom, a waiting room, a bus) sit next to a stranger. Carefully observe how this person reacts to your presence, and report your findings to the class.

4. Can your speaking voice be easily understood? As a test of your intelligibility, the instructor may ask you to deliver a short speech with your back to the audience. Stand in approximately the same position where you normally do when speaking to the class.

SUGGESTIONS FOR FURTHER READING

Judee K. Burgoon and Thomas Saine, *The Unspoken Dialogue: An Introduction to Nonverbal Communication* (Dallas: Houghton Mifflin Company, 1978).

Joseph A. DeVito, Jill Giattino, and T.D. Schon, *Articulation and Voice: Effective Communication* (Indianapolis: The Bobbs-Merrill Company, Inc., 1975).

Mark L. Knapp, *Essentials of Nonverbal Communication* (New York: Holt, Rinehart, and Winston, 1980).

Dale G. Leathers, *Nonverbal Communication Systems* (Boston: Allyn and Bacon, Inc., 1976).

Albert Mehrabian, *Silent Messages: Implicit Communication of Emotions and Attitudes* 2nd ed. (Belmont, Ca.: Wadsworth Publishing Co., 1981).

CHAPTER 11

Speaking to Inform

An important function of public speaking is the communication of knowledge. Through informative speeches, people are able to give others the benefit of their learning and expertise. The main purpose of a speech to inform, then, is to secure understanding among listeners. Creating understanding is not a matter of parading knowledge or pontificating before an audience on endless facts and figures. People seek information and understanding from speakers only in the face of perceived needs. Like all other oral transactions, informative speeches depend upon the speaker's sensitivity to listeners' purposes, knowledge, and attitudes.

Why have your listeners come to hear your message? What kinds of information do they need and expect? How can you help them remember the information you are conveying? How can you keep them from losing interest or becoming inattentive through the course of the presentation? How can you make seemingly abstract information relevant to their everyday lives? To the extent that you are able to deal strategically with these and similar questions, you will achieve your primary goal in an informative speech—to communicate knowledge and understanding.

In this chapter we will discuss the types and characteristics of informative speeches. Then we will consider strategies for structuring the types of informative speeches in ways which will improve your chances for reaching common understandings with audiences.

TYPES OF INFORMATIVE SPEECHES

Informative speeches take many forms. Four of these forms—*reports, instructions, demonstrations,* and *lectures*—occur so frequently, however, that they merit special attention.

Oral Reports

Academic reports, committee reports, and executive reports are typical of this kind of informative speech. Scientists and scholars announce their research findings at professional conventions or in radio and television interviews. Committees in business, industry, and government carry out special research or advisory tasks and then present oral reports to their parent organizations and bureaus. Board chairpersons report annually to stockholders on the past year's activities and accomplishments. The oral report is, therefore, a staple kind of informative speech in a society such as ours which is organized into so many groups and subgroups, each with special concerns, tasks, and responsibilities. We will have more to say about this sort of discourse in Chapter 15.

Oral Instructions

In a complex culture, job instructions, class instructions, and instructions for the performance of special tasks play a vital role. Teachers instruct students in ways of preparing assignments. Supervisors tell their subordinates how a task should be performed. Leaders explain to volunteer workers their duties in a fund-raising drive or a cleanup campaign. For convenience, such instructions usually are given to a group of people rather than to individuals, and, even when written, may need to be accompanied by oral explanations which amplify and clarify printed material. The feedback mechanisms provided in public speaking are especially important and valuable in this type of communication process.

Demonstrations

Often, however, as in the case of oral instructions, we have to do more than "tell." We also have to "show" people how to carry out the desired actions. A demonstration speech is one in which a speaker describes to an audience the steps involved and the physical and mental skills required for carrying out a certain task. A supervisor will need to lay out office procedures for new employees. An instructor in an art class will need to give careful, step-by-step instructions in how to prepare a canvas. Speakers offering demonstrations must be clear, efficient, comprehensive, orderly, and verbally and visually coordinated.

Lectures

Characteristic of this type of informative communication are lectures on travel and public affairs, classroom lectures, and "talks" at club meetings, study conferences, and institutes. The purpose of a lecture is to increase the audience's understanding or appreciation of a particular field of knowledge. More specifically, lecturers tend to be *explainers;* they are often called upon to define unclear or new concepts and terms, to indicate how a certain situation arose, or to point out the implications of some old or new policy. For instance, a business person might define the notion of "management-by-objectives," a historian might tell a group of students what social-cultural forces converged to create the American Revolution, and a social worker might lecture to an audience of citizens on the impact of the current welfare system.[1]

ESSENTIAL FEATURES OF INFORMATIVE SPEECHES

Four qualities should characterize any speech to inform: (1) *clarity*, (2) *the association of new ideas with familiar ones*, (3) *concreteness*, and (4) *the motivation of the audience*.

Clarity

This quality is largely the result of effective organization and the careful selection of words. Informative speeches achieve maximum clarity when your listeners can follow you and understand what you are saying.

Observe the following rules when organizing your speech: *(a)* Do not have too many points. Confine your speech to three or four principal ideas, grouping whatever facts or ideas you wish considered under these headings.

---

[1]Demonstration speeches, reports, and explanative speeches are treated in more detail in Bruce E. Gronbeck, *The Articulate Person: A Guide to Everyday Public Speaking*, 2nd ed. (Glenview, Ill.: Scott, Foresman and Company, 1983), Part II, "Informing" (Chaps. 6 and 7).

Even if you know a tremendous amount about your subject matter, remember that you cannot make everyone an expert in a single speech. *(b)* Clarify the relationship between your main points by observing the principles of coordination. Word your transitions carefully—"Second, you must prepare the chair for caning by cleaning out the groove and cane holes," "To test these hypotheses, we set up the following experiment." Such transitions allow auditors to follow you from point to point. *(c)* Keep your speech moving forward according to a well-developed plan; do not jump back and forth between ideas, charging ahead and then backtracking.

As you select the words to convey your message, remember to: *(a)* Use a precise, accurate vocabulary when you can do so without getting too technical. In telling someone how to finish off a basement room, you might say, "Next, take one of these long sticks and cut it off in this funny-looking gizmo with a saw in it, and try to make the corners match." An accurate vocabulary helps your listeners remember what supplies and tools to get when they approach the same project: "This is a ceiling molding; it goes around the room between the wall and the ceiling to cover the seams between the paneling and the ceiling tiles. You make the corners of the molding match by using a mitre box, which has grooves that allow you to cut 45 degree angles. Here's how you do it." *(b)* Simplify when possible, including only as much technical vocabulary as you need. Try not to make a speech on the operation of a two-cycle internal combustion engine sound as if it came out of a lawnmower mechanic's operational manual. *(c)* Use reiteration when it clarifies complex ideas, but don't simply repeat the same words. Seek rephrasings that will help solidify ideas for those who had trouble getting them the first time, thusly: "Unlike a terrestrial telescope, a celestial telescope is used for looking at moons, planets, and stars; that is, its mirrors and its lens are ground and arranged in such a way that it focuses on objects thousands of miles, not hundreds of feet, away from the observer."

Association of New Ideas with Familiar Ones

Audiences grasp new facts and ideas more readily when they are able to associate them with what they already know; therefore, in a speech to inform, always try to connect the new with the old. If you are giving instructions or describing a problem, relate your materials to procedures or problems with which your listeners are familiar. A college dean talking to an audience of manufacturers on the problems of higher education presented his ideas under the headings of raw material, casting, machining, polishing, and assembling. He thus "translated" the central ideas into an analogy his audience would understand and appreciate. Indeed, if a speech to inform is to meet the needs and satisfy the curiosities of audiences, *the association of new ideas with familiar ones may well represent the informative speaker's principal intellectual task.*

Concreteness

In a speech to inform, concreteness is as important as clarity. A lecture or report should be packed with facts—with names and references to actual places, events, and experiences. In presenting facts, however, observe these two precepts: (1) Do not multiply details unnecessarily. Present statistics in round numbers, especially if they involve large and complicated sets of data; outline the general course of historical change or development rather than recount each minute incident; do not belabor a story or illustration until your listeners' attention is drawn completely away from the point you wish to emphasize. Facts are indispensable, but excessively detailed facts are confusing. (2) Again, as we emphasized in Chapter 9, whenever possible, support your presentation of factual information with charts, diagrams, models, or other visual materials. If the members of your audience can see what you are describing, they usually can assimilate the details more readily.

Motivation of the Audience

Finally, you must be able to motivate the audience to listen. This is an essential feature of good informative speeches that many people ignore. Many of us blithely assume that because *we* are interested in something, *they* also will want to hear about it. To you, stamp-collecting may be an interesting, relaxing, and profitable hobby, but until your listeners are likewise convinced that it is, they will yawn through your speech on American commemoratives.

Keep in mind, therefore, what we have said about attention (Chapter 2) and motivation (Chapter 4) even when preparing informative speeches: (*a*) Use the factors of attention to engage the members of your audience, to draw them into your speech. (*b*) Once you have captured them initially, be sure to build in motivational appeals, reasons why they should want to know what you are about to tell them. If you indicate that your talk will increase their interpersonal effectiveness, provide them with additional income, reduce their confusion about important matters, and the like, you will be going a long way toward making your speech relevant and compelling.

Remember, too, that the Motivated Sequence can be used often when building an informative speech. (Look ahead to Chapter 12, pp. 237–263.)

The Attention Step should pique their curiosity, the Need Step can effectively engage their motive drives, and then the Satisfaction Step can provide them with the information which channels those drives.

STRUCTURING INFORMATIVE SPEECHES

Now that we have described the various types of informative speeches and treated their essential features, it is time to examine ways in which you can structure them. Of course, many of the organizational patterns we described earlier can be used, but, traditionally, some of these patterns are better suited to particular types of informative speeches than others.

Oral Reports

Introduction.   Oral reports are "called for" by some group, committee, or class; the audience, therefore, generally knows what it expects and why. In introducing oral reports, then, you need not spend much time motivating your listeners—they already are. Rather, you should concentrate upon (1) reminding them of what they asked for, should their memories be short; (2) describing carefully the procedures you used in gathering the information; (3) forecasting the development of various sub-topics so they can follow you easily; and (4) pointing ahead to any action they are expected to take in light of your information. The key to a good introduction for an oral report, thus, is *orientation*—reviewing the past (their expectations and your preparations), the present (your goal now), and the future (their responsibilities once you are done). A report is "given to" an audience for some purpose, and neither you nor they should ever forget that.

Body.   The principle for organizing the body of an oral report can be stated clearly: *Select an organizational pattern which best reflects the audience's needs.* Have you been asked to provide them with a history of some group or problem? Use a chronological pattern. Do they want to know how some state-of-affairs came to be? Try a cause-effect format. Have you been asked to discuss an organizational structure for the group? A topical pattern would allow you to review the constitutional responsibilities of each officer. If you were asked to examine the pros and cons of various proposals and to recommend one to the group, the elimination pattern as we discussed it in Chapter 6 is the way to go, as in the following example:

     I. My committee was asked to compare and contrast various ways of doing a final examination in this speech class, and to recommend a procedure to you. [*the reporter's "charge"*]

      A. First, we interviewed each one of you.

      B. Then, we discussed the pedagogical virtues of various exam proce-
dures with our instructor.

      C. And next, we deliberated as a group, coming to the following conclu-
sions. [*orientation completed*]

  II. Like many students, we first thought we should recommend a take-home
essay examination as the "easiest" way out.

      A. But, we decided our wonderful textbook is filled with so much detailed
and scattered advice that it would be almost impossible for any of us to
answer essay-type questions without many, many hours of worry,
work, and sweat.

      B. We also wondered why a course which stresses oral performance
should test our abilities to write essays.

 III. So, we next reviewed a standard, short-answer, in-class final.

      A. While such a test would allow us to concentrate upon the main ideas
and central vocabulary which has been developed in lectures, readings, and discussion, it would require a fair amount of memorization.

      B. And, we came back to the notion that merely understanding communi-
cation concepts will not be enough when we start giving speeches
outside this classroom.

 IV. Thus, we recommend that you urge our instructor to give us an oral
examination this term.

      A. We each could be given an impromptu speech topic, some resource
material, and ten minutes to prepare a speech.

      B. We could be graded, in this way, on both substantive and communica-
tive decisions we make in putting together and delivering the speech.

      C. Most important, such a test would be consistent with this course's
primary goal—and could be completed quickly, almost painlessly.

Conclusion.   Most oral reports end with conclusions which mirror the
introduction. A mention often is made again of the report's purpose, a
review of the main points is presented, committee members (if there are
any) are thanked publicly, and then either a motion to accept the committee
recommendations (if there are any) is offered or, in the case of more
straightforwardly "informative" reports, questions from the audience are
called for. Conclusions to reports—when done well—are quick, firm,
efficient, and pointed.

Demonstrations and Instructions

Introduction.   In most situations where you will be called on to give
instructions or offer a demonstration, you will need to spend little time
piquing curiosity or motivating people to listen. After all, if you are

Lectures represent a common kind of informative speech, especially in educational settings. When presenting lectures aim for: maximum clarity; concreteness; the association of new ideas with old ones; the motivation of your audience; a speaking rate which allows listeners to absorb the information easily; and, as illustrated in this picture, the coordination of verbal and visual materials.

instructing your listeners in a new office procedure or giving a workshop on how to build an ice boat, you already have the prerequisite interest and motivation—otherwise, they would not have come. If your listeners' attendance is not voluntary (as can be the case in speech communication classrooms!), then of course you will have to pay attention to motivational matters, but normally you must concentrate your introduction on two other tasks: (1) *Preview* your speech. If, say, you are going to take the members of your audience through the seven steps involved in making a good tombstone rubbing, give them an overall picture of the process before you start describing each operation in detail. (2) *Encourage* them to follow along, even through some of the more difficult steps. A process like tombstone rubbing, for example, looks easier than it is; many are tempted to quit listening and trying along the way. If, however, they are forewarned and are promised special help with the difficult techniques, they are more likely to bear with you.

Body. As we suggested earlier, you will find that most speeches of demonstration and instruction are packaged in a chronological and/or spatial pattern, simply because you are teaching people a serial process you want them to be able to carry out on their own. A nonsequential organizational pattern would be very confusing.

In other words, speakers usually have little trouble organizing the body of this type of speech. Their problems are more likely to be technical ones: *(a) The problem of rate.* If the glue on some project needs to set before you can go on to the next step, what do you do? You cannot just stand there and wait for it to dry. You need to have preplanned some material for filling the time—perhaps additional background, perhaps a brief discussion of what problems one can run into at this stage. Preplan your remarks carefully for those junctures; otherwise, you are likely to lose your audience. *(b) The problem of scale.* How can you show various embroidery stitches to an audience of twenty-five? When dealing with minute operations, you often must increase the scale of operation. In this example, you might use a large piece of poster board or even a 3' by 4' piece of cloth stretched over a wood frame. By using an oversized needle and yarn instead of thread, and stitches measured in inches instead of millimeters, you could more easily make your techniques visible to all audience members. At the other extreme, as in the case of a speech on how to make a homemade solar heat collector, you probably would be well-advised to work with a scaled-down model. *(c) The coordination of verbal and visual materials.* Both instructions and demonstrations usually demand that speakers "show" while "telling." To keep yourself from becoming flustered or confused, be sure to practice talking while doing—offering demonstrations while explaining to others what you are doing. Decide where you are going to stand when showing a slide so that the audience can see both you and the image; practice talking about your aerobic exercise positions while you are actually doing them; work a dough press in practice sessions as you tell your mythical audience how to form professional-looking cookies. If you do not, you will inevitably get yourself into trouble before your real audience.

Thinking through such procedural and technical problems you can face might lead to a speaking outline like the following one on planting tomatoes:

Coordinate verbal and visual materials	I. First, you must select a variety of tomato seed which is suited to various geographical, climatological, agricultural, and personal factors. [*display chart, showing varieties in columns along with their characteristics*] A. Some tomatoes grow better in hard soils, some, in loose soils. B. Some varieties handle shade well, some, direct sunlight. C. Some are well suited to short growing seasons, others, to long seasons. D. Each variety tends to resist certain diseases such as blight better than others.

II. Once you have selected a variety (or maybe even two, so that they mature at different times), next you must start the seeds.

Coordinate verbal and visual materials

A. Prepare a mixture of black dirt, peat moss, and vermiculite as I am doing. [*do it, indicating proportions*]

B. Fill germination trays, pots, or cut-off milk cartons with the germination soil, and insert seeds. [*do it*]

Reduce time delay (rate)

C. With watering, sunlight, and patience, your plants will grow. I can't show you that growth here today, but I can use these seedlings to illustrate their care along the way. [*bring out half-grown and fully grown seedlings*]

Coordinate verbal and behavioral actions

1. When the seedlings are about an inch or two tall, thin them. [*demonstrate*]
2. At about six inches [*show them*], you can transplant them safely.
3. But, you'll know more about which plants are strong if you wait until they are ten to twelve inches tall. [*show them plants of different strengths*]

D. Now, you are ready to transplant the seedlings to your garden.
1. Carefully de-pot the seedlings, being sure not to damage the root network. [*demonstrate*]

Coordinate visual and verbal materials; enlarge materials

2. Put each seedling in a hole already prepared in your plot; this diagram shows you how to do that. [*show an enlarged diagram which illustrates hole size and depth, a mixture of peat moss and vermiculite in the bottom, and spacing of plants*]
3. Pack the garden soil firmly, but not so hard as to crush the roots.

Coordinate verbal and visual materials; reduce size of materials

4. Water it almost every day for the first week.
5. Put some sort of mulching material—grass clippings, hay, black sheets of plastic—between the rows if weeds are a problem. [*another diagram or picture*]

E. Once you know your plants are growing, cage or stake each plant. [*show sketches of various styles of cages or stakes, discussing the advantages of each*]

Conclusion.   Conclusions for informative speeches usually are composed of three parts: (1) First, *summaries* are offered. Most audiences need this review, which reminds them to ask questions about procedures or ideas they do not understand fully. (2) Second, some *bolstering* has to take place. People trying their hands at new processes or procedures usually get into trouble the first few times, and need to be reassured that this is natural and can be overcome. (3) Finally, *future help* should be offered. What sounded so simple in your talk can be much more complicated in execution. So, if possible, make yourself available for later assistance: "As you fill out your registration form, just raise your hand if you're unsure of anything and I'll be happy to help you." Or, point to other sources of further information and assistance: "Here's the address of the U.S. Government Printing Office, whose pamphlet X1234 is available for only a dollar; it will give you more details"; "If you run into a filing problem I haven't covered in this short orientation to your job, just go over to Mary McFerson's desk, right over here. Mary's experienced in these matters and is always willing to help." These sorts of statements not only offer help, but assure your audience members that they won't be labeled as dull-witted if they actually have to ask for it.

Lectures (Explanations)

Introduction.   Introductions to lectures or explanatory speeches may well have to rely on many of the techniques we have described thus far. You may have to raise curiosity in some instances (e.g., how many of your classmates wonder about the causes of the American Revolution at ten o'clock in the morning?). You might also have to generate a need or desire to listen, again, especially if your topic seems distant or irrelevant. And, too, if the explanation offered in the lecture is going to be somewhat complex, a forecast of coming ideas is almost mandatory. Finally, you may well need to encourage your listeners to follow along, telling them you will go into greater detail especially in the sections of greatest difficulty.

Body.   Most explanations fit well into causal and topical organizational patterns. If you are trying to explain how or why something operates the way it does, either cause-effect or effect-cause orders work very well. Or, if you are trying to explain how some problem can be or should be solved, you might find it advantageous to use a straightforward problem-solution format, especially if your listeners are unsure what the solution might be. These organizational patterns are well suited to explanatory speeches because, as we noted earlier, explanations seek to interrelate phenomena and/or ideas.

Conclusion.   Typically, conclusions of good explanations develop additional implications or call for particular actions. If, for example, you have explained how contagious diseases spread through a geographical area, you probably will want to conclude that speech by discussing a series of actions which could be taken to halt the process of contagion. Or, in explaining what courts are starting to mean by the idea of "children's rights," you might close by asking your listeners to consider what the idea *should* mean to them—how they should change their thinking and their behaviors toward six-year-olds. Do not simply sit down when you have completed the explanation; reinforce its importance to your listeners by treating its implications. In that way, it will gain considerably more meaning for them and will more likely be remembered.

Overall, you should visualize the structure of an explanatory lecture in the following terms:

Introduction
I. Introduction of topic, using one of the beginnings described in Chapter 7.
II. Reasons the audience should be motivated to listen:
   A. First reason,
   B. Second reason, etc.
III. Forecast of the development of the body of the speech.

Body
I. First cause or problem, with developmental material;
II. Second cause or problem, with developmental material, etc.
III. First effect or aspect of solution;
IV. Second effect or aspect of solution, etc.

Conclusion
I. Summary
II. Treatment of implications (in the case of speeches in the causal pattern) or indication of desired actions (in the cause of problem-solution patterns).
III. Formal closing, using one of the ending tactics described in Chapter 7.

A SAMPLE SPEECH TO INFORM

The following text is Joyce Chapman's speech, "The Geisha," one she delivered when she was a freshman at Loop College, Chicago. It illustrates well most virtues of a good informative speech: (1) It provides enough detail and explanations to be clear. (2) It works from familiar images of geishas, adding new ideas and information in such a way as to enlarge audience members' conceptions. (3) Its organizational pattern—a topical pattern—makes it both easy to follow and coherent. (4) And, it includes the sorts of motivational appeals to make an audience want to listen.

THE GEISHA[2]

Joyce Chapman

[INTRODUCTION]

Personal
Reference

As you may have already noticed from my facial features, I have Oriental blood in me and, as such, I am greatly interested in my Japanese heritage. One aspect of my heritage that fascinates me the most is the beautiful and adoring Geisha.   /1

I recently asked some of my friends what they thought a Geisha was, and the comments I received were quite astonishing. For example, one friend said, "She is a woman who walks around in a hut." A second friend was certain that a Geisha was, "A woman who massages men for money and it involves her in other physical activities." Finally, I received this response, "She gives baths to men and walks on their backs." Well, needless to say, I was rather surprised and offended by their comments. I soon discovered that the majority of my friends perceived the Geisha with similar attitudes. One of them argued, "It's not my fault, because that is the way I've seen them on TV." In many ways my friend was correct. His misconception of the Geisha was not his fault, for she is often portrayed by American film producers and directors as: a prostitute, as in the movie, *The Barbarian and the Geisha,* a streetwalker, as seen in the TV series, "Kung Fu," or as a showgirl with a gimmick, as performed in the play, *Flower Drum Song.*   /2

Central Idea

A Geisha is neither a prostitute, streetwalker, or showgirl with a gimmick. She is a lovely Japanese woman who is a professional entertainer and hostess. She is cultivated with exquisite manners, truly a bird of a very different plumage.   /3

Orientation

I would like to provide you with some insight to the Geisha, and, in the process perhaps, correct any misconception you may have. I will do this by discussing her history, training, and development.   /4   [BODY]

First Point:
History

The Geisha has been in existence since 600 A.D., during the archaic time of the Yakamoto period. At that time the Japanese ruling class was very powerful and economi-

---

[2]"The Geisha" by Joyce Chapman, *Communication Strategy: A Guide to Speech Preparation* by Roselyn L. Schiff et al. Copyright © 1981 by Scott, Foresman and Company.

cally rich. The impoverished majority, however, had to struggle to survive. Starving fathers and their families had to sell their young daughters to the teahouses in order to get a few yen. The families hoped that the girls would have a better life in the teahouse than they would have had in their own miserable homes. /5

During ancient times only high society could utilize the Geisha's talents because she was regarded as a status symbol, exclusively for the elite. As the Geisha became more popular, the common people developed their own imitations. These imitations were often crude and base, lacking sophistication and taste. When American GIs came home from World War II, they related descriptive accounts of their wild escapades with the Japanese Geisha. In essence, the GIs were only soliciting with common prostitutes. These bizarre stories helped create the wrong image of the Geisha. /6

Second Point: Training

Today, it is extremely difficult to become a Geisha. A Japanese woman couldn't wake up one morning and decide, "I think I'll become a Geisha today." It's not that simple. It takes sixteen years to qualify. /7

At the age of six a young girl would enter the Geisha training school and become a Jo-chu, which means housekeeper. The Jo-chu does not have any specific type of clothing, hairstyle, or make-up. Her duties basically consist of keeping the teahouse immaculately clean (for cleanliness is like a religion to the Japanese). She would also be responsible for making certain that the more advanced women would have everything available at their fingertips. It is not until the girl is sixteen and enters the Maiko stage that she concentrates less on domestic duties and channels more of her energies on creative and artistic endeavors. /8

The Maiko girl, for example, is taught the classical Japanese dance, Kabuki. At first, the dance consists of tiny, timid steps to the left, to the right, backward and forward. As the years progress, she is taught the more difficult steps requiring syncopated movements to a fan. /9

The Maiko is also introduced to the highly regarded art of floral arrangement. The Japanese take full advantage of the simplicity and gracefulness that can be achieved with a few flowers in a vase, or with a single flowering twig. There are three main styles: Seika, Moribana, and Nagerie. It takes at least three years to master this beautiful art. /10

During the same three years, the Maiko is taught the

ceremonious art of serving tea. The roots of these rituals go back to the thirteenth century, when Zen Buddhist monks in China drank tea during their devotions. These rituals were raised to a fine art by the Japanese tea masters, who set the standards for patterns of behavior throughout Japanese society. The tea ceremony is so intricate that it often takes four hours to perform and requires the use of over seventeen different utensils. The tea ceremony is far more than the social occasion it appears to be. To the Japanese, it serves as an island of serenity where one can refresh the senses and nourish the soul. /11

One of the most important arts taught to the Geisha is that of conversation. She must master an elegant circuitous vocabulary flavored in Karyuki, the world of flowers and willows, of which she will be a part. Consequently, she must be capable of stimulating her client's mind as well as his esthetic pleasures. /12

Third Point:
Development
Having completed her sixteen years of thorough training, at the age of twenty-two, she becomes a full-fledged Geisha. She can now serve her clients with duty, loyalty, and most important, a sense of dignity. /13

The Geisha would be dressed in the ceremonial kimono, made of brocade and silk thread. It would be fastened with an obi, which is a sash around the waist and hung down the back. The length of the obi would indicate the girl's degree of development. For instance, in the Maiko stage the obi is longer and is shortened when she becomes a Geisha. Unlike the Maiko, who wears a gay, bright, and cheerful kimono, the Geisha is dressed in more subdued colors. Her make-up is the traditional white base, which gives her the look of white porcelain. The hair is shortened and adorned with beautiful, delicate ornaments. /14

As a full-fledged Geisha, she would probably acquire a rich patron who would assume her sizable debt to the Okiya, or training residence. This patron would help pay for her wardrobe, for each kimona can cost up to $12,000. The patron would generally provide her with financial security. /15

The Geisha serves as a combination entertainer and companion. She may dance, sing, recite poetry, play musical instruments, or draw pictures for her guest. She might converse with them or listen sympathetically to their troubles. Amorous advances, however, are against the rules. /16

[CONCLUSION]
So, as you can see the Geisha is a far cry from the back-rubbing, streetwalking, slick entertainer that was described by my friends. She is a beautiful, cultivated, sensitive, and refined woman.   /17

GROUP PROJECTS

1. Listed below are possible subjects for a speech. Select three of these subjects for a speech to inform (general purpose), and list what you think would be appropriate specific purposes. Using the same subjects for a speech to persuade (general purpose), list what you think would be appropriate specific purposes. What are the differences between the specific purposes for the two types of speeches? Are there any similarities?

    Financing higher education   Use and abuse of drugs
    Cooperative housing on campus   American cities
    Health food   The political process in America

For each of the subjects you selected above, write an appropriate central idea and proposition statement. How do your central idea statements differ from your propositions? Compare your specific purposes and central ideas and propositions with those of members of a small task group. Do the central ideas seem strictly informative, or could there be some kind of ultimately persuasive goal hidden in the central ideas?

2. Assume that you were to deliver a report describing each of the topics listed below. Divide into small groups to discuss (1) the group or agency responsible for hearing and taking action on each report; (2) the sources of information you would use in preparing each report; and (3) the method of organizing the data you might find.

    (a) Is a new library (or other university facility) needed?
    (b) Should a particular elementary school be closed in response to declining enrollments?
    (c) What is the present state of the university's health care system?
    (d) What can be done to cut gasoline consumption by university vehicles?

3. How would you go about explaining the topic of rabies vaccinations for pets to each of the following groups listed below? Work with three or four classmates to formulate the specific purpose of each speech, to suggest a pattern of organization, and to propose specific ideas that ought to be included.

    (a) A junior 4-H club studying the grooming and training of dogs
    (b) A city council meeting at which a new vaccination ordinance to include cats is to be discussed
    (c) Members of your speech class
    (d) A group of students at the Pre-Vet Club

INDIVIDUAL PROJECTS

1. Plan a two- to four-minute speech in which you will give instructions. For instance, you might explain how to calculate your life-insurance needs, how to "door knock" for a political candidate, or how to make a charter or group flight reservation. This exercise is basically descriptive, so limit yourself to use of a single visual aid.

2. For a varied round of four- to six-minute informative speeches, the class can alternate among these three types of presentations:

(a) The *demonstration* speech represents a highly coordinated effort at using verbal and nonverbal communication to illustrate or explain the operation of a device, the use of a product, or the steps in a process. Make sure that the object or the product or the tangible essentials of the process you are demonstrating are visible to everyone in your audience. Possible topics might include the following: fundamentals of self-defense, process of transplanting seedlings, basic tennis strokes.

(b) The *opposing positions* speech is an exercise in clearly and impartially presenting two sides of an issue. The communicator seeks to describe and summarize conflicting philosophies, solutions to some problem, or whatever. Prepare and deliver a speech of this type on one of the following topics or a similar one: the pros and cons of birth control, suggested alternatives to the piston engine, alternative grading systems, the strip-mining controversy.

(c) Explain or give a definition of an *unfamiliar or complex concept* such as one of the following: est, class-action suit, marriage contracts, charismatic movement, wholesale price index, Zen Buddhism, truth in labeling. Use visual supporting materials when they will enhance your presentation.

3. Since history courses have a way of getting rushed at the ends of terms, you may not have spent much time studying events since World War II. Unfortunately, even though you have lived through events such as the agitation at the Democratic National Convention in 1968, the collapse of South Vietnam, the Senate Watergate hearings, you may not have paid careful attention to them. To get a better idea of the historical factors that have influenced your parents' and your own lives, prepare a six- to eight-minute report on a historical event since World War II.

SUGGESTIONS FOR FURTHER READING

Lewis Donohew and Leonard Tipton, "A Conceptual Model of Information Seeking, Avoiding, and Processing," in *New Models for Communication Research,* ed. Peter Clarke, Sage Annual Reviews of Communication Research, Vol. 2 (Beverly Hills: Sage Publications, Inc., 1973), pp. 243–68.

Werner J. Severin and James W. Tankard, Jr., *Communication Theories: Origins*

Methods Uses, Humanistic Studies in The Communication Arts (New York: Hastings House, Publishers, 1979), Chapter 4, "Information Theory."

W. V. Quine and J. S. Ullian, *The Web of Belief* (New York: Random House, Inc., 1970), Chapter 7, "Explanation."

Magdalen D. Vernon, "Perception, Attention, and Consciousness," in *Foundations of Communication Theory*, ed. Kenneth K. Sereno and C. David Mortensen (New York: Harper & Row, Publishers, 1970), pp. 137–51.

Otis M. Walter and Robert L. Scott, *Thinking and Speaking: A Guide to Intelligent Oral Communication*, 4th ed. (New York: Macmillan Publishing Co., Inc., 1979), Chapters 10–12, "Thinking and Speaking About Problems," "Thinking and Speaking About Causes," and "Thinking and Speaking About Solutions."

CHAPTER 12

Speaking to Persuade and Actuate

Speeches to persuade are attempts to bring about changes in people's psychological states or behaviors. To be sure, a successful informative speech affects listeners in some way, altering their conceptions of the world or, in the case of instructions and demonstrations, the way they do things. The central focus of informative speeches, however, always is upon "information" and transmitting it to others. In contrast, the central focus of persuasive speeches is upon "psychological or behavioral change," or, in the case of actuative speeches, on actions you wish auditors to take as a result of altered beliefs, attitudes, and values.

Think back to Chapter 4's discussion of beliefs, attitudes, and values. You could present speeches to others on, say, why some people believe in Extra Sensory Perception, why those people are suspicious of so-called "scientific" investigations of ESP, and even why they value "psychic power" as a tool for integrating people and even nations. It would be one thing to *tell* an audience about the beliefs, attitudes, and values of "ESP-freaks"; but, it would be a very different communicative task were you to attempt to *persuade* an audience to accept those beliefs, attitudes, and values themselves, or even to go to the monthly meetings of a local ESP club.

The persuader is making quite a different demand upon an audience than the informer. The informative speaker is satisfied when listeners understand what has been said; the persuasive speaker is never happy until the audience *internalizes* (adopts as its own credo) or *acts upon* the speech. The demand of the persuader, the thrust of the speech, is upon personal change.

Although the purpose of a persuasive speech is to win belief or produce action, an unwilling decision is of little value. Beliefs which people are forced to accept may soon be abandoned; actions done unwillingly are usually done inefficiently and without any sense of reward or accomplishment. To persuade successfully, therefore, not only must you make your listeners believe or do something, but you also must make them *want* to believe or do it. For this reason, two subsidiary purposes of persuasive speaking must be kept in mind: (1) to provide the audience with motives for believing by appealing to certain of their basic needs or desires, and (2) to satisfy their understanding by convincing them that the proposition you recommend will make the satisfaction of these desires possible.

We will begin this chapter, therefore, with a discussion of motive needs and the motivational appeals speakers can use to tap those needs. Then, we will examine the Motivated Sequence as an organizational pattern which allows you to efficiently combine motivational appeals with claims to belief, attitude, value, and action to persuade the audience or move them to action.

ANALYZING THE NEEDS AND DESIRES OF THE LISTENERS

As we have said, a speech must be related to listeners' interests and desires. For your purposes as a public speaker, these interests and desires may be thought of productively as *motive needs.*

The Concept of Motive Needs

We may think of a *need* as some desire, want, or uneasiness which individuals sense or think about when considering their own situation. That need may arise from physiological considerations—pain, lack of food, or an uncomfortable temperature in a room—and it may come about for sociocultural reasons, as when you feel left out of a group or wonder whether your peers judge you to be a "good" person. If that need is deeply felt, it may impel you to do something about your situation, for example to eat, to adjust the thermostat, to ask to be let into a group. In these sorts of situations, you have been motivated to act. A *motive need*, then, is a tendency to move or act in a certain direction, an impulse to satisfy a psychological-social want or a biological urge.

A Classification of Motive Needs

The classification of fundamental human needs most often cited today is, perhaps, the one developed by psychologist Abraham H. Maslow.[1] Maslow presents the following categories of needs and wants which impel human beings to think, act, and respond as they do:

1. *Physiological Needs*—for food, drink, air, sleep, sex, etc.—the basic bodily "tissue" requirements.
2. *Safety Needs*—for security, stability, protection from harm or injury; need for structure, orderliness, law, and predictability; freedom from fear and chaos.
3. *Belongingness and Love Needs*—for abiding devotion and warm affection with spouse, children, parents, and close friends; need to feel a part of social groups; need for acceptance and approval.
4. *Esteem Needs*—for self-esteem based on achievement, mastery, competence, confidence, freedom, independence; desire for esteem of others (reputation, prestige, recognition, status).
5. *Self-Actualization Needs*—for self-fulfillment, actually to become what you potentially can be; desire to actualize your capabilities; being true to your essential nature; what you *can* be you *must* be.[2]

These "needs," according to Maslow, function as a *prepotent hierarchy;* that is, lower-level needs must be largely fulfilled before higher-level needs become operative. Persons caught up in the daily struggle to satisfy physiological and safety needs will, for example, have little time and energy left to strive for "esteem" or "self-actualization." Once these basic requirements of living are satisfied, however, higher-level drives take over. We should note, moreover, that as individuals we tend to move upward or downward between one level and another as our life progresses or regresses. Maslow's category of basic human needs and the hierarchical order in which they stand are illustrated in "A Hierarchy of Motive Needs," page 241.

And finally, it should be noted that motives do not always automatically produce certain courses of action. Physiologically, you may sense a sharp feeling of pain from not having eaten for two days; yet, because of social-cultural needs or pressures, you will not gobble down a chocolate cake when presented with one, but rather will sit politely with fork and napkin.

[1]Abraham H. Maslow, Motivation and Personality, New York: Harper & Row, 1954.

[2]In the 1970 revision of his book, *Motivation and Personality*, Maslow identified two additional needs—the needs to know and understand and the aesthetic needs—as higher need states which frequently operate as part of self-actualization needs.

The need for social approval may control the way one satisfies physiological needs. Nevertheless, the hierarchy of prepotency is of considerable use in conceptualizing human motivation, even if individuals vary in the ways they manifest those needs.

Motivational Appeals Useful to the Persuasive Speaker

Recognizing the power of motive needs to impel human action, one may ask: How can I as a public speaker go about creating, using, and satisfying such needs? How can I translate these basic needs, wants, or desires into verbal acts—into effective public communication? The answer to both of these questions is: With the use of motivational appeals.

A *motivational appeal* is either (1) a *visualization* of some desire and a method for satisfying it, or (2) an *assertion* that some entity, idea, or course of action can be or ought to be linked with an impulse-to-human-action— that is, a motive.

Suppose, for example, that you had been dating a person some time, and decided one evening that it was time to declare your love. As the evening progressed, you thought about how you were going to talk to your friend. You even created little "movies" in your head—perhaps full pieces of dramatic dialogue—as you rehearsed your speech. Will I be suave, casual, or a stumbling fool? Will I find the words, the looks, the actions to move my beloved? Will the person respond to me with tears or laughter, flippantly or seriously? Here we see the power of visualization. In visualizing various scenarios, you playacted yourself and your speech through a variety of motivational appeals: Is the *fear* of rejection worth the possibility of mutual declarations of *love?* Will *aggressiveness* work better than quiet appeals to *companionship?* By a process of intrapersonal visualization you thus assembled a group of motivational appeals potent enough to move your "audience," your beloved, and you organized those appeals into little stories you could tell.

At other times, instead of visualizing courses of action for yourself or your listener, you may simply try to attach motivational concepts directly to other concepts. Technically, this verbal process is called *attribution.*[3] Suppose, for example, that you had avoided going to church because you thought of churches as *conformist, authoritarian, dominating, repulsive,*

---

[3]For a fuller discussion of *attribution,* see Philip G. Zimbardo, Ebbe B. Ebbesen, and Christina Maslach, *Influencing Attitudes and Changing Behavior,* 2nd ed. (Reading, Mass.: Addison-Wesley Publishing Company, 1977), esp. pp. 72–80.

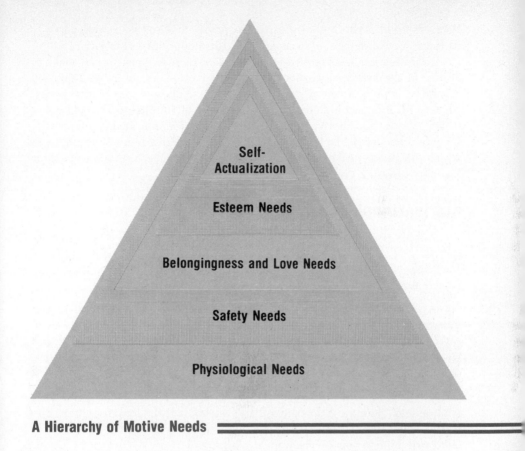

A Hierarchy of Motive Needs

and *destructive* institutions. One night, however, you went to a religious meeting, one where the preacher talked about the *adventure* of living a God-based life, the *beauty* of God's creation, the *reverence* one must feel in living a full life, the *endurance* one must have in overcoming doubts. You decided, upon reflection, that you had misconstrued the church's motivation and even misanalyzed yourself. You became a devout churchgoer. What happened? You changed the attributes of "churchness" in your own mind. Instead of attributing conformity/authority/dominance/etc., to that institution and ideal, you began attributing adventure/beauty/reverence/etc., to personal religion. Conversion was effected, and your behavior changed.

Motivational appeals, therefore, are verbal attempts to make salient and relevant a series of motives within an audience, within an idea or proposal under discussion, or within a countervailing force which you think is keeping listeners from accepting an idea or proposal. Such appeals work visually (through verbal depiction) or assertively (through verbal association).

Following is a list of motivational appeals which the speaker may make to arouse in the listener a particular feeling, emotion, or desire and thereby stimulate or perhaps set at work one or more of the primary *motive needs*. This list must be incomplete, because there are an infinite number of human wants, needs, and motives—and combinations thereof. It does, however, include some of the specific desires, drives, feelings, and sentiments to which practiced speakers often appeal in order to effectively motivate their listeners toward a given belief or action.[4]

Motivational Appeals

Achievement and display. "The successful businessman knows . . . ," "To make maximum use of your talents, act today to . . . ." Such appeals depend upon people's interest in making a mark, in developing or actualizing themselves.

Acquisition and saving. In this era of "me-ism," as seen in the growth of assertiveness training workshops, investment clubs, special savings plans offered by banks, etc., the appeal to personal savings and reward is potent. Rewards can be described in materialistic, social, spiritual, or personal terms.

Adventure and change. "Taste the High Country!" cries the beer commercial. "Join the Army and see the world" says the local recruiter. The human soul yearns for release; the human body seeks risk as a way of validating human worth. The appeal works.

Companionship and affiliation. Yet, also, we all need others—their presence, their touch, and their recognition of who we are. Thus, we all upon occasion listen and respond to such appeals as "We care about you . . . ," "Join our group and find fellowship with kindred souls," and "You are one of a select group we're extending this invitation to . . . ."

Creativity. As Maslow noted, the height of self-actualization is a

---

[4]For somewhat fuller discussion of these and other motive needs, see Douglas Ehninger, Bruce E. Gronbeck, Ray E. McKerrow, and Alan H. Monroe, *Principles and Types of Speech Communication*, 9th ed. (Glenview, Ill.: Scott, Foresman and Company, 1982), Chap. 6, "Determining the Basic Appeals"; and Bruce E. Gronbeck, *The Articulate Person: A Guide to Everyday Public Speaking*, 2nd ed. (Glenview, Ill.: Scott, Foresman and Company, 1983), Chap. 9, "Moving to Action."

sense of individualized abilities and talents. The ads that urge you to "Draw Me" so as to get a "scholarship" to a correspondence school art course, and the cookbooks which insist you become a "gourmet" by following step-by-step recipes are appealing to your sense of creativity.

Curiosity.   Children tear open alarm clocks to find out where the tick is, and adults crowd the sidewalks to gaze at a celebrity. Curiosity sometimes is "idle," yet often is the driving force behind such "high achievers" as experimenters, scholars, and explorers.

Deference.   When we perceive that others have wisdom, experience, or expertise superior to our own, we defer to their knowledge and judgment. The successful use of testimony as a form of supporting material depends upon listeners' deference.

Destructiveness.   In times of high agitation and anger, most of us respond to appeals which ask us to tear apart, to batter, to destroy. In times of war, "the enemy" must be destroyed; in times of interpersonal argument, ideas must suffer the same fate. If you think through the moral implications of urging destruction and, normally, couple it with more positive appeals as well, you will find the appeal a potent weapon.

Endurance and tradition.   We all are sensitive to our own relatively short span of earthly existence, and to all of the others who came before us, building the great social and physical monuments to life. Hence, we all are susceptible to appeals to our family, group, and social traditions as (1) entities for which we have responsibility and (2) guides to our own behavior.

Fear.   Humans have a broad range of fears—of failure, of death, of speechmaking, of inadequacy, of triumph by another. Fear is powerful, and productive of both good (as when an individual is driven to achievement and bravery) and evil (as when fear-based prejudice produces bestial behavior toward others). Use it carefully and cautiously.

Fighting and aggression.   Because human groups and societies tend to be hierarchical, our natural biological urge to fight for our own rights and territory becomes translated into appeals to personal and social competition. So, ad after ad tells you how "to get ahead of the crowd" or "to beat your competition to the punch"; and, many a group leader urges action so "we can win" or "we can beat them [competing groups] on this issue." No one wants to lose.

Imitation and conformity.   At times, people's sense of belonging-ness becomes so strong that they feel psychological pressure to be "one of the crowd." Commercials stressing what "the ingroup does," what the "successful businessman wears," and what "all true Americans believe" contain appeals to conformity.

Independence and autonomy.   Yet, as often you hear, "Be your own person; don't follow the crowd." Appeals to "know yourself," "be yourself," and "stand on your own two feet"—like the appeal to adventure—draw their force from our struggles to at least occasionally stand apart from others.

Loyalty.   Periodically, we all want to celebrate our membership in groups and societies. In times of crisis, therefore, speakers often call for "tests of loyalty," for extraordinary actions which visibly demonstrate individuals' adherence to group standards for belief and action. You can ask listeners to be loyal to family, friends, organizations, states, geographical regions, their country.

Personal enjoyment.   Like appeals to creativity, curiosity, and independence, appeals to personal enjoyment depend more or less on our "selfish" instincts. While undoubtedly we often act as group members, at least as often we will take some course of action because it promises us personal comfort and luxury; aesthetic enjoyment; recreation and rest; relief from home and work restraints; and just plain fun.

Power, authority, and dominance.   Like its first cousin, the appeal to fighting and competition, the appeal to power/authority/dominance depends for its potency upon our sense of aggressiveness. But, unlike the appeal to fighting and competition, this appeal moves beyond "mere winning" to *control:* People with power and authority control objects or other people. Thus, when President Jimmy Carter called his energy policy "the moral equivalent of war," he was urging us to control our energy needs; when the public service announcement says that "Cancer can be beaten in your lifetime," it is asking you to act from a sense of domination.

Pride.   Appeals to pride—a sense of our own or our group's worth— can drive us to collective or individual achievement. Such appeals tighten one's loyalties to groups, and, when coupled with appeals to adventure, creativity, and/or independence, move individuals to great personal exertion.

Reverence or worship.   Many times in our lives we recognize our own inferiority—our inferiority to others of superior qualities, to institutions we admire, to nature and the cosmos, and to deities which humble us in their magnitude and eternity. Beyond deference, a sense of reverence or worship leads to *submission*. Such reverent submission can take three forms: *hero worship*, *reverence for institutions*, and *divine worship*, conceived of both religiously and philosophically (as when eighteenth-century philosophers worshipped Nature).

Revulsion. The fragrance of a flower garden attracts people; the odor of a refuse heap repels. Similarly, in symbolic terms, you can attract people by verbally depicting the aesthetic pleasures they'll enjoy by acquiring or doing something, or by visualizing in strong images objects of disgust or loathing. (See "imagery" in Chapter 8.) So, by picturing the unsanitary conditions of slums or the horrors of war, you often can mobilize people to action. Beware only that you don't make such descriptions so gruesome that your appeal to revulsion turns them disgustedly against you. Be impressive without offending the deeper sensibilities of listeners.

Sexual attraction. A staple of advertising trying to sell you deodorant, hair rinse and spray, beer and liquor, and sundry other sundries is the sex appeal. "Sex sells," note the ad agents. Actually, as you look closely at such appeals, you'll find the core of the appeals lies not so much in bodily functions per se as in a more general idea of "personal attractiveness." Especially over the last decade, as our masculine and feminine consciousnesses have been raised, we have come to reject most objectionally blatant appeals to libidinous appetites. But we all listen to messages which promise to enhance our personal physical and psychological attractiveness and well-being.

Sympathy and generosity. While we often (cynically) assume that most people are selfish at root, yet we know that, on many occasions, we all can be shamed or drawn to reach out for others. All appeals to giving, to support of others, and to self-sacrifice in the name of the "common good" are predicated on the assumption that your *social self* (that part of you bonded to others) will overcome your *private self* (that part of you which is self-centered) when the right appeal is made. "Reach out and touch someone," "Give that others might live," "There but for the grace of God go I"—such appeals form the heart of many an actuative speech.

You may have noticed that this list contains certain appeals which seem to contradict each other: for example, fear against the drive for adventure; defense against the desire for power/authority/dominance; and so on. Remember, in this regard, that the human being is an inconsistent and changeable creature who, at different times, may pursue quite different ends or goals.

Using Motivational Appeals

In practice, motivational appeals—instead of acting singly—often act in combination. Suppose you were deciding whether to buy a particular suit or dress. What would influence your decision? One thing, obviously, would be price—*saving;* another would be comfort and appearance—the *personal enjoyment* to be derived from wearing it; a third consideration might be style—*imitation;* a fourth, individuality of appearance— *independence.* And finally, all these items together would raise the question of *pride:* Would other people think the clothes in good taste; would they envy your selection? Some of these influences might be stronger than others, and some might conflict, but all of them probably would affect your choice, and you would buy the dress or suit which made the strongest total appeal.

Because motivational appeals are thus interrelated, when building a speech it is a good idea to employ them in combination rather than singly. However, if the variety is too great, you may dissipate the effect. Generally, therefore, try to select the two or three appeals which you think will have the greatest effect on your hearers and concentrate on these, allowing others to be secondary or incidental. Be sure also that you do not inadvertently use conflicting appeals—for instance, do not urge your listeners to do something because of the *adventure* involved but describe the situation so vividly that they come to *fear* the act or its consequences. To avoid this, select as the main points of your speech those ideas that contain strong appeals and then examine them closely for pertinence and consistency.

Recently a representative of a College Union Board, in urging students to take advantage of a Union-sponsored summer tour of Europe, built her talk around these three points:

Acquisition and saving	I. The tour is being offered for the very low price of $1500 for three weeks.
Independence	II. There will be a minimum of supervision and regimentation.
Companionship	III. You will be traveling with your friends and fellow students.

In the complete development of her speech, she also emphasized the educational value of the experience *(self-advancement)* and said that a special mountain-climbing expedition was being planned *(adventure).*

Above all, don't let your attempt to motivate your listeners be too obvious, because that might make them reject your proposal. Do not say, "I want you to *imitate* Jones, the successful banker," or "If you give to this cause, we will print your name in the newspapers so that your *reputation* as a generous man will be known to everybody." Instead, merely suggest these results through the descriptions and illustrations you use. Remember, too, that people generally are ashamed to acknowledge publicly certain motives which privately may be very powerful, such as greed, fear, imitation, or pride. Therefore, when appeals to these and similar motivational factors are used in a speech, they must be carefully framed and supplemented by others which people are publicly willing to admit as the cause of their actions.

DEVELOPING A PERSUASIVE SPEECH: THE MOTIVATED SEQUENCE

When you have a persuasive goal, various sorts of supporting materials, a list of possible motivational appeals, and some thoughts about your audience's beliefs, attitudes, and values clearly in mind, it is time to think about organizing the materials—about "packaging." And, as we have been suggesting, a most important consideration in structuring materials is people's psychological tendencies—ways in which individuals' own motivations and circumstances favor certain kinds of structuring frameworks-for-ideas. Basically, we can say that human beings follow their own motives-to-action along one of two perceptual paths:

1. We may tend toward a *world-* or *problem-orientation.* The American philosopher John Dewey early in this century recognized this tendency when he devised his "psycho-logic"—a pattern for thought he called "reflective thinking." In Dewey's view, individuals tend to (and sometimes do) follow a systematic procedure for solving problems. First, said Dewey, people become aware of a specific lack or disorientation—some situation with which they are, for one reason or another, dissatisfied. Second, they examine this difficulty in their world to determine its nature, scope, causes, and implications. Third, they search for new orientations or operations that will solve the problem or satisfy the need. Fourth, they compare and evaluate the possible solutions that have occurred to them. And, fifth, they select the solution which, upon the basis of their foregoing reflections, seems most likely to put their minds at rest and to handle the real-world dimensions of the problem.[5] Dewey, in other words, adapted the so-called "scientific method" to individual and group problem-solving.

2. Our other tendency is to be more *self-centered,* more *motivation-centered.* Salespersons and advertisers began recognizing this principle in

---

[5]John Dewey, "Analysis of Reflective Thinking," *How We Think* (Boston, Mass.: D. C. Heath & Company, 1910), p. 72.

Political campaigns—for causes, for candidates—are largely matters of presenting speeches to persuade and actuate. Campaign speeches may be delivered one-on-one or one-to-many, printed up, electronically broadcast. Campaigners must get their audiences (1) to internalize points of view so as to make preferential judgments, and then, through voting or joining, (2) to act positively on those judgments.

the 1920s. They realized that you and I buy a particular automobile, not simply to get from here to there, but also to create a certain image; we buy this or that style of clothes to identify ourselves with others who wear certain sorts of trousers and coats; we buy furniture that is both functional and decorative. In other words, our personal motivations, hopes, fears, and desires often control the ways we act and the goods we consume.

Alan Monroe (1903–1975), the original author of this textbook, knew Dewey's work well and had himself worked in the 1920s training sales personnel. As he thought about Dewey's "psycho-logic" and the various sales techniques he had taught people to employ, Monroe discovered he could unite both sets of procedures—one set based on the personalized scientific method, and the other rooted in an understanding of human motivation—to form a highly useful organizational pattern. Since 1935, that structure has been called "Monroe's Motivated Sequence."[6] In this, the 50th anniversary edition of Monroe's textbook, we will devote the rest of this chapter to it.

---

[6]Anyone interested in how Alan Monroe conceived of and first used the motivated sequence—then a revolutionary idea—should see the first edition, Alan H. Monroe, *Principles and Types of Speech* (Chicago, Ill.: Scott, Foresman and Company, 1935), esp. pp. vii–x.

The Motivated Sequence: Its Five Basic Steps

The motivated sequence derives its name partly because it follows Dewey's problem-solution format for thinking and partly because it makes attractive analyses of those problems and their solutions by tying them to human motives. That is, in terms of our preceding discussion, the motivated sequence is simultaneously problem-oriented and motivation-centered.

Thus, the motivated sequence is composed generally of five basic steps in the presentation of verbal materials (see figure, page 252–3):

1. *Attention:* The creation of interest and desire.

2. *Need.* The development of the problem, through an analysis of things wrong in the world and through a relating of those wrongs to individuals' interests, wants, or desires.

3. *Satisfaction.* The proposal of a plan of action which will alleviate the problem and satisfy the individuals' interests, wants, or desires.

4. *Visualization.* The verbal depiction of the world as it will look if the plan is put into operation.

5. *Action.* The final call for personal commitments and deeds.

A SAMPLE SPEECH TO PERSUADE USING THE MOTIVATED SEQUENCE

Let us consider a speech which attempts to motivate the audience by employing the five steps: Attention, Need, Satisfaction, Visualization, and Action. It was prepared and presented in the annual contest of the Interstate Oratorical Association by Mr. Todd Ambs, Eastern Michigan University.

"THE SILENT KILLER"[7]
Todd Ambs

Attention step
For many Americans, life can seem to be a maze of numbers. We use many numbers so often that to be without them seems almost impossible. How long could college students survive without their student numbers? How many businesses could operate without a phone number? How many of you have

---

[7]"The Silent Killer" by Todd Ambs. Reprinted from *Winning Orations* (1980) by special arrangement with the Interstate Oratorical Association, Larry Schnoor, Executive Secretary, Mankato State College, Mankato, Minnesota.

never had use for your social security number? The answers to these questions are easy. But there is one other set of numbers that could set us on the road to preventing an estimated 300,000 deaths and over two million serious illnesses each year, if we would only pay attention to them. For no student number, phone number, or social security number will ever be as vital to you as your blood pressure reading.   /1

The human blood pressure is a veritable measuring stick of good health. Normal blood pressure, that is anything between 90/70 to 140/90, is generally a good indication of normal health. Unfortunately, over 25 million Americans do not have a blood pressure within this range. They suffer from high blood pressure, or hypertension.   /2

Indeed, according to the Department of Health, Education, and Welfare, this year, 310,000 Americans will perish from illnesses whose major contributing factor is hypertension. Two million will suffer strokes, heart attacks, and kidney failure as a direct result of hypertension. Even more startling is the realization that of that 25 million, 11 million aren't even aware of their condition. According to Dr. Theodore Cooper, Director of the Heart and Lung Institute, "Hypertension can be brought under control through proven treatment which is neither unduly hazardous, complicated or expensive."   /3

Need step
Before we can fully understand the magnitude of the problem though, we need to know what high blood pressure does to the body. When the pressure of the blood becomes too great for the arterial walls, high blood pressure results. This is somewhat like giving your circulatory system a headache. Fatty tissues, salts and fluids build up and the heart must be made to work harder than it should to keep the blood flowing properly. In this case, however, one tiny time pill won't relieve the pressure, or the irreparable damage that follows.   /4

That information may sound familiar to many of you. But then, why is hypertension still responsible for one out of every eight deaths in this country!   /5

The National High Blood Pressure Council attempted to answer that question when they said: "Half of those who have high blood pressure don't even know that they do. Of those who do, only half are being treated, only half again of those have their blood pressure under control. Patients and physicians alike just don't seem to take this condition very seriously."   /6

Such carefree attitudes leave many people's lives just hanging in the balance because high blood pressure has no symptoms. Contrary to popular belief, high blood pressure is not confined to trapeze artists, overactive children, or the Annie Hall's of the world. There is, in fact, no direct correlation between tension and nervousness and high blood pressure. The only way you can tell if you have high blood pressure is to get it checked. As Dr. Frank Finnerty, author of the book, *High Blood Pressure—The Silent Killer,* put it: "You can look great and feel healthy and have been living for years with the hidden time bomb of high blood pressure doing internal damage to your body." For Bill, a 49-year-old account executive, the time bomb was about to explode. One minute he was walking along seemingly in the best of health. The next he was on the ground clutching his chest. The heart attack would be the last event in Bill's life. He would never know the anguish that his family would suffer when they discovered that high blood pressure, a totally preventable condition, had caused his death. The silent killer had quietly destroyed life again.   /7

A routine physical could have saved Bill's life. And it could save yours. But unfortunately, our hectic, fast-paced lifestyles often provide easy excuses for not getting that needed physical. Lack of time, money, and the ever-popular lack of awareness can all be easy rationalizations for our failure to diagnose and treat hypertension. And our health care systems have failed to adjust to this reality at home, or especially on the job. A recent major manufacturing study found that on the average, businesses spend over $300 per employee per year, for illnesses caused by hypertension. Dr. Andrea Foote and Dr. John Erfurt, the country's leading specialists in hypertensive care, painted the picture in this light: "The current inadequacy of treatment suggests that the problem is a matter of social organization and lies primarily in the inability of the health care delivery system to provide health care for this disease."   /8

And here we reach the apex of the problem. Simple diagnosis must be followed by constant treatment if hypertension is to be controlled. Unfortunately, many people do not continue this vital treatment. Mike Gorman, Executive Director of the Citizens for the Treatment of High Blood Pressure, estimates that at least 50% of those diagnosed drop out of treatment after a few months. One man who had a severe attack of high blood pressure on his vacation came home, followed a steady treatment plan, and brought his pressure down. After a while, he foolishly decided to try foregoing the medication. Within a month, he had a stroke which left him with irreversible brain damage. This man should have known better. He was a doctor, who was about to be nominated to the A.M.A. presidency. Unbelievably, a man who had frequently prescribed treatment for hypertension, and ignored his own warnings! The precautions must be heeded; anyone can be a victim.   /9

Satisfaction step
Obviously then, the public needs to be made aware of the dangers of hypertension, health care systems should be improved to provide adequate health care for the disease, and finally, hypertensives must realize that constant treatment is essential to effective control.   /10

Thankfully, the goals I have mentioned are not just mere ideals proposed by a few specialists in hypertensive care. In 1972, the National Heart, Lung and Blood Institute organized the National High Blood Pressure Education Program, a program that all of us can get involved in. Their goal is to alert people to the dangers of hypertension through location, diagnosis, and

1 At current
consumption
rates, we
will run out
of fossil
fuels in
twenty years.

2 An advanced,
technological society
will be destroyed
unless
effective
measures
are adopted.

3 The solution to the
energy crisis requires a
three-pronged plan:
fuel conservation,
alternative energy
sources, and regulated
allocation of energy.

The Motivated Sequence

treatment. The results have been astounding. According to the National Center for Health Statistics, 290,000 people leading normal lives today would have died, were it not for the Hypertensive Education Program. Over eight million people now have their blood pressure under control, a 100% increase since 1972.   /11

And it touches all sectors of society, for the Hypertensive Education Program is nationwide. Here in Michigan, for instance, you can contact Steve Renke at the University of Michigan's hypertensive care unit in Ann Arbor, if you want to help.   /12

Visualization step

But we cannot rest on the laurels of this program. A disease which claims the lives of over 300,000 people annually is hardly under control. Doctors Foote and Erfurt have found that blood pressure control, for employed people, can best be carried out in the work setting. Their Worker Health Program was tested at four different job sites. As a result, 92% of the hypertensives at these jobs have their blood pressure under control, and the cost to the businesses involved has been cut from $300 per employee to $6.21. The program has been so successful that Blue Cross/Blue Shield of Michigan and Connecticut are now undergoing pilot programs of their own, based on the Worker Health Program.   /13

On the local level there are things you can do as well. In 1970, Savannah, Georgia, had the infamous title of Stroke Capital of the World. Today,

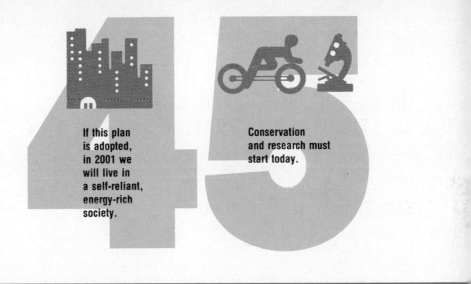

If this plan
is adopted,
in 2001 we
will live in
a self-reliant,
energy-rich
society.

Conservation
and research must
start today.

Savannah has 14 permanent blood pressure reading stations and the stroke toll in that city has been cut in half. A program, like one of these, can work in your community.   /14

Action step
So often, those of us in forensics use persuasive ploys instead of getting right to the heart of the problem. As a result, we tend to perform, instead of persuade. And you in turn as an audience listen, but don't hear. *Please,* if you do nothing else today, hear what I'm saying. There are people in this country who are dying because they have high blood pressure and there is not enough being done about it. You could be one of the 11 million Americans who has high blood pressure and does not even know it. If you are lucky enough to not be inflicted with the malady of hypertension, certainly someone that you know is. Don't let yourself or someone you know become a number on a fatality sheet. Get your blood pressure checked and save a life, your own.   /15

Observe that in his speech Mr. Ambs (1) called attention to his subject by referring to "everyday" numbers in people's social environment; (2) pointed out—by means of expert testimony, statistics, and poignant examples—the crucial need to bring hypertension under control; (3) demonstrated in the satisfaction step that a successful plan can be launched to sap hypertension's killer power; (4) via a series of examples visualized the financial and medical benefits produced by the plan; and (5) personalized the call for action by referring both to the situation in which the speech was delivered and to the special circumstances of the listeners.

USING THE MOTIVATED SEQUENCE TO STRUCTURE ACTUATIVE SPEECHES

Because speeches calling for action place great demands upon speakers, we can use them to fully illustrate ways the Motivated Sequence functions.

Step 1. Getting Attention

It has been said that all too frequently the attitude of the people about to hear someone give a speech is "Ho-hum." Obviously, you must change this attitude at the very beginning if you hope to persuade your listeners to believe or to act. The methods for effecting this change are described in Chapter 7. A review of pages 145–152 will remind you how startling statements, illustrations, questions, and other supportive materials can be used to focus wide-awake attention on what you have to say. You can't persuade an audience unless you have their attention.

Step 2. Showing the Need: Describing the Problem

When you have captured the attention of your listeners, you are ready to make clear why the policy you propose is needed. To do this, you must show that a definite problem exists; you must point out what is wrong with things as they are and through facts and figures make clear just how bad the situation is. For example, "Last month our plant at Littleton produced only 200 carburetors rather than the 300 scheduled. As a result we have had to shut down our main assembly line at Metropolis three times, with a loss of more than $60,000."

In its full form, a need or problem step requires a fourfold development: (1) *Statement*—a definite, concise statement of the problem. (2) *Illustration* —one or more examples explaining and clarifying the problem. (3) *Ramification*—additional examples, statistical data, testimony, and other forms of support showing the extent and seriousness of the problem. (4) *Pointing*—making clear to the listeners how the problem directly affects them. You will not, however, invariably need to use all four of these developmental elements. "Statement" and "pointing" should always be present, but the inclusion of "illustration" and "ramification" will depend upon the amount of detail required to impress the audience. But whether you use the complete development or only a part of it, the need step is exceedingly important in your speech, for it is here that your subject is first definitely related to the needs and desires of your listeners.

Step 3. Satisfying the Need: Presenting the Solution

The solution or satisfaction step in a speech urging the adoption of a policy has the purpose of getting your listeners to agree that the program you propose is the correct one. Therefore, this step consists of presenting your proposed solution to the problem and proving this solution practicable and desirable. Five items are usually contained in a fully developed satisfaction step: (1) *Statement*—stating the attitude, belief, or action you wish the audience to adopt. (2) *Explanation*—making sure that your proposal is understood. (Often diagrams or charts are useful here.) (3) *Theoretical demonstration*—showing by reasoning how your proposed solution meets the need. (4) *Reference to practical experience*—supplying examples to prove that the proposal has worked effectively where it has been tried. (Use facts, figures, and the testimony of experts to support this contention.) (5) *Meeting objections*—forestalling opposition by answering any objections which might be raised against the proposal.

Just as certain items may at times be omitted from the need step, so also one or more of these phases may be left out of the satisfaction step if the situation warrants. Nor must the foregoing order always be followed exactly. Occasionally, objections can best be met by dealing with them as they arise in the minds of the listeners; in other situations, the theoretical demonstration and reference to practical experience may be combined. If the satisfaction step is developed properly, however, at its conclusion the audience will say, "Yes, you are right; this is a practicable and desirable solution to the problem you pointed out."

Step 4. Visualizing the Results

The function of the visualization step is to intensify, or raise desire. It should picture for the audience how conditions will be in the future (1) if the policy you propose is adopted, or (2) if the policy you propose is not adopted.

Because it projects the thinking of the audience into the future, it might just as correctly be called the "projection" step.

This projection may be accomplished in one of three ways: by the *positive* method, the *negative* method, or the method of *contrast*.

The Positive Method.   When using this method, you describe conditions as they will be in the future if the solution you propose is carried out. Make such a description vivid and concrete. Select a situation which you are quite sure will arise. Then picture your listeners in that situation actually enjoying the conditions which your proposal will produce.

The Negative Method.   This method describes conditions as they will be in the future if your proposal is not carried out. It pictures for your audience the evils or dangers which will arise from failure to follow your advice. Select from the need step the most undesirable aspects of the present situation, and show how these conditions will be aggravated if your proposal is rejected.

The Method of Contrast.   This method combines the two preceding ones. The negative approach is used first showing the disadvantages accruing from failure to adopt your proposal; then the positive approach is used, showing the advantages accruing from its adoption. Thus, the desirable situation is thrown into strong contrast with the undesirable one.

Whichever method you use—positive, negative, or contrast—remember that the visualization step must stand the test of reality: the conditions you picture must be capable of attainment. Moreover, they must be made vivid. Let your listeners actually see themselves enjoying the advantages or suffering the evils you describe. The more clearly you can depict the situation, the more strongly the audience will react.

The following excerpt illustrates how a speaker urging homeowners to carry adequate property insurance might develop a visualization step by the method of contrast:

> Suppose that while you and your family are watching television some warm summer evening, a tornado warning is suddenly flashed on the screen and you are told to go at once to a safe corner of your basement. You gather your children in your arms and hurry down the steps. As the sky grows dark and the wind howls, you huddle together, hoping against hope that your lives will be spared.
>
> Eventually the storm passes, and you emerge from your shelter. At first you can only think how fortunate you and your family are to have escaped injury. But then you begin to look about you. Although you and your loved ones have survived, in other ways you have not been so lucky. The roof of your house has

been entirely blown off and the walls reduced to kindling. Your home is a total loss!

Then with a shock you realize that your insurance will not even begin to cover the damage. In addition to the expense of moving to an apartment and buying new furniture, you will need to buy another house. Not only will your hard-earned savings disappear, but you will have to go heavily into debt for many years to come.

Suppose, on the other hand, that your house had been fully insured. How different the picture would be! Although the inconvenience and trauma caused by the storm still would be present, one great worry would be taken off your mind. You would know you had the money to buy and furnish a new home, and to do so without any financial sacrifice on your part. So far as money matters were concerned, you would be able to pick up your life and carry it forward exactly as you had planned.

Step 5. Requesting Action or Approval

The function of the action step in a policy speech is to translate into overt action the desire created in the visualization step. This step commonly takes the form of a challenge or appeal, an inducement, or a statement of personal intention as described in Chapter 7. A review of pages 152–157, where these endings are discussed, will suggest their appropriateness as methods for developing this actuative phase.

Beware, however, of making the action step too long or involved. Someone has given this formula for successful public speaking: "Stand up; speak up; shut up." It is well here to emphasize the final admonition; finish your speech briskly and sit down.

Overall, of course, this description of the motivated sequence should be viewed as a *flexible* arrangement; it merely *suggests* the general pattern to be followed. The number of main points within each step and the number and order of subordinate or supporting ideas will vary from speech to speech and cannot be determined in advance. Sometimes the restatement will be omitted from the attention step; sometimes, instead of the method of contrast, you will use only a negative or a positive projection in the visualization step; and sometimes other modifications will be in order.

Once you have determined the general plan, however, write out the points of the outline as complete sentences, following the suggestions for phrasing and outline form given in Chapter 6 (pages 132–143). See also that each part of the talk performs the function required of it: that the attention step catches attention, that the need step points out a serious problem, and so on.

❝❞ A SAMPLE OUTLINE FOR AN ACTUATIVE SPEECH

An abbreviated outline[8] for an actuative speech arguing that students be given greater voice in the management of their college might, for example, take this form:

CITIZENS WITHOUT VOTES

Specific purpose:	To urge students to secure a greater voice in the decisions affecting their college lives.

Attention step	I. "Taxation without representation" was the rallying cry of our Revolutionary forebears.
	   A. It epitomized the plight of the voteless citizens of the American colonies.
	   B. It stirred them to action against "the mother country."

Need step
(Statement)
(Illustration)
	II. Today as students at Old Ivy College, we are voteless citizens of our academic community.
	   A. We have no voice in determining the fees that are assessed against us.
	     1. Tuition is set by the Board of Trustees.
	     2. Other charges are fixed by the Business Office.

(Illustration)	B. We have no voice in determining academic requirements.
	     1. Degree programs are established by the Faculty.
	     2. Grading policies are determined by the Dean.

(Illustration)	C. We have no voice in the government of our residence halls.
	     1. Rooms and roommates are assigned arbitrarily by the Director of Dormitories.
	     2. Policies affecting visiting privileges and study periods are set by the hall counselors.

(Ramification)	D. We are therefore not only voteless but also powerless.
Satisfaction step *(Statement)*	III. This state of affairs must end. A. We students should be given a voice in determining the fees we are charged.
(Explanation)	1. We should be allowed to make recommendations to the Board of Trustees.

---

[8]In an outline for a full-length speech, each of the steps may contain two or more major points or ideas (I, II, III, etc.) and also a number of subordinate or supporting points. We have "skeletonized" this outline to highlight its structure.

2. We should have student representatives who are allowed to meet regularly with officials in the Business Office.

(Statement)   B. We students should be given a voice in determining the establishment of academic policies.

(Explanation)   1. We should have a voting representative on the Committee on Curriculum.

2. We should be consulted whenever a change in grading policies is contemplated.

(Statement)   C. We should be granted complete control of our residence halls.

(Explanation)   1. Democratically elected dormitory councils should assign rooms and roommates.

2. All residents should vote on policies affecting visiting privileges and study periods.

(Practical experience)   IV. Fair and just policies of a similar nature already have been successfully instituted at many other colleges.

A. At Mountain Top College, representatives of the Student Senate sit on all faculty committees.

B. At Seaside College, students have complete control of their residence halls.

(Meeting the main objection)   V. In all cases where students have been given such authority, they have proved responsible.

A. They have discharged their duties faithfully and fairly.

B. They have acted conscientiously and with consistently good judgment.

Visualization step (Positive projection)   VI. The proposed reforms would bring two important benefits to Old Ivy.

A. They would provide important new inputs and insights into solving the many serious problems our college faces.

B. They would heal the misunderstandings and breaches now developing between students and faculty/administration.

Action step   VII. Begin action here and now to secure adequate student representation in college affairs.

A. You owe it to yourself as a student.

B. You owe it to the college community of which you are a member.

VIII. Raise your voices loud and strong in a modern-day variation of that old revolutionary war cry: "No relaxation until we get representation!"

USING THE MOTIVATED SEQUENCE TO STRUCTURE PERSUASIVE SPEECHES

When seeking to change listeners' attitudes and/or values—their positive or negative judgments about people, practices, institutions, or philosophies—you can adapt the basic pattern of the Motivated Sequence to your purposes as follows:

1. *Getting attention:* Capture the attention and interest of the audience.

2. *Showing the need:* Make clear that a judgment concerning the worth of the person, practice, or institution is needed. Do this by showing *(a)* why a judgment is important to your listeners personally, or *(b)* why it is important to the community, state, nation, or world of which they are a part.

3. *Satisfying the need: (a)* Set forth the criteria upon which an intelligent judgment may be based. *(b)* Advance what you believe to be the correct judgment and show how it meets the criteria.

4. *Visualizing the results:* Picture the advantages that will accrue from agreeing with the judgment you advance or the evils that will result from failing to endorse it.

5. *Requesting action or approval:* Appeal for the acceptance of the proposed judgment and for a determination to retain it.

A SAMPLE OUTLINE FOR A PERSUASIVE SPEECH

Each of the five steps in the basic pattern of the Motivated Sequence, adapted as suggested above, is illustrated in the following speech outline:

CONTRIBUTE TO CHARITIES WISELY[9]

Specific purpose: To persuade listeners to evaluate carefully the efficiency and effectiveness of the charitable organizations to which they contribute.

---

[9]This outline is based on a speech given by Steve Favitta, Central Missouri State University in 1978. We have omitted the supporting materials, but most may be found in "New CT Ratings on 53 Charities," *Changing Times*, November 1976; and "United Way: Are the Criticisms Fair?" *Changing Times*, October 1977. This altered outline is used with the permission of Mr. Favitta. Text supplied courtesy of Professor Roger Conaway and Professor Dan Curtis.

Attention step
(Startling
statement)

I. In 1975, Americans gave over 11.6 billion dollars to charitable organizations, not counting contributions to religious and educational institutions, but some experts have estimated that 116 million dollars was wasted because it went to fraudulent or poorly managed organizations.

Need step

II. There are differences in the ways charities distribute their funds.

(Example to
describe the
problem)

    A. Example of a charity which uses 94 percent of its contributions for administration.

    B. Example of a charity—United Way—which distributes ninety cents out of every dollar collected.

(Call for
evaluation)

III. Unless we all simply decide to stop giving to charities, we must come up with criteria for evaluating organizations and procedures for investigating them.

Satisfaction step
(Criteria)

IV. How, then, can you evaluate charities?

    A. Fund-raising and administrative costs should total less than 50 percent of the total public contributions.

    B. An effective charity should be controlled by an active, unsalaried governing board, with no paid employees serving as voting members of that board.

    C. It should use reputable promotional and fund-raising methods.

    D. It should publicly disclose a complete and independently audited annual financial report. (Each of these criteria could be justified by appeals to authority and example.)

(Indication of how
criteria can be
applied)

V. These criteria can be applied by both governmental units and individuals.

    A. Both Florida and Pennsylvania have laws governing what percentage of their total contributions charities can spend on fund raising.

    B. The federal government similarly regulates charities soliciting in more than one state.

    C. As an individual, you also can check into charities you might wish to support.

        1. Ask for an annual report before contributing.

        2. The Council of Better Business Bureaus publishes a rating list.

        3. The National Information Bureau discloses pertinent information.

Visualization step   VI. If both government and individuals do their investigative
                             jobs properly, imagine the benefits which would accrue
                             from the extra money spent on those who need it.
                             A. The number of poor that could be fed and clothed
                                would increase.
                             B. Additional medical and health care facilities could be
                                built.
                             C. Research into killing and crippling diseases could
                                proceed with more vigor.

Action step   VII. You have the power to direct your contributions to the
                             most beneficial charities.
(Summary)   A. Keep the evaluative criteria—efficiency, disinterest-
                                edness, fairness, and openness—in mind when you
                                receive a call for help.
(Appeal)   B. And when you give, open your heart, your pocket-
                                book, and, yes, your mind—give, but give wisely.

GROUP PROJECTS

1. What motivational appeals might you employ in addressing each of the following audiences? Be ready to discuss your responses.

   (a) A group of farmers taking part in a tractorcade
   (b) A meeting of predental students
   (c) Women at a seminar on nontraditional employment opportunities
   (d) Meeting of a group of local elementary and secondary classroom teachers
   (e) Group gathered for an old-fashioned Fourth of July picnic

2. Collect radio, television, and magazine ads that use fear appeals. Meet in small groups to discuss which of these advertisements are most effective and why. To what audiences are these ads directed? Do any of these ads have secondary or tertiary motivational appeals? If so, are these appeals carefully integrated to form a consistent persuasive message?

3. As a small group, examine closely the texts of several political speeches, advertisements for goods and services, and brochures describing social organizations or clubs. Category by category (speeches, advertisements, organizational brochures), list the motives appealed to in each type of persuasive discourse. Upon critical inspection, do you find any common patterns in these motive appeals? Do politics, business, and social services each appeal to certain motives more often than others? Do these three types of persuasion appeal principally to one or two levels in Maslow's prepotent hierarchy; and, if so, what do these facts lead you to conclude about each type of persuasion?

▶ INDIVIDUAL PROJECTS

1. Present a five- to eight-minute speech, the purpose of which is to persuade members of your speech class to take a recommended action. Show that a problem or situation needing remedy *actually* exists. Show your listeners why *they* (and not someone else) should be concerned, and why you think a specific action on their part will be a concrete, influential move toward a remedy. On a future "check-up" day, see how many members of the audience actually have taken the recommended action. For example, you may urge an audience to *sign a petition* proposing that graduating seniors should be excused from their final examinations or that the college should establish a cooperative bookstore. Or, you may ask members of your class to *write letters* or send mailgrams to *their congressional representatives* urging that all election campaigns should be financed publicly or that Bill X should be passed. (Be sure to tell them who their representatives are and where they can be reached.) Or, you can ask members to *attend a meeting* of a newly organized campus group to *participate* in an activity such as giving blood during the next visit to the Red Cross Bloodmobile.

2. In a brief persuasive speech, attempt to alter your classmates' impression or understanding of a particular term. To begin with, you must analyze their current attitude toward the topic. If the prevalent attitude toward the term is negative, how are you going to change that impression, or vice versa? Sample topics include the following: constitutional monarchy, pesticide, closed shop, natural gas deregulation, open housing, compulsory health insurance, party politics, physical handicaps, the volunteer army.

3. Wayne C. Minnick [*The Art of Persuasion*, 2nd ed. (Boston: Houghton Mifflin, 1968), p. 232] writes: "Emotion is an aroused 'feeling state' that accompanies an unusual degree of motivation. Persuasive communications that evoke emotional reactions are successful in some cases and ineffectual in others. The degree of emotional response evoked seems to interact with such factors as credibility to determine persuasiveness." Read Martin Luther King, Jr.'s "I Have a Dream" speech and appraise its effectiveness in securing an emotional response from the audience. Use Minnick's Chapter 9, pages 232–251, as a basis for a paper discussing King's use of emotion.

4. Work with two of your classmates. The three of you will choose a purpose— e.g., give blood during the upcoming blood-donation marathon, go see *The Rocky Horror Picture Show* (or some other movie which may raise considerations of propriety), urge the passage of a bill increasing local taxes for education, do not cross the "lines" to shop at a store being picketed by union employees—and then choose which of you will prepare an address for a hostile audience, for a neutral audience, and for a favorable audience. You may consult each other in planning the speeches. Be prepared to deliver your speeches on the same day so that the class can discuss the differences in approaches.

SUGGESTIONS FOR FURTHER READING

Erwin P. Bettinghaus, *Persuasive Communication*, 3rd ed. (New York: Holt, Rinehart & Winston, 1980).

Ernest G. Bormann, *Communication Theory* (New York: Holt, Rinehart & Winston, 1980), Chapter 1, "The Development of Contemporary Communication Theory."

Stephen Littlejohn, "A Bibliography of Studies Related to Variables of Source Credibility," in *Bibliographical Annual in Speech Communication: 1971*, ed. Ned A. Shearer (New York: Speech Communication Association, 1972), pp. 1–40.

Werner J. Severin and James W. Tankard, Jr., *Communication Theories: Origins Methods Uses*, Humanistic Studies in The Communication Arts (New York: Hastings House, Publishers, 1979), Chapter 12, "Beginnings of Attitude Change Research," and Chapter 13, "Further Developments in Attitude Change."

Philip G. Zimbardo, Ebbe B. Ebbesen, and Christina Maslach, *Influencing Attitudes and Changing Beliefs*, 2nd ed. (Reading, Mass.: Addison-Wesley Publishing Company, 1977).

CHAPTER 13

Public Reasoning and Argumentation

In argument, a speaker offers specific, identifiable reasons for, and seeks acceptance of, a particular claim in opposition (usually) to a claim or claims advanced by others. Argument is considered the lifeblood of democratic institutions. Decision-making by means other than executive fiat and brute power requires the freedom to advance and appraise arguments for and against specific claims. Because there seldom are certain, absolute answers to most questions of public belief, attitudes, values, and policies, a group or country must depend upon public debate to make enlightened, thoughtfully examined, decisions.

The word "argument" is ambiguous in everyday usage. Some people are afraid of arguing ("I want to discuss this with you, not argue about it"). Others see argumentation as a process of verbal attack and parry ("Now *that* was a good fight [or argument]!"). Attacking and fighting often are associated with the word "argument" in our minds, and understandably so. But yet, argument—public reasoning—as a type of communication and decision-making process is quite different from attack and warfare. In this chapter, therefore, we will first review the characteristics of argument that differentiate it from fighting, and then discuss the bones or skeleton of a unit-of-argument, and conclude with discussions of proper and improper (fallacious) reasoning.

ARGUMENT AS A TYPE OF COMMUNICATION

What makes argument special is not that it is a *fight*, which it is; not that you ordinarily are *attacked*, which you are; and not even that it is perfectly *logical*, which frequently it is not. Rather, what distinguishes argument from other communicative forms is the fact that it is *rule-governed*. In this chapter we will focus on the specialized rules that govern *an act of arguing* with other people. Instead of merely offering information or trying to persuade others that you are right and they are wrong, *the act of arguing commits you to communicating according to certain rules*, especially *social conventions* and *technical regulations*.

Social Conventions

In this and most other societies, there are unstated yet potent *conventions* or habitual *expectations* which govern argument. That is, when you decide to argue with another person, you are making, generally, commitments to four standards of judgment or four of these conventions:

Convention of bilaterality. Argument is explicitly bilateral: it requires at least two people or two competing messages. The arguer, implicitly or explicitly, is saying that he or she is presenting a message which can be examined and evaluated by others. Now, the seller of toothpaste seldom invites this kind of critical examination of the product; Procter and Gamble is in the business of persuasion, not argumentation. A U.S. senator, in contrast, assumes a party label and pits a proposed solution to some social problem against solutions proposed by others, thus specifically calling for counteranalysis or counterargument. The arguer invites reasoned inquiry in return.

Convention of self-risk. By at least implicitly calling for a critique of your ideas and propositions from others, you assume certain risks, of course. There is always the risk of failure, naturally; but you face that risk any time you open your mouth. More important in argument there is the risk of being proven *wrong*. For example, when you argue that a federal system of welfare is preferable to a state- or local-based system of relief, you face the possibility that your opponent will convince *you* that local control creates fewer problems and more benefits than does federal control. The bright light of public scrutiny often can expose your own as well as your opponent's weaknesses and shortcomings. That risk is potent enough, indeed, to make many people afraid of arguing publicly.

The fairness doctrine. Arguers also commit themselves to some version of what the radio and television industry calls the "fairness" doctrine. The fairness doctrine of the Federal Communication Commission maintains that all competing voices ought to be given equal access to the airways to express their viewpoints. Similarly, arguers say, in effect, "You may use as much time as I have (or as much time as you need) to criticize my claims and reasons." This is why, for example, most legislative bodies are reluctant to cut off debate by invoking cloture rules even in the face of political filibustering. Our legislative bodies are committed to the fairness doctrine: the idea that debate (argument) ought to be as extended and as complete as possible so that all considerations can be aired, considered, and defended.

Commitment to rationality. Arguers commit themselves to rationality, to a willingness to proceed logically. That is, when you argue, you are at least implicitly saying, "Not only do I believe X, but I have *reasons* for doing so." When you argue, for instance, that nonreturnable bottles should be banned by state law, someone else has the right to say "No" (the convention of bilaterality) and the right to assert a contrary proposition (the fairness doctrine). But—in addition—all parties to the argument have a right to ask, "*Why* do you believe that?" (the convention of rationality). As an arguer, you are committed to *giving reasons*, reasons that you think support your claim and ought to be accepted by unsure or doubtful listeners. Argument, therefore, is a rational form of communication, not in the sense that speakers often use syllogisms or other strictly logical structures, but in the sense that all arguers believe they have good reasons for the acceptance of their claims. They are obligated to provide those reasons; they cannot get away with saying, "Oh, I don't know—I just feel that is true." When reasons are given, if they are relevant to the claim being advanced and if they are acceptable to the audience hearing the claim defended, then the arguer will have met the commitment to rationality.

Technical Rules

In some cases, arguers are committed not only to generalized conventions or accepted bases of argument, but also to arguing in accordance with particular formalized procedures or unusual technical strictures. At a monthly meeting of a hobby club, for example, you may well find that you are expected to offer motions and amendments according to *Robert's Rules of Order.*[1] In many

---

[1]From *Robert's Rules of Order, Newly Revised.* Eds. Sarah Corbin Robert, Henry M. Robert III, James W. Cleary, William J. Evans. Copyright © 1970 by Henry M. Robert III, Trustee for the Robert's Rules Association.

Political debates often illustrate the social conventions governing public argument: (1) Opposing positions are advanced *(bilaterality)*. (2) Candidates allow others to examine and critique their ideas publicly *(self-risk)*. (3) Opponents are given equal time *(fairness doctrine)*. (4) Candidates are expected to give "good reasons" for their positions *(commitment to rationality)*.

formal meetings, Robert's or some other set of parliamentary procedures are used. Parliamentary procedures are technical rules. They limit *what* you can say (some motions are "out of order"), *how* you can say it (you may not be allowed to defend an idea unless your motion is seconded), and even *when* you can say it (everything you say must be germane to the motion under consideration). The essential details of parliamentary procedure for handling motions are shown in the chart on pages 286–287. Argumentation in legislatures and courtrooms is governed by such specifically defined rules, as it is in many clubs and other decision-making organizations.

In other settings and contexts, arguers are expected to follow somewhat different, but analogous, technical rules. The social scientist who has made a study, say, of the effect of source credibility upon the persuasiveness of messages must report the results in a specific way. The "scientific method" is, in effect, a set of rules—rules of procedure, statistical rules for proper measurement, and rules of inference: what we can infer about the whole society as the result of a limited experiment carried out on a small portion of that society. The social scientists who—in offering reports of their findings—do not carefully define, scrupulously measure, and statistically compare data, and who then draw broad conclusions about the universe from a limited study, will not be listened to or published. The argument, as social scientists view their work, would not be "proper," and the report would be rejected. Various academic and business disciplines thus lay out their own rules for arguing; rules which must be followed if you are going to engage in argument in a given profession or field.[2]

THE ANATOMY OF AN ARGUMENT

You can approach the question of argumentation's "anatomy" at three levels. The overall process of arguing, with proponents and opponents taking turns in addressing each other, represents the "gross anatomy" of argumentation. This process is initiated with an "argumentative" or "constructive" speech; it progresses when someone offers a "refutative" speech; it continues then through a series of "rebuttals" until some sort of decision is reached via voting or consensus. At a narrower level, you can examine the anatomy of a single argumentative speech, noting that (1) the introduction should set out the position and suggest criteria for judging a claim supported or unsupported; (2) the body should be organized around the series of reasons which support the claim, and (3) the conclusion should summarize the position and indicate why it is superior to the opposing view.

In this chapter, however, we will examine the anatomy of argument essentially at the "cellular" level, concerning ourselves primarily with how a "unit-of-argument" is built. Basically, an argument consists of (a) the *claim* or proposition to be defended, (b) the relevant *evidence* you can accumulate in support of that claim or proposition, and (c) the *reasoning pattern* (sometimes called the inference) you use to connect the evidence to the claim. Let us examine each of these elements separately, then together.

Types of Claims

Most argumentative speeches assert that in the opinion of the speaker (1) something is or is not the case; (2) something is desirable or undesirable; or (3) something should or should not be done. Such judgments or recommendations, when formally addressed to others, are called the speaker's *propositions* or *claims*. The first step in constructing a successful argument is to clearly determine the nature of the claim you wish to establish.

---

[2]See Richard Rieke and Malcolm O. Sillars, *Argumentation and the Decision Making Process*, 2nd ed. (Glenview, Ill.: Scott, Foresman and Company, 1984); Stephen Toulmin, Richard Rieke, and Allan Janik, *An Introduction to Reasoning* (New York: Macmillan, 1979), Chaps. 13–17.

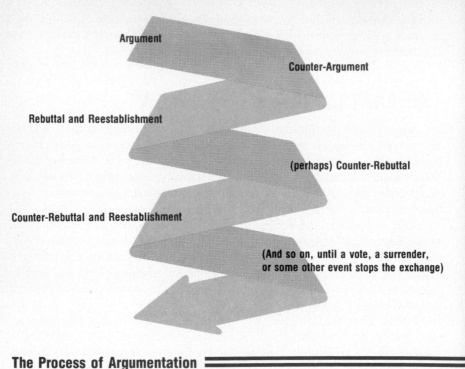

Argument

Counter-Argument

Rebuttal and Reestablishment

(perhaps) Counter-Rebuttal

Counter-Rebuttal and Reestablishment

(And so on, until a vote, a surrender, or some other event stops the exchange)

The Process of Argumentation

Claims of Fact. If you were trying to convince your listeners that "price controls on raw agricultural products result in food shortages," you would be presenting a factual claim—asserting that a given state of affairs exists or that something is indeed the case. When confronted with a claim of this sort, two questions are likely to arise in the mind of a thoughtful listener:

1. *By what criteria or standards of judgment should the truth or accuracy of this claim be measured?* If you were asked to determine a person's height, you would immediately look for a yardstick or other measuring instrument. Listeners likewise look for a standard when judging the appropriateness of a factual claim. In the example given above, before agreeing that price controls result in shortages, the members of your audience would almost certainly want to know what you as a speaker mean by "shortages." Does it mean "the disappearance, for all practical purposes, of a given kind of food" or merely "less of that food than everyone might perhaps desire"? Against what standard, precisely, is the accuracy of the claim to be judged?

2. *Do the facts of the situation fit the criteria as set forth?* Does the amount of produce and other raw agricultural products presently on supermarket shelves fall within the limits set by your definition of "shortages"? First, get your listeners to agree to certain standards or measurements for judgment and then present evidence to show that a given state of affairs meets these standards. Then you will, in most instances, be well on your way toward winning their belief.

Claims of Value.   When, instead of asserting that something is or is not so, you assert that something is good or bad, desirable or undesirable, justified or unjustified, you are advancing a claim of value—a claim concerning the intrinsic *worth* of the belief or action in question. Here, as in the case of claims of fact, it is always appropriate to ask: (1) *By what standards or criteria is something of this nature to be judged?* (2) *How well does the item in question measure up to the standards specified?* We may, for example, assert that the quality of a college is to be measured by the distinction of its faculty, the excellence of its physical plant, the success of its graduates in securing positions, and the reputation it enjoys among the general public; and then proceed to argue that because the college we are concerned with meets each of these tests, it is indeed a good one.

Claims of Policy.   A claim of policy recommends a course of action you want the audience to approve. Typical examples are: "Federal expenditures for pollution control *should be* substantially increased"; "The student senate *should have* the authority to expel students who cheat." In both instances, you are asking your audience to endorse a proposed "policy" or course of action. When analyzing a policy claim, four subsidiary questions are relevant:

1. *Is there a need for such a policy or course of action?* If your listeners do not believe that a change is called for, they are not likely to approve your proposal.

2. *Is the proposal practicable?* Can we afford the expenses it would entail? Would it really solve the problem or remove the evil it is designed to correct? Does such a policy stand a reasonable chance of being adopted? If you cannot show that your proposal meets these and similar tests, you can hardly expect it to be endorsed.

3. *Are the benefits your proposal will bring greater than the disadvantages it will entail?* People are reluctant to approve a proposal that promises to create conditions worse than the ones it is designed to correct. Burning a barn to the ground may be a highly efficient way to get rid of rats, but it is

hardly a desirable one. The benefits and disadvantages that will accrue from a plan of action always must be carefully weighed along with considerations of its basic workability.

4. *Is the offered proposal superior to any other plan or policy?* Listeners are hesitant to approve a policy if they have reason to believe that an alternative course of action is more practicable or more beneficial.

From what has been said about the three types of claims, you should now be able to see the importance of knowing exactly the kind of claim you are seeking to establish. Is it a claim of policy, fact, or value? If it is a claim of policy, do you need to answer all four of the basic questions listed above, or is your audience likely to accept one or more of them without proof? If yours is a claim of fact or value, what criteria should you use as bases for judgment; and how well are they met by the evidence?

Finally, unless there are sound reasons for delay, you should announce early in your speech the claim you are going to support or oppose. If your listeners do not see the precise point on which they will be asked to judge, your strongest arguments and appeals probably will prove useless.[3]

Evidence

By "evidence" per se we are referring to nothing more complicated than the kinds of supporting materials reviewed in Chapter 5. Thus, explanations, comparisons and contrasts, illustrations, specific instances, statistics, and testimony represent types of evidence as well as, more generally, types of supporting materials.

For the arguer, the question of *kinds* of evidence should cause no problem; you simply must go out and find it, as you have been doing throughout this course. But, questions concerning the *selection of relevant evidence* is another matter. The question is complex because evidence is supporting material which must be "relevant" to some claim in both logical and psychological terms: (1) It must seem relevant *rationally* to the type of claim being advanced, and (2) yet it also must be relevant *motivationally* to members of the audience.

Rationally Relevant Evidence. As our analysis of types of claims should suggest, the rational requirements for evidence are related to the

---

[3]A full discussion of the logical grounding of claims in evidence and reasoning is presented in Douglas Ehninger and Wayne Brockriede, *Decision by Debate,* 2nd ed. (New York: Harper & Row, Publishers, 1978).

types of claim being defended. So, for example, testimony and definitions are kinds of evidence useful in defending your selection of standards of judgment of fact- and value-based claims; while statistics, examples, and illustrations are useful when you must urge that the situations being discussed "fit" the criteria or standards you set out. Or, when defending policy claims, you often must document "needs-for-a-change" with statistics, examples, and testimony; practicality arguments with comparisons and contrasts; propositions concerning benefits with explanations and illustrations; and, claims about the superiority of your policy, again, with comparisons and contrasts. The point is this: As you sort through the questions we have asked about each type of claim, you should be asking yourself, "What type of evidence is logically relevant in support of that type of claim?"

Motivationally Relevant Evidence. But your evidence must be more than rationally relevant. You also must answer a perhaps tougher question: "What sort of evidence will this audience accept as relevant to its decision-making?" And, in turn, buried in that question are two sub-questions:

1. *What type of evidence will this audience demand?* The social scientists we referred to earlier will demand, from a fellow scientist reporting on an experimental study, operational definitions of key concepts, expert testimony from other researchers who have investigated the same phenomena, examples of ways in which the experiment was carefully controlled, statistical tests and inferences, and perhaps comparisons between this study and the others which have been done in the same area. "Mere" examples or illustrations, or even figurative analogies, will not be accepted as proof. In contrast, were you evaluating a novel for an audience of literary buffs, examples, illustrations, figurative analogies, etc., would be much more forceful as "proof" than statistical counts of words or even the testimony of other literary critics. Careful audience analysis will help you determine what type of evidence is needed psychologically to move your particular group of listeners.

2. *Which actual pieces of evidence of a given type will this audience prefer?* This is an even harder question to answer. Whom should you quote if you decide to use testimony? What comparisons and contrasts will make sense to this audience? Should you use "big city" or "small town," classical or contemporary, nearby or faraway examples? In dealing, say, with the problem of a federal farm program, should you use a highly personalized or a general illustration?

To answer these and similar questions about evidence, you need to analyze your audience: A homogeneous, "home town" audience probably would prefer "local" experts, everyday comparisons, local, nearby examples, and an illustration about a farmer who lives outside of town. A heterogeneous audience (such as the people making up your class audience) probably would prefer more generally recognized authorities, more college-student oriented comparisons, geographically varied examples, and illustrations dealing with farmers from several parts of the country. And, Democrats will want Democratic experts, Republicans, GOP authorities; a Chamber of Commerce audience will like business illustrations; a Future Farmers of America audience, agricultural illustrations; and so on. You cannot always, of course, wholly tailor your evidence to your audience's demographical or psychological characteristics; but always, at least, attempt to take them into account.

In sum, it is one thing to discover evidence, another to select it. Select it with both your claim and your audience in mind.

Reasoning (Inferences)

The third element of a unit of argument is that element which "connects" the evidence with the claim. This is called reasoning or inference. *Reasoning* is a process of connecting something which is known or believed (the evidence) to some concept or idea (the claim) you wish others to accept. "Patterns of reasoning," therefore, are habitual ways in which a culture or society uses inferences to connect that which is accepted to that which is being urged upon them. Basically, there are five basic reasoning patterns.

Reasoning from Examples.   Often called *inductive* reasoning, reasoning from instances or examples is a matter of examining a series of particular examples or known occurrences (evidence) and drawing a general conclusion (claim). The inference in this reasoning pattern can be stated: "What's true of particular cases is true of the whole class." This represents a kind of mental inductive "leap" from specifics to generalities. So, for example, the Food and Drug Administration will study the effects of cyclamates on a few people and discover a larger than normal incidence of cases of visceral cancer (the examples or evidence). With an inductive leap they'll move to the factual claim, "Cyclamates can cause visceral cancer in the general population," and hence ban them. You use a similar pattern of reasoning every time you drive home during rush hour. After trial and error, you decide that Street A is the best one to take home between 5:00 and 5:30 p.m., and Street B, between 5:30 and 6:00 p.m. After enough instances, in other words, you arrive at a generalization and act upon it.

Reasoning by Parallel Case. Another common reasoning pattern involves thinking, not in terms of generalizations, but solely in terms of closely similar events. Your city, for example, probably designed its transit system or its parking lots by examining the transit systems or parking arrangements in cities very much like it. The evidence was the occurrences in a *parallel* town; the claim was that certain policies ought to be implemented in your city; while the inference ran something like, "What worked in City A will work here because of similarities." As a parent, you employ reasoning from parallel case every time you say, ever so sanctimoniously, "Don't run into the street. Remember what happened to Jamie Johns when she did?" Obviously, you're not generalizing (for not everyone who goes into a street will be struck down). Instead you are asserting that Jamie and your child are parallel cases—that they have enough features in common to increase the likelihood of another accident in the neighborhood.

Reasoning from Sign. A third reasoning pattern uses an observable mark or symptom as proof for the existence of a state of affairs. You reason from sign when you note the rash or spots on your skin (the evidence) and decide you have measles (the claim). The rash doesn't "cause" measles; rather, it's a sign of the disease. Detectives, of course, are notorious reasoners-from-sign. When they discover someone had motive, had access, and had a weapon in his or her possession (the signs), they move to the claim that the person might be the murderer. Your doctor works the same way every time she asks you to stick out your tongue, looking for signs of trouble. These signs, of course, are circumstantial evidence—and could be wrong. Just ask detectives and doctors. The inference, "This evidence is a sign of a particular conclusion," is one you have to be careful with. This sort of reasoning works pretty well with natural occurrences (ice on the pond is always a sign that the temperature has been below 32 degrees Fahrenheit). But reasoning from sign can be troublesome in the world of human beings (as when we take people's skin color as a sign that they are lazy/dishonest/rhythmical). Yet we often have to use signs as indicators; otherwise we could not project our economy, predict our weather, and forecast the rise and fall of political candidates.

Reasoning from Causal Relation. Reasoning from causal relation involves associating known antecedents (that which comes before or "pushes") with certain consequents (that which comes after as a result of the "push"). Such cause-effect reasoning is important enough, you'll remember, that it is frequently used as a basic pattern for organizing speeches. Its power derives from the hope we have that our world is a regularized, predictable one in which every occurrence has a cause. Hence, if crime rises in your community, there's an immediate scramble to find the causes—drugs, economic deterioration, inept law enforcement, or bad street lighting. Instead of reasoning from certain effects back to possible causes, we also can reverse the process by reasoning from causes to possible effects. When the Great Plains are threatened with drought, the government moves immediately to head off bad effects by stockpiling grain, by arranging for airlifts of hay for animals, by raising beef import quotas, and by planning for emergency loans to build irrigation projects. The evidence and the claim, therefore, are the identified causes and effects, while the inference is the simple but important generalization, "Every cause has an effect."

Reasoning from Generalization or Axiom. A final kind of reasoning pattern, often called *deduction,* is essentially the reverse of reasoning from instances (induction). Even as a child you probably were taught that buying goods in large quantities saves money (the generalization or evidence). Therefore, because discount stores purchase goods in quantity, you will be able to save money shopping there (the claim deduced from the evidence). Or, to take the classic example, because all people are mortal (generalization or axiom), and because Socrates is a person, therefore Socrates is mortal (the claim). Note that the inference can garner its power from one of two sources: in the first case, it is justifiable because of *experience* (by shopping around a lot we arrived at the generalization); and in the second, the generalization really is a *definition* (i.e., one of the innate characteristics of human beings is mortality). In other words, we accept the first inference because of uniformities in the world, and the second because of ways we use words such as *human* and *mortal.*

These five forms of reasoning are judged "logical" or "rational" in this culture, and hence are the primary means for connecting evidence with a claim.

TESTS FOR REASONING

Because argumentative speaking is preeminently a reason-giving communicative activity, and because the reasoning process is really the fulcrum on which the entire argument turns, it is essential that you test your reasoning. This testing is a quasi-logical activity; you engage it, not simply to discover your logicalness, but more simply to protect yourself as both a generator and a consumer of arguments. Each form of reasoning has its own tests or questions to which it must respond if an argument is to be found sound. Consider the following questions as you construct your own arguments and listen to those of others:

Reasoning from Examples

1. *Have you looked at enough instances to warrant generalizing?* (You don't assume spring is here because of one warm day in February.)

2. *Are the instances fairly chosen?* (You certainly hope your neighbors don't think you've got a rotten kid just because he picked one of their flowers; you want them to judge your son only after seeing him in many different situations.)

3. *Are there important exceptions to the generalization or claim which must be accounted for?* (While it is generally true, from presidential election studies, that "As Maine goes, so goes the nation," there have been enough exceptions to that rule to keep Maine losers campaigning hard even after that primary.)

Reasoning from Parallel Case

1. *Are there more similarities than differences between the two cases?* (City A and City B may have many features in common—size, location, etc.; yet they probably also have many features in which they differ—perhaps in the subgroups that make up their populations, the degree of industrial development, and the like. Too many differences between the two cases will rationally destroy the parallel.)

2. *Are the similarities pointed out the relevant and important ones?* (So there are two tads in your neighborhood who are the same age, live on the same block, and wear the same kinds of clothes; but are you therefore able to assume that one is a saint simply because the other is? Probably not, because more relevant similarities would include their home lives, their school backgrounds, their relationships with siblings, and so forth. Comparisons must be made on relevant and important similarities.)

Reasoning from Sign

1. *Is the sign "fallible"?* (As we noted already, many signs are merely circumstantial, as in the case of the murderer and racial examples above. Be extremely careful not to confuse sign reasoning with causal reasoning. If sign reasoning were infallible, your weather forecaster would never be wrong!)

Reasoning from Causal Relation

1. *Can you separate causes and effects?* (We often have a difficult time doing this. Do higher wages cause higher prices, or is the reverse true? Does a strained home life make a child misbehave, or is it the other way around?)

2. *Are the causes strong enough to have produced the effect?* (Did Jimmy Carter's winning smile really give him the election, or was that an insufficient cause? There probably were much stronger and more important causes.)

3. *Did intervening events or persons prevent a cause from having its normal effect?* (If the gun's not loaded, no matter how hard you pull the trigger you won't shoot anything. Even if droughts normally drive up food prices, that might not happen if food has been stockpiled, if spring rains left enough moisture in the soil, or if plenty of cheap imported foods are available this year.)

4. *Could any other cause have produced the effect?* (Although crime often increases when neighborhoods deteriorate, increased crime rates can be caused by any number of other changes—alterations in crime-reporting methods, increased reporting of crimes which have been going on for years, or closings of major industries. We rationally must sort through all the possible causes before championing one.)

Reasoning from Generalization or Axiom

1. *Is the generalization true?* (Remember how long sailors set certain courses on the assumption that the world was flat, or the number of years parents in this country accepted as gospel Benjamin Spock's generalizations about childrearing.)

2. *Does the generalization apply to this particular case?* (If a small neighborhood store has a sale, it may well offer better prices than discount houses. Or the old saw "Birds of a feather flock together" certainly applies to birds, but perhaps not to human beings.)

DETECTING FALLACIES IN REASONING

As we noted in Chapter 2 and as we have suggested here, one of your jobs as a listener and as a person who often will be called upon to answer to arguments of others is to evaluate the claims, evidence, and reasoning of other speakers. Whether you are evaluating speakers' claims as a "mere" listener or whether you are judging those claims so you can respond publicly, you must be able to think sensibly through what has been said. In part you are looking for ways in which others' ideas and reasons are relevant to your own situation and worldview. And, in part you are trying to examine the soundness—the logical foundations—of their thought. A *fallacy* is a flaw in the rational properties of an argument or other inference. Although this textbook is no place to present a complete course in logical fallacies, we at least can review some of the basic errors in reasoning that often are presented, and urge you to attack them in your own mind or in your refutative speeches. We can break down such fallacies into three categories: *fallacies in evidence*, *fallacies in reasoning*, and *fallacies in language*.

Fallacies in Evidence

These fallacies occur in the management of ideas or supporting materials. Three of them stand out:

Hasty Generalization (faulty "inductive leap"). A hasty generalization is one made on the basis of too little evidence. Has the arguer really examined enough typical cases to make a claim? Urging the closing of a hospital because two people have successfully brought malpractice suits against it is probably an example of a hasty generalization.

False Division. A false division is an attempt to argue that some process or idea can be subdivided in only one particular way, when in fact there are numerous alternative divisions or additional properties or ideas that are being ignored. When someone argues there are only three ways to rejuvenate your community's uptown district, be on the lookout. "Only" often is signal of a possible false division; there well may be other plans worth considering.

Genetic Fallacy. Many people argue for an idea by discussing its origins (see "definition," pp. 167–169). They may suggest that it is "rooted in sacred traditions" and trace its ancestry back to respected sources. Many people who defended the ideas of slavery in the nineteenth century talked about the Founding Fathers and the seemingly racist ideas in the Bible; such arguments suggest that an idea "must" be true because it's been around in respected circles for a long time. But, times change; new values arise to replace old ones. Genetic definitions may help us understand some concept, but they hardly are "proof" of correctness or justice.

In addition, the other tests-of-reasoning we reviewed earlier can be applied to other categories-of-evidence. Be on your guard against what are called "the material fallacies."

Fallacies in Reasoning

We already have reviewed some of the sources of fallacious reasoning. Five additional "logical fallacies" should be mentioned:

Appeal to Ignorance (argumentum ad ignoratiam). People often argue with double-negatives ("You *can't* prove that it *won't* work"), or may even attack an idea because of gaps in human knowledge ("We can't write laws about euthanasia because we know so little about death"). Both of these strategies are appeals to ignorance. Sometimes, we simply must act on the basis of knowledge we have, despite our ignorance. In answering such arguments, you often can cite parallel cases and carefully constructed arguments from example to overcome this appeal.

Appeal to Popular Opinion (argumentum ad populum). Many an argument begins, "Everyone knows . . ." So, "Everyone knows the world is flat." "Everyone knows that blacks are inferior to whites." These appeals to popular opinion may be useful in setting out *valuative* claims, but, when used as the basis for *factual* claims, especially, they are fallacious. (To make them "legal," the word "knows" must be changed to "thinks," "believes," or "values." If you *know* that, you won't advance the claims we just did!)

Sequential Fallacy (post hoc, ergo propter hoc). Literally translated "after this, therefore because of this," the sequential fallacy is one to look for in arguments from causal relations; it's based on the assumption that because one event occurred after another, the first must have caused the second. Given that intervening causes often intercede between two events, one must be most careful in asserting a cause-effect relationship. Watch for this fallacy.

Begging the Question (petitio principii). Begging the question is simply rephrasing an idea and then offering it as its own reason. If someone argues, "Marijuana smoking is immoral because it just isn't right," that person has begged the question—simply rephrasing the claim (it is immoral) to form a reason (it just isn't right). Especially in the case of claims of value, watch for *petitio principii*.

Either-or (two-valued) Logic. We often hear, "either it is or it isn't," "either it's good or it's bad," "either you're for us or against us." All these statements are examples of two-valued logic or either-or reasoning. Now, sometimes such reasoning applies, as when you say, "Either that's a dog or it isn't." A so-called "A or non-A" ("dog" or "non-dog") argument is perfectly acceptable. But, that is different from an "A or B" argument: "Either you're for Proposition 12 (A) or you're against it (B)." "Either you must fight (A) or surrender (B)." Either-or reasoning of this type ignores compromises, additional alternatives, or even combinations of both A and B—Proposition 13, perhaps, or negotiation rather than fighting or surrender.

Fallacies in Language

Finally, certain fallacies creep into people's speeches simply because of the ways words are used. Because word meanings are so slippery, language can be used sloppily or manipulatively. Five so-called "linguistic fallacies" appear often in public debate.

Ambiguity.   Ambiguity is the fallacy of using one word with two or more meanings in the same context. So, suppose you heard: "The end of a thing is its perfection; death is the end of life; therefore, death is the perfection of life." Here, the word "end" has been used ambiguously; in the first statement, "end" means "goal," but in the second, it means "final state." Watch out for shifting meanings.

Nonqualification.   It is all too easy to drop out some important qualifications as an argument progresses. Words such as "maybe," "might," and "probably" tend to fall by the wayside. An expert may have said "*Perhaps* this is the best answer," or "Plan A will work *if* Committees X, Y, and Z get behind it." If arguers use such pieces of expert testimony but drop out the qualifications, the argument is verbally distorted.

Is-Faults.   One of the trickiest verbs in English is "is." "John is a man" and "John is a radical" are grammatically equivalent sentences; but in the first case we are identifying an essential characteristic of John, and in the second, specifying a changeable attribute of his thinking. Learn to distinguish between the "is" of classification and the "is" of attribution, especially in condemnatory speeches (and advertisements).

Persuasive Definition.   In the heat of a dispute, many advocates try to win by persuading you to accept their definition of an idea, especially a value or an abstract concept. Two clear signals of a persuasive definition are "true" and "really." "True liberty consists of freedom from governmental regulation"; "a real university education is one which leads to a post-college job." In both cases, you are being asked to accept someone's arbitrary definition; if they get you to accept the definition, the argument is over.[4]

---

[4] For a fuller discussion of persuasive definitions, see Charles L. Stevenson, *Ethics and Language* (New Haven: Yale University Press, 1944), Chap. 9, "Second Pattern of Analysis: Persuasive Definitions."

Name-Calling.   Name-calling is a general label for several kinds of attacks on people instead of on their arguments. *Argumentum ad hominem* is an attack on the special interests of a person: "You can't offer a fair analysis of 'right to work' questions because you are a union member." *Argumentum ad personam* is an attack upon some personal characteristic of someone: "You are a sniveling liar (or Irishman or male)." Even liars, Irishmen, and males occasionally offer solid argumentative analyses. *Ideological appeals* give some idea or person a political-evaluative label: "The Kaiser medical plan is really communistic socialized medicine and thus un-American." This appeal attaches a value-label to an idea rather than examining its merits and operational faults; arguments, whomever their source, ought to be judged on their own features, not personalities and ideologies.

These are only some of the material, logical, and linguistic fallacies which creep into argument. Should you wish a fuller list, check with a good basic logic book.[5] Even armed with knowledge of only these thirteen fallacies, however, you should be able to construct some ideas for refutative speeches and to protect yourself against unscrupulous demagogues, sales personnel, and advertisers.

❝❞ A SAMPLE ARGUMENT

The role of argument in public decision-making perhaps is never clearer than in televised presidential debates between candidates from different parties. These debates are worthy of your inspection because they illustrate the virtues and vices, the rational bases and yet the fallacious turns, and the sheer struggle for public confidence which underlie public debate.

On Tuesday, October 28, 1980, the League of Women Voters sponsored the second in a series of debates between then-President Jimmy Carter, the Democratic candidate, and former Governor of California, Ronald Reagan, the Republican candidate for the presidency. As you conclude this chapter, read over the segment from that debate which follows, transcripts from their discussion of the nuclear arms control issue. Be sensitive to (1) their selection and adaptation of evidence, (2) their reasoning patterns which attempt to make various kinds of evidence relevant especially to attacks upon

---

[5]An excellent logic textbook of use here is Irving M. Copi, *Introduction to Logic*, 5th ed. (New York: Macmillan Publishing Co., Inc., 1978), esp. Chaps. 2 and 3.

each other, (3) and their employment even of fallacies (especially name-calling, persuasive definition, and the sequential fallacy) in this exchange.

The panelist posing the question was Marvin Stone, Editor of *U.S. News and World Report*. The debate format allowed each participant the chance to comment on the question, with two follow-up opportunities to refute the opponent or extend his own analysis of the question.

PRESIDENTIAL DEBATE, 1980[6]

MR. STONE: Governor Reagan—arms control: The President said it was the single most important issue. Both of you have expressed the desire to end the nuclear arms race with Russia, but by methods that are vastly different. You suggest that we scrap the Salt II treaty already negotiated, and intensify the build-up of American power to induce the Soviets to sign a new treaty—one more favorable to us. President Carter, on the other hand, says he will again try to convince a reluctant Congress to ratify the present treaty on the grounds it's the best we can hope to get.

Now, both of you cannot be right. Will you tell us why you think you are?

GOVERNOR REAGAN: Yes. I think I'm right because I believe that we must have a consistent foreign policy, a strong America, and a strong economy. And then, as we build up our national security, to restore our margin of safety, we at the same time try to restrain the Soviet build-up, which has been going forward at a rapid pace, and for quite some time.

The Salt II treaty was the result of negotiations that Mr. Carter's team entered into after he had asked the Soviet Union for a discussion of actual reduction of nuclear strategic weapons. And his emissary, I think, came home in 12 hours having heard a very definite *nyet*. But taking that one no from the Soviet Union, we then went back into negotiations on their terms, because Mr. Carter had cancelled the B-1 bomber, delayed the MX, delayed the Trident submarine, delayed the Cruise missile, shut down the Missile Man—the three—the Minute Man missile production line, and whatever other things that might have been done. The Soviet Union sat at the table knowing that we had gone forward with unilateral concessions without any reciprocation from them whatsoever.

Now, I have not blocked the Salt II treaty, as Mr. Carter and Mr. Mondale suggest that I have. It has been blocked by a Senate in which there is a

[6]"An NBIC-Verified transcriptional record of the Second Debate of the Series of Presidential Debates sponsored by the League of Women Voters Education Fund" from *The Pursuit of the Presidency 1980*, David Broder et al. Copyright © 1980 by the Washington Post Company. Reprinted with permission.

Democratic majority. Indeed, the Senate Armed Services Committee voted 10 to 0, with seven abstentions, against the Salt II treaty, and declared that it was not in the national security interests of the United States. Besides which, it is illegal, because the law of the land, passed by Congress, says that we cannot accept a treaty in which we are not equal. And we are not equal in this treaty for one reason alone—our B-52 bombers are considered to be strategic weapons; their Backfire bombers are not.

MR. SMITH: Governor, I have to interrupt you at that point. The time is up for that. But the same question now to President Carter.

MR. STONE: Yes. President Carter, both of you have expressed the desire to end the nuclear arms race with Russia, but through vastly different methods. The Governor suggests we scrap the Salt II treaty which you negotiated in Vienna . . . or signed in Vienna, intensify the build-up of American power to induce the Soviets to sign a new treaty, one more favorable to us. You, on the other hand, say you will again try to convince a reluctant Congress to ratify the present treaty on the grounds it is the best we can hope to get from the Russians.

You cannot both be right. Will you tell us why you think you are?

PRESIDENT CARTER: Yes, I'd be glad to. Inflation, unemployment, the cities are all very important issues, but they pale into insignificance in the life and duties of a president when compared with the control of nuclear weapons. Every president who has served in the Oval Office since Harry Truman has been dedicated to the proposition of controlling nuclear weapons.

To negotiate with the Soviet Union a balanced, controlled, observable, treaty and then reducing levels of atomic weaponry, there is a disturbing pattern in the attitude of Governor Reagan. He has never supported any of those arms control agreements—the limited test ban, Salt I, nor the Antiballistic Missile Treaty, nor the Vladivostok Treaty negotiated with the Soviet Union by President Ford—and now he wants to throw into the wastebasket a treaty to control nuclear weapons on a balanced and equal basis between ourselves and the Soviet Union, negotiated over a seven-year period, by myself and my two Republican predecessors.

The Senate has not voted yet on the Strategic Arms Limitation Treaty. There have been preliminary skirmishings in the committees of the Senate, but the Treaty has never come to the floor of the Senate for either a debate or a vote. It's understandable that a senator in the preliminary debates can make an irresponsible statement, or, maybe, an ill-advised statement. You've got 99 other senators to correct that mistake, if it is a mistake. But when a man who hopes to be president says, take this treaty, discard it, do not vote, do not debate, do not explore the issues, do not finally capitalize on this long negotiation—that is a very dangerous and disturbing thing.

MR. SMITH: Governor Reagan, you have an opportunity to rebut that.

GOVERNOR REAGAN: Yes, I'd like to respond very much. First of all, the Soviet Union . . . if I have been critical of some of the previous agreements, it's because we've been out-negotiated for quite a long time. And they have managed, in spite of all of our attempts at arms limitation, to go forward with the biggest military build-up in the history of man.

Now, to suggest that because two Republican presidents tried to pass the Salt treaty—that puts them on its side—I would like to say that President Ford, who was within 90 percent of a treaty that we could be in agreement with when he left office, is emphatically against this Salt treaty. I would like to point out also that senators like Henry Jackson and Hollings of South Carolina— they are taking the lead in the fight against this particular treaty.

I am not talking of scrapping. I am talking of taking the treaty back, and going back into negotiations. And I would say to the Soviet Union, we will sit and negotiate with you as long as it takes, to have not only legitimate arms limitation, but to have a reduction of these nuclear weapons to the point that neither one of us represents a threat to the other. That is hardly throwing away a treaty and being opposed to arms limitation.

MR. SMITH: President Carter?

PRESIDENT CARTER: Yes. Governor Reagan is making some very misleading and disturbing statements. He not only advocates the scrapping of this treaty—and I don't know that these men that he quotes are against the treaty in its final form—but he also advocates the possibility, he said it's been a missing element, of playing a trump card against the Soviet Union of a nuclear arms race, and is insisting upon nuclear superiority by our own nation, as a predication for negotiation in the future with the Soviet Union.

If President Brezhnev said, we will scrap this treaty, negotiated under three American presidents over a seven-year period of time, we insist upon nuclear superiority as a basis for future negotiations, and we believe that the launching of a nuclear arms race is a good basis for future negotiations, it's obvious that I, as president, and all Americans, would reject such a proposition. This would mean the resumption of a very dangerous nuclear arms race. It would be very disturbing to American people. It would change the basic tone and commitment that our nation has experienced ever since the Second World War, with all presidents, Democratic and Republican. And it would also be very disturbing to our allies, all of whom support this nuclear arms treaty. In addition to that, the adversarial relationship between ourselves and the Soviet Union would undoubtedly deteriorate very rapidly.

This attitude is extremely dangerous and belligerent in its tone, although it's said with a quiet voice.

MR. SMITH: Governor Reagan?

GOVERNOR REAGAN: I know the President's supposed to be replying to me, but sometimes, I have a hard time in connecting what he's saying with

(debate text continues on page 288)

PARLIAMENTARY PROCEDURE FOR HANDLING MOTIONS

Classification of motions	Types of motions and their purposes	Order of handling	Must be seconded	Can be discussed	Can be amended	Vote required [1]	Can be reconsidered
Main motion	(To present a proposal to the assembly)	Cannot be made while any other motion is pending	Yes	Yes	Yes	Majority	Yes
Subsidiary motions [2]	To postpone indefinitely (to kill a motion)	Has precedence over above motion	Yes	Yes	No	Majority	Affirmative vote only
	To amend (to modify a motion)	Has precedence over above motions	Yes	When motion is debatable	Yes	Majority	Yes
	To refer (a motion) to committee	Has precedence over above motions	Yes	Yes	Yes	Majority	Until committee takes up subject
	To postpone (discussion of a motion) to a certain time	Has precedence over above motions	Yes	Yes	Yes	Majority	Yes
	To limit discussion (of a motion)	Has precedence over above motions	Yes	No	Yes	Two-thirds	Yes
	Previous question (to take a vote on the pending motion)	Has precedence over above motions	Yes	No	No	Two-thirds	No
	To table (to lay a motion aside until later)	Has precedence over above motions	Yes	No	No	Majority	No
Incidental motions [3]	To suspend the rules (to change the order of business temporarily)	Has precedence over a pending motion when its purpose relates to the motion	Yes	No	No	Two-thirds	No
	To close nominations [4]	[4]	Yes	No	Yes	Two-thirds	No
	To request leave to withdraw or modify a motion [5]	Has precedence over motion to which it pertains and other motions applied to it	No	No	No	Majority [5]	Negative vote only
	To rise to a point of order (to enforce the rules) [6]	Has precedence over pending motion out of which it arises	No	No	No	Chair decides [7]	No
	To appeal from the decision of the chair (to reverse chair's ruling) [6]	Is in order only when made immediately after chair announces ruling	Yes	When ruling was on debatable motion	No	Majority [1]	Yes
	To divide the question (to consider a motion by parts)	Has precedence over motion to which it pertains and motion to postpone indefinitely	[8]	No	Yes	Majority [8]	No

287

	Motion	Description				Nc	Two-thirds	Negative vote only
Privileged motions	To object to consideration of a question	In order only when a main motion is first introduced	No	No	No	No	Chair decides	No
	To divide the assembly (to take a standing vote)	Has precedence after question has been put	No	No	No	No	Chair decides	No
	To call for the orders of the day (to keep meeting to order of business) [6, 9]	Has precedence over above motions	No	No	No	No	No vote required	No
	To raise a question of privilege (to point out noise, etc.) [6]	Has precedence over above motions	No	No	No	No	Chair decides [7]	No
	To recess [10]	Has precedence over above motions	Yes	No [10]	No [10]	Yes	Majority	No
	To adjourn [11]	Has precedence over above motions	Yes	No [11]	No [11]	No [11]	Majority	No
	To fix the time to which to adjourn (to set next meeting time) [12]	Has precedence over above motions	Yes	No [12]	No [12]	Yes	Majority	Yes
Unclassified motions	To take from the table (to bring up tabled motion for consideration)	Cannot be made while another motion is pending	Yes	No	No	No	Majority	No
	To reconsider (to reverse vote on previously decided motion) [13]	Can be made while another motion is pending [13]	Yes	When motion to be reconsidered is debatable	Yes	No	Majority	No
	To rescind (to repeal decision on a motion) [14]	Cannot be made while another motion is pending	Yes	Yes	Yes	Yes	Majority or two-thirds [14]	Negative vote only

1. A tied vote is always lost except on an appeal from the decision of the chair. The vote is taken on the ruling, not the appeal, and a tie sustains the ruling.
2. Subsidiary motions are applied to a motion before the assembly for the purpose of disposing of it properly.
3. Incidental motions are incidental to the conduct of business. Most of them arise out of a pending motion and must be decided before the pending motion is decided.
4. The chair opens nominations with "Nominations are now in order." A member may move to close nominations, or the chair may declare nominations closed if there is no response to his/her inquiry, "Are there any further nominations?"
5. When the motion is before the assembly, the mover requests permission to withdraw or modify it, and if there is no objection from anyone, the chair announces that the motion is withdrawn or modified. If anyone objects, the chair puts the request to a vote.
6. A member may interrupt a speaker to rise to a point of order or or of appeal to call for orders of the day, or to raise a question of privilege.
7. Chair's ruling stands unless appealed and reversed.
8. If propositions or resolutions relate to independent subjects, they must be divided on the request of a single member. The request to divide the question may be made when another member has the floor. If they relate to the same subject but each part can stand alone, they may be divided only on a regular motion and vote.
9. The regular order of business may be changed by a motion to suspend the rules.
10. The motion to recess is not privileged if made at a time when no other motion is pending. When not privileged, it can be discussed. When privileged, it cannot be discussed, but can be amended as to length of recess.
11. The motion to adjourn is not privileged if qualified or if adoption would dissolve the assembly. When not privileged, it can be discussed and amended.
12. The motion to fix the time to which to adjourn is not privileged if no other motion is pending or if the assembly has scheduled another meeting on the same or following day. When not privileged, it can be discussed.
13. A motion to reconsider may be made only by one who voted on the prevailing side. It must be made during the meeting at which the vote to be reconsidered was taken, or on the succeeding day of the same session. If reconsideration is moved while another motion is pending, discussion on it is delayed until discussion is completed on the pending motion; then it has precedence over all new motions of equal rank.
14. It is impossible to rescind any action that has been taken as a result of a motion, but the unexecuted part may be rescinded. Adoption of the motion to rescind requires only a majority vote when notice is given at a previous meeting; it requires a two-thirds vote when no notice is given and the motion to rescind is voted on immediately.

what I have said or what my positions are. I sometimes think he's like the witch doctor that gets mad when a good doctor comes along with a cure that'll work.

My point I have made already, Mr. President, with regard to negotiating: it does not call for nuclear superiority on the part of the United States. It calls for a mutual reduction of these weapons, as I say, that neither of us can represent a threat to the other. And to suggest that the Salt II treaty that your negotiators negotiated was just a continuation, and based on all of the preceding efforts by two previous presidents, is just not true. It was a new negotiation because, as I say, President Ford was within about 10 percent of having a solution that could be acceptable. And I think our allies would be very happy to go along with a fair and verifiable Salt agreement.

MR. SMITH: President Carter, you have the last word on this question.

PRESIDENT CARTER: I think, to close out this discussion, it would be better to put into perspective what we're talking about. I had a discussion with my daughter, Amy, the other day, before I came here, to ask her what the most important issue was. She said she thought nuclear weaponry—and the control of nuclear arms.

This is a formidable force. Some of these weapons have ten megatons of explosion. If you put 50 tons of TNT in each one of railroad cars, you would have a carload of TNT—a trainload of TNT stretching across this nation. That's one major war explosion in a warhead. We have thousands, equivalent of megaton, or million tons, of TNT warheads. The control of these weapons is the single major responsibility of a president, and to cast out this commitment of all presidents, because of some slight technicalities that can be corrected, is a very dangerous approach.

GROUP PROJECTS

1. How influential are political debates in presidential campaign years? Break the class into a series of groups. Some groups will analyze the 1960 Kennedy-Nixon debates; others, the 1976 Carter-Ford debates. One group will prepare background reports on the 1960 debates using Sidney Kraus, ed., *The Great Debates;* two more will prepare similar reports using Lloyd Bitzer and Theodore Reuter, eds., *Carter vs. Ford,* and Sidney Kraus, ed., *The Great Debates, 1976.* (These sources also will include complete texts of the debates.)

2. Break the class into two groups. One group will prepare an outline for a speech favoring the military draft, and the other group, for a speech opposing it. Then, exchange outlines, and search each other's outlines for fallacies. Having done that, prepare a speech refuting the other group's arguments.

3. Each person will examine magazine, newspaper, radio, and TV ads, for appeals illustrating various of the fallacies discussed in this chapter. Do particular types of appeals seem to dominate in the advertising perused? If so, why do you think those particular types are favored by advertisers? Turn your list in to your instructor, who will share the ads with the class, and, if desired, grade your work.

INDIVIDUAL PROJECTS

1. Prepare a ten-minute argumentative exchange on a topic involving you and one other member of the class. Dividing the available time equally, one of you will advocate a claim: the other will oppose it. Adopt any format you both feel comfortable with. You may choose: (a) a Lincoln/Douglas format—the first person speaks four minutes; the second, five, and then the first person returns for a one-minute rejoinder; (b) an issue format—you both agree on, say, two key issues, and then each one of you speaks for two and a half minutes on each issue; (c) a debate format—each speaker talks twice alternatively, three minutes in a constructive speech, two minutes in rebuttal; and (d) a heckling format—each of you has five minutes, but during the middle of each speech, the audience or your opponent may ask you questions.

2. Turn the class into a parliamentary assembly; decide on a motion or resolution to be argued; and then schedule a day or two for a full debate. This format should use particular argumentative roles: advocate, witness, direct examiner, cross-examiner, summarizer. It allows each speaker to be part of a team; what you do affects not only yourself but also other speakers on your side of the argument. [For guidance in the use of this format, see John D. May, ed., *American Problems: What Should Be Done? Debates from "The Advocates"* (Palo Alto, Ca.: National Press Books, 1973)].

SUGGESTIONS FOR FURTHER READING

Douglas Ehninger, *Influence, Belief, and Argument: An Introduction to Responsible Persuasion* (Glenview, Ill.: Scott, Foresman and Company, 1974).

Bruce E. Gronbeck, *The Articulate Person*, 2nd ed. (Glenview, Ill.: Scott, Foresman and Company, 1983), Chapter 10, "Arguing," and Chapter 11, "Refuting," pp. 213–247.

Richard D. Rieke and Malcolm O. Sillars, *Argumentation and the Decision Making Process,* 2nd ed. (Glenview, Ill.: Scott, Foresman and Company, 1984).

J. Michael Sproule, *Argument: Language and Its Influence* (New York: McGraw-Hill, 1980).

Stephen Toulmin, Richard Rieke and Allan Janik, *An Introduction to Reasoning* (New York: Macmillan, 1979).

CHAPTER 14

Speaking on Special Occasions

Speeches to inform and persuade represent the two kinds of talk you most often will be called upon to make. Many occasions, however, require special types of speeches. These sorts of occasions call in part for information, and in part, sometimes, for persuasive efforts, yet they require more as well: they represent occasions for demonstrating and even celebrating *group solidarity or membership.* You are familiar with many such occasions—funeral speeches for friends and fallen heroes; tributes paid to outstanding humanitarians, artists, and professionals, as in the case of Nobel Prize speeches; speeches of good will offered by representatives of business and government to visitors or to members of a local cooking club; keynote addresses at conventions or conferences.[1]

These occasions can stretch the oratorical skills of speakers to their fullest because of all the pomp and ceremony associated with them. Other occasions demand somewhat simpler, more everyday speaking skills. Because in this chapter we are only introducing speaking on special occasions,

---

[1]For a much fuller examination of speeches which celebrate and remember special occasions in society, see Bruce E. Gronbeck, *The Articulate Person: A Guide to Everyday Public Speaking,* 2nd ed. (Glenview, Ill.: Scott, Foresman and Company, 1983), Preview IV, "Ritual, Ceremony, and Public Communication," and Chapter 12, "Celebrating and Remembering Special Occasions."

we will concentrate upon those simpler occasions. We will discuss the times when you must (1) introduce someone to a group, (2) offer a speech of courtesy such as a welcome or an acceptance, (3) nominate someone for an office or other high position, and (4) entertain an audience.

SPEECHES OF INTRODUCTION

Speeches of introduction are usually given by the chairperson. Sometimes, however, they are presented by another person who is especially well acquainted with the featured speaker.

Purpose: Creating a Desire to Hear the Speaker

If you are invited to give a speech of introduction, remember that your main object is to create in the listeners a desire to hear the speaker you are introducing. Everything else should be subordinate to this aim. Do not bore the audience with a long recital of the speaker's biography or with a series of anecdotes about your acquaintance with him or her. Above all, do not air your own views on the subject of the speaker's message. You are only the speaker's advance agent; your job is to "sell" that person to the audience. Therefore, you must try (1) to arouse curiosity about the speaker and the subject in the minds of the listeners so that it will be easy to capture their attention, and (2) to motivate the audience to like and respect the speaker so they will tend to respond favorably to the forthcoming information or proposal.

Formulating the Content

Usually the better known and more respected a speaker is, the shorter your introduction can be; the less well known he or she is, the more you will need to arouse interest in the speaker's subject and to build up his or her prestige. When presenting a speech of introduction, observe these principles:

Be brief.   To say too much is often worse than to say nothing at all. For example, if you were to introduce the President, you might simply say, "Ladies and gentlemen, the President of the United States." The prestige of the person you introduce will not always be great enough for you to be so brief, but it is always better to say too little than to speak too long.

Talk about the speaker.   Who is he? What is her position in business, education, sports, or government? What experiences has he had that qualify him to speak on the announced subject? Build up the speaker's identity, tell what he knows or what she has done, but do not praise his or her ability as a speaker. Let speakers *demonstrate* their skills.

Emphasize the importance of the speaker's subject.   For example, in introducing a speaker who will talk about the oil industry, you might say: "All of us drive automobiles in which we use the products made from petroleum. A knowledge of the way these products are manufactured and marketed is, therefore, certain to be valuable to our understanding and our pocketbooks."

Stress the appropriateness of the subject or of the speaker.   If your town is considering a program of renewal and revitalization, a speech by a city planner is likely to be timely and well received. If an organization is marking an anniversary, the founder may be one of the speakers. Reference to the positions these people hold is obviously in order and serves to relate the speaker more closely to the audience.

Use humor if it suits the occasion.   Nothing serves better to put an audience at ease and to create a friendly feeling than congenial laughter. Take care, however, that the humor is in good taste and does not come at the expense of someone else. In particular, do not risk offending the speaker whom you are introducing or detract from his or her prestige.

❝❞ A SAMPLE SPEECH OF INTRODUCTION

Under all circumstances, remember that the four primary virtues of a speech of introduction are *tact, brevity, sincerity,* and *enthusiasm.* These virtues are illustrated in the following introduction prepared by Barbara Miller.

INTRODUCING A CLASSMATE[2]
Barbara Miller

We all have come to know Greg Latham in this class. When we introduced ourselves during the first week of class, you learned that Greg was raised on an Illinois farm, later moving to Chicago when farming became a losing proposition for the five members of his family. Greg's dual background—rural and urban—has obviously affected him strongly, as you can tell from various topics he's addressed in speeches to us. The farmer in him emerged when he delivered his first speech, the one classifying various types of pesticides. He changed into a city slicker, however, in his visual-aids speech—the clever

---

[2]A speech of introduction given at the University of Iowa, winter term, 1980. Reprinted with the permission of Ms. Miller.

battleplan for making your way through and around Chicago's expressway and tollway systems. Three weeks ago, in the group discussion on health care, he once again put on his straw hat and bib overalls, speaking out strongly for the need to increase health care facilities in rural areas.

Today, we will see Greg combine his double background. If you followed the state legislature's recent public hearings, if you read the front page of *The State Journal* last week, or if you saw ABC's special report on foreign investments in American land two nights ago, the term "agribusiness" became a part of your vocabulary. Agribusiness, which involves the consolidation of farming operations within corporate structures, may well profoundly affect each of us within a decade. Greg this morning will trace those direct effects upon your daily life in his speech, "Agribusiness: Panacea or Pandora's Box?"

SPEECHES OF COURTESY: WELCOMES, RESPONSES, ACCEPTANCES

Most speakers will have occasion to give a speech for courtesy either on behalf of themselves or on behalf of an organization they represent.

Typical Situations

Speeches for courtesy are given to fulfill one of three obligations:

Welcoming visitors.   When a distinguished guest is present, someone —usually the presiding officer—should extend a public greeting.

Responding to a welcome or a greeting.   An individual so welcomed must express appreciation.

Accepting awards.   An individual who is presented an award for some special accomplishment is obligated to acknowledge this honor. Sometimes the award is made to an organization rather than to an individual, in which case someone is selected to respond for the group.

Purpose: Expressing Sentiment and Creating Good Feeling

The speech for courtesy has a double purpose. The speaker not only attempts to express a sentiment of gratitude or hospitality, but also to create an aura of good feeling in the audience. Usually the success of such a speech

Especially on such special occasions as acceptances, or even more formal occasions such as dedications, tributes, and commemorations, speakers sometimes are thrust into highly formal settings. These settings often are surrounded with pomp and ceremony. On such occasions, speakers must be doubly aware of the need to meet audiences' expectations and to observe group traditions.

depends upon satisfying the listeners that the appropriate thing has been said. Just as courtesies of private life put people at ease, so public acts of courtesy create good feeling in the recipient and the audience.

Formulating the Content

The scope and content of a speech for courtesy should be guided by the following principles:

Indicate for whom you are speaking. When you are acting on behalf of a group, make clear that the greeting or acknowledgment comes from everyone and not from you alone.

Present complimentary facts about the person or persons to whom you are extending the courtesy. Review briefly the accomplishments or qualities of the person or group you are greeting or whose gift or welcome you are acknowledging.

Illustrate; do not argue. Present incidents and facts that make clear the importance of the occasion, but do not be contentious. Avoid areas of disagreement. Do not use a speech for courtesy as an opportunity to air your own views on controversial subjects or to advance your own policies. Rather, express concretely and vividly the thoughts which already are in the minds of your listeners.

SPEECHES OF NOMINATION

A somewhat curious blend of informative and persuasive purposes, speeches of nomination are used in most groups when they are about to change or transfer leadership.

Purpose: Reviewing Accomplishments and Urging Endorsement

The informative half of the nominator's tasks involves a review of the nominee's accomplishments, normally in terms which are relevant to the sought-after office and to the audience's general beliefs, attitudes, and values. So, a nomination speech for someone wishing to be treasurer of a local political-action group would have to review that person's fiscal abilities and his or her commitment to group goals and actions. This review, however—instead of standing as an end in itself—must contribute to the principal goal of the speech: obtaining the listeners' endorsement of that individual.

Formulating the Content

Long-winded nomination speeches fall flat on listeners' ears. And, given their informative and persuasive goals, focus your remarks by observing the following rules:

Stress relevant traits.   The competencies and backgrounds you review should be relevant to the office sought and to listeners' perceptions of the group's goals and commitments, as we have noted. Be selective.

Give special emphasis to the nominee's commitments.   Frequently, especially in political organizations, many individuals have the same qualifications for some office. To make your nominee stand out from the crowd, therefore, you may have to assemble examples which show how deeply committed he or she is to the organization; don't simply assert commitment, but instead, demonstrate it concretely.

Concentrate upon the positive, not the negative.   Some are tempted in a nomination speech, not simply to forward their own candidates, but to attack other candidates as well. That strategy usually backfires because it indicates to some listeners your small-mindedness, and because it creates overt discord at a time when a group is looking for solidarity and commitment.

Finally, as you probably have observed, in political conventions the name of a proposed candidate often is withheld until the very end of the nominating speech in order to heighten the drama of the situation and to avoid premature demonstrations. This practice, should not, however—except in very special circumstances—be used elsewhere. In most situations, before you come to the concluding phase of your speech, most of your listeners probably will guess whom you are talking about anyway. As a mere trick of rhetoric, the device is too obvious to be genuinely effective.

SPEECHES TO ENTERTAIN

To entertain, amuse, or divert is frequently the purpose of an after-dinner speech, but talks of other kinds also may have the enjoyment of the listener as their principal end. Often a travel lecture, although it also presents a great deal of factual material, has as its overall purpose entertaining an audience with exciting or amusing tales of adventures in a strange land. Club meetings, class reunions, and similar gatherings of friends and associates also provide occasions for the sharing of fond memories. In these situations, the speaker may depend chiefly on humor, interesting anecdotes, or curious bits of information.

Purpose: Informing or Persuading in an Entertaining Manner

While humor—often in the form of exaggerated descriptions, puns, irony, unexpected turns of phrase, jokes, and the like—is usually a primary element in a speech to entertain, such a speech is more than a string of unrelated one-liners. One story or observation should lead naturally into the next, and all material should serve to bring out a central point around which the speech is built. Use stories and anecdotes to develop a common theme—some sentiment of loyalty or appreciation for the group addressed or even a serious thought concerning your subject. Thus, you need to choose illustrations, comparisons, and the like carefully, and connect them to your central idea.

Formulating the Content

When arranging speech materials mainly to entertain, develop a series of illustrations, short quotations or quips, and stories, each following the other in fairly rapid succession and each bearing upon the central theme. As a point of departure, at least, consider building a speech to entertain in the following steps:

1. Relate a story or anecdote, present an illustration, or quote an appropriate verse.

2. State the essential idea or point of view implied by your opening remarks.

3. Follow with a series of additional stories, anecdotes, or illustrations that amplify or illuminate your central idea. Arrange these supporting materials so that they are thematically or tonally coherent.

4. Close with a striking or novel restatement of the central idea you have developed. As in Step 1, you may use a bit of poetry, a startling quotation, or a final brief anecdote to provide the necessary "clincher" and sum up your speech as a whole.

❝❞▶ A SAMPLE SPEECH TO ENTERTAIN

By organizing your materials in the way listed above, you not only will provide your listeners with entertainment, but you will also help them remember your theme or central idea. The speech which follows illustrates the four steps we have described.

A CASE FOR OPTIMISM[3]
Douglas Martin

I'm sure you have heard the verse that runs:

Poem	'Twixt optimist and pessimist
Embodying	The difference is droll:
Contrast Used	The optimist sees the doughnut,
as Opening	The pessimist, the hole.
Statement	The longer I live, the more convinced I am of the truth of this poem. Life, like a doughnut, may seem full, rich, and

---

[3]Based in part on material taken from *Friendly Speeches* (Cleveland: National Reference Library).

enjoyable, or it may seem as empty as the hole in the middle. To the pessimist, the optimist seems foolish. But who is foolish—the one who sees the doughnut or the one who sees the hole?

Contrast

Somebody else pointed out the difference between an optimist and a pessimist this way: An optimist looks at an oyster and expects a pearl; a pessimist looks at an oyster and expects ptomaine poisoning. Even if the pessimist is right, which I doubt, he probably won't enjoy himself either before or after he proves it. But the optimist is happy because he always is expecting pearls.

Illustration

Pessimists are easy to recognize. They are the ones who go around asking "What's good about it?" when someone says "Good morning." If they would look around, they would see *something* good, as did the optimistic merchant whose store was robbed. The day after the robbery a sympathetic friend asked about the loss. "Lose much?" he wanted to know. "Some," said the merchant, "but then it would have been worse if the robbers had got in the night before. You see, yesterday I just finished marking everything down 20 percent."

Illustration

There is another story about the happy-go-lucky shoemaker who left the gas heater in his shop turned on overnight and upon arriving in the morning struck a match to light it. There was a terrific explosion, and the shoemaker was blown out through the door almost to the middle of the street. A passerby, who rushed up to help, inquired if he were injured. The shoemaker got up slowly and looked back at the shop, which by now was burning briskly. "No, I ain't hurt," he said, "but I sure got out just in time, didn't I?"

Testimony (Pro and Con)

Some writers have ridiculed that kind of outlook. You may recall the fun Voltaire made of optimism in *Candide:* "Optimism," he said, "is a mania for maintaining that all is well when things are going badly." A later writer, James Branch Cabell, quipped: "The optimist proclaims that we live in the best of all possible worlds; the pessimist fears this is true."

These writers, I suppose, couldn't resist the urge to make light of optimists; but I, for one, refuse to take *them* seriously. I like the remark by Keith Preston, literary critic and journalist: "There's as much bunk among the busters as among the boosters."

Beginning the Summary

Optimism, rather than the cynicism of Voltaire, is the philosophy I like to hear preached. There was a little old lady who complained about the weather. "But, Melissa," said her

friend, "awful weather is better than no weather." So quit
complaining, I say, and start cheering; there is always
something to cheer about. And stop expecting the worst. An
optimist cleans his glasses before he eats his grapefruit.

Restatement   Give in to optimism: don't fight it. Remember the dough-
nut. And, as Elbert Hubbard advised:
As you travel on through life, brother.
Whatever be your goal.
Keep your eye upon the doughnut
And not upon the hole.

GROUP PROJECTS

1. Speeches of nomination often follow the motivated sequence. In the
attention step, the speaker indicates his or her intention to place a name in
nomination for a given office; in the need step, the qualifications needed by a person
holding the office are examined; in the satisfaction step, the nominee's qualifications
are shown to meet the needs indicated; in the visualization step, expected accomplishments of the nominee are projected; and, in the action step, the nominee's name
is formally put into nomination, often with a call for endorsement. Examine one or
more speeches of nomination—frequently found in collections of speeches, in
summaries of national party conventions, and in *The New York Times*—to see if you
can discern the motivated sequence at work. Was it altered in any way? Why?
Compare your findings with those of your classmates.

2. Work in groups of two or three. Develop a role-playing situation similar to
the examples suggested below. Prepare appropriate speeches to fit the situations.

(*a*) Professor Mercer has been selected as the outstanding emeritus professor of Midlands University. The president of the Alumni Association will present
the award at the annual homecoming luncheon, and Professor Mercer will
accept her plaque.

(*b*) At the annual state 4-H awards presentation, the master of ceremonies
introduces the president of the university where the convocation is being held.
The president extends a welcome to the 2,000 4-H'ers, and the chairperson of
the state 4-H council responds to the welcome.

(*c*) It took a six-month campaign to save an 1850s cemetery from becoming
part of the parking lot of a soon-to-be-built shopping center. Mr. Alex Blank,
head of the state historical society, will present a citation to the county historical
society for its important role in saving the cemetery. The president of the county
group, Mrs. Nita Hamm, will accept the award on behalf of all who worked in
the campaign.

3. What is the precise nature of the increasingly popular "roast"? Work with members of a small group to formulate guidelines for conducting a "roast"; and then pick an appropriate individual (a classmate or other real person or a fictitious individual), and start applying the verbal "heat."

INDIVIDUAL PROJECTS

1. Your instructor will prepare a list of special-occasion, impromptu speech topics, such as:

  (a) Student X is a visitor from a neighboring school; introduce him/her to this class.
  (b) You are Student X; respond to this introduction.
  (c) Dedicate your speech-critique forms to the state historical archives.
  (d) You have just been named Outstanding Classroom Speaker for this term; accept the award.

You will have between five and ten minutes in which to prepare, and then will give a speech on a topic assigned or drawn from the list. Be ready also to discuss the techniques you employed in putting the speech together.

2. Using the four-step procedure laid out on pages 297–298, prepare and present to a classroom audience a one-point speech to entertain based on one of the following topics or a similar one:

  (a) You can't take it with you
  (b) How to swallow a pill
  (c) What this country really needs is _____
  (d) The great American gesture
  (e) Professors I have known
  (f) The inevitables of life

3. During the next round of classroom speeches, you may be asked to introduce one of your classmates. Follow the suggestions in this chapter; and, after learning the speaker's topic, plan an introduction that will emphasize the importance of the subject.

SUGGESTIONS FOR FURTHER READING

Donald C. Bryant, Karl R. Wallace, and Michael C. McGee, *Oral Communication: A Short Course in Speaking,* 5th ed. (Englewood Cliffs, N.J.: Prentice-Hall, Inc., 1982), Chapter 11, "Special Forms: Occasional Speeches, The Public Interview, Committee Discussion," pp. 184–205.

James H. Byrns, *Speak for Yourself: An Introduction to Public Speaking* (New York: Random House, 1981), Chapter 26, "Speaking for Special Occasions," pp. 286–293.

Douglas Ehninger, Bruce E. Gronbeck, Ray E. McKerrow, and Alan H. Monroe, *Principles and Types of Speech Communication*, 9th ed. (Glenview, Ill.: Scott, Foresman and Company, 1982), Chapter 18, "Speeches on Special Occasions," pp. 329–348.

Bruce E. Gronbeck, *The Articulate Person*, 2nd ed. (Glenview, Ill.: Scott, Foresman and Company, 1983), Preview Four, "Ritual, Ceremony, and Public Communication," pp. 248–257.

Rudolph F. Verderber, *The Challenge of Effective Speaking*, 5th ed. (Belmont, Ca.: Wadsworth Publishing Company, 1982), Chapter 18, "Adapting to Special Occasions," pp. 355–364.

CHAPTER 15

Interviewing and Group Communication

The worlds of business and the professions (law, medicine, engineering, education, journalism, and most of the other occupations licensed or certified by states or organizations) run on communication skills. Experience after experience, survey after survey, demonstrate that corporate and organizational workers will be successful only to the extent that they can write, talk, and listen effectively.[1]

Now, the great bulk of the communication skills we have reviewed thus far are directly applicable to careers in business and the professions; one of your challenges once you move outside school will be to adapt what you have learned here to specific career demands. Yet, because your communicative life in the "outside world" is composed of more than formal speeches, you need additional advice on forms of oral communication which are not part of speeches to inform and persuade. Thus, in this chapter we will look not only at special forms of public speaking associated with business and professional tasks (oral reports and conference presentations), but, as well, we will introduce you to what are the essential day-to-day communicative challenges of businesspeople and professionals—interviewing and group discussion.

---

[1]For a comprehensive listing of studies investigating the role of communication skills in job-related success, see Samuel L. Becker and Leah R. V. Ekdom, "That Forgotten Basic Skill: Oral Communication," *Association for Communication Administration Bulletin*, #33 (August, 1980).

INTERVIEWS

While there are many specific kinds of interviews, generally all interviews fall into one of three categories. An *informational interview* is one wherein the parties are exchanging concepts, ideas, or brute information. For example, polling agencies conduct survey interviews to find out how people assess the performance of the president or what they think about a new line of products. Almost all companies, too, conduct employment (also termed "selection" or "entrance") interviews of prospective employees, to discover their qualifications, personalities, talents, and desires, in turn, telling them about the company. Similarly, school administrations, faculty members, and admissions officers interview would-be students for much the same reasons. And, architects, lawyers, doctors, engineers, etc., conduct interviews to see if their services match a prospective client's or patient's needs.

In an *evaluative interview*, one party seeks to interpret and judge the performance of another or of some object. You may have had an "oral test" in school, for example. Or, in the case of businesses, employees periodically are called in by their supervisors for an "appraisal" interview on their job performance or the company's image, or on some new office procedure needing examination. Likewise, most other professionals must periodically evaluate their progress with clients and patients by using evaluative interviews.

In a *persuasive interview*, one person is trying to convince another, in a one-on-one situation, to use a certain product, to accept a particular idea, to vote for a candidate, etc. Thus, faculty members sometimes try to convince you to enroll for a course, major in a discipline, or cooperate in some project. Or, you may find someone at your door trying to persuade you to attend a religious meeting, buy a vacuum cleaner, or vote for Jones in the upcoming election.

Common Features of All Interviews

All interviews, regardless of type, have certain features in common:

1. *Interviews are purposive.* People engaged in an interview are seeking to gather or express particular ideas, opinions, evaluations, or proposed courses of action. As we will see, the specific purpose of the interview controls what is said and how it is said during the time available for the exchange.

2. *Interviews usually are structured.* Any interview has a beginning, a middle, and an end, whether or not these divisions are formally fixed. The

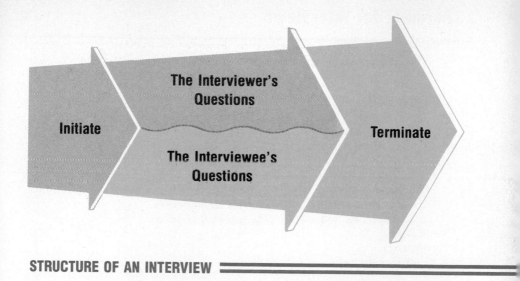

The Interviewer's
Questions

Initiate

The Interviewee's
Questions

Terminate

STRUCTURE OF AN INTERVIEW

beginning of an interview normally sets its purposes and limits, allows the participants to establish mutual rapport, and lets both parties know what to expect in the course of the interaction. In the middle of an interview, there is an exchange of information, opinions, values, feelings, arguments. And, at the end, there usually is some sort of summary, mutual exchange of perspectives, final appeals, perhaps a projection for a future meeting, and an exchange of parting courtesies.

Interviews are structured substantively as well. That is, one or both of the parties usually come with prepared questions. So, in the informational interview we described in Chapter 5 (pages 106–107), the interviewer had prepared a list of questions in order to acquire the desired information from the interviewee. Employment and appraisal interviews are instances where both parties may have preplanned questions which are used to structure the transaction.

3. *Interviews are interactive processes.* There is a definite pattern of "turn-taking" in interviews, which allows the parties to concentrate upon one item at a time and which helps guarantee that the exchange benefits both participants. The interactive pattern of interviews means that both parties must be extraordinarily careful listeners, for one person's comments should affect the next comment of the other. The pattern also demands that one be able to look ahead and plan when to bring up a particular idea or opinion.

Formats for Interviews

The structure of interviews varies with the purposes to be achieved in them. An informational interview has a simple, straightforward structure.

INFORMATIONAL INTERVIEW

Opening:
1. Mutual greeting
2. Discussion of purposes
   a. Reason information is needed
   b. Kind of information wanted
Informational Portion:
1. Question #1, with clarifying questions if needed
2. Question #2, with clarifying questions if needed
3. [etc.]
Closing:
1. Summary by one or both parties
2. Final courtesies (promise to show interviewee any use made of the information, thanks and good wishes)

In some situations, this structure may need to be more complicated. In an employment interview, for example, where the exchange of information is two-way, the main portion may be subdivided. See, for example, the sample employment interview in Appendix II (pp. 366–371). In that interview and in most employment interviews, the body of the exchange is divided into two sub-stages: interviewer questioning and interviewee questioning. Sometimes, even the closing contains another stage; in addition to summaries and final courtesies, informational interviews in the employment situation, if the rest has gone well, will include negotiations between the prospective hiree and the company regarding job conditions, follow-up interviews and visits, and the like.

When informational interviews contain negotiations, they tend to be more like evaluative interviews. Evaluative interviews, because they call for interpretive criteria and commentary, tend to have a more complicated structure than informational interviews.

EVALUATIVE INTERVIEW

Opening:
1. Mutual greeting
2. Discussion of purposes
   a. Reason for evaluation
   b. Use to which the evaluation will be put
   c. Kinds of evaluative criteria to be used

Evaluative Portion:
1. Evaluative criterion #1, along with data upon which the evaluation is based
2. Evaluative criterion #2, along with data upon which the evaluation is based
3. [etc.]

Interpretive Portion:
1. Overall judgment of the person, process, or product being evaluated
2. Effect that judgment may have on the person's, process's, or product's future

Closing:
1. Summary, to verify accuracy
2. Final courtesies (promise to show interviewee any use or record made of the evaluation, perhaps plan for future evaluations on a preset schedule, final thanks)

Evaluative interviews are especially sensitive exchanges. The interviewee often feels threatened by the evaluative process, especially if it is an appraisal interview carried on by a superior at work. The interviewer, too, has to take care to keep an open mind and a sympathetic demeanor, to be sure the exchange is productive and not destructive. Above all, the purpose and possible future consequences of the interview at all times must be clear and explicit, to reduce hedging and fear.

A persuasive interview has a structure which is similar in many respects to the informational interview.

PERSUASIVE INTERVIEW

Opening:
1. Mutual greeting
2. Discussion of purposes
   a. Reason it is being conducted
   b. Gains the interviewee can make by participating

Informational Portion:
1. Information about the interviewee
2. Probing of needs and interests of interviewee

Persuasive Portion:
1. Ways in which the product or course of action can meet the needs and interests of the interviewee
2. Discussion of doubts or questions the interviewee has after the presentation of the product or action

Closing:
1. Summary, with probe of the probability that the interviewee will buy the product or take the desired action
2. Final courtesies

Notice that the middle portion of the interview is split into informational and persuasive segments. This occurs because interviewers trying to sell a product (insurance, a used car, a new brand of coffee) or course of action (a trip to Europe, a political party, a religious meeting) first need to assess the personality and needs of the interviewee before trying to show the person that the product or action will be satisfying. Thus, an insurance agent gathers as much information as possible about the family before offering a particular policy to meet its needs; a travel agent inquires about your financial situation, preferences in transportation, and personal interests before offering you a package deal.

Types of Interviewing Questions

Because the communicative hearts of interviews are made up of questions and answers, a skilled interviewer must be practiced in phrasing and organizing useful questions. Six types of questions are often asked:

Primary questions introduce some topic or area-of-inquiry, while *follow-up questions* probe more deeply or call for elaboration. Thus, in an employment interview, "What college courses prepared you for this job?" might be a primary question, and "Tell me more about the 'Introduction to Computer Sciences'" would signal a follow-up. One also has to be able to frame *direct questions* ("How long did you work at your last company?") as well as *indirect questions* ("What do you want to be doing in five years?"). Direct questions allow you to gather information in a hurry, while indirect probes let you see interviewees "thinking on their feet," structuring materials and responses, and exploring their own minds. And, careful interviewers use both *open* and *closed questions*. A closed question—"Have you had experience as a clerk, a typist, a buyer, or a sales representative?"— specifies a range of responses; while an open question—"What are you looking for in a job?"—allows the interviewee to control the categories of response. Closed questions require little effort from the interviewee and are easy to "code" or record; open questions allow interviewers to observe the interviewees' habits, to let them feel in control of the interaction. Note, of course, that these types of questions overlap: you can use a direct or indirect, an open or closed, question as your primary question; a closed question can be used in direct ("Are you a freshman, sophomore, junior, or senior?") or indirect ("Would you rather be a manager, a supervisor, or a line worker in five years?") ways.

And overall, it is important to know that primary, direct, and closed questions tend to produce a lot of "hard" information quickly; follow-up, indirect, and open questions produce more thought, interpretation, and grounds for understanding and analyzing interviewees and their motivations, capacities, and expectations. As you plan interviews, you must learn to blend questions of all six types. This is called building an *interview schedule.*

An interview schedule is your effort to organize specific questions in such a way as to systematically elicit the materials and opinions you are looking for. Like any other organizational pattern, an interview schedule should have a rationale, one which (1) permits you to acquire systematic information or opinion, and (2) seems reasonable to the interviewee, avoiding confusing repetitions and detours. Interview schedules normally are built in one of two forms—the *traditional* and the *branching schedule:*

TRADITIONAL SCHEDULE OF QUESTIONS

I. "How many speech communication courses did you take at Jackson University?" (primary, direct, open question)
  A. "Are those quarter-hour or semester-hour courses?" (secondary, direct, closed question)
  B. "What kinds of practical experiences in communication with others did you get in the public speaking class?" (secondary, direct, open question)
    1. "What are your strengths as a speaker?" (secondary, indirect, open question)
    2. "What communication skills do you still feel a need to work on?" (secondary, direct, open question)
    3. "Would you say you're better at platform speaking or at informal-but-purposive chit-chat?" (secondary, direct, closed question)

BRANCHING SCHEDULE OF QUESTIONS

1. "Did you take courses in speech communication while attending Jackson University?"

IF YES: IF NO:

2. "Did you take courses in   2. "What kinds of non-school
   public speaking?"   experiences in public speaking
                                         have you had?" (etc.)

IF YES: IF NO:

3. "Did you get any practical   3. "Did you give oral reports

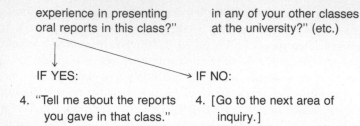

experience in presenting   in any of your other classes
oral reports in this class?"   at the university?" (etc.)

IF YES: IF NO:

4. "Tell me about the reports   4. [Go to the next area of
   you gave in that class."   inquiry.]

Notice that the traditional schedule of questions uses an organizational pattern that first extracts information and then follows with more thoughtful or probing questions. This sort of pattern allows the interviewee to think through his or her experiences concretely before you ask for self-reflection or evaluation; were that pattern reversed, the interviewee might be asked to evaluate some experience before having recalled it clearly, most likely producing a less-than-complete evaluation. Notice, too, the mixing of types of questions, to keep the interaction progressing.

A branching schedule is used in situations where the interviewer knows rather specifically what he or she is looking for. Survey or polling interviewers very often use this kind of schedule. In our example, an employment interviewer is using a branching schedule to guarantee complete exploration of all experiences the interviewee has had relevant to a job requirement—the presentation of oral reports to others. In a complete branching schedule, the "IF NO" questions likewise would have "branches" beneath them, but perhaps you can see how one works from our abbreviated example. A branching schedule also can be used by groups to organize an agenda for a decision-making session, because it gets "yes-no" group agreements systematically; when used in that way, it often is called a "decision tree."

No matter what type of questions you use and no matter what specific organizational pattern for questions is devised, the important points to remember are these: (1) Plan your questions before going into an interview, so that you know your goals and proceed toward them with dispatch. (2) Organize your questions in a manner which seems rational and which prepares interviewees adequately before asking them to make abstract, complex evaluations of themselves or the world.

Communicative Skills for Successful Interviewers

From this discussion of interviewing and structures for communicating, it becomes clear that adept interviewers must have certain communicative skills:

A good interviewer is a good listener. Unless you take care to understand what someone is saying and to interpret the significance of those comments, you may well misunderstand the person. Because questioning and answering are alternated in an interview, there is plenty of opportunity to clarify remarks and opinions. You can achieve clarification only if you are a good listener. (See Chapter 2.)

A good interviewer is open. Many of us may have become extremely wary of interviewers. We are cynical enough to believe that they have *hidden agenda*—unstated motives or purposes—which they are trying to pursue. Too often interviewers have told interviewees they "only want a little information," when actually they are selling magazine subscriptions or a religious ideal. If, as an interviewer, you are "caught" being less than honest, your chances for success are vastly diminished. If you are engaging in a persuasive interview, or if the evaluative interview could influence someone's future, it is better to state that honestly than to misrepresent yourself. Frankness and openness should govern all aspects of your interview communication.

A good interviewer builds a sense of mutual respect and trust. Feelings of trust and respect are created by revealing your own motivation, by probing the other party and getting the person to talk, and by expressing sympathy and understanding. Sometimes, of course, your assumptions of integrity and good will can be proved wrong. To start with suspicion and distrust, however, is to condemn the relationship without giving it a fair chance.

Interviewing is a dimension of communication which is both challenging and fascinating. Those wishing to explore the communicative dynamics of interview communication are encouraged to read more about it elsewhere.[2]

DISCUSSIONS

As we suggested earlier, businesses and other professional organizations depend heavily on oral communication for their successful operation. Indeed, it even can be said that what makes an organization an organization (and not a collection of isolated individuals) is the opportunity for face-to-face oral interaction—the exchanging of information, ideas, beliefs, perceptions, interpretations, and thoughts about what to do in any given situation. Businesspeople and professionals are constantly calling on committees, task

---

[2]See, for example, Charles J. Stewart and William B. Cash, Jr., *Interviewing: Principles and Practices*, 3rd ed. (Dubuque, Ia.: William C. Brown, Publishers, 1982).

forces, and more informal groups to formulate ideas, evaluate courses of action, and put proposals into effect. These exchanges generally are termed "group discussions." *A group discussion is a shared, purposive communication transaction in which a small group of people exchange and evaluate ideas and information in order to understand a subject or solve a problem.*

As this definition suggests, there are two major sorts of discussions: In a *learning or study discussion,* participants seek to educate each other, to come to a fuller understanding of some subject or problem. A number of people interested in art or literature or coin-collecting, for example, may gather monthly to share thoughts and expertise; book clubs, transcendental meditation groups, and Sunday School classes are learning groups. Businesses use such discussions to educate new employees or to explore problems creatively.

In an *action or decision-making group,* participants are trying to reach an agreement on what the group as a whole should believe or do, or are looking for ways to implement a decision already made. In discussions of this kind, conflicting facts and values are examined, differences of opinion are evaluated, and proposed courses of action are explored for their feasibility and practicality, in an effort to arrive at a common judgment or consensus. So, a neighborhood block association may gather periodically to decide on projects to undertake. A city council must decide what to do with its federal revenue-sharing funds. A subcommittee in a business may be asked to find ways to expand markets. Once such decisions are made, these groups may meet later as action teams, discussing ways to implement their plans.

Essentials for the Participant

For the participant in group communication the most important requirement is a *knowledge of the subject* being considered. If you know what you are talking about, you will be forgiven many faults. Of equal importance and usefulness is an *acquaintance with the other members of the group,* but it may not always be possible for you to know a great deal about them. To the extent that you can acquaint yourself with their values and interests, you will be able to judge more accurately the importance of their remarks and to determine more fairly the role you must play in order to make the group process profitable. Equally important is *close attention to the discussion* as it progresses. Unless you listen to what is going on, you will forget what already has been said or lose track of the direction in which the thinking of the group seems to be moving. As a result, you may make foolish or irrelevant comments, require the restatement of points already settled, or misunderstand the positions taken by other participants.

The worlds of business and the professions run on communication. Corporate and organizational workers are successful to the extent that they can write, talk, and listen. Oral interviews, discussions, reports, and panel presentations are the lifeblood of the workplace. Every speech preparation and speech presentation skill discussed in this book is needed by employer and employee alike.

Essentials for the Leader

If a discussion is to prove fruitful, the leader of the group must be alert, quick-witted, and clear-thinking—able to perceive basic issues, to recognize significant ideas, to sense the direction an interchange is taking, to note common elements in diverse points of view, and to strip controversial matters of unnecessary complexity. Moreover, a good discussion leader must be capable of the *effective expression* needed to state the results of the group's analyses clearly and briefly, or to make an essential point stand out from the others.

Another important quality of a discussion leader is *impartiality*. The leader must make sure that minority views are allowed expression and must phrase questions and comments fairly. In this way, a spirit of cooperation and conciliation will be promoted among participants who may differ from one another vigorously. Discussion groups are no different from other groups in preferring leaders who are fair. There is no place for a leader who takes sides in a personal argument or who openly favors some of the members at the expense of others. To help ensure that all may participate in a democratic, representative way—especially if the discussion is a formal, decision-making one—the leader should have a working knowledge of parliamentary procedure and the commonly employed motions. For a brief discussion of parliamentary procedure and a table of such motions, review pages 286–287.

Finally, a discussion leader should have an *encouraging or permissive attitude* toward the participants. There are times, especially at the beginning of a discussion, when people are hesitant to speak out. Provocative questions may stimulate them to participate, but even more helpful is a leader whose manner conveys confidence that the members of the group have important things to say about an important subject.

DEVELOPING THE DISCUSSION PLAN

When people communicate in groups, much time can be lost by needless repetition or by aimless wandering from point to point. A carefully developed discussion plan will guard against this danger.

Ideally, the entire group should cooperate in framing the discussion plan; but if this is impossible, the leader must take the responsibility for formulating it. In the pages immediately following, we shall consider separate plans for learning discussions and decision-making discussions. Although these can be used in most situations, at times they may have to be modified because of peculiarities in the composition of the group or because in a decision-making discussion the problem already has received considerable attention, either by individuals or by the group in earlier meetings.

A Plan for Learning Discussions

Sometimes a learning discussion concerns a book or parts of it, or is based upon a study outline or syllabus prepared by an authority in a given field. In such cases, the discussion generally should follow the organizational pattern used in the resource. The ideas in the book or outline, however, should be related to the experience of the individuals in the group; and an effort should be made to give proper emphasis to the more important facts and principles. When the group finds that previously prepared outlines are out of date or incomplete, the leader and/or the other participants should modify them to bring the missing information or points of view into the group's considerations.

When learning discussions are not based upon a book or outline, the leader and/or the group must formulate their own plan. The first step in this process is to *phrase the subject for discussion as a question.* Usually the question is framed before the actual discussion begins. If not, the leader and the members of the group must work it out together. Ordinarily, it is phrased as a question of fact or of value. (See pages 77–79.) Questions of fact, such as "What are the essentials for effective discussion?" or "What is our community doing to combat the increasing crime rate?" seek an addition to or a clarification of knowledge within the group; questions of value, such as "Is civil disobedience ever justified as a form of social protest?" or "Is our Middle Eastern policy effective?" seek judgments, appraisals, or preferences. The following suggestions should help you develop a satisfactory discussion plan for both types of questions.

Introduction.   The introduction consists of a statement of the discussion question by the leader, together with one or two examples showing its importance or its relation to individuals in the group.

Analysis.   In this step the group explores the nature and meaning of the question and narrows the scope of the discussion to those phases which seem most important. These considerations are pertinent:

1. Into what major topical divisions may this question conveniently be divided? (See pages 119–144 for some suggestions.)
2. To which of these phases should the discussion be confined?
    a. Which phases are of the greatest interest and importance to the group?
    b. On which phases are the members of the group already so well informed that detailed discussion would be pointless?

At this point the leader summarizes for the group, listing in a logical sequence the particular aspects of the questions that have been chosen for discussion.

Investigation.   In the investigative phase of the discussion, the members focus on the topics they have chosen in the preceding step. Under *each topic,* they may consider the following questions:

1. What terms need definition? How should these terms be defined?
2. What factual material needs to be introduced as background for the discussion (historical, social, geographic, etc.)?
3. What personal experiences of members of the group might illumi nate and clarify the discussion?

4. What basic principles or causal relationships can be inferred from consideration of this information and these experiences?

5. Upon which facts or principles is there general agreement and upon which points is information still lacking or conflicting?

Final Summary. At the close of the discussion, the leader briefly restates (1) the reasons which have been given for considering the question important and (2) the essential points which have been brought out under each of the main topics. A summary need not be exhaustive; its purpose is merely to review the more important points and make clear their relationships to each other and to the general subject.

A Plan for Decision-Making Discussions

Decision-making discussions characteristically raise questions of policy. (See pages 271–272) Examples of such questions are "What can be done to give students a more effective voice in the affairs of our college?" and "How can our company meet competition from foreign imports?"[3] As you will see in the following suggested procedure, answering such questions also requires answering subsidiary questions of fact and of value.

The steps in the ensuing plan for decision-making discussions are adapted from John Dewey's analysis of how we think when we are confronted with a problem.[4] Although presented here in some detail, this plan is only one of several possible ways of deciding upon a course of action and, therefore, is intended to be suggestive rather than prescriptive. Any plan that is developed, however, probably should follow—in general—a problem-solution order. Moreover, steps in the plan always should be stated as a series of questions.

Defining the Problem. After introductory remarks by the leader touching on the general purpose of the discussion and its importance, the group should consider:

---

[3]Not all discussions of this kind deal with problems or policies over which the group has immediate control. For example, a decision-making group may discuss "Should we deemphasize intercollegiate athletics?" or "What can the government do to ensure a stable food supply at reasonable prices?" The systematic investigation of these subjects, however, requires substantially the same steps as for matters over which the group has direct control. The only difference is that instead of asking, "What shall we *do?*" the group, in effect, asks, "What shall we *recommend* to those in authority?" or "What *would* we do if we ourselves were in positions of authority?"

[4]See Chapter 7, "Analysis of Reflective Thinking," in *How We Think* by John Dewey (Boston: D. C. Heath & Company, 1933). Cf. pp. 247–249 of this textbook, where these steps are discussed in connection with the development of a speech to persuade.

1. How can the problem for discussion be phrased as a question? (*Note:* Usually the question has been phrased before the discussion begins. If not, it should be phrased at this time.)
2. What terms need defining?
   a. What do the terms in the question mean?
   b. What other terms or concepts should be defined?

Analyzing the Problem. This step involves evaluating the problem's scope and importance, discovering its causes, singling out the specific conditions that need correction, and setting up the basic requirements of an effective solution. The following sequence of questions is suggested for this step:

1. What evidence is there that an unsatisfactory situation exists?
   a. In what ways have members of the group been aware of the problem, how have they been affected by it, or how are they likely to be affected?
   b. What other people or groups does the situation affect, and in what ways are they affected?
   c. Is the situation likely to improve itself, or will it become worse if nothing is done about it?
   d. Is the problem sufficiently serious to warrant discussion and action at this time? (If not, further discussion is pointless.)
2. What are the causes of this unsatisfactory situation?
   a. Are they primarily financial, political, social, or what?
   b. To what extent is the situation the result of misunderstandings or emotional conflicts between individuals or groups?
3. What specific aspects of the present situation must be corrected? What demands must be met, what desires satisfied?
   a. What evils does everyone in the group wish corrected?
   b. What additional evils does a majority in the group wish corrected?
   c. What desirable elements in the present situation must be retained?
4. In light of the answers to Questions 1, 2, and 3 above, by what criteria should any proposed plan or remedy be judged?
   a. What must the plan do?
   b. What must the plan avoid?
   c. What restrictions of time, money, etc., must be considered?
5. In addition to the above criteria, what supplementary qualities of a plan are desirable, though not essential?

At this stage the leader summarizes the points agreed upon thus far. Particularly important is a clear statement of the agreements reached on Questions 4 and 5, since the requirements there set forth provide the standards against which proposed remedies are judged. Moreover, agreement regarding criteria tends to make further discussion more objective and to minimize disagreements based upon personal prejudices.

Suggesting Solutions. In this step, every possible solution is presented. The group asks:

1. What are the various ways in which the difficulty could be solved? (If the group is meeting to discuss the merits of a previously proposed plan, it asks: What are the alternatives to the proposed plan?)
   a. What is the exact nature of each proposed solution? What cost, actions, or changes does it entail or imply?
   b. How may the various solutions best be grouped for initial consideration? It is helpful to list all solutions, preferably on a blackboard.

Evaluating the Proposed Solutions. When the discussants have presented all possible solutions which have occurred to them, they examine and compare these solutions and try to agree on a mutually satisfactory plan. The following questions may be asked:

1. What elements are common to all the proposed solutions and are therefore probably desirable?
2. How do the solutions differ?
3. How do the various solutions meet the criteria set up in Questions 4 and 5 of the analysis step? (This question may be answered either by considering each plan or type of plan separately in the light of the criteria agreed upon, or by considering each criterion separately to determine which solution best satisfies it.)
4. Which solutions should be eliminated and which ones retained for further consideration?
5. Which solution or combination of solutions should finally be approved?
   a. Which objectionable features of the approved solution or solutions should be eliminated or modified?
   b. If a number of solutions are approved, how may the best features of all the approved solutions be combined in a single superior plan?

As soon as agreement is reached on these matters, the leader sums up the principal features of the accepted plan. In groups which have no authority to act, this statement normally concludes the discussion.

Deciding How to Put the Approved Solution into Operation. When a group has the power to put its solution into operation, the following additional questions are pertinent:

1. What persons or committees should be responsible for taking action?
2. When and where should the solution go into effect?
3. What official action, what appropriation of money, etc., is necessary? (*Note:* If several divergent methods of putting the solution into effect are suggested, the group may need to evaluate these methods briefly to decide on the most satisfactory one.)

When these matters have been determined, the leader briefly restates the action agreed upon to be sure it is clear and acceptable to the group.

As we conclude this examination of group discussion, one final point must be made: *The key to successful group communicative experiences is interdependency.* Even though people take turns talking, often disagreeing with each other, occasionally worrying whether the leader has been too autocratic or too laissez-faire, and even sometimes having to quit talking for the moment out of sheer frustration—even though a discussion can exhibit as much competition as it does cooperation, it ultimately is an interdependent activity. It could not produce results without everyone feeling that all of the others are important contributors to the final product.

This means, more practically, that participants must be *good listeners;* must be *ready to contribute;* must help leaders *solve conflicts.* It means that leaders, likewise, must not only *build the agenda, open and run the discussion,* and *bring it to a close;* but they, too, must be ever sensitive to the socioemotional needs of the participants, bringing reticent members "into" the group, reducing conflict before it becomes disruptive, and creating an atmosphere wherein people feel good about their group experiences. If both discussants and leaders promote a sense of interdependency, group communicative experiences in business and the professions will be positive and productive.

ORAL REPORTS

An *oral report* is a speech in which one assembles, arranges, and interprets information gathered in response to a request. Thus, as we noted, a business firm may ask one of its members to assemble statistics on employment, sales, or cost overruns; a congressional committee may call in outside experts to offer testimony; a club may ask its treasurer to report on patterns or trends in its finances over a specified period; or a college might ask its registrar to report to the faculty on steps the school can take to recruit more students with particular backgrounds or interests. As these examples indicate, we may usefully think of two basic types of reportive speeches: the *factual report* concentrates upon assembling, arranging, and interpreting raw information; and the *advisory report* makes a set of recommendations based on information which has been prepared.

Techniques for Making Oral Reports

Making reports to groups, large or small, does not differ substantially from delivering a successful informative speech. But, unlike the speech to inform, the report is normally made in response to a specific request from others who expect to use information they have asked you for. Therefore, as a reporter, you should be aware of certain restrictions. Above all, bear in mind your role as an *expert*—the *source* of predigested information for a group of people who, in turn, will act upon it. That role carries with it tremendous responsibilities. It demands that you prepare with special care and that you present your material with clarity and balance. The success of a business firm, the government's legislative program, or your club's future—all may depend upon your reporting abilities. Therefore, keep the following guidelines in mind as you prepare and deliver your report:

The information you present must be researched with great care. Although you may be asked only to present a series of statistical generalizations in a short, five-minute report, your research must be extensive and solid. You must assemble your material "cleanly," free of bias or major deficiency. A quarterly report for a business which relies solely on material gathered from only one of the business's territories may not only be partial, but also skewed. Furthermore, even though you may be asked only to report the bare facts or "bottom lines" of your information, in a question-and-answer session you could be asked to expand upon what you say—to supply the figures on which you based your statistical conclusions. So have all of your information available even if you have only a short time for your actual presentation.

When making recommendations rather than merely reporting information, be sure to include a complete rationale for the advice you present. Suppose, for example, that you have been called upon by your student-government council to recommend ways to spend certain developmental monies. First, you will need to gather information on certain needs: Does this campus require additional buses (and should you, therefore, recommend further subsidy for public transportation)? Could it use more student-sponsored scholarships? Might it profit from a "careers week" in which recruiters from various businesses, industries, and other endeavors put on special seminars for interested students? To make recommendations on these needs, you must have financial information on the costs incurred in filling each demand. Second, you will need to assemble data on student interest, based on interviews and patterns of usage observed in the past. Third, in order to make sound recommendations, you then will have to rank-order the options open to the group. Fourth, you will need to build a rationale for your rank-ordering, including answers to such questions as: What student needs will each course of action meet? Why do you consider one need more pressing than the other? Why should student government, and not some other college or university agency, act to meet that need? Were student goverment to act on a specific need, what other kinds of university, community, or governmental supports would be forthcoming over the short and long term?

Answers to such questions would provide the rationale for a decision. This is important for two reasons: (1) Such a rationale enhances your *image* or *credibility* because it demonstrates your ability to think through and rationally solve problems. Unless your credibility is strong, your recommendations have little chance for action. (2) More importantly, if your rationale is a good one, it probably will be adopted by the audience as a whole; for the audience, in turn, has constituencies—the student body, specific organizations represented on the government council, etc.—to which it must answer when it takes action. In other words, by not only making recommendations but also offering reasons, you allow your auditors to meet objections, to urge the action, etc., in the important second step of persuasion—the appeal to secondary audiences.

Make full use of visual aids when making reports. Because reports often have to be short and to the point and yet contain a great amount of information, the reporter must decide how to present a maximum amount of useful material in the shortest period of time. The advice on the employment of visual aids presented in Chapter 9 (pages 181–194) is germane. Use each aid to its maximum advantage. Were you to give the speech to the student-government council mentioned earlier, for example, you might (1) offer statistical data on a mimeographed handout, with summaries in the form of bar or pie graphs; (2) audiotape and replay sample student interviews; (3) employ a brief slide show to help the audience visualize either the problems or the solutions (for example, slides of "career days" at other schools); (4) exhibit a flipchart with diagrams of proposed bus routes, a floor plan for a ballroom setup for a career-days fair, or an organizational chart delineating the sources of scholarship money currently available on campus; or (5) hand out a dittoed sheet containing the wording of a motion you would introduce to make your recommendations official. Under these circumstances, you could limit your remarks to those aspects of the report best enhanced by your voice—the rationales or persuasive appeals. The employment of such visual aids, therefore, would help to keep you within the assigned time limit and would make full use of both the verbal and the visual communication channels.

Whatever you do, stay within the boundaries of your report-making charge. As a reporter, you are a conduit—a pipeline between the audience and some subject of interest. You therefore must be highly sensitive to the audience's expectations: Were you charged with gathering information only? Or were you told what kind of information to bring in? Did your instructions say to assemble recommendations for action? Were you to include financial and impact analyses along with those recommendations? Most reporters are given a charge—a duty to perform. If you depart too far from that charge—if you make recommendations when you are expected only to gather information, *or* if you only gather information when you have been asked to make recommendations—you are likely to create ill will among your listeners. When this occurs, your work often will be for naught; you will have failed as a reporter. So, clarify the boundaries within which you are operating; when given a task, ask for relevant instructions. In that way, as you carry out your duties, you probably will satisfy the group and, consequently, will also increase (or at least not decrease) your own credibility and status.

PRESENTATIONS IN TEAMS: PANELS AND SYMPOSIA

When a group is too large to engage in effective roundtable discussion or when its members are not well enough informed to make such discussion profitable, a *panel* of individuals—from three to five, usually—may be selected to discuss the topic for the benefit of others, who then become an audience. Members of a panel are chosen either because they are particularly well informed on the subject, or because they represent divergent views on the matter at issue.

Another type of audience-oriented discussion is the *symposium.* In this format, several people—again, from three to five, usually—present short speeches, each focusing on a different facet of the subject or offering a different solution to the problem under consideration. Especially valuable when recognized experts with well-defined points of view or areas of competence are the speakers, the symposium is the discussion procedure commonly employed at large-scale conferences and conventions.

Various modifications of the panel and the symposium are possible, and sometimes the two formats may be successfully combined. Frequently, the set speeches of the symposium are followed by an informal exchange among the speakers. Then the meeting might be opened for audience questions, comments, and reactions. The essential characteristic of both the panel and the symposium is that a few people discuss a subject or problem while many people listen.

When you are asked to participate in a panel or symposium, remember that the techniques you employ do not vary substantially from those used for any other type of speech. Bear in mind, however, that you are participating as a member of a *group* who is centering its remarks, information, and

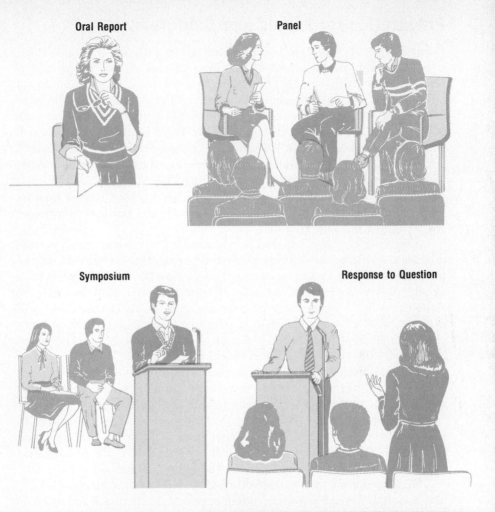

Oral Report

Panel

Symposium

Response to Question

Group Presentation Formats

opinions upon a specific topic or problem. You, therefore have an obligation to function as *part of a team,* to do what you can to coordinate your communicative behaviors with the efforts of others in order to give your audience a full range of viewpoints and options. Thus, in an important sense you must sacrifice part of your individual freedom and latitude for the greater good of all. With this important caution in mind, we can proceed to discuss techniques useful in preparing for and participating in group and conference presentations.

Preparation for Panels and Conferences

Because in panels and conferences you are one of a team of communicators, it is important that you take others into account as you prepare your remarks. This taking-into-account involves considerations which you do not have to face in other speaking situations. First, *you have to fit your comments into a general theme.* If, say, the theme of your panel is "The State of American Culture at the Beginning of Its Third Century," not only will you be expected to mention "American," "culture," "two hundred years," and the like, but probably you will also be expected to say something about where society has been over those two hundred years, where you think it is today, and how you see it evolving. The theme, in other words, goes far toward dictating how you will treat your subject, and perhaps even forces you to approach it in a particular way.

Also, *remember that you may be responsible for covering only a portion of a topic or theme.* In most symposia and panels, the speakers divide the topic into parts to avoid duplication and to provide an audience with a variety of viewpoints. For example, if you are discussing the state of American culture, you might be asked to discuss education, while others will examine social relations, the state of science and technology, leisure time, etc., thus dividing the theme *topically.* Or, alternatively, you might be asked to discuss *problems* (depersonalization, the "plastic" world, the limits of the work force) while other participants examine *solutions* (individual, corporate, ethical, political). Part of your preparation, therefore, involves coordinating your communicative efforts with those of others.

The more you know about the subject under discussion, the better. To be ready for any eventuality, you must have a flexibility born of broad knowledge. For each aspect of the subject or implication of the problem you think may possibly be discussed, make the following analysis:

First, review the facts you already know. Go over the information you have acquired through previous reading or personal experience and organize it in your mind. Prepare as if you were going to present a speech on every phase of the matter. You will then be better qualified to discuss any part of it almost spontaneously.

Second, bring your knowledge up to date. Find out if recent changes have affected the situation. Fit the newly-acquired information into what you already know.

Third, determine a tentative point of view on each of the important issues. Make up your mind what your attitude will be. Do you think that Hemingway was a greater writer than Faulkner? If so, exactly how and why? What three or four steps might be taken to attract new members into your club? On what medical or health-related grounds should cigarette-smoking be declared illegal? Stake out a tentative position on each question or issue that is likely to come before the group, and have the facts and reasons that support your view clearly in mind. Be ready to state and substantiate your opinion at whatever point in the discussion seems most appropriate, but also be willing to change your mind if information or points of view provided by other participants show that you are wrong.

Fourth—and finally—to the best of your ability anticipate the effect of your ideas or proposals on the other members of the group or the organization of which the group is a part.   For instance, what you propose might make someone lose money or force someone to retract a promise that has been made. Forethought concerning such possibilities will enable you to understand opposition to your view if it arises and to make a valid and intelligent adjustment. The more thoroughly you organize your facts and relate them to the subject and to the people involved, the more effective and influential your contributions to the discussion will be.

Participating in Panels and Conferences

Your style and vocal tone will, of course, vary according to the nature and purpose of the discussion as a whole, the degree of formality that is being observed, and your frame of mind as you approach the task. In general, however, *speak in a direct, friendly, conversational style.* As the interaction proceeds, differences of opinion are likely to arise, tensions may increase, and some conflict may surface. You will need, therefore, to be sensitive to these changes and to make adjustments in the way you voice your ideas and reactions.

Present your point of view clearly, succinctly, and fairly.   Participation in a panel or conference should always be guided by one underlying aim: to help the group think objectively and creatively to analyze the subject or solve the problem at hand. To this end, you should organize your contributions not in the way best calculated to win other people to your point of view, but rather in the way that will *best stimulate them to think for themselves.* Therefore, instead of stating your conclusion first and then supplying the arguments in favor of it, let your contribution recount how and why you came to think as you do. Begin by stating the nature of the problem as you see it; outline the various hypotheses or solutions that occurred to you as you were thinking about it; tell why you rejected certain solutions; and only after all this, state your own opinion and explain the reasons that support it. In this way, you give other members of the group a chance to check the accuracy and completeness of your thinking and to point out any deficiencies or fallacies that may not have occurred to you. At the same time, you will also be making your contribution in the most objective and rational manner possible.

Maintain attitudes of sincerity, open-mindedness, and objectivity. Above all, remember that a serious discussion is not a showplace for prima donnas or an arena for verbal combatants. When you have something to say, say it modestly and sincerely, and always maintain an open, objective attitude. Accept criticism with dignity and treat disagreement with an open mind. Your primary purpose is not to get your own view accepted, but to work out with the other members of the group the best possible choice or decision that all of you together can devise, and as a team to present a variety of viewpoints to the audience.

RESPONSES TO QUESTIONS AND OBJECTIONS

In most meetings (and at other times as well), listeners are given a chance to ask speakers questions. Panelists frequently direct questions to each other; professors ask students to clarify points made in classroom reports; clubs' treasurers often are asked to justify particular expenditures; political candidates normally must field objections to positions they have taken.

Sometimes, questions require only a short response—a bit of factual material, a "yes" or "no," a reference to an authoritative source. These sorts of questions need not concern us. But at other times, questions from listeners can require a good deal more, specifically: (1) Some questions call for *elaboration and explanation.* So, after an oral report, you might be asked to elaborate on some statistical information you presented, or called upon to explain how some financial situation arose. (2) Other questions call for *justification and defense.* Politicians often must defend stands they have taken. In open hearings, school boards seeking to cut expenditures justify their selection of school buildings to be closed. At city council meetings, the city manager often has to defend ways council policies are being implemented. In these two situations, a "speech" is called for in response to questions and objections.

Techniques for Responding to Questions

Questions calling for elaboration and explanation are, in many ways, equivalent to requests for an informative speech. That is, think about them as you would any situation wherein you are offering listeners ideas and information in response to their needs and interests. This means:

Give a "whole" speech. Your response should include an introduction, a body, and a conclusion. Even though you may be offering an impromptu speech (see Chapter 10), you nonetheless are expected to structure ideas and information clearly and rationally. A typical pattern for an elaborative remark might look like this:

1. Introduction: a rephrasing of the question, to clarify it for the other audience members; an indication of why the question is a good one; a forecast of the steps you will take in answering it.
2. Body: first point, often a brief historical review; second point, the information or explanation called for.
3. Conclusions: a very brief summary (unless the answer was extraordinarily long); a direct reference to the person asking the question, to see if further elaboration or explanation is called for.

Directly address the question as it has been asked.   Nothing is more frustrating to a questioner than an answer which misses the point or which drifts off into territory irrelevant to the query. Suppose, after you have advocated a "pass-fail" grading system for all colleges, you are questioned about how graduate schools can evaluate potential candidates for advanced degrees. The questioner is calling for information and an explanation. If, in response, you launch a tirade against the unfairness of letter grades or the cowardice of professors who refuse to give failing grades, you probably will not satisfy the questioner. Better would be an explanation of all the other factors—letters of recommendation, standardized tests, number of advanced courses taken, etc.—in addition to grade point averages that graduate schools can employ when evaluating candidates. If you are unsure what the point of the question is, do not hesitate to ask before you attempt an answer.

Be succinct.   While you certainly do not want to give a terse "yes" or "no" in response to a question calling for detail, neither should you talk for eight minutes when two minutes will suffice. If you really think a long, complex answer is called for, you can say, "To understand why we should institute a summer orientation program at this school, you should know more about recruitment, student fears, problems with placement testing, and so on. I can go into these topics if you would like, but for now, in response to the particular question I was asked, I would say that . . ." In this way, you are able to offer a short answer, yet are leaving the door open for additional questions from auditors wishing more information.

Be courteous.   During question periods, you may well be amazed that one person asks a question you know you answered in your oral report, and another person asks for information so basic you realize your whole presentation probably went over his or her head. In such situations, it is easy to become flippant or overly patronizing. Avoid those temptations. Do not embarrass a questioner by pointing out you have already answered that query, and do not treat listeners like children. If you really think it would be a waste of the audience's time for you to review fundamental details, simply say that the group does not have time to discuss them, but that you are willing to talk with individuals after the meeting to go over that ground.

Techniques for Responding to Objections

A full, potentially satisfying response to an objection is composed of two sorts of verbal-intellectual activities. *Rebuttal* is an answer to an objection or counterargument, and *reestablishment* is a process of rebuilding the ideas originally attacked. (See Chapter 13.)

Suppose, for example, that at an office meeting you propose your division institute a "management-by-objectives" system of employee evaluation. With this approach the supervisor and employee together plan goals for a specified period of time; so, you argue, it tends to increase productivity, it makes employees feel they are in part determining their own future, and it makes company expectations more concrete. During a question period, another person might object to management-by-objectives, saying that such systems are mere busywork, that supervisors are not really interested in involving underlings in work decisions, and that job frustration rather than job satisfaction is the more likely result.

You then return to the podium, *rebutting* those objections with the results of studies at other companies much like your own (reasoning from parallel case); those studies indicate that paperwork is not drastically increased, that supervisors like having concrete commitments on paper from employees, and that employee satisfaction must increase because job turnover rates usually go down (reasoning from sign). Furthermore, you *reestablish* your original arguments by reporting on the results of interviews with selected employees in your own company, almost all of whom think the system would be a good one.

In this extended illustration, we see most of the principal communicative techniques used by successful respondents:

Be both constructive and destructive when responding to objections. Do not simply tear down the other person's counterarguments. Constructively bolster your original statements as well. Reestablishment not only rationally shores up your position, but it psychologically demonstrates your control of the ideas and materials, thereby increasing your credibility.

Answer objections in an orderly fashion. If two or three objections are raised by a single questioner, sort them out carefully and answer them one at a time. Such a procedure helps guarantee that you respond to each objection, and it helps listeners to sort out the issues being raised.

Attack each objection in a systematic fashion. A speech which rebuts the counterarguments of another ought to be shaped into a series of steps, to maximize its clarity and acceptability. A so-called "unit of rebuttal" proceeds in four steps:

1. State the opponent's claim which you seek to rebut. ("Joe has said that a management-by-objectives system won't work because supervisors don't want input from their underlings.")
2. State your objection to it. ("I'm not sure what evidence Joe has for that statement, but I do know of three studies done at businesses much like ours, and these studies indicate that . . .")
3. Offer evidence for your objection. ("The first study was done at the XYZ Insurance Company in 1976; the researchers discovered that . . . The second . . . And, the third . . .")
4. Indicate the significance of your rebuttal. ("If our company is pretty much like the three I've mentioned—and I think it is—then I believe our supervisors will likewise appreciate specific commitments from their subordinates, quarter by quarter. Until Joe can provide us with more hard data to support his objection, I think we will have to agree . . .")

Keep the exchange on an impersonal (intellectual) level. All too often counterarguments and rebuttals degenerate into name-calling exchanges. We all are tempted to strike out at objectors. When you become overly sensitive to attacks upon your pet notions and other people feel similarly threatened, a communicative free-for-all can ensue. Little is settled in such verbal fights. Reasoned decision making can occur only when the integrity of ideas is paramount. And the calm voice of reasonableness is more likely to be listened to than emotionally charged ranting.

In sum, answering questions and responding to objections can be a frightening experience. Many of us feel threatened when we are made accountable for what we say by questioners and counterarguers. Yet, we must overcome our natural reticence in such situations if we are to weed out illogic, insufficient evidence, prejudices, and infeasible plans of action from our group deliberations.

*   *   *   *   *

We have now come full circle. We have reviewed in *Principles of Speech Communication* most of the forms of everyday public oral communication. We have concentrated upon the steps through which a public speaker proceeds when constructing and delivering informative, persuasive, and more specialized sorts of speeches. And we have examined in less detail the kinds of public discourses which comprise the world of work and social interaction, a discussion of which began this book.

While you cannot learn everything there is to know about public oral communication in a single course or in one brief book, you now are ready to take up the challenges of public oral expression. As you think through the rhetorical decisions you must make each time you rise to speak, we hope you will find a wealth of personal fulfillment and public service. You then will be putting the principles of speech communication to work in your life. If you do, we will have accomplished our purposes.

 GROUP PROJECTS

1. Divide into groups of four or five, and select a topic for a learning or decision-making discussion. Each group should prepare a panel forum which will be presented in front of the class. Allow approximately twenty-five minutes for the panel discussion, fifteen for the forum with the audience, and ten for critiques of the presentation. Following are some suggested topics:

(*a*) How effective is our freshman-orientation program?

(*b*) How are American cities solving their traffic problems?

(*c*) What makes a novel/play/film great?

(*d*) What are the social and ethical implications of organ-transplant surgery?

(*e*) How can we reconcile the demands of both the ecological and the energy crises in this country?

(*f*) What can be done about America's child-abuse problems?

(*g*) Is protest dead on the campuses of American colleges?

(*h*) How should the basic speech communication course be taught?

(*i*) Is it possible to put into law reasonable controls over pornography?

(*j*) What has the United Nations accomplished?

(*k*) Can individual citizens ever make their collective voices heard in Washington?

2. Work with several of your classmates to develop an agenda for a one-hour seminar in time management. Prepare your seminar with a specific audience in mind—students, housewives, secretaries, managers, etc. Alan Lakein's *How to Get Control of Your Time and Your Life* (New York: New American Library, 1974) and Donna Goldfein's *Everywoman's Guide to Time Management* (Millbrae, Cal.: Les Femmes Publishing, 1977) are useful sources to help you spot time wasters and to give you information on goal setting and planning. Your instructor may want your group to actually conduct these seminars in class or in another controlled situation.

3. Examine recent financial reports to shareholders or to the public. For instance, ask a business that has a profit-sharing plan for a copy of its most recent report. Or examine financial reports published in your local newspaper for a bank, the school district, or city or county governmental expenditures. Collect a number of

these financial reports so that each small group can study two or three and discuss just what the statistics mean. Each group is responsible for designing a five-minute report describing the statistical data used in one of the financial statements. What kinds of statistical generalizations would be appropriate for an audience composed of shareholders, bank stockholders, citizens attending an open meeting of the school board, etc.?

4. In this assignment you will conduct mock press conferences. Divide into small groups; each person in the group will decide upon a specific role to play. Determine the person you will pretend to be and the nature of the situation. Then, you will work alone to develop a brief statement announcing some upcoming activity, event, etc. Other members of the group should work individually to formulate potential questions for each situation. After you present your statement, your group will take the major responsibility for questioning you. You should develop a role/situation similar to these:

(*a*) You are the President of the United States. Make an announcement indicating that Congress has passed an important piece of legislation.

(*b*) As the chairman of the board of directors of a large firm, you will indicate that the company has just signed an important contract with China or some other nation.

5. Your instructor will divide the class into dyads. Meet briefly with your partner to decide on the type of interview and the specific situation that you will simulate, as well as who will be the interviewer and who the interviewee. Develop a series of questions to use in a ten-minute interview.

6. Along with several members of your class, consider the following situations, and then formulate specific questions which an interviewer might use to get information, to evaluate performance, or to persuade. What types of questions—direct, indirect, open, closed—did you choose and why?

(*a*) The interviewee worked only six months at the last job listed on his or her resumé.

(*b*) The interviewer wants to know how many employees are using manual rather than electric typewriters with a correcting feature.

(*c*) How does an interviewer ascertain whether Jane realizes that her work has become progressively poorer?

(*d*) The interviewer seeks to account for a switch in a major from predentistry to accounting.

(*e*) How does an interviewer determine what problems an employee has encountered in learning the new systems for billing?

INDIVIDUAL PROJECTS

1. Investigate a local problem. Designate a particular audience which would be likely to receive a report on this matter. Use the principles discussed in this chapter to explain the nature, dimensions, and causes of the problem. Make sure that you

reveal the type of charge at the outset of the speech, that you are clear about where and how you obtained information, and that, although you will not recommend a specific solution, you suggest workable solutions. A brief period for questions should follow the speech. Provide your instructor with an outline of your report.

2. Assume that a particular campus or local organization has asked for your services in making their meetings more efficient. You will actually attend a meeting of this organization and take notes during the proceedings. Then, you will formulate recommendations for improving the parliamentary and/or discussion skills which were exhibited. Pretend that the class is that organization, and deliver a ten-minute advisory report. After your presentation, the class will ask questions.

3. Assume that, as part of a mythical National Student Week, you have been asked to arrange on your campus a panel discussion or symposium to which all students and faculty members will be invited. *(a)* Select a subject you think would be of interest to such an audience. *(b)* Assuming you have a moderate budget to allow you to invite at least two "outside" persons of prominence, indicate whom you would ask to participate. *(c)* When and where would you hold the meeting? *(d)* How long would it last? *(e)* Which public-discussion format would you employ?

4. Choose a question for a panel discussion or symposium. Carefully research the question, and choose five references which you consider to be the best. Plan a brief report in which you justify your choice of these materials, explain the general nature of the materials, and indicate how they will be useful in a discussion on this question. Be prepared to answer questions relating to your choice of materials.

5. Pick a topic that is very important to you. The class will ask questions about the topic. After you have answered questions for a few minutes, the class will discuss the effectiveness of your responses. Also, consider how effective the questions were and whether there were questioners who made you feel especially comfortable, either in the way they asked the question or in the feedback they provided you.

 # SUGGESTIONS FOR FURTHER READING

Steven A. Beebe and John T. Masterson, *Communicating in Small Groups: Principles and Practices* (Glenview, Ill.: Scott, Foresman and Company, 1982).

Alfred Benjamin, *The Helping Interview*, 2nd ed. (Boston: Houghton Mifflin Company, 1974).

Patricia Hayes Bradley and John E. Baird, Jr., *Communication for Business and the Professions* (Dubuque, Ia.: William C. Brown Company Publishers, 1980).

Lois J. Einhorn, Patricia Hayes Bradley, and John E. Baird, Jr., *Effective Employment Interviewing: Unlocking Human Potential* (Glenview, Ill.: Scott, Foresman and Company, 1982).

Charles J. Stewart and William B. Cash, Jr., *Interviewing: Principles and Practices*, 3rd ed. (Dubuque, Ia.: William C. Brown Company Publishers, 1982).

APPENDIX I

Communication and Your Career*

Nancy L. Harper and John Waite Bowers

Understanding communication processes and skill in communicating are fundamental in nearly every kind of work. Some careers (for example, public relations) require specialized study of particular aspects of communication while others (for example, management) may require only a more general background in theory and basic skills. Even if communication skills are applicable only to selected portions of your future jobs, however, chances are you won't be successful if you cannot communicate.

The information included here about specific communication careers, the role of communication in all kinds of careers, and a strategy called "clustering" can help you make decisions about

careers and about your college years in general. The study of communication uniquely prepares you for certain kinds of work and at the same time is valuable preparation for *all* kinds of work. Whatever you might major in at college and whatever career aspirations you may have, courses in communication will be useful. The skills and information taught in communication departments are fundamental to earning a living (not to mention to living in general).

Research on hiring practices supports these observations. For instance, a recent nationwide survey shows that oral communication skills are more important than any other single factor in both getting a first job and being promoted later on. Speaking skills are con-

---

*Based on a manuscript, "Academic Clustering for a Career: How to Make College Relevant to Your Future," copyright 1981 Nancy L. Harper and John Waite Bowers.

sistently shown to be more important than factors we normally think of, such as grade-point average, letters of reference, and the reputation of the school.[1]

Public speaking ability is not the only communication skill that is critical to getting, keeping, and advancing in a job. A Midwest College Placement Association survey of employers shows that skills developed in courses such as interpersonal, group, and organizational communication; rhetorical criticism; persuasion and argumentation—to name just a few—are high on the list of qualities employers look for. Notice the rank ordering of results of this study in the table. The employers were asked to rank skills and qualities in terms of their importance in hiring decisions. The table shows, on a four-point scale (where 4 = very important), those that were assigned a "4" by 14 percent or more of the respondents. You will notice that oral communication ranks first, followed closely by a number of "presentational" and thinking skills of the sort taught in communication courses.

Careers for Communication Majors

The study of communication prepares you uniquely for certain kinds of work. One of the most common questions college students ask about any major is, "Once I get my degree, what can I do with it?" Or, "Are there any jobs for X majors?" The answer, of course, is that a particular kind of degree does not necessarily lead to a particular kind of

WHAT EMPLOYERS LOOK FOR IN HIRING[2]

Skills and Qualities	Percentage of "4" Rankings
Oral communication	83%
Responsibility	79%
Interpersonal skills	74%
Self-discipline	65%
Problem-solving skills	64%
Decision-making skills	63%
Self-confidence	59%
Written communication skills	59%
High energy	53%
Leadership ability	52%
Ability to work under pressure	42%
Organizational skills	42%
Ability to meet public	37%
Selling/promoting skills	31%
Appearance	30%
Math skills	29%
Research skills	14%

career. Majoring in communication, or anything else for that matter, will not guarantee you a job.

But communication majors do remarkably well in finding jobs that are satisfying and that make use of their special knowledge and skills. The range of these jobs is unusually diverse. Communication is a large field, encompassing a variety of skill areas as well as the study of specialized and general theories of human behavior. Communication departments offer

---

[1]Gustav W. Friedrich, "Speech Communication as a Required University Course," *Association for Communication Administration Bulletin*, October 1982, pp. 7–9.

[2]Lanna Hagge-Greenberg, "Report on the Liberal Arts Employer Survey: Opportunities for the Liberal Arts Graduate," Midwest College Placement Association, August 1979, p. 17.

courses in interpersonal, group, and organizational communication; persuasion, debate, and argumentation; public speaking and business and professional speaking; media production and mass communication theory. Many offer specialized courses in research methods, public relations and advertising, oral interpretation of literature, voice improvement for personal and professional (for example, theatre/broadcasting) development. Some even provide courses in areas such as family, political, scientific, and medical communication.

A number of studies have examined the kinds of jobs communication graduates get, and you can read about these in several of the books and articles listed in the following bibliography. Some common settings include business and industry, educational institutions, government agencies, hospitals and health organizations, mass media concerns, political organizations, private foundations, professional associations, research and consulting firms, and social service organizations.

Job titles within these various settings are even more diverse. In order to avoid generating endless lists, we have grouped the kinds of careers most likely to interest communication majors into six categories, or "clusters": (1) *Arts and Entertainment,* (2) *Corporate Communication,* (3) *Human Resources Management,* (4) *Political Professions,* (5) *Publishing,* and (6) *Training and Organizational Consulting.*

Each of these clusters contains a variety of related careers and an even larger number of specific jobs. We will describe each cluster briefly and cite some of the job titles each includes. If you want more information about any of the career areas, or about jobs within them, you can find detailed advice in sources listed for each cluster in the bibliography.

Arts and Entertainment (Performance, Production, and Management). If your interests and talents tend toward the artistic or performing aspects of communication studies, you may want to investigate these career opportunities. Mass media industries, theatrical production companies, community arts associations, media consulting firms, and a variety of governmental and business organizations offer careers that may interest communication majors. Typical jobs include script writing and editing, graphic and scene design, lighting, costuming, and makeup, video, audio and film production, and photography.

In addition to production and performance, these same organizations offer extensive opportunities in "arts management." The arts establishment has a growing need for stage, house, box-office, and publicity managers, talent agents, gallery or museum managers, program managers, arts outreach coordinators, exhibit coordinators, arts education consultants, agents, period style consultants, directors of development, and the like.

Depending on their organization's size, these "organizers" may raise funds and monitor the budget, develop audiences, stage special events, arrange travel and accommodations—in short, do everything required of managers in business and more. Some combine performing and management, as in local repertory companies. While some universities offer graduate programs in arts management, many managers start in entry-level positions as performers or members of the crew and work their way into management.

If this aspect of arts and entertainment especially interests you, look at the management skills cluster discussed later. If the production/performance areas are more attractive, the visual design and media skills cluster discussed later should be helpful.

Corporate Communication (Advertising, Audio-Visual Services, Public Relations). If your interests and abilities tend more toward the pragmatic uses of oral and written communication or the persuasive uses of media, you may want to investigate opportunities in business, government, and industry. Corporate communication careers include internal and external information services, audio/video or film production for personnel training and orientation, and marketing and media management. Each of these in turn comprises a variety of specific jobs. Some sample entry-level job titles are: print production clerk, type director, proofreader, typesetter, copywriter trainee, public relations aide, advertising assistant, art staff assistant, brand promotion assistant, production assistant, research trainee, management trainee, advertising account representative.

A sample of advanced job titles includes: director of development, director of media relations, print production manager, broadcast coordinator, public relations director, editor, industrial relations director, employee development specialist, director of corporate communication, manager of internal communication, art director, sales manager.

Human Resources Management (Personnel). Career opportunities in human resources management have grown rapidly and are expected to continue growing to meet the changing demands of business and the changing needs of management. One area of expanding responsibility is in making jobs more meaningful, more rewarding, and more challenging for workers. There are other responsibilities as well: meeting the pressures of governmental regulations; developing organizational structures according to the changing needs of business; dealing with unemployment; testing the competencies and skills of job applicants; securing and training qualified professional and managerial personnel; implementing employment services (safety programs, training, pension, and other benefit plans); and providing equal opportunity regardless of age, race, religion, and gender.

Human resources management includes a range of occupations, all of which revolve around people and problems involved in attracting and maintaining an effective workforce. Typical occupational categories are: employment and manpower planning, personnel development and communication, wage and salary administration, personnel research, employee services, labor relations, equal opportunity/affirmative action, and human resources information systems. These occupations comprise a variety of specific jobs and are practiced in almost every kind of public and private organization.

Advanced jobs are often filled from within the organization, so you should be prepared to work your way up to them by beginning in entry-level positions as a sales person, office worker, service representative, or management trainee. Many organizations offer training programs to employees who have an appropriate background or demonstrate aptitude.

Some sample entry-level job titles are: employment interviewer, test administrator, job analyst, personnel assistant, trainer, group facilitator. Some sample advanced job titles are: employment manager, training director, wage and salary administrator, benefits coordinator, safety director, industrial psychologist, equal opportunity coordinator, labor relations director, employee relations manager, personnel director.

Political Professions. Historically, politics has been attractive to communication majors. Political professions include a range of jobs in addition to national, state, and local elective office. Those most likely to interest communication specialists include campaign manager; political consultant to business, industry, or government agencies and offices; field representative; fund raiser; political organizer, commentator, or pollster; consumer advocate or researcher; speech writer or media expert. Entry is almost always through some kind of apprenticeship, such as volunteer worker, and is dependent upon the individual's talents and knowledge.

There are many opportunities in the federal bureaucracy, where you must follow established procedures. A newsletter, "Trends in Federal Hiring," published by the Civil Service Commission, provides information about job openings by agency and region, and specifies application procedures.

The Civil Service Commission also provides information about the Professional and Administrative Career Examination (PACE). This examination is the primary means for establishing eligibility for federal employment at the junior professional level. It is also important to know that the most common way to obtain legislative aide jobs is by personally contacting a member of the House of Representatives or Senate or a congressional staff member.

Opportunities in state and city government sectors are encouraging. Some states recruit on the basis of a general aptitude test (besides the requirement of a bachelor's degree). Graduates may gain employment in city government as an assistant to a city manager or a director of public works or, with experience, an administrative specialist.

American political parties also offer numerous opportunities to people who are able and willing to participate in local party activities, to manage campaigns, to canvass voters, and to organize money drives. Grass-roots participation is helpful, often necessary, for advancement within the major parties.

Community organizations also provide opportunities. Locally organized groups are influential in reform, particularly on issues of local planning, environment, school integration, etc. People who act as city council or school board members, aldermen or members of commissions are generally employed elsewhere. Although these jobs are part-time and low-paying, they provide direct access to the political system and a chance to affect policy decisions.

Publishing. The first publishing careers to come to mind are in the book, magazine, and newspaper industries, but governmental agencies, social service organizations, and many large institutions that are not commonly thought to deal in the printed word are big employers in the publishing world. Publishing careers include research, writing, editing, design, illustration, production, advertising, sales, and management. Entry into these careers usually means starting in sales or as an assistant. You might seek, in addition to the general skills associated with these jobs, familiarity with the use of computers for editing, typesetting, and design. Advancement is a matter of assuming increased responsibility for coordinating projects—usually in editorial, art, or advertising.

Training and Organizational Consulting. The increasing demand for the services of professional consultants stems largely from the growing burdens imposed on managers in recent years. Issues that consultants deal with range from inflation, urban renewal, and race relations to energy and pollution problems and the shortage of essential raw materials. In short, a consultant requires the knowledge and skills to aid an organization in a period of explosive change.

Job titles and specific duties may vary, but typically the trainer or consultant focuses on assessing the current "health" of the organization and designing and implementing educational programs (1) to orient new employees to the organization's history, policies, benefits, and formal and informal procedures; (2) to train new employees in technical and operational skills required in particular jobs; and (3) to guide current employees as they identify and acquire the skills they need for advancement.

Consulting positions can be found in private business (banks, department stores, manufacturing firms), in service organizations (universities, hospitals, groups such as Junior Achievement), and in local and state governmental agencies.

Within the six career clusters, therefore, are to be found a great variety of specific employment opportunities, all of which require communication training to varying degrees.

Communication Skills for Careers

You have undoubtedly noticed that the six communication career clusters overlap to some extent, at least in the skills they require. For instance, if you have a strong interest in video production, you probably noticed that you could employ that interest in any of the six clusters. And you probably can think of additional settings in which you could make use of such skills—for instance, in an environmental profession (making documentaries for the Environmental Protection Agency perhaps), a health profession (making training tapes to help physicians learn to interview patients), or a potentially infinite variety of other areas.

We have found it useful to identify general clusters of "communication skills," groupings of skills that are useful across a range of careers. All of these clusters are areas that you can specialize in within a communication major or take as concentrations in conjunction with another professional or liberal arts major. Whatever you major in, though, you probably should plan to take some coursework in each communication skill area—*Speaking and Writing, Language Computer Processing, Management, Social Science Research,* and *Visual Design and Media Production.*

Speaking and Writing Skills. A recent survey asked three groups—college alumni, college students, and employers—about the relative importance of various aspects of college work. *All three groups perceived communication—speaking and writing —as among the most important skills that might be learned in college.*[3] Furthermore, about half of those surveyed were *dissatisfied* with the policies of the colleges and universities from which they graduated vis-à-vis communication skills. Incredible though it may seem, some colleges and universities require no work in speaking and writing.

The failure to require work in speaking is especially unfortunate because many college students are so apprehensive or anxious about speaking that they will not take a speech course by choice even though they know they need one. People avoid, if they can, the things they fear. A survey at the University of Pittsburgh revealed that "public speaking anxiety" was the *leading* "personal problem for which students perceive they need help." ("Dependence on drugs" was the problem least frequently cited.) You should take college work in speaking, *especially if you don't want to.*

In order to assure that you get some balanced coursework in this area, you will probably want to take one or more courses from each category of the following outline. Such courses are likely to be found in departments with names like communication, speech, rhetoric, English, or journalism. But you may need to look around carefully; They may also be found in places such

as business, engineering, and education. Also, some departments offer their own specialized writing courses, often called "seminars" or "writing for —————." As a general rule, be sure to look for both major and elective courses that encourage oral reports, discussions, papers, and essay exams. Nearly every course you take *can* be an opportunity to improve your communication skills.

I. Speaking
  A. Formal—Look for courses with titles such as "principles of speech," "public speaking," "public communication," "speaking in public," "speech communication," "debate," "argumentation," "persuasion," "rhetoric."
  B. Informal—Look for courses with titles such as "discussion," "group discussion," "group communication," "interpersonal communication," "interviewing," "conference methods."

II. Writing
  A. General—Look for courses with titles such as "English composition," "rhetoric," "expository writing," "purposive writing," "writing for public purposes."
  B. Specialized—Look for courses called such things as "business writing," "technical writing," "scientific writing," "journalistic writing," "advertising," "news reporting," "magazine writing."

Language Computer Processing Skills. Understanding computers and

---

[3]Samuel L. Becker and Leah R. V. Ekdom, "That Forgotten Basic Skill: Oral Communication," *Association for Communication Administration Bulletin,* August 1980, pp. 12-25.

what they can or cannot be made to do is rapidly becoming a necessity. Whatever you want to do with your life, you probably will find computers involved. Authors use computers to compose articles and books, and publishers use computers to print them. Computers help small and large businesses keep track of their inventories and their profits and expenses. You also should consider learning at least a little about computers in general and about using computers to handle language in particular because statistics indicate that "information processing" is rapidly becoming *the* most transferable skill. More people spend more time handling information—getting it, recording it, retrieving it, sending it—than ever handle the objects or products the information is about. Many people in banking or agribusiness, for instance, never touch money or wheat; they deal almost exclusively with written records of their product.

Courses that can help you develop such skills can be found in a variety of departments. In addition to computer science, you might look in mathematics, English, linguistics, speech pathology, audiology, business, education, and, of course, communication. Also, check the university's computing center to see if they offer "short courses" or workshops and laboratories.

Management Skills. "Management" is a broad term used to refer to all levels of decision-making and responsibility in organizations. Our society is a highly organized one; it is almost impossible to play or work in isolation. Face-to-face accommodation is an everyday necessity. On social occasions, someone has to decide that enough people are gathered to begin a game of volleyball, where the boundaries will be, which side will serve. In work situations, someone has to decide that certain things must get done, how, when, and by whom. Even kinds of activities that we think of as essentially individual require organization and therefore management. Writing a book is a solitary activity—in part. The actual writing usually occurs in isolation. But before, during, and after, people organize to decide on approach, deadlines, stylistic conventions, and format.

You can undoubtedly think of hundreds of examples of the pervasiveness of organizations and management. Management skills are needed everywhere people try to get something done together. Prospective employers look for evidence of "leadership potential." Most of the qualities employers report as influencing their hiring decision (see Table 1) are managerial. Certainly advancement in a career is normally thought of as "moving up" to more responsible positions. The study of communication is excellent preparation for decision-making roles. Some special supplementary coursework of the sort recommended in this cluster can help you learn management skills and provide the kind of evidence you need to present yourself as someone with growth potential.

In addition to communication departments, management courses can often be found in departments of psychology, sociology, guidance, and counseling. They may also be found in business, engineering, economics, political science, social work, and even in home economics and physical and recreation education.

I. Leadership—Look for courses with

words like "leadership," "management," "procedure," "persuasion," "policy," "motivation," and "attitude" in their titles.

II. Interpersonal and group behavior—Look for courses with any of the following terms in their titles: "organization(al)," "negotiation," "bargaining," "group," "interpersonal," "relation(al)," "conflict," "human rights," "counseling," "sex roles," "interaction," "guidance."

Social Scientific Research Skills. The daily newspapers are full of reports of social scientific research: reports on the comparative satisfaction of Americans with their jobs, with the President, with the school system. Social scientific research is carried out to determine whether a new movie or a new kind of soap is likely to sell. When profits fall in a business or industry, social scientific research is employed to search for reasons. When new regulations are proposed, social scientific research is employed to identify probable consequences. As with the other areas represented in the communication skills clusters, social scientific research pervades all aspects of our lives.

Knowing how to conduct a public opinion poll, how to describe a population (say an audience or a group of potential buyers) in terms of characteristics critical to a proposed action or product, and how to interpret the results of others' attempts, is certainly a valuable skill. Like the other skill areas, social scientific research does not require a major commitment. You undoubtedly will encounter such research constantly in your courses. A few research methods courses will make you a better interpreter of such research

and give you the basic tools for becoming proficient, including computer skills in some places. And having such skills gives you something concrete to offer a prospective employer who is trying to decide whether to hire you or someone with a similar background but no research skills.

The most likely departments for such courses—in addition to communication—are psychology, economics, education, sociology, statistics, and mathematics. Equally relevant courses may also be found in biology, business, geography, geology, history, political science, and social work.

I. Computer—Look for courses with "computer," "programming," "data processing" or terms like these in their titles.

II. Quantitative—Look for courses with terms in their titles like "quantitative analysis," "statistical analysis," "statistical methods," "research methods," "sampling," "public opinion polling," "mathematical models," "probability," "experimental design."

III. Special topics—Look for titles such as "research methods in . . . (a particular subject, for example, marketing)," or "measurement problems in . . ." or "field techniques in . . ." or "research practicum in . . ."

Visual Design and Media Production Skills. Visual design and media production skills can work for you in much the same way as social scientific research skills. They can help to set you apart from a crowd of job applicants, and they can be used in whatever you decide to do with your life. Being

341

a good critic of design and media can also, of course, enrich your life outside of work. Magazines, books, movies, television programs are the staple of our entertainment lives and are the subject of a surprisingly high percentage of social conversation. The largest "publishers" (of print and audio-visual products) in the world are governmental agencies and private business and industry. Even if you work in the accounting office, the way your results are interpreted graphically and visually can be extremely important to you. And if you are knowledgeable, you probably can have some impact. Certainly, if you will occupy any sort of management position, knowing something about "information packaging" will be important.

You need not become a photographer or filmmaker or graphic designer, but taking a few courses to improve your critical skills (so you can recognize why a photograph or film or design is good) and learning something about the process of making such products can give you extra flexibility that can make the difference when you apply for a first job or when you think about moving up or over later in your life.

In addition to communication, these courses can be found in departments of broadcasting, film, theatre, journalism, art, English, instructional design, and even engineering.

I. Audio—Look for courses with words like "broadcasting," "radio," "audio," "sound," "media" in their titles.

II. Film—Look for courses with "film" or "cinema(tic)" in their titles.

III. Graphics—Look for courses with "graphic(s)," "print(ing)," "lettering," "typography" in their titles.

IV. Photography—Look for courses with terms like "photography," "photocommunication," "visual communication" in their titles.

V. Video—Look for courses with terms like "video," "electronic production," "broadcasting," "media" in their titles.

Planning for Careers

Now that you have some idea of the kinds of careers communication students tend to find attractive, and of the communication skills that are generalizable to a wide variety of kinds of work, the remaining question is "How can you use this information to make the most of your years at college?" One answer is to be systematic in deciding what courses, and other experiences, will be most interesting and useful to you. The model we have developed, "clustering," is an approach that a number of students have found helpful. Wherever you are in your thinking about college and careers, you should find the five steps in this model provide a useful strategy that is simple, though not necessarily easy. Clustering requires that you do some hard thinking about yourself and some careful study of resources available to you both in school and in various career areas.

Step 1. Begin by identifying your interests and abilities—what you like to do, what courses and activities you enjoy, and what you are or are likely to become good at—and deduce from that process the kinds of work that might be satisfying to you. We call this an *aspiration* or a *career goal*. We do not mean by these terms a *job*. We mean a general category of kinds of things people do to make a life (not just a living). Arts management, personnel training, politics, public relations, and advertising (the career clusters discussed earlier) are some of the kinds of things that we have identified as likely to be interesting to communication graduates.

Step 2. Once you have an idea of what you might like to do and would be good at, you need to determine what knowledge and skills you especially need to acquire in order to attain that goal. We call these *competencies.* Typical competencies (sets of knowledge and skills) can be found by examining the categories we used to organize course suggestions in the communication skills clusters: for instance, photography, leadership, interpersonal and group communication.

Step 3. Once you have a general career goal and know the central competencies required for it, you need to identify the *kinds of* courses and other experiences that will be most interesting and useful to you. This requires learning as much as possible about the structure of your college or university and about various ways of getting things done in it. Many factors will influence the way you pick courses: availability of certain academic degree programs, majors and minors, general requirements of the college or university, minimum and maximum term credit limits, prerequisites, and preferences you have or will develop about course size, timing, methods of instruction, certain professors, etc. Availability of internships or cooperative education programs, part-time work, and student and community organizations will influence other kinds of activities you might select to help you develop the competencies you define as central.

Step 4. Clustering (that is group-ing) your interests, abilities, aspirations, desirable competencies, likely courses, and extracurricular options gives you a basis for *choosing among the alternatives* available. You have a range of choices about what to major and/or minor in, what courses will fulfill the requirements of the major and minor, what courses will fulfill general college requirements for graduation, and what courses you can take as electives. Faculty and staff advisers and special service offices such as career planning or "pre-major" advising can help you make these choices. But no matter how much help is available, *you* still have to make the decisions. You will be better able to seek appropriate advice, interpret conflicting advice, and make satisfying decisions if you have done the necessary research in steps 1, 2, and 3.

Step 5. Finally, clustering enables you to develop a *plan of study,* a systematic outline of what you want to do (courses you want to take, activities you want to be involved in) while you are attending college. You can never anticipate everything and—we hope—you will grow and change while you are in school, so this plan will be tentative. It will have many "if . . . then's" and "either . . . or's" and "maybe's" in it. But it will give you a picture of where your clustering has led you. Formulating a plan, you should discover, makes it easier to decide on specifics when the time comes and—strange as it may sound—also makes it easier to change your mind later.

As a process, then, clustering is simple and straightforward. The kind of research you need to do, the self-examination, is not easy. But students who have done it indicate that the effort pays off in increased confidence and sense of purpose. Clustering will not guarantee you a job. No strategy or person—except maybe your cousin in the hardware business—can do that. But, it can make you feel better about what you are doing.

Also, clustering can give you an advantage when you begin your first job search. The plan you work out and follow will serve as an excellent guide for preparing your first resumé—often an arduous process. (See references in the "General" section of the bibliography for samples and for additional guidelines.) Clustering should make you better able to explain yourself to others—not only to prospective employers, but to co-workers, and to your parents and friends. More important, perhaps, you should be able to focus on the kinds of first jobs that will be satisfying in themselves and that will lead to other equally satisfying jobs. You are less likely to find yourself making money but hating the way you make it.

The ability to use symbols effectively—to communicate well—is unique among the skills that human beings can develop: It is a skill that will never become obsolete. In "Communication and Your Career," we have demonstrated that this skill is the center of many careers, and that it can be centrally important to most careers.

Communication *study* is as important as communication *skill*. Human beings not only think and talk, but they also think about and talk about talk. Communication as a discipline seeks to explain communicative behavior as well as to teach it. As a student of communication, you can learn to understand the variety of strategies people use in communicating, that is, to assess and predict outcomes and make informed choices among alternative strategies. This learning, unlike technical "performance" skills, allows you to adopt to new situations in life and in your career. It will never be exhausted.

Communication knowledge and skills are fundamental to earning a living—and to living itself.

BIBLIOGRAPHY

General Career Planning Resources

Bolles, Richard N. *The Three Boxes of Life, and How to Get Out of Them: An Introduction to Life/ Work Planning.* Berkeley, Ca.: Ten Speed Press, 1978.

Bolles, Richard N. *What Color Is Your Parachute? A Practical Manual for Job-Hunters and Career Changers.* Berkeley, Ca.: Ten Speed Press, 1978.

Dunphy, Philip C., et al. *Career Development for the College Student.* Cranston, R. I.: The Carroll Press, 1973.

Figler, Howard. *The Complete Job-Search Handbook.* New York: Holt, Rinehart and Winston, 1979.

Figler, Howard. *PATH: A Career Workbook for Liberal Arts Students.* Cranston, R.I.: The Carroll Press, 1975.

Fox, Marcia. *Put Your Degree to Work: A Career-Planning and Job Hunting Guide for the New Professional.* New York: W. W. Norton and Co., 1979.

Frigley, Bert. *How to Get a Job.*

Homewood, Il.: ETC Publications, 1974.

Gale, Barry and Linda Gale. *The National Career Directory: An Occupational Information Handbook.* New York: Arco, 1979.

Holland, John. *Making Vocational Choices: A Theory of Careers.* Englewood Cliffs, N.J.: Prentice-Hall, 1973.

Lathrop, Richard. *Who's Hiring Who.* Berkeley, Ca.: Ten Speed Press, 1977.

Medley, H. Anthony. *Sweaty Palms: The Neglected Art of Being Interviewed.* Belmont, Ca.: Wadsworth Publishing Co., 1978.

Plan Now for Your Life After College. Washington, D.C.: U.S. Government Printing Office, 1978.

Renetzky, Alvin. *Directory of Career Resources for Women: A Guide to Career Resources and Opportunities for Women.* Santa Monica, Ca.: Ready Reference Press, 1979.

Renetzky, Alvin, and Gail Schlachter, eds. *Directory of Internships, Work Experience Programs, and On-the-Job Training Opportunities.* Thousand Oaks, Ca.: Ready Reference Press, 1976.

Shingleton, John, and Robert Bao. *College to Career: Finding Yourself in the Job Market.* New York: McGraw-Hill, 1977.

U.S. Bureau of Labor Statistics. *The Occupational Outlook Handbook.* Washington, D.C.: U. S. Government Printing Office, 1980.

U.S. Department of Labor. *Guide for Occupational Exploration.* Washington, D.C.: U.S. Government Printing Office, 1979.

U.S. Department of Labor Employment and Training Administration. *Dictionary of Occupational Titles,* 4th ed. Washington, D.C.: U.S. Government Printing Office, 1977.

Resources for the Career Clusters

Arts and Entertainment

Allosso, Michael. *Exploring Theatre and Media Careers.* Washington, D.C.: U.S. Government Printing Office, 1976.

American Theatre Association. *The Summer Theatre Directory.* Washington, D.C.: American Theatre Association, Current Ed.

Ball, Victoria. *Opportunities in Interior Design and Decoration.* New York: Union Publishing and Distributing, 1963.

Ballinger, Raymond A. *Opportunities in Graphic Arts Careers.* New York: Union Publishing and Distributing, 1963.

Berlyn, David. *Your Future in Television Careers.* Skokie, Il.: Vocational Guidance Manuals, 1975.

Biegeleisen, Jacob Israel. *Careers and Opportunities in Commercial Art.* New York: E. P. Dutton, 1963.

Blanchard, Nina. *How to Break into Motion Pictures, Television, Commercials, and Modeling.* New York: Doubleday, 1978.

Degen, Clara, and Betty Stearns, eds. *Careers in Music.* Kalamazoo, Mi.: American Music Conference, 1976.

Denis, Paul. *Opportunities in the*

Dance. Skokie, Il.: Vocational Guidance Manuals, 1980.

Dubman, Sheila, et al. *Exploring Visual Arts and Crafts Careers*. Washington, D.C.: U.S. Government Printing Office, 1976.

Johnson, Bervin, et al. *Opportunities in Photography*. Skokie, Il.: Vocational Guidance Manuals, 1979.

London, Mel. *Getting into Film*. New York: Ballantine Books, 1977.

Loney, Glenn. *Your Future in the Performing Arts*. New York: Richards Rosen Press, Inc., 1980.

Moore, Dick. *Opportunities in Acting Careers*. Skokie, Il.: Vocational Guidance Manuals, 1975.

Piper, Robert J. *Opportunities in an Architecture Career*. New York: Universal Publishing and Distributing, 1966.

School of Visual Arts. *Careers in Visual Arts*. New York: Visual Arts Press, 1978.

Summer, Elyse. *Career Opportunities in Crafts*. New York: Crown Publishers, 1977.

Corporate Communication: Advertising, Audio-Visual Production, Public Relations

Bishop, Robert L., ed. *Public Relations, a Complete Bibliography*. Ann Arbor, Mi.: Publications Distribution Service, 1974.

Clarke, George Timothy. *Opportunities in Advertising Careers*. New York: Universal Publishing and Distributing Corp., 1968.

Davis, Martyn P. *A Career in Advertising*. London: Museum Press, 1963.

Dubman, Sheila, *Exploring Visual Arts and Crafts Careers*. Washington, D.C.: U.S. Government Printing Office, 1976.

Fujita, Neil S. *Aim for a Job in Graphic Design/Art*. New York: Richards Rosen Press, 1979.

Gould, Jay R., and Wayne A. Losans. *Opportunities in Technical Communications*. Skokie, Il.: Vocational Guidance Manuals, 1980.

Hill, John W. *The Making of a PR Man*. New York: McKay, 1963.

Hansen, Mary Lewis. *Exploring Writing Careers*. Washington, D.C.: U.S. Government Printing Office, 1976.

Henkin, Shepard. *Opportunities in Public Relations*. Skokie, Il.: Vocational Guidance Manuals, 1977.

Mertes, John E. *Corporate Communications: The Promotional View*. Norman, Ok.: University of Oklahoma Press, 1972.

Newsom, Doug. *This is PR: The Realities of Public Relations*. Belmont, Ca.: Wadsworth Publishing Co., 1976.

Olsson, David, and Raphael Harold. *Opportunities in Packaging Science*. Skokie, Il.: National Textbook Co., 1979.

Vance, Adrian. *Audiovisual Production*. New York: Amphoto, 1979.

Wallington, C. James. *Jobs in Instructional Media*. Washington, D.C.: Association for Educational Communications and Teaching, 1970.

Human Resources Management: Personnel

The Art of Motivating People. Waterford, Ct.: Bureau of Business Practice, 1975.

Beach, Dale S. *Personnel: The Management of People at Work.* New York: Macmillan, 1980.

Bittel, Lester R. *What Every Supervisor Should Know: The Basics of Supervising Management.* New York: McGraw-Hill, 1980.

Cayer, N. Joseph. *Managing Human Resources: An Introduction to Public Personnel Administration.* New York: St. Martin's Press, 1980.

Heneman, Herbert G., III, and Donald P. Schwab, eds. *Perspectives on Personnel/Human Resources Management.* Homewood, Il.: R.D. Irwin, 1978.

Mack, David. *Opportunities in Personnel Management Careers.* New York: Vocational Guidance Manuals, 1970.

Traynor, William J. *Opportunities in Personnel Management.* Skokie, Il.: National Textbook Co., 1978.

Political Professions

Baxter, Neale. *Opportunities in Government Service.* Skokie, Il.: VGM Career Horizons, 1980.

Clark, C.P., ed. *Minority Opportunities in Law for Blacks, Puerto Ricans, and Chicanos.* New York: Richards Rosen Press, Inc., 1979.

Duncan, James P., Jr. *Your Future in Foreign Service Careers.* New York: Richards Rosen Press, Inc., 1979.

Pre-Law Handbook/The Official Guide to ABA-Approved Law Schools. Princeton, N.J.: Association of American Law Schools, 1974.

Publishing

Bohne, Harald. *Publishing: The Creative Business.* Toronto: University of Toronto Press, 1973.

Education for Publishing Committee. *The Accidental Profession: Education, Training, and the People of Publishing.* American Association of Publishers, 1977.

Labbel, John. *Opportunities in Publishing Careers.* Louisville, Ky.: Vocational Guidance Manuals, 1975.

Training and Organizational Consulting

Lusterman, Seymour. *Education in Industry.* New York: The Board, 1977.

Oana, Katherine. *Opportunities in Counseling and Guidance.* Skokie, Il.: VGM Career Horizons, 1979.

Pollack, Sandy. *Alternative Careers for Teachers.* Harvard, Ma.: Harvard Common Press, 1979.

Traynor, William J. *Opportunities in Personnel Management.* Skokie, Il.: VGM Career Horizons, 1978.

Watson, Charles E. *Management Development Through Training.* Reading, Ma.: Addison-Wesley, 1979.

APPENDIX II

Sample Speech Materials

A SPEECH TO INFORM

Some speeches to inform give listeners detailed information, instructions, background data, and the like. For example, "The Geisha" (pp.231–234) provides historical background and descriptions of geishas' duties for an audience essentially ignorant of both. Some speeches to inform, however, try to orient audiences. Rather than concentrating upon detail, they offer "ways of thinking about and looking at" some idea, event, or object.

Architect Myron Goldsmith's speech, "We Shape Our Buildings, and Thereafter They Shape Us," is an example of an informative speech which concentrates upon orientation. It was delivered as an introduction to a symposium presented to the citizens of Columbus, Indiana. The purpose of the symposium was to present the revised Master Plan for that city. Goldsmith's speech introducing the symposium had as its primary purpose orientation—showing the participants the value of the dual concerns for utility and aesthetic appeal in the architectural environment. Notice that Mr. Goldsmith (1) uses his introduction to stress the importance of his subject and to forecast the development of the speech; (2) carefully divides the body of his talk into "utilitarian" and "aesthetic" considerations; and (3) presents a short conclusion (because the other members of the symposium presumably will develop more particular conclusions). The resulting speech is short, clear, and efficient.

WE SHAPE OUR BUILDINGS, AND THEREAFTER THEY SHAPE US
Myron Goldsmith

The theme of our symposium is "We Shape Our Buildings, and Thereafter They Shape Us." I would like to explore the truth of that statement in terms of architectural merit and the architecture of your community.   /1

Scholars all over the world study the impact of environment on human behavior. It is a new and burgeoning field of research activity for anthropolo-gists, sociologists, psychologists, and communication specialists. For these scholars, it is a fresh area of inquiry that is enjoying a surge of attention and scrutiny. It is widely covered and discussed in journal literature, in publications, and in symposiums such as the one we enjoy today.   /2

But the impact of environment on human behavior is *not* a new idea to

348

architects: It's something we've known for hundreds of years. I will address its significance in reference to the two broad aspects or dimensions of architecture—the utilitarian and the aesthetic—and I will explain why I think great architecture combines both of these. /3

First, the utilitarian. In the field of domestic architecture, we know that some houses are easier and more pleasant to live in than others and promote positive interaction among family members. The large kitchen of our past and its legacy in the post-World-War II family room encourage family interaction. On the other hand, a too-formal and forbidding room can discourage use. A similar effect occurs in a neighborhood. Arrangement of houses in a common cul de sac promotes interaction among families and children in the cul de sac. Or, dwellings can be set back—behind fences, through gates. Such devices provide greater privacy and security; they convey messages that say: Stay Out. /4

In places of work, we know that a pleasant, well-organized factory or office fosters better efficiency, happier employees, and less absenteeism. The layout of a building can promote or restrict accessibility to people. In some banks, for example, the president is in the open, accessible to any person who wants to discuss something. The opposite can also be true, where top executives are on the upper floor of a building, reached only through a battery of receptionists and secretaries, or even in a separate building with separate dining and parking facilities. This too affects interaction, the style of management, and the priorities of the corporation. /5

I know of a conglomerate that was nearly ruined because all the top managers of the constituent companies were moved to a single, isolated building on the theory that the interaction of the top management was the most important priority. For them, horizontal communication at the upper echelons was more important than vertical communication. And meanwhile, no one was minding the company store. /6

In other words, we have learned and are learning by trial and error about architectural spaces—public and private, accessible and formal. We understand more about what makes a building function well and efficiently. /7

What about the aesthetic? In the best architecture, the utilitarian is combined with the aesthetic. And when that occurs, architecture represents more than the sum of its parts. While it is easy to define and evaluate the functional aspect, it is much more difficult to define and evaluate the aesthetic aspect. To do this, we must be able to recognize and make informed judgments about aesthetics and decide how much we are willing to invest in it. The return may be many times the investment in the improved quality of life. /8

How does the aesthetic aspect serve us and our community? Does it only give people pleasure? Or does it meet other basic human needs as well? The most dramatic example of this concept is the church or cathedral. How can one explain Chartres Cathedral, built 700 years ago in a town the size of Columbus, Indiana? What prompted the prodigious effort in engineering and craftsmanship, in art and architecture? What made those people build a nave over 120 feet high, the height of a 12-story building, and towers almost

300 feet high? If the utilitarian dimension was the sole criterion, they could have built a nave 15 to 20 feet high. But there were other things at stake in the 13th century—the glory of God and civic pride, to name but two. The worship of God was heightened and exalted by the beauty of man's unparalleled artistic achievement. And the pride of the community was enhanced by the size, the proportions, and the majesty of the cathedral—bigger and more beautiful than its counterpart in Paris, only 40 miles away. /9

But we need not go to thirteenth century France to see a proper example of the combination of the utilitarian and the aesthetic in historic architecture. Your own county courthouse, built in 1874, is a good example. Not to put it in the same class as Chartres, but it is a fine building. It provides centralized, efficient working space for the county functions, but it also aesthetically represents a good example of late nineteenth century civic architecture. Buildings constitute a large part of the tangible reality we experience. Size and scale are not necessarily the measure of their significance. /10

Your own town is a notable example of the impact of a distinguished architectural environment on the quality of community life: where informed clients and distinguished architects have confronted with honesty and solved with integrity the problems of space and use, where the functional and aesthetic aspects of architecture have forged a standard of excellence that any community in the world might envy. Through a combination of clear vision, good fortune, and unusual circumstances, you have provided for your citizens the finest our profession has to offer in churches, schools, and buildings—public, commercial, and industrial. You have given your young people something beautiful to grow up with, and you have given your own population something beautiful to live with. /11

So, then, what value do we place on the environment where we live and work and learn? How important is it that the community as well as the leadership—clients, architects, teachers, and business people—are knowledgeable about architecture and have some aesthetic judgments? It is of immense value and in Columbus you are better informed about architecture than any city I know of. Columbus is the proper training ground for the architects and clients of the future. You shape your buildings, and thereafter they shape you. /12

SPEECHES TO PERSUADE AND TO ACTUATE

The following speech, delivered to a joint session of Congress on December 8, 1941, was President Franklin Delano Roosevelt's message requesting a declaration of war against Japan. Round-the-clock negotiations with Japan had been suddenly disrupted when, on Sunday morning, December 7, the Japanese launched a massive, surprise attack on Pearl

Harbor, Hawaii, sinking eight American battleships and other smaller craft and leveling planes and airfields.

The nation was numbed; Congress was indignant; and the President moved quickly. The joint session was held in the House chamber. The galleries were overflowing, and the speech was broadcast worldwide.

Notice that this message contains only a short attention step (because the surprise attack created all of the necessary attention), a longer need step (paragraphs 2–11) which details the situation in the Pacific, and a short satisfaction step (paragraph 12) which only hints at American military strategy. The visualization step (paragraphs 13–17) attempts, in heroic fashion, to steel the nation for war, and it is followed by a concise, sharply drawn action step. The President's strategies seem clear. The fact that the need and visualization steps receive detailed development shows his concern for (1) providing an informational base for the action, (2) offering a psychological orientation to wartime thinking, and (3) justifying the commencement of hostilities.

 FOR A DECLARATION OF WAR AGAINST JAPAN*
Franklin Delano Roosevelt

TO THE CONGRESS OF THE UNITED STATES: Yesterday, December 7, 1941—a date which will live in infamy—the United States of America was suddenly and deliberately attacked by naval and air forces of the Empire of Japan. /1

The United States was at peace with that nation and, at the solicitation of Japan, was still in conversation with its government and its Emperor, looking toward the maintenance of peace in the Pacific. Indeed, one hour after Japanese air squadrons had commenced bombing in Oahu, the Japanese Ambassador to the United States and his colleague delivered to the Secretary of State a formal reply to a recent American message. While this reply stated that it seemed useless to continue the existing diplomatic negotiations, it contained no threat or hint of war or armed attack. /2

It will be recorded that the distance of Hawaii from Japan makes it obvious that the attack was deliberately planned many days or even weeks ago. During the intervening time the Japanese government had deliberately sought to deceive the United States by false statements and expressions of hope for continued peace. /3

·The attack yesterday on the Hawaiian Islands has caused severe damage to American naval and military forces. Very many American lives have been lost. In addition, American ships have been reported torpedoed on the high seas between San Francisco and Honolulu. /4

*Originally published in the *Congressional Record*, 77th Congress, 1st Session, Volume 87, Part 9, pp. 9504–9505, December 8, 1941.

Yesterday the Japanese government also launched an attack against Malaya. /5

Last night Japanese forces attacked Hong Kong. /6

Last night Japanese forces attacked Guam. /7

Last night Japanese forces attacked the Philippine Islands. /8

Last night the Japanese attacked Wake Island. /9

This morning the Japanese attacked Midway Island. /10

Japan has, therefore, undertaken a surprise offensive extending throughout the Pacific area. The facts of yesterday speak for themselves. The people of the United States have already formed their opinions and well understand the implications to the very life and safety of our nation. /11

As Commander-in-Chief of the Army and Navy I have directed that all measures be taken for our defense. /12

Always will we remember the character of the onslaught against us. /13

No matter how long it may take us to overcome this premeditated invasion, the American people in their righteous might will win through to absolute victory. /14

I believe I interpret the will of the Congress and of the people when I assert that we will not only defend ourselves to the uttermost but will make very certain that this form of treachery shall never endanger us again. /15

Hostilities exist. There is no blinking at the fact that our people, our territory, and our interests are in grave danger. /16

With confidence in our armed forces—with the unbounded determination of our people—we will gain the inevitable triumph—so help us God. /17

I ask that the Congress declare that since the unprovoked and dastardly attack by Japan on Sunday, December 7, a state of war has existed between the United States and the Japanese Empire. /18

Sometimes, a problem you wish to discuss seems a million miles from audience members. In such situations, how can you engage their sympathies and propensities to act? Sheer statistics seldom work; eloquent exhortation may not be enough, either. Personalized illustrations, however, may do the trick.

This was the approach Molly Timmins of Buena Vista College used when attempting to get an audience to do something about state custody laws and child stealing. Note, too, the structure of her speech: Paragraphs 1–3 seek to gain attention; paragraphs 4–16 develop the need; and, satisfaction is provided in paragraphs 17–18. But then, to personalize her appeals even more than she had this far into her speech, Ms. Timmins combines the visualization and action steps in paragraphs 19–22, so that she herself is both the visual exemplar and the reason why action is called for.

THERE'S A COLD SILENCE AND
THINGS ARE NEVER LIKE THEY USED TO BE*
Molly Timmins

On a bright, sunny April morning, five year old Johnny burst out the front door. His mother stood in the door smiling, waved to him and watched as he scampered out of sight. School was only two blocks away, a five, sometimes ten minute walk for a curious little boy like Johnny. /1

Kindergarten let out at 11:30, and when Johnny wasn't home at 11:45, his mother didn't worry. Knowing Johnny, she said to herself, he will probably pop in any moment, with a crumpled bunch of crocuses in his hand. /2

At noon, Johnny's mother began to look out the front door. At 12:30, she called the school calmly, perhaps she reasoned, he was still enjoying the warm sunshine on the playground. That's when her nightmare began; for Johnny never showed up—he had been abducted by his father before he even got to school. /3

A fictional story? No! Last year as many as 100,000 children were stolen from their homes. Officials say that 20 percent of these children will never be heard from again. What these cases have in common, is that in each one the kidnapper was one of the children's own divorced or separated parents, whose act is not even technically considered a crime. /4

The problem with child stealing is that it is pervasive and the parent who is left to wait and wonder will tell you, "there's a cold silence and things are never like they used to be." /5

What makes a parent steal his own child? A counsel for the New York based Citizens League on Custody Kidnapping says, "the main motive is revenge, not love of the child, It's to hurt the other parent, the custodial parent." /6

The most horrible of all are the children who are beaten, emotionally abused, and abandoned by the parent who took them. A good example of this, is the Arizona mother who, after an eight month search, discovered that her children had been abandoned by their father, then bounced from one foster home to another, finally being adopted by a couple of another race. /7

Two problems arise out of parental child stealing. First, the legal system doesn't recognize parental kidnapping as a serious crime. While many states will charge the child stealers with a misdemeanor, only a handful will charge them with a felony. Some 40 states have adopted the Child Custody Jurisdiction Act, which makes other states enforce one another's custody decrees. But in spite of these statutes, lawyers will tell you it is still easy to ignore a custody order in one state and start new legal proceedings in another. /8

*"There's a Cold Silence and Things Are Never Like They Used to Be" by Molly Timmins. Reprinted from *Winning Orations, 1982*, by special arrangement with the Interstate Oratorical Association, Larry Schnoor, Executive Secretary, Mankato State College, Mankato, Minnesota.

If you find this hard to believe ask Bobbie Lawrence from San Francisco. Her son was snatched off the school playground by his father, whom he'd not seen in seven years, and another man. They fled to Oklahoma, where the father petitioned the court for custody of the boy. Custody was granted, despite the fact that the mother had been given custody both in Arizona, where the divorce was granted, and in California, where she and her son lived.   /9

Lawrence did get her son back, but not because she had convinced anyone that her ex-husband's action was criminal. She got him back on a legal technicality—the Oklahoma court failed to notify her of the custody hearing. /10

During this time you would think Lawrence would have received help. Instead she was shuffled between the police department and the district attorney's office, with neither agency anxious to take command. /11

What is wrong with our courts and state legal systems? According to Senator Malcolm Wallop of Wyoming, "at the state level, there is no uniform approach to child stealing. It is exceedingly difficult and in most cases impossible to enforce the laws beyond the state border." In most states child-stealing is considered a domestic affair, not a serious crime. /12

Not only are the children caught in a legal tug-of-war between conflicting state laws, they are also caught in an emotional and psychological tug-of-war between parents. When both parents love the child, this struggle is understandable, even though damaging to the child. But when the motive is revenge, the psychological and emotional abuse of the children is intolerable. /13

Clinical psychologist Eugene Evens of Tucson, in treating small children who have been abducted and returned, says, "the common element of their reactions are an intense clinging and an incredible fear. They are frightened it will happen to them again." /14

A similar thing happened to Bobbie Lawrence. Once her son was returned to her, he refused to go to school. When she finally persuaded him to go to school, the principal told her that he hid under a staircase all day. For protection he carries a safety pin with him, and he has recurring nightmares that his father is climbing through his bedroom window to steal him again.   /15

A rare case? Hardly! Chicago child psychiatrist, Ner Littner, says that between 10 and 40 percent of the kidnapped victims become seriously disturbed. One such severe case occurred in Illinois. A girl, six, was taken away by her father, at night, leaving the state by bus. Now a teenager, she reacts to depression by going to the same bus terminal at night, picking up an older man and going off with him for two or three days. The shock of being kidnapped is one that stays with a child for a lifetime. One child who was kidnapped twenty years ago, still has daily nightmares about it. /16

What can be done to combat this serious crime? We could demand that each state charge child stealers with a felony. This would make some think twice about getting revenge. We should all encourage our state legislatures to pass the Parental Kidnapping Prevention Act, now before Congress, which would require all states to honor and enforce one another's custody decrees. /17

But even if we could get stricter laws passed, more and more divorced parents will undoubtedly, someday, be faced with the painful shock of having their children stolen. /18

Some of you are probably saying to yourselves, "OK, what does this have to do with me?" Since statistics show us that 50 percent of all marriages today end in divorce, every one of *you* could sometime in the future become a potential child stealer, or have your child stolen from you. It is up to each one of us to become aware of this problem and to think about how we would handle it. /19

I, like many of you, never was too concerned over child stealing. I never thought it could possibly involve me. Three years ago I was proven wrong. My ex-husband took my daughter, Stacy, to Minneapolis, on one of his visitations. He told me he was going to do this. When I reminded him that the custody decree stated he could not take her out of the county, he went to his lawyer. /20

Now, imagine what it was like for me to be driving home that day from classes and meeting them on the highway. I immediately called my lawyer who assured me he would get them back. I waited seven hours, only to find out my lawyer had gone out of town and left a message with his wife that my husband had obtained a court order, from a different judge, allowing him to take Stacy. /21

I had three days to wait and wonder if I would ever see her again. I was one of the lucky ones. My ex-husband chose not to put Stacy through such an emotional trauma. As sociologist Agopions tells it, "when someone steals your child, it's like a shadow that follows you everywhere. You are always looking, always searching. There's a cold silence and things are never like they used to be." /22

AN ARGUMENTATIVE SPEECH (CLAIM OF POLICY)

Often, it is not enough simply to argue in favor of some policy. Especially if you are challenging a generally valued institution with your policy claim, you have to be careful to (1) undermine (refute) the current policy of that institution, and yet (2) not destroy the overall credibility of the valued institution. This sort of problem was faced by Timothy L. Sellnow of St. Cloud State University when he proposed changes in the federal Food and Drug Administration's policy on artificial hearts.

Note his responses to his challenges: Paragraphs 1–3 introduce the subject matter and forecast the speech's developmental pattern; paragraph 4 finishes the orientation by describing an artificial heart. Then, Mr.

Sellnow devotes paragraphs 6–11 to a refutation of the FDA's refusal to allow the University of Utah to do an artificial heart transplant. Furthermore, in offering and defending an alternative policy in paragraphs 12–16, he is very careful to protect the FDA's general reputation even while asking for changes. All that remains, then, is a quick call for action in paragraphs 14, 15, 18, and 19. As you read this speech, also be sensitive to the valuative premises Mr. Sellnow uses as foundations for his policy claim.

Arguments like those offered here apparently worked; the University of Utah surgical team was allowed to transplant an artificial heart into Dr. Barney Clark in December 1982.

A MISSING BEAT*
Timothy L. Sellnow

"It's a miracle! The greatest single development in the battle against our nation's number one killer." These were the words chosen by doctors and journalists across the country to describe one of history's greatest developments in medical technology. The world watched in disbelief as the amazing function of the Artificial Heart was displayed through the mass media. The artificial heart's creators watched in disbelief as the American Food and Drug Administration refused to allow the use of this device. /1

The impact of this FDA decision can easily be seen through the current studies of the National Heart, Blood and Lung Institute which claims that 50,000 Americans per year could be given artificial hearts. This figure may seem inflated until one considers the fact that heart diseases will kill over a million Americans this year alone. /2

My goal today is to prove to you that the FDA is making a grave mistake by holding up the therapeutic application of the artificial heart. To do so, first I'll explain the artificial heart's function. Second, I'll present the FDA's arguments against the artificial heart along with upholding arguments by the heart's backers. Finally, I'll offer a practical solution to this problem. /3

What is this new weapon in the arsenal of heart therapy? Experimentation with the artificial heart has continued over the past two decades. The particular heart in question is the Jarvik-7, developed by American Dr. Robert Jarvik. This mechanical heart is composed of plastic and aluminum and fits in the space left by a person's original heart. It is powered by a small air compressor connected by narrow tubes outside the body. This compressor is designed to be easily wheeled or

*"A Missing Beat" by Timothy L. Sellnow. Reprinted from *Winning Orations, 1982*, by special arrangement with the Interstate Oratorical Association, Larry Schnoor, Executive Secretary, Mankato State College, Mankato, Minnesota.

placed in a wheel chair. It is keeping dogs, goats, and calves alive and active indefinitely, and its two temporary trials with humans were both highly successful. /4

Why then if this device is safe and in such demand has the FDA banned its use? The FDA offers several basic reasons. First is a concern over when and how doctors would decide to implant the device. The FDA also wondered whether the proposed patient consent forms accurately describe the kind of life the implant recipient should expect. Finally, the FDA believes the proposal does not go into enough detail on what information will be gathered after the implant. /5

If you're thinking that much of this reasoning sounds more technical than medical, you're right. Wayne Pines, a spokesman for the FDA, told a *New York Times* reporter that, "The main problem is with the study plan, not with the actual heart." It's sad to think that doctors helplessly watch 3,000 Americans a day die of heart disease, while our FDA worries about study plans. /6

Dr. Jarvik and the rest of the University of Utah's research team have some powerful arguments to counter the FDA's concerns. They first address the issue of when and how the artificial heart would be used. Dr. Willem Kolff, overall director of the research team, stated that the decision to use the heart would come only in the operating room when the heart of a patient who has undergone conventional surgery cannot be revived. Only when all known means for reviving the natural heart fail, and the doctors would ordinarily give up, will they turn to artificial hearts. / 7

Next, the team turns to the FDA's concern about the consent form. First,

Dr. William DeVries, the team's chief surgeon, is careful to point out that no heart will be forced on anyone. All patients must give approval before undergoing serious heart surgery of any kind. DeVries says the patient and his spouse or family would be counseled before surgery, letting them know all risks and limitations involving the artificial heart. He says, ". . . only families deemed likely to cope well with such circumstances will be considered." /8

The research team's response to the FDA's challenge of observing their patients closely after the implant is, in their opinion, obvious. The Utah researchers feel they are very close to such developments as an electrically powered heart which could allow a patient full mobility and eliminate any outside equipment. Developments such as these are absolutely impossible without the close monitoring and analysis of all artificial heart recipients. /9

At this point, two other questions arise. Could enough artificial hearts be produced to meet the tremendous demand, and how will recipients pay for it? Will enough artificial hearts be produced? With FDA approval, mass production of the artificial heart could begin immediately. In fact, Dr. DeVries maintains that up to 5,000 successful operations could be performed within approximately a year of the heart's approval. This is a sharp contrast to the 30 annual organic transplants performed today. /10

Cost will certainly be an obstacle in the beginning, but because the artificial heart can be produced in mass production, and requires no continuous hospitalization, the Utah medical crew believes the cost will steadily drop after its approval. With FDA approval, further financial support would be given by such insurance agencies as Blue Cross and Blue Shield, and the artificial heart's research and use would receive extensive government financial assistance. /11

Now that you are aware of the evidence that the artificial heart can work, and that it is in great need, the only question remaining is how to solve this controversy. I would like to offer a solution aimed at the immediate problem, as well as future benefits. /12

The most immediate compromise that can be reached with the FDA is to use the artificial heart as temporary substitute for patients awaiting an organic heart for transplant. Though the Utah experts are ready for its permanent use, they are willing, and anxious to begin the implant process with even this short-term measure. Thus they can continue perfecting the artificial heart while saving human lives. The heart's creators are ready to save lives, now we must urge the FDA to do the same. /13

It is up to each one of us to stay informed, and speak out to friends and family about the artificial heart, and the immediate necessity for its acceptance. Ask your doctor about it and urge him to actively support the artificial heart as well. The way is open for us to take a direct part in this issue. Call or write your local chapter of the FDA and urge others to do so. Sounds like the first step to nearly every solution, right? That may be so, but in this case it bears special weight. Already the organized opposition to this FDA ruling has become so great, that the FDA is publicly considering allowing the artificial heart's use in a closely monitored experiment involving seven hopeless heart patients. With our support and pressure, that number can grow from 7 to the 5,000 the artificial heart can reach now, and the 50,000 the device can reach annually in the near future. /14

You can individually aid the cause by continuing your financial support of such research organizations as the American Heart Association, one of the many organizations which gives its full fledged support for the immediate use of the artificial heart. /15

In the long run, some changes need to be made in the FDA's methods. I'm not denouncing the FDA as an administration. I'm not even asking them to stop anything. Instead, the FDA needs to add a clause to their current policy for dealing with therapeutic devices. Today, the FDA is forced to say yes or no to the regular use of a medical device. What is needed is an intermediate clause that would allow the FDA to say no to a device they feel needs more work, yet allow its use in people who otherwise stand no chance for survival. This step would at least lessen the blow of such FDA decisions as with the artificial heart. /16

Finally, for your own benefit, make sure your health insurance includes coverage of such therapeutic operations, and take care of your own heart. /17

These actions and changes will not only aid in the development of the artificial heart, they will benefit whatever medical breakthroughs lie ahead. /18

Please join in this effort. So many people stand to benefit, maybe even you. I'll leave you with the words of Dr. Steven Fredman: "In matters of the heart, procrastination is hardly the best policy." /19

A SPEECH OF ACCEPTANCE

Anyone who has watched a Motion Picture Academy Award ceremony can testify that speeches of acceptance often are stumbling, halting affairs with a profusion of thanks and embarrassment. Actually, however, the formality and dignity of the occasion invite exceptional—even profound—discourse. While accepting an award or gift, a speaker can, for example, strive to inspire others to the pinnacle he or she has reached. William Faulkner (1897–1962), renowned novelist and critic of the human race, endeavored to provide that type of inspiration when, on December 10, 1950, he accepted the Nobel Prize for Literature. Since he had no reputation as a lecturer, the public might well have expected a lesser speech filled with the kind of pessimism so characteristic of his novels. Instead he greeted his listeners with a positive and stirring challenge to improve humankind.

   Notice that Mr. Faulkner quickly pinpoints a particular audience— "the young men and women writing today"—to whom he directs much of his speech. Then, through a series of contrasts, he articulates the attitudes that are appropriate and useful to the artist, after which he concludes his remarks with a moving visualization step aimed at crystallizing the duties and obligations of writers for all time. Study this speech with your thoughts trained especially on Chapter 8, "Wording the Speech," and Chapter 14, "Speaking on Special Occasions."

ON ACCEPTING THE NOBEL PRIZE FOR LITERATURE*
William Faulkner

I feel that this award was not made to me as a man, but to my work—a life's work in the agony and sweat of the human spirit, not for glory and least of all for profit, but to create out of the materials of the human spirit something which did not exist before. So this award is only mine in trust. It will not be difficult to find a dedication for the money part of it commensurate with the purpose and significance of its origin. But I would like to do the same with the acclaim too, by using this moment as a pinnacle from which I might be listened to by the young men and women already dedicated to the same anguish and travail, among whom is already that one who will some day stand here where I am standing.   /1

   Our tragedy today is a general and universal physical fear so long sustained by now that we can even bear it. There are no longer problems of the spirit. There is only the question: When

   *William Faulkner, "On Receiving the Nobel Prize" from *The Faulkner Reader*. New York: Random House, Inc., 1954.

will I be blown up? Because of this, the young man or woman writing today has forgotten the problems of the human heart in conflict with itself which alone can make good writing because only that is worth writing about, worth the agony and the sweat. /2

He must learn them again. He must teach himself that the basest of all things is to be afraid; and, teaching himself that, forget it forever, leaving no room in his workshop for anything but the old verities and truths of the heart, the old universal truths lacking which any story is ephemeral and doomed—love and honor and pity and pride and compassion and sacrifice. Until he does so, he labors under a curse. He writes not of love but of lust, of defeats in which nobody loses anything of value, of victories without hope and, worst of all, without pity or compassion. His griefs grieve on no universal bones, leaving no scars. He writes not of the heart but of the glands. /3

Until he relearns these things, he will write as though he stood among and watched the end of man. I decline to accept the end of man. It is easy enough to say that man is immortal simply because he will endure: that when the last ding-dong of doom has clanged and faded from the last worthless rock hanging tideless in the last red and dying evening, that even then there will still be one more sound: that of his puny inexhaustible voice, still talking. I refuse to accept this. I believe that man will not merely endure: he will prevail. He is immortal, not because he alone among creatures has an inexhaustible voice, but because he has a soul, a spirit capable of compassion and sacrifice and endurance. The poet's, the writer's, duty is to write about these things. It is his privilege to help man endure by lifting his heart, by reminding him of the courage and sacrifice which have been the glory of his past. The poet's voice need not merely be the record of man, it can be one of the props, the pillars to help him endure and prevail. /4

A COMMENCEMENT ADDRESS (SPEECH TO ENTERTAIN)

As we noted in Chapter 14, an entertaining speech should have at its core a message of importance for the audience. This can become a special problem for comedians called to address audiences at usually-serious occasions. It certainly was a problem for Dick Cavett, former gag-writer, stand-up comic, and now host of PBS's "Dick Cavett Show," when he was asked to deliver the commencement address at Vassar College, May 27, 1979.

Mr. Cavett was concerned with the ceremonial demands of a commencement speech (see paragraphs 1–4). Yet, he obviously knew that, given his usual speaking style and reputation, the audience expected him to be "funny" even if he wanted to make a serious point regarding the personal and social uses of the English language. The resulting speech demonstrates his skills; it is appropriate to the occasion, humorous enough to meet audience expectations, and yet serious enough to leave listeners with significant advice. As you read over the speech, note what he does to guarantee that the humor is always subordinated to the central idea, and his use of transitions to keep the address from becoming only a string of one-liners.

IS ENGLISH A DYING LANGUAGE?*
Dick Cavett

Mrs. Villard, President Smith, members of the faculty, students of Vassar, and friends: /1

The last college commencement I attended was my own. That, as President Smith mentioned, was at Yale in 1958. So if I get rattled here this morning, don't be surprised if I suddenly take out my handkerchief and launch into a chorus of "Bright College Years." /2

Actually, that was not only the last commencement I attended, but the only other one I've ever attended; so my whole sense of these affairs comes from that single experience. I gather that the speaker in my position is expected to address himself to some vaguely uplifting topic that has a bearing on the academic career you graduates are leaving behind you, but also looks ahead to some problem that awaits you, some challenge that will be put to you to try to make the world a better place. In 1958 I seem to remember being urged to go out and do something about the Cold War. And, as you can see, the results speak for themselves. /3

Anyway, those are the requirements as I understand them. And I'm sorry to tell you I have a topic that meets them perfectly. But don't worry— I don't think I'll use it. After all, the world would little note nor long remember what I might say here about "Ethical Dilemmas in Ecology During a Nuclear Age." /4

Instead, let me begin on what, for me, is firmer ground: humor, or at least a humorist. James Thurber was talking at a party with an actress he knew. She was telling him about the troubles of a mutual friend. The friend, she said, had had her apartment broken into so many times that she finally had to have it "burglarized." Thurber thought about that for a moment and said, "Wouldn't it have been simpler for her just to have it alarmed?" /5

Now, there's more than a joke here, as Thurber was quick to point out when he told this story in one of his essays. "Ours is a precarious language," he said, "in which the merest shadow line often separates affirmation from negation, sense from nonsense,

*"Is English a Dying Language?" by Dick Cavett. Given at Vassar College Commencement, May 27, 1979. Reprinted by permission of Dick Cavett.

and one sex from another." In his later years, when he was blind, Thurber took in the world mostly through his hearing, and what he heard, acutely, was how our language was being mangled. He wrote often about "The Spreading You-Know" and other blights that he wished would pass "from the lingo into limbo." Even the sound and the fury, he said, had become the unsound and the fuzzy. /6

Thurber was one of a long line of people who have confirmed what George Orwell wrote nearly 35 years ago—that "most people who bother about the matter at all would admit that the English language is in a bad way." We can confirm it ourselves, every day. /7

We can confirm it when we take an airplane, and the pilot doesn't tell us he expects a bumpy ride; he says he anticipates experiencing considerable turbulence. Or we open a newspaper and read that a government office isn't going broke; it's undergoing a budget shortfall situation. Or we hear a policeman who doesn't say the suspect got out of the car; he relates that the alleged perpetrator exited the vehicle. /8

We can confirm it when we encounter viable, meaningful, beautiful, "in" buzz-words; for example, "input," "interface," and "thrust," which, as somebody said, shouldn't be used in public but might be all right in private among consenting adults. /9

We can confirm it when we hear people using "disinterested" as if it meant the same thing as "uninterested"; or "infer" as if it meant the same thing as "imply." To confuse any such pair is to take two distinct, useful words

and blur them into a single, useless smudge. Every time it happens the language shrinks a little. /10

Of course, I work in television, which is one of the designated disaster areas of language. In the past 11 years I've conducted thousands of hours of interviews, during which I've probably been an accessory to, or committed myself, all the known violations. I shouldn't even talk about this subject unless I'm granted complete immunity. Television is, among other things, a machine for turning nouns into verbs. I "host" a show. It's "funded" by the Chubb Corporation and "aired" by PBS. And naturally I always hope it will be "successed." /11

I could go on and on. The phrase "between you and I" appears, like an upraised pinkie, whenever people who should know better try for refinement. We seem to be stuck with that barbarous abbreviation "Ms.," which doesn't abbreviate anything, except common sense. The "you-know" is still spreading. /12

Worst of all is the fact that the very authorities we might expect to shore up these collapsing standards—the experts in linguistics, the dictionary makers, the teachers of English—are in many cases leading the onslaught. It's as if, in the middle of a coup, we turned to the palace guard for help and saw them coming at us with bayonets. /13

I had several linguistics professors on a series of shows about language earlier this season. They assured me that things like grammar, syntax and spelling were mere superficial details that shouldn't be allowed to interfere with the deeper importance of self-expression. In fact they suggested that, in matters of language, rules and standards of any kind were snobbish, authoritarian and downright undemocratic. Most of them were apostles of a group called the Council on College Composition and Communication, which a few years ago put out a policy statement advocating "the student's right to his own language," no matter what dialect, patois, slang or gibberish it might be. This idea could revolutionize education. I keep waiting for other departments to pick it up: the student's right to his own math, the student's right to his own history, and so on. /14

In Browning's poem "The Grammarian's Funeral," the grammarian himself was dead, obviously. Today the grammarian is underground in a different sense. A man named Richard Mitchell, who teaches English at Glassboro State College in New Jersey, publishes a monthly broadside called *The Underground Grammarian,* which is his one-man guerilla war on jargon, cliches and fuzziness. The point is, his chief target is not the Philistine outside the ivied wall, but his own colleague, the English teacher sitting in the library— excuse me, I mean the language skills instructor sitting in the learning resources center. /15

Yes, the English language *is* in a bad way. In my business there's a famous phrase characterizing the Broadway theater as a "fabulous invalid." To me, that's exactly what the language has become. My late friend, the writer Jean Stafford, once described its symptoms in the following clinical terms: /16

"Besides the neologisms that are splashed all over the body . . . like the daubings of a chimpanzee turned loose

with finger paints, the poor thing has had its parts of speech broken to smithereens . . . and upon its stooped and aching back it carries an astounding burden of lumber piled on by the sociologists and the psychologists, the Pentagon, the admen, and, lately, the alleged robbers and bug planters of Watergate. The prognosis for the ailing language is not good. I predict that it will not die in my lifetime, but I fear that it will be assailed by countless cerebral accidents and massive strokes and gross insults to the brain and finally will no longer be able to sit up in bed and take nourishment by mouth." /17

Members of the class of 1979, I can imagine you saying to yourself, "I'm sorry the language is ailing, but there's nothing I can do. It doesn't affect me anyway, since that's not my field. I can still get through the day. I can always get my meaning across." /18

At this point the sharper students among you will recognize that I have come around the back way and snuck up on my subject. For I am here this morning to say it *does* affect you, and there *is* something you can do. No matter what you majored in, you're still English majors. We're all English majors, willy-nilly, until the day we join Browning's grammarian. The breakdown of language isn't just something that happens to language. It's something that happens to us, and to our lives. /19

Let's go back for a moment to Thurber and the actress at the party. They were, as Thurber put it, on the shadow line, close to losing rational touch with each other. Of course, it wouldn't have mattered all that much if they had. There are many occasions when it doesn't matter all that much if words and meaning part company—if an undertaker advertises coffins with a "lifetime guarantee," for example; or if the New York Times prints this sentence about Nelson Rockefeller: "He was chairman of the Museum of Modern Art, which he entered in a fireman's raincoat during a recent fire, and founded the Museum of Primitive Art." /20

But E. B. White, who found that sentence in the Times, reminds us that muddiness of meaning isn't always such harmless fun. "Muddiness," White says, "is not merely a disturber of prose, it is a destroyer of life, of hope: death on the highway caused by a badly worded roadsign, heartbreak among lovers caused by a misplaced phrase in a well-intentioned letter, anguish of a traveler not being met at a railroad station because of a slipshod telegram." /21

You will live a lot of your lives on this mundane, practical level, exchanging gossip at a party, giving and taking directions, making and breaking plans. If your language is faulty, then these transactions will be faulty. Each of you literally will be in danger of not knowing what the other is talking about. Reconsider for a minute: can you really get through the day? Can you really always get your meaning across? When the gravedigger catches Hamlet out in a bit of muddiness, Hamlet says to his friend Horatio, "We must speak by the card, or equivocation will undo us." E. B. White believes it, and so do I. /22

Beyond this practical level, there are two other levels on which the breakdown of language affects you. One is moral and esthetic. Language is "the defining mystery of man," in George Steiner's phrase. It is the index to our civilization, the history of our race, the living web of our shared values and emotions. But it doesn't only define man generally and culturally. Specifically and personally it defines men, or rather, persons. The cardinal virtues of language are: clarity; simplicity; precision; vigor, if possible; and, on good days, gracefulness. What you ask of yourselves in each of those categories will define the terms by which you perceive things, by which you think, by which you register on the world around you. It will also define the terms by which other people judge you. /23

I'm not talking about language as an ornament, or about having a good prose style the way you might have a good backhand. I don't mean something external like Gucci stripes. I mean some outward sign of an inner dimension. Come to think of it, Gucci stripes probably are an outward sign of an inner dimension. But anyway, consider the phrase, "I could care less." It means exactly the opposite of what it's intended to mean. If you could care less, then you do care. But people use the phrase as a corruption of "I couldn't care less," which apparently is now too much trouble to say. And I judge their inner dimensions accordingly. The woman who says to me, "I could care less," is numb to logic and meaning. She simply isn't thinking about what she's saying, and I don't want to have anything to do with her—even if she is my wife. /24

Finally, the breakdown of language affects you politically, and I'm using the word in the broad sense that George Orwell used it in the essay I quoted at the beginning, "Politics and the English

Language." By politics I think Orwell meant that whole way we order our public life and common welfare. When politics in this sense is decayed, language tends to be decayed too. This was true in Nazi Germany. It's true today in Soviet Russia. Part of what Solzhenitsyn and other Russian dissidents are protesting is the repression of the mother tongue, the debasement of words like "truth" and "freedom" into Newspeak, the twisting of a term like "insane" until it means any thought that departs from the Party line. /25

Alas, we have more of that kind of decay in the West, specifically here in America, than we like to think. Vietnam taught us that, if nothing else. When soldiers bombard a village, drive the peasants into the countryside, burn their huts, machine-gun their cattle and then call it "pacification," how different is that from Newspeak? /26

Orwell wasn't sure whether politics debased the language, or vice versa, or whether it was a cycle. Our language "becomes ugly and inaccurate because our thoughts are foolish," he said, "but the slovenliness of our language makes it easier for us to have foolish thoughts." What Orwell *was* sure of was that the condition was curable, that we could shake off dead verbiage and mindless orthodoxy. /27

If one simplifies one's English, he said, "one can think more clearly, and to think clearly is a necessary first step towards political regeneration. . . . When you make a stupid remark its stupidity will be obvious, even to yourself. Political language . . . is designed to make lies sound truthful and murder respectable, and to give an appearance of solidity to pure wind. One cannot change this all in a moment, but one can at least change one's own habits, and from time to time one can even, if one jeers loudly enough, send some worn-out and useless phrase . . . into the dustbin where it belongs." /28

"If one jeers loudly enough . . ." That takes me back, again, to Thurber. What appeals to me about that moment at the party is that Thurber not only skewered the actress's verbal absurdity, but he did it with humor. If I've raised any laughter here this morning, it hasn't been to reconcile you to the follies and abuses I've been talking about. It's been to hold them up to ridicule, to shame the people who commit them, and to render them so silly and contemptible that you won't commit them yourselves. /29

There are other ways to achieve the same ends. There are a thousand ways. Humor is mine. The important thing is for you to find yours. /30

Thank you. /31

AN EMPLOYMENT INTERVIEW

As we noted in Chapter 15, an employment or job-seeking interview essentially is an informative exchange between a potential employer and a potential hiree. These can be stressful situations, especially if one or the other of the parties is unprepared. But, if the interviewer has a strong sense of goals—a sense for what kinds of information a face-to-face meeting will add to data already recorded in application forms, letters-of-recommendation, college transcripts, and resumes—and if the interviewee has a clear picture of his or her career goals, strengths and weaknesses, preparation and talents, then the employment interview can be a mutually satisfying communicative event. They do not, of course, always lead to hiring and employment, but they can be productive if both parties are ready.

The following abbreviated interview occurs between Sharon Young, an applicant for a Management Trainee position, and Leonard Michaels, Personnel Director of Management Operations with Parker House Restaurants. It occurs at Parker House's corporate headquarters in Columbus, Ohio. As you read through the transcript, note not only the major segments (opening, body, closing), but also the sub-divisions of the body. The first segment (paragraphs 9–54) explores Sharon's background and work-related interpersonal talents; the second (paragraphs 55–64), a job description; and the third (paragraphs 65–79), questions the interviewee has. Further, as you read through the transcript, try to outline the schedule-of-questions being used especially by Mr. Michaels, noticing how he integrates both primary and secondary as well as open and closed questions.

MANAGEMENT-TRAINEE EMPLOYMENT INTERVIEW*

Opening

MICHAELS: Hi! *(Smiles)* Sharon Young? /1

YOUNG: Yes. /2

MICHAELS: *(Greets applicant with a handshake)* I'm Len Michaels, Personnel Director for Parker House Restaurants and I'll be interviewing you today for the Management Trainee position you applied for. Won't you have a seat? /3

YOUNG: Thank you. /4

MICHAELS: *(Asks an "ice breaker" question)* Did you have any problem finding the office? /5

YOUNG: No, not really. When I was here before to complete the application form, I asked the secretary if this was where they'd hold the interviews and she said yes. So I didn't have any problems at all. /6

MICHAELS: Very good. *(The interviewer now makes a transition to the body of the interview)* What I'd like to do this afternoon is find out something about you—your educational and work background. Then I'd like to discuss the qualifications for this job and, finally, I'd be happy to answer any questions that

---

*This transcript was prepared by Paul Seland, Niagara County Community College. Reprinted by permission of the author.

you may have about Parker House in general and the management trainee position in particular. /7

YOUNG: Fine, I am ready to go. /8

Body

MICHAELS: As a starting point, could you please tell me what you think you could offer Parker House? /9

YOUNG: Well, I'm a self-starter and I work well with most types of people. I pick things up very quickly and I have had specific work experience with Burger World, two summers, and two years with The Fisherman's Restaurant. The psychology, communication, accounting, and management courses that I completed in college should also help me as a manager at Parker House. /10

MICHAELS: What were some of your duties at Burger World? *(Interviewer is seeking work experience information)* /11

YOUNG: The first summer I worked the grill and the friers, took orders, and worked the register. The second summer I was shift supervisor for the afternoon-evening shift and I cashed out all the registers and made the bank deposits. /12

MICHAELS: And your duties at Fisherman's? /13

YOUNG: The first year I worked in the kitchen preparing dinners and salads. Then one of the hostesses quit and I took over her position and helped Mr. Mann with the daily deposits and the books. /14

MICHAELS: That sounds like a pretty varied experience. Did you encounter any problems while you were at Fisherman's? /15

YOUNG: I am not sure what you mean by problems . . . Do you mean personal problems or work-related problems? *(The applicant asks for clarification when unsure of the question)* /16

MICHAELS: I mean work-related problems. /17

YOUNG: There were times when reservations got backed up and so you had to ask customers if they would like to have a drink at the bar while they waited for their table to become available. Sometimes one of the kitchen crew wouldn't show for some reason and we'd have to pitch in and help. Things like that . . . nothing serious though. /18

MICHAELS: You mentioned Mr. Mann, was he the owner? /19

YOUNG: Yes, he and his wife owned the restaurant. /20

MICHAELS: What did Mr. Mann do about the people who didn't show for work? /21

YOUNG: If they had a legitimate excuse but did not call before their shift, he gave them a warning. If it happened again—as it did once—he would fire them. /22

MICHAELS: I take it that you've never fired anyone? /23

YOUNG: No, I haven't. /24

MICHAELS: Would you be able to terminate or fire anyone? *(The interviewer is trying to discover how the applicant would handle this conflict situation)* /25

YOUNG: *(Pause)* If there were just cause, I guess I could. Does Parker House have a specific policy on this, Mr. Michaels? /26

MICHAELS: We can cover that later in the interview, but Sharon, what I'd like to explore with you for a moment is what your feelings would be if you had to fire someone. /27

YOUNG: Sure. *(Pause)* If someone had done something against company policy, like *not* showing for a shift and *not* calling, then the employee would warrant termination. If, for example, the person did a sloppy job of cleaning a stove . . . I'd *tell* them and *show* them how it was to be done, and then I'd have them *show me* how it was to be done. I would explain to them that the sloppy work should not happen again. If it did, then you'd have to let them go. /28

MICHAELS: If a customer complained that his food was not cooked properly how would you handle it? *(Again, another question which seeks to determine how the applicant would handle a conflict situation)* /29

YOUNG: If his food was not done, I'd find out what was not cooked properly. I'd apologize and find out how the customer wanted it cooked. I'd then ask the cook to prepare it to the customer's specifications and I'd make sure to offer another apology after the dinner was returned to the customer. I'd make sure to check back later and find out if everything was satisfactory. /30

MICHAELS: On your resumé you list that you have a two-year degree from Lock City Community College in New York and a B.A. from Columbus College. *(Pause)* /31

YOUNG: Right. /32

MICHAELS: What courses do you think would be helpful in managing a Parker House restaurant? *(Interviewer is attempting to discover what educational experiences would be related to this position)* /33

YOUNG: The psychology courses would be helpful in understanding customers and employees. The public speaking course helped me to gain confidence in myself and helped me to improve my communication ability. The interpersonal communication course helped me learn how to resolve conflicts between myself and others and how to work with other people. The management courses would certainly be relevant for organizing, hiring, training, and managing employees. The economics and accounting courses have given me a background for the bookkeeping and the food ordering aspects of the job. /34

MICHAELS: Umm hum. I see. *(Pause)* Any other courses that you could think of that would be helpful? /35

YOUNG: I took two non-credit food preparation courses at Lock City College, one in dinner preparation and the other in dessert preparation. *(Pause)* When I was a freshman in high school my mother said I had something to learn about cooking. /36

MICHAELS: Does your mother think that you've improved? /37

YOUNG: Oh yes!! *(Smiles)* She helped me a lot, and those courses and then Fisherman's have given me a pretty good foundation. /38

MICHAELS: Is there anything about cooking that you really dislike? /39

YOUNG: Nothing major, but I never did get the hang of lemon meringue pies. /40

MICHAELS: *(Smiles and nods)* I take it that you enjoy cooking? /41

YOUNG: Very much! I like to experiment with foods. But I also enjoy being "out front," meeting people, making them feel comfortable. /42

MICHAELS: How would you rate the education you received from Columbus? /43

YOUNG: Columbus has an excellent business management program and I am glad that my father got transferred. I was a little apprehensive about the move at first and about attending Columbus. However, the academic training and experiences I received from Columbus supported the foundation courses that I took at Lock City College. /44

I think the grades I earned at both colleges reflect just as much about my capabilities as they do about the schools' educational programs. The teachers, for the most part, were sensitive to student needs, were challenging and motivating, and were realistic and practical in what they taught. /45

I also got to learn something about myself, who I was, and what I wanted to do with my life. *(pause)* Probably the most important factors of college life are that it helps you to understand yourself and other people and how to get along with and work with other people. /46

MICHAELS: *(Smiles)* What about strengths and weaknesses; we all have them. What would you say is your biggest strength? /47

YOUNG: I like to be organized, to anticipate problems and how to solve them. And I like working with people. /48

MICHAELS: Why do you like to work with people? *(Interviewer probes for more specific information)* /49

YOUNG: *(Pause)* I can't really put my finger on it, but I worked with a lot of different people all my life. I guess I got this from home. There was always someone at the house—neighbors, friends, relatives, and so forth. In high school and college I was working with people to solve mutual problems—like on the Student senates at Lock City College and Columbus College. /50

MICHAELS: What's your biggest weakness? /51

YOUNG: *(Pause)* I don't like people who are gossips. One of my best friends got hurt by gossip stories that weren't true. And I guess I get short-tempered with people who constantly slack-off; who do just enough to squeak by in doing a job. /52

MICHAELS: I see. Excluding *age, racial background,* and *gender* characteristics, what types of people do you like to work with most? *(Notice that the interviewer is tacitly telling the applicant that he does not wish to pursue material which might be classified as unlawful according to the Civil Rights Act of 1964)* /53

YOUNG: I like to work with people who are organized; who try to do a job right the first time rather than having to do it over again. I like to work with people who are willing to "hop" right in and help others if a problem occurs. I guess I *prefer* to work with people who are *willing* to work with others. It doesn't matter if they are quiet or outgoing, but, like I said, I can work with a lot of different types of people. /54

MICHAELS: Let me tell you about this management trainee position and what Parker House can offer *you.* /55

We start all of our management trainees out with a twelve-week, intensive, training orientation. This pamphlet outlines in detail *(smiles and hands applicant the pamphlet)* what the training sessions are all about. /56

369

Basically, you will be rotated through all of the basic operations and procedures that all of our restaurants follow: cooking, dishes, register, waitressing, hosting, record and bookkeeping, ordering, scheduling, employee evaluations, and supervision. /57

During these three months you are on probationary status and if you do *not* work out you can be terminated. The pay for these three months would be $265.00 per week. Room and board will be paid for by the company during this three-month orientation and the day you begin your training you'll be covered by our medical and dental insurance policies. /58

After the orientation program you will be assigned to a Parker House restaurant in the greater Columbus area for a period of nine months. What happens during these nine months is explained in another pamphlet. *(Hands the material to the applicant and smiles)* /59

Essentially, during these nine months you will be a shift supervisor and you will work very closely with the manager of the restuarant—sort of like the "buddy-buddy" system. The manager will reinforce what you learned in the orientation sessions. For these nine months your pay will be elevated to $300.00 per week. /60

After one year with the company you will be eligible for a one-week paid vacation. In the second year you *could* be offered an assistant manager position with an area restaurant with a *minimum* pay of $350.00 per week. /61

Finally, after the second year you *could* move up to manager status by bidding on a restaurant—bidding is done by *seniority*—and this move *may* involve a relocation on your part. /62

Well, Sharon, I guess that's the best summary I can offer of our policy for trainees, supervisors, and managers. Is it too much to digest too quickly? /63

YOUNG: No, Mr. Michaels, it seems to fit together very nicely. /64

MICHAELS: I have a lot of information about you, Sharon. Would you have any questions that *you* might want to ask? /65

YOUNG: During the twelve-week orientation, what type of hours would I be working? /66

MICHAELS: Sessions start at 8:45 a.m. You'll spend two hours in class and one hour in the kitchen. Then there's a lunch break. When you return from lunch there are another two hours of class and a one-hour demonstration. Finally, you have a one-hour classroom summary and then dinner. /67

Trainees usually spend a couple of hours in the evening preparing for the next day's orientation sessions. The remaining part of the evening is free time as are Saturday afternoons and Sundays. /68

YOUNG: So, there are classes on Saturday mornings? /69

MICHAELS: Yes, classes are held from 10 until noon. /70

YOUNG: I see. What about shift hours for the nine months following the orientation? /71

MICHAELS: Sharon, the schedule would be determined by the restaurant manager. However, you would be working one of the three shifts during those nine months. *Most likely* you would start on the 11 p.m. to 7 a.m. shift because that would be the shift with the least amount of activity. Then you would be eased slowly into the busier shifts. /72

YOUNG: What about relocation, you mentioned that it was possible. Where do you have plans for expansion? /73

MICHAELS: Within the next two years we will be adding restaurants in the Virginia, North Carolina, and northern and southern Florida areas. We also would like to expand in western New York and eastern Ohio. /74

It is *premature* to ask, but would you have a preference for a particular area? /75

YOUNG: Oh, *(pause)* I would not mind western New York. That's where I was born and raised. Florida would be nice—the weather is nice most of the year. *(Long pause)* Would there be any special requirements for clothing? /76

MICHAELS: No, not really. The only thing we require of our management trainees, supervisors, and managers is that they dress neatly, wear business attire, and dress conservatively on the job. *(Long pause; the interviewer looks at his watch)* Would there be any further questions that you would have at this time? /77

YOUNG: *(Having seen the interviewer's clue that the interview was coming to a close)* No, Mr. Michaels, I think that you have answered all the questions that I had. However, I would like to reinforce what I said earlier about my qualifications for this position. *(pause)* /78

(Smiles) I think that the varied experiences that I have had in the restaurant business would help me considerably. I also believe that my educational preparation and my ability to comprehend things quickly would give me a solid foundation for the management trainee position. These two factors and my ability to work well with people should make me a strong candidate. *(Pauses and smiles)* /79

Closing

MICHAELS: It's been a pleasure meeting with you today, Sharon, and discussing your qualifications for the position. As you know we haven't finished our personal interviews with all of the candidates, but I am sure that we will have made our decisions by late Monday of next week. I will be contacting you by phone on Tuesday morning and let you know our decision at that time. /80

In the meantime, if you have any questions, please don't hesitate to call me at the number on my business card. *(Hands candidate his business card)* /81

YOUNG: I appreciate your time, Mr. Michaels, and the opportunity to discuss my career goals with you. I'll be home on Tuesday morning to accept your call personally. Thanks again. *(Candidate extends her hand and shakes the interviewer's hand)* /82

MICHAELS: Take care, Sharon, and have a good evening. /83

Index

Aural channel, 13, 195, 207
Authoritative definition, 168
Authority, motivational appeal, 244
Authority, tests of, 104–6
Autonomy, motivational appeal, 244
Axiom, reasoning, 276;
   tests, 278

Baird, John E. Jr., 332n
Balanced coverage, criteria for speech, 119
Ball, Victoria, 345n
Ballinger, Raymond A., 345n
Bao, Robert, 345n
Barker, Larry L. 26n 46n
"Barriers Come Tumbling Down, The," 147–48
Barriers to listening, 26–28
Basic needs, 238, 239. See also Motive needs
Baumgartel, Howard, 2n
Baxter, Neale, 347n
Beach, Dale S. 347n
Becker, Alicia, 150, 150n
Becker, Samuel L., 2n, 303n, 339n
Beebe, Steven A., 332n
Begging the question, 280
Beginning the speech, 145–152;
   aims of introductions, 145–47; apology, 149; developing introductions, 147–52; fit with body, 157–58; humorous anecdote, 147, 150–51, 152; illustration, 147, 151–52; personal reference, 147, 148–149, 152; quotation, 147, 150, 152; referring to subject or occasion, 147–48, 152; rhetorical question, 147, 149, 152; sample, 158–59; startling statement, 147, 149–50, 152
Behavior change, 237, 238, 240–41
Beliefs, 237, 238;
   audience analysis, 72–73
Beliefs of listeners, 53
Believability of speaker, listening, 33
Belongingness needs, 239
Bem, Daryl, 93n
Benefits, claim of policy, 271–72
Benefits coordinator, careers, 337
Benjamin, Alfred, 332n
Berlo, David K., 58n
Berlyn, David, 345n
Bettinghaus, Erwin P., 264n
Biederman, Irving, 18n
Biegeleisen, Jacob Israel, 345n
Bilaterality, argument, 266
Bisconti, Ann Stouffer, 2n
Bishop, Robert L. 346n
Bittel, Lester R., 347n
Bitzer, Lloyd, 22n
Blanchard, Nina, 345n
Bloomer, Carolyn M., 182n
Bockman, Jane, 173, 174n
Body
   in argument, 269; demonstrations and instructions, 226–28; lecture, 229; oral report, 224–25; response to questions, 326–27; sample informative speech, 231–33; sample speech, 66–67; use to communicate, 62–63; using in delivery, 207–17
Body language. See Nonverbal communication

Bohue, Harald, 347n
Bolles, Richard, N., 344n
Bormann, Ernest G., 264n
Bosmajian, Haig, 207n
Boulding, Kenneth, 180n
Bowers, John Waite, 93n, 178, 178n, 333
Bradley, Bert E., 160n
Bradley, Patricia Hayes, 332n
Branching schedule, interview questions, 309–10
Brevity, speech of introduction, 292–93
Brisel, George A., 98, 98n
Brockreide, Wayne, 272n
Brown, B.L., 201n
Brown, Charles T., 58n
Brown, Michael, 102
Brown, Roger, 162n
Bryant, Donald C., 144n, 160n, 301n
Burgoon, Judee, 94n, 218n
Burgoon, Michael, 12, 94n
Business speaking, 335
Byrns, James H. 302n

Califano, Joseph, 98, 98n
Campbell, James H., 180n
Capaldi, Nicholas, 118n
Careers, 333–44;
   for communication majors, 334–38; communication skills for, 338–42; planning for, 342–44
Carmichael, Carol A., 2n
Carter, Jimmy, 282
"A Case for Optimism," 298–300
Cash, William B., 311n, 332n
Causal patterns 121–22
Causal relation, 275–76;
   tests for reasoning, 277–78
Cause-effect, 121–22, 280;
   sample, 121
Causes, series, 130
Cavett, Dick, 361–65
Cayer, N. Joseph, 347n
Central idea, 51, 55–58, 297, 298. See also Thesis statement
   sample, 57; sample informative speech, 231; wording, 56–57
Challenge, conclusion, 153–54, 157
Change, motivational appeal, 242
Channels, 12–13
Chapman, Joyce, 230, 231
Characteristics of informative speech, 221–24;
   association of ideas, 221, 222–23; clarity, 221–22; concreteness, 221, 223; motivation of audience, 221, 223–24
Characteristics of listeners, 26–28
Charts, 183, 185, 187, 223
Chronological patterns, 120, 140, 226
Chute, Alan, G. 183n
Claims, 265, 269–73, 274, 277, 278–79, 280;
   fact, 270–71; policy, 271–72; sample speech, 355–58; value, 271
Clarity, informative speech, 221–22
Clark, C.P., 347n
Clarke, George Timothy, 346n
Classification of motive needs, 239–40
Classification of motivational appeals, 242–45

374

Dresser, William R., 118n
Dubman, Sheila, 346n
Duncan, James P. Jr., 347n
Dunphy, Philip C., 344n
DuPont, Pierre S., 155, 155n
Dwyer, F.M., 183n
Dynamism, credibility, 9

Ebbesen, Ebbe B., 240n 264n
Education, and audience analysis, 70
Effective gestures, 214
Effective language style, 167
Effective listening, 30–43
Effective speaking styles, 161–66;
    accuracy, 162–63, 165; appropriateness, 162,
    165; coherence, 162, 163–65; simplicity, 162,
    163, 165
Effective speech, criteria, 119
Effective voice, 198–205
Effect-to-cause, 121–22
Ehninger, Douglas, 242n, 272n, 289n, 302n
Ehrlich, Paul R., 105
Einhorn, Lois J., 332n
Eisenberg, Abne M., 180n
Either-or-logic, 280–81
Ekdom, Leah R.V., 2n, 303n, 339n
Ekman, Paul, 207n, 212, 212n
Elimination order, 123, 125–26
Elliot, Jason, 175, 175n
Ellsworth, P., 212n
Ely, Donald P., 182n
Emphasis, voice, 203–4
Employment interview, sample, 365–71
Emotional characterizers, 205
Emotional color, voice, 198, 205–6
Emotions, nonverbal communication, 208, 216
Encoding messages, 161
Ending the speech. See Conclusion
Endurance, motivational appeal, 243
Entertain, speech to, 297–300
Enumeration, topical pattern, 122
Enunciation, 200
Environment, listening, 31
Equal opportunity, 336, 337
Essentials for discussion participant, 312
Essentials of effective speaking styles, 161–66
Essentials for discussion leader, 313–14
Establish mood, aim of conclusion, 152–53
Esteem needs, 239
Ethnic background, audience analysis, 70–71
Ethos, 9, 105, 183
Etymological definition, 168
"Eulogy for Wernher Von Braun," 166
Evaluating solutions, 318
Evaluation form, classroom speech, 44
Evaluative interviews, 304, 306–7, 311
Evidence, 269, 272–74, 279;
    argument, 272–74; fallacies, 279
Examining language, 161
Examples, 61, 183;
    illustrative, 131; reasoning, 274; speech to in-
    form, 52; tests for reasoning, 277
Exemplar definition, 168–69
Explanation, 114, 116, 229, 230;

response to questions, 326; satisfaction step,
    255, 258–59; supporting materials, 96–97
Expository speech. See Informative speech
Expression, group leader, 313
Extemporaneous delivery, 197
Eye contact, 216

Face-to-face intereaction, 311–12
Facial expression, 208, 212–13, 216
Fact, claim of, 270–71, 280
Factors of attention, 36–42, 223
Facts, 61, 183, 223;
    audience analysis, 72
Factual illustration, 100
Factual report, 319
Fairness doctrine, 266–67
Fallacies, 278–82
Fallacious reasoning, 265
Fallacy, 277;
    genetic, 279
False division, 279
Familiarity, factor of attention, 39–40
Familiarity-acceptance order, 123–24
Fast, Julius, 207n
Faulkner, William, 359–60
Faulty "inductive" leap, 279
Fear of speaking. See Speech fright
Fear, motivational appeal, 243
Features of informative speech, 221–24
Features of interviews, 304–5
Feedback, 12, 15;
    audience, 196, 197; nonverbal, 208
Feliciano, G.D., 183n
Fighting, motivational appeal, 243
Figler, Howard, 344n
Final summary, 164, 165;
    discussion plan, 316
Finding speech topics, 384. See also Topics, find-
    ing
Fixed beliefs, audience analysis, 73
Flexibility, of expression, 197
Focusing, aim of conclusion, 152
Follow-up questions, 308
"For a Declaration of War Against Japan," 351–52
Force, vocal, 204
Forecast, in introduction, 152
Formal perspective, 170
Formats for interviews, 306–8
Forms of supporting materials, 96–104
Forward movement, criteria for effective speech,
    119
Foster, Edward, 2n
Fox, Marcia, 344n
Frankel, 201n
Friedrich, Gustav, 5n, 334n
Friesen, Wallace, V., 212, 212n
Frigley, Bert, 345n
Fry, Maurine, 183n
Fujita, Neil S., 346n
Full-content outline, 137–42;
    sample, 137–41
Full-sentence outline, 134
Functions of visual materials, 182–83

Gale, Barry 345n
Gale, Linda, 345n Garey, Doris B., 162n
"The Geisha," 230–34
Gender, audience analysis, 70
Generalizations, 274–75, 277
General purpose, 51–54, 57;
    actuate, 53–54; inform, 52–53; persuade, 53–54
General Semantics, 162
Genetic definition, 168
Genetic fallacy, 279
Generosity, motivational appeal, 245
Geographical patterns, 120–21
Gerlach, Vernon S., 182n
Gestalt psychologists, 181–82
Gestures, 208, 213–15, 216;
    adapt to audience, 216; arousal, 213; condensation, 213; conventional, 213; definiteness, 214; descriptive, 213; effective, 214; indicators, 213; pictorialization, 213; relaxation, 214; timing, 214–15; vigor, 214
Giattino, Jill, 218n
Gibson, 144n
Goals of speech. See Purpose
Goffman, Erving, 212n
Goldsmith, Myron, 348–50
Goodwill, in introduction, 146
Gould, Jay R., 346n
Government documents, 61
Grady, Henry W., 40
Graphs, 183, 187, 321
Gray, Hanna, 151, 151n
Greeting, Baxter, 46n
Greeting, Corinne, 46n
Gronbeck, Bruce E., 5n, 18n, 68n, 94n, 221n, 242n, 289n, 291n, 302n
Group communication, 335
Group discussion, 303, 311–19
Group membership, audience analysis, 70
Group members, acquaintance, 312
Group presentation, 322–23
Group solidarity, speeches for, 291
Guidelines for argument, 270
Gumperz, John J. 14n
Gustatory imagery, 171, 173–74, 176;
    example, 173–74

Habits, listening, 26–28
Habitual pitch level, 202
Hagge-Greenberg, Lanna, 334n
Hall, Carl, 104
Hall, Edward T., 4, 4n, 207n, 209, 209n, 216
Hancock, John, 188
Hansen, Mary Lewis, 346n
Haring, Marilyn J. 183n
Harms, L.S., 3n 197n
Harold, Raphael, 346n
Harper, Nancy L., 333
Harrison, Randall, P., 208n
Hart, Thomas, 118n
Hasty generalization, 279
Hearing and listening, 24
Heckert, Richard, 154–55, 155n
Heidt, E., 182n
Henneman, Hubert G. III, 347n

Henkin, Shepard, 346n
Hepler, Hal W., 180n
Hibbitt, George W., 173n
Hierarchy of motive needs, 239, 241
Hilgard, Ernest, R., 182n
Hill, John W., 346n
Hiring practices, and communication, 333–334
Holland, John, 345n
Hoover, Ryan, 111n
Hopper, Robert, 3n, 197n
Horn, George F., 194n
Hughey, Jim D., 68n
Human resources information systems, 336
Human resources management, 335, 336–37
"Human Side of Managing Complexity, The," 155
Human sound, production and reception, 24–25
Humor, factor of attention, 41–42
Humor, speech of introduction, 293
Humorous anecdote, 147, 150–51, 152
Hunger, imagery, 175
Hunt, Gary T., 160n
Hymes, Dell, 14n
Hypothetical illustration, 99–100, 115

Ideas, association in informative speech, 221, 222–23
Ideas, outline form, 133
Ideological appeals, 282
Ideologies, 78
Ignorance, appeal to, 280
Illustrations, 61, 96, 115, 223, 298, 299;
    in conclusion, 153, 156, 157; factual, 100; guide for choosing, 100; hypothetical, 99–100; in introduction, 147, 151–52; need step, 254, 258; speech to inform, 52
Illustrative examples, 131
Image, speaker, 9
Imagery, 167, 171–76, 245;
    auditory, 171, 173, 176; gustatory, 171, 173–74, 176; kinesthetic, 171, 175, 176; olfactory, 171, 174, 176; organic, 171, 175, 176; tactual, 171, 174, 176; visual, 171, 172–73, 176
Imitation, motivational appeal, 243–44
Immediacy, phrasing main points, 127, 128
Impartiality, group leader, 30–31, 313–14
Impartiality, oral report, 320
Implied meaning, 169
Impromptu speech, 196, 326–27
Inclusive illustration, 156
Independence, motivational appeal, 244
Indentation, outline form, 134
Indicators, gestures, 213
Indirect questions, 308
Inducement, 153, 156, 157;
    supplied in conclusion, 153, 157; sample, 156
Inductive reasoning, 274
Inferences. See Reasoning
Inferred meaning, 169
Inform, general purpose, 52–53
Informal speechmaking, 1–2
Information, speech to entertain, 297
Information, speech of nomination, 296
Informational interview, 304, 306
Informative report. See Oral report

376

316; response to, 326–330
Quine, W.V., 236n
Quotation, 147, 150, 152, 153, 155, 157;
in introduction, 147; sample, 150, 155; using in
conclusion, 153

Ramification, need step, 254, 258
Raoul-Duval, Michael, 103, 103n
Rate, 199–200, 202, 203, 227, 228
Rationale, wording central idea, 56
Rationality, argument, 267
Rationally relevant evidence, 272–73
Rational support, 185
Read delivery, 196–97
Reagan, Ronald, 282
Reality, factor of attention, 38–39
"Reality 101," 64–67
Reasoning, 265;
and argument, 267; detecting fallacies, 278–82;
fallacious, 265, 280–81; pattern, 269; tests,
276–78; types, 274–76
Rebuttal, response to objection, 328
Receiver orientation, 58
Reception of human sound, 24–25
Recommendations, oral report, 320–21
Recording information, 111–12
Reestablishment, response to objection, 328
Reference to practical experience, satisfaction step,
255
Referring to subject or occasion, 147–48, 152
Reflective thinking, 247
Refutation. See Objections
Regulate, purpose of nonverbal communication,
211, 216;
gestures, 216–17
Rehearsal, 62
Rein, Irving J., 194n
Reiteration, 170–71, 222;
of speech purpose, 141
Relaxation, gestures, 214
Relevant belief and attitude statements, audience
analysis, 84–86
Rencher, A.C., 201n
Renetzky, Alvin, 345n
Rephrasing, 170
Reportive definition, 167
Reports, 110;
oral. See Oral reports
Reputation of speaker, listening, 33
Requirements of outline form, 132–34
Requirements of speech occasion, 145
Research, oral report, 320
Research methods, 335
Resonance, 205
Responses
to questions and objections, 326–30; speeches of
courtesy, 294–96
Restatement, 114, 141, 298, 300;
reiteration, 170–71; rephrasing, 170
Results, series, 130
Retention, listener, 161–62
Reverence, motivational appeal, 244–45
Revulsion, motivational appeal, 244–45
Rhetorical principles, 6

Rhetorical question, in introduction, 147, 149, 152
Rhetorical vocabulary, 6
Rieke, Richard, 118n, 269n, 290n
Robert's Rules of Order, 267–68
Roosevelt, Franklin Delano, 351, 352
Rosenberg, B.G., 207n
Rough outline, 134, 135–36
Rules, communication, 14
Rules, of speech occasion, 60
Rules, technical, 267–69
Ruch, Floyd L., 39n

Safety needs, 239
Saine, Thomas, 218n
Salomen, Gavriel, 182n
Sample outline
actuative speech, 258–259; demonstration and
instructions, 227–28; informative speech,
114–15; lecture, 230; oral report, 224–25; persuasive speech, 115–17, 260–62
Sample Speeches
acceptance, 357–60; actuative, 353–55; argumen-
tative, 355–58; claim of policy, 355–58; Com-
mencement Address, 360–65; employment inter-
view, 365–71; to entertain, 298–300, 360–65;
informative, 230–34; of introduction, 293–94;
motivated sequence, 249–53; persuasive,
350–55
Sanford, William P., 176n
Satisfaction, actuative speech, 255
Satisfaction step, 249, 251–52, 258–59, 260, 261
Satterthwaite, Les, 182n, 194n
Saving, motivational appeal, 242
Scale, demonstration speech, 227, 228
Schaillol, Charles, 176n, 178
Schedule of interview questions, 309–10
Schlachter, Gail, 345n
Schon, T.D., 218n
Schramm, Wilbur, 183n
Schuller, Charles F., 194n
Schwab, Donald P., 347n
Scientific method, 247, 268
Scott, Robert L., 236n
Securing goodwill, 146
Security needs, 239
Segments, statistics, 102–3
Seibert, David R., 8n
Seiler, William J., 183n
Self-actualization needs, 239
Self-analysis, 30–33
Self-confidence and control, 19–21
Self-examination, nonverbal communication, 215
Self-image, speaker, 8
Self-risk, argument, 266
Selecting method of delivery, 195–97
Selecting subject, 47–51, 384;
audience expectation, 49, 50–51; audience inter-
est, 48, 50; comprehension level of audience,
49, 50; speaker interest, 48, 50; speaker knowl-
edge, 48, 50; time limit, 48–49, 50
Selection of visual materials, 184–92;
audience, 191–92; communicative potential,
184–85; integration with verbal materials, 185,
188–91; personality, 184; occasion, 191–92

Visual materials, 12–13, 114, 216, 223, 227, 228; audience, 191–92; communicative potential, 184–85; functions, 182–83; integration with verbal materials, 185, 188–91; occasion, 191–92; oral report, 321; personality, 184; persuasiveness, 183; practice, 192–93; selection, 184–92; types, 186–87; use of, 184–92

Visual message, 207
Vital, factor of attention, 42
Vividness, phrasing main points, 127–28
Vocabulary, 222
Vocal control, practicing, 207
Vocal energy, 203
Vocal force, 204
Vocalized pauses, 205
Vocal stereotypes, 201
Vocal tone, participation in panels, 325
Voice, used to communicate, 197–207; control, 207; effective, 198–205; emotional color, 198, 205–6; intelligibility, 198–201; stress patterns, 198, 203–5; variety, 198, 202–3
Voice improvement, 335
Volume, vocal, 199, 203
Von Braun, Wernher, 165, 166

Walker, Russell, 64
Wallace, Karl R., 144n, 160n, 301n
Wallington, C. James, 346n
Walter, Otis, 16n, 236n
Warrants. See Reasoning

Watson, Charles E., 347n
Watson, Kittie W., 46n
Weaver, Carl, 26n, 46n
Weaver, W.J., 201n
Welcomes, speech of courtesy, 294–96
Wells, H.G., 175n
"We Shape Our Buildings, and Thereafter They Shape Us," 348–50
White, Noel D., 68n
Whole, parts, 130
Wilcox, Roger P., 144n
Williams, Frederick, 3n, 102n, 197n
Williams, Robin M., 78n
Winegar, Kathy, 151, 152n
Wittich, Walter, A., 194n
Wolfe, Tom, 173, 173n
Wolvin, Andrew D., 29n, 46
Word choice, 222n, 223
Wording main points. See Main points
Working model, 216
Worship, motivational appeal, 244–45
Worth, Sol, 183n
Wycoff, Edgar, B., 183n

Yeager, W. Hayes, 176n
Your Self, visual material, 186

Zimbardo, Philip G., 39n, 264n, 240n
Zimmerman, George I., 8n
Zusne, Leonard, 182n

Subject Categories

Aids to Choosing Speech Topics

The beginning speaker often has difficulty in selecting a suitable speech subject. If you find yourself in this situation, we suggest that you study the following list of subject categories. These categories are not speech subjects; rather, they are *types or classes of material in which speech subjects may be found.* To decide upon a suitable subject for a public speech, consider them in terms of your own interests and knowledge, the interests of your audience, and the nature of the occasion on which you are to speak.

 PERSONAL EXPERIENCE

1. Jobs you have held.
2. Places you have been.
3. Military service.
4. The region you come from.
5. Schools you have attended.
6. Friends and enemies.
7. Relatives you like—and dislike.
8. Hobbies and pastimes.

FOREIGN AFFAIRS

1. Foreign-policy aims.
   - What they are.
   - What they should be.
2. The implementation of policy aims.
3. Ethics of foreign-policy decisions.
4. History of the foreign policy of the United States (or of some other nation.)
5. Responsibility for our foreign policy.
6. How foreign policy affects domestic policy.
7. War as an instrument of national policy.
8. International peace-keeping machinery.

DOMESTIC AFFAIRS

1. Social problems.
   - Crime.
   - The family: marriage, divorce, adjustments.
   - Problems of cities.
   - Problems of rural areas.
   - Problems of races and ethnic groups.
   - Problems of juveniles or the aged.
   - Child abuse.
   - Abortion, adoption.
   - The drug culture.
   - Sexual mores.
   - Pollution.
2. Economic problems.
   - Federal fiscal policy.
   - Economically deprived persons and areas.
   - Fiscal problems of state and local governments.
   - Taxes and tax policies.
   - Inflation and price controls.
   - Unemployment.
   - International monetary affairs.
   - Energy.
3. Political problems.
   - Powers and obligations of the federal government.
   - Relations between the federal government and the states.
   - Problems of state and local governments.
   - Parties, campaigns, and nominating procedures.
   - The courts
     —Delays in justice.
     —The jury system.
   - Congress versus the President.
   - Careers in government.